D1274101

VOLUME 2: PROFESSIONAL DEVELOPMENT

SPECIALIZED STUDY OPTIONS

U.S.A.

1986-1988

A guide to short-term educational programs in the United States for foreign nationals

Edrice Howard, Editor

The Institute gratefully acknowledges special grant support from the United States Information Agency, which made publication of this book possible.

INSTITUTE OF INTERNATIONAL EDUCATION
809 UNITED NATIONS PLAZA, NEW YORK, N.Y. 10017

Production Editor: Ellen L. Goodman

Associate Editors: Carol Weeg, Anne K. Wolf

Cover Design: Krista Van Laan

Proofreader: Lynn Anderson

With special thanks to Olga Melbardis, who assisted in our preliminary
research efforts.

Second Edition
Specialized Study Options U.S.A.
Volume II: Professional Development
Copyright © 1986 by the Institute of International Education.
All rights reserved.
Printed in the United States of America.
ISBN: 87206-141-8

Institute of International Education
809 United Nations Plaza
New York, NY 10017-3580

CONTENTS

INTRODUCTION

Specialized Study Options U.S.A. 1986-88 is the successor to two earlier IIE directories to short-term training in the United States, *Specialized Study Options U.S.A. 1984-86* and *Summer Learning Options 1983-85*. Preliminary discussions with U.S. Information Service (USIS) educational advisers overseas revealed that data on more advanced training would be particularly helpful to them. In planning the new edition, then, IIE determined that a two-volume division based on academic prerequisites would be more appropriate to their needs than the previous seasonal arrangement.

Accordingly, the 1986-88 edition of *Specialized Study Options* is divided into Volume I, *Technical Education*, which lists programs that require only a high school diploma as a prerequisite for enrollment, and Volume II, *Professional Development*, which describes more advanced programs—those requiring at least an associate's degree or a corresponding level of academic or nonacademic study for admission.

These volumes include programs in nearly every field of study available at colleges and technical schools in the United States, with business and technical subjects most heavily represented. Both books, however, contain a wide variety of interdisciplinary programs which were frequently difficult to categorize for placement in an appropriate section. For this reason, a field of study index has been added to each volume.

Inclusion Criteria

The study programs described in these books meet several criteria: they are from two weeks to one year in duration, they recur on a definable basis, and they are either intended for, or open to, non-U.S. citizens. The institute's advisory committee believed that these limitations would help to ensure that *Specialized Study Options U.S.A.* would provide the information of greatest use to foreign nationals, who would often have to travel long distances at substantial expense to participate in short-term training.

As in the earlier editions, English-language programs for foreign nationals have generally not been included, because they are fully described in another IIE publication, *English Language and Orientation Programs in the United States*. The only exceptions to this rule are courses in technical English, teaching English, and those devoted to literature, composition, or writing.

Programs in general clerical and secretarial skills, word processing, hairdressing, and cosmetology are also excluded, because of the numbers of programs involved and the wide availability of such training abroad. Nor do the books include programs geared to secondary school students, since the focus is on postsecondary courses of study for adults and professionals.

Survey Method

In preparing the 1986-88 edition, IIE surveyed approximately 24,000 institutional contacts, including the nearly 1,000 sponsors of programs listed in the previous editions.

Surveys for the earlier edition were largely targeted at the institutional level. Technical schools were surveyed in this manner again in 1986, because the high rate of response to previous surveys from National Assocation of Trade and Technical Schools (NATTS) member institutions demonstrated the effectiveness of this approach.

Responding to the needs of USIS educational advisers, the institute made a special effort to expand the number of entries of advanced short-term training opportunities. And, to this end, colleges and universities were surveyed differently in 1986 than in 1983 and 1984. In 1986, IIE surveyed at both the institutional and departmental levels in order to elicit as many responses from academic institutions as possible. The new approach was successful. Several hundred additional advanced study programs are listed in the 1986-88 edition than in the two earlier volumes combined.

The Institute made use of mailing lists or membership directories made available by the following educational and professional associations:

American Assembly of Collegiate Schools of Business
Association for Education in Journalism and Mass Communications
American Association of Colleges for Teacher Education
American Association of Teacher Educators in Agriculture
American Council on Education
American Economic Association
American Nurses Association
American Physical Therapy Association
American Psychological Association
American Society for Quality Control
American Society for Engineering Education
Association for Library and Information Science Education
Association of American Law Schools
Association of American Medical Colleges
Association of Collegiate Schools of Architecture
Association of Collegiate Schools of Planning
Association of Independent Colleges and Schools
Association of Schools of Public Health
Association of University Programs in Health Administration
Council for Noncollegiate Continuing Education
Council on Social Work Education
Council on the Continuing Education Unit
National Association for Foreign Student Affairs
National Association of Schools of Public Affairs and Administration
National Association of Trade and Technical Schools
National Research Council
North American Association for Environmental Education
North American Association of Summer Sessions
Population Association of America
Society for Public Health Education
U.S. Department of Agriculture
University Film and Video Association

Some research resources, notably the National Research Council in the sciences and the U.S. Department of Agriculture in agriculture-related fields, were especially helpful in reaching academic departments and/or professional schools in several fields.

IIE also used its own reference resources to survey programs in: area studies, aviation, banking and finance, computer sciences, development education, executive education, hotel and restaurant management, international agriculture, international business, international education, nonprofit organization administration, publishing, and tourism.

Other Study Opportunities

Although IIE made every effort to cover all major fields of interest to foreign nationals in these books, some fields are less represented than others. This certainly does not mean that short-term study in these subjects does not exist in the United States.

Frequently, short-term training is too brief to meet our two-week minimum criterion for inclusion. Many fields abound in two- to four-day seminars and workshops designed to help professionals update and expand their knowledge. In other areas, short-term training is not available as recurring courses or seminars, but may be provided at national or regional conferences and may focus on different topics each year.

Corporations and professional associations often offer specialized training in their fields, although their programs are generally closed to individuals who are not employees or members of the organization. It may be worthwhile to investigate such offerings, however; exceptions can sometimes be made through special arrangement.

It may also be helpful to note that many organizations will develop special study programs for groups of foreign nationals, providing minimum participation requirements are met. Some of these study opportunities are listed in these guides, but many more are undoubtedly available.

Foreign nationals who wish to investigate the multitude of shorter—or longer—training opportunities available should consult the list of professional associations in the appendix at the back of this book. The information services of these organizations can often provide guidance on continuing education in a given field and a more complete picture of opportunities for short-term study in the United States today.

HOW TO USE THIS BOOK

This book is a compendium of short-term study programs offered by U.S. colleges, universities, trade and technical schools, and other organizations. Ranging in length from two weeks to one year, these programs are all open to non-U.S. students. Some study programs are, in fact, designed especially for students from other countries.

The information in the program listings was supplied by the sponsoring institutions, in response to a survey mailing conducted early in 1986. IIE has made every effort to organize and list this information accurately, in order to make this book as helpful as possible.

As you use this book, however, there are several points to bear in mind. In many cases, information had to be considerably abridged to fit our editorial style and space constraints. In other cases, circumstances may dictate changes in program information; some programs may be drastically altered or cancelled. At times, certain categories of information were not provided to us by the program sponsor; this is indicated in the text by the phrase "not given." It is also important to realize that IIE does not *evaluate* either the study programs listed here or the organizations that sponsor them.

For these reasons, we recommend that you use this book as a general guide to programs of study in the U.S. When you find a program that interests you, write directly to the sponsor for full, current information before you begin making travel arrangements. Better still, write to several program sponsors so that you will have a real basis to analyze and compare similar programs.

You will also find it helpful to read through this section thoroughly; it explains how the program listings are organized and the phrasing and terminology used in them.

Overall Organization of the Program Listings

The programs are arranged by fields of study. Each chapter is devoted to a specific subject, such as agriculture or business, with general programs in the field listed first. Programs that fall into a particular subfield are listed next. The chapters are arranged alphabetically by subject, as are the subsections of each chapter. Within each chapter section, the programs are listed alphabetically by the names of the sponsoring institutions.

Program Number, Sponsor Name, and Program Title

The top line of each listing gives the program number and the name of the sponsoring organization. Programs are numbered consecutively throughout each chapter. The number is preceded by a letter differentiating the programs in that chapter from those in other chapters.

The second line of each listing gives the program title, if any. This will not always appear, as some programs have no specific title.

Specialization

This section is used to describe the program more completely. It may indicate specific subjects taught in the program or features that the sponsor wishes to emphasize.

Dates

Some programs have specific beginning and ending dates that are similar each year. In other cases, we have provided the length of the program and approximate starting dates, e.g., "Six weeks: classes begin monthly."

The term "rolling" is frequently used; it indicates either that a program has frequent starting dates (weekly, for example) or that a student may enter the program at virtually any time.

Location

The city and state in which the program is held are given first; this may differ from the location of the sponsoring organization. Additional information indicates whether the program is held "on campus" (in a building owned/operated by the sponsor), at a "professional work site" (a workplace appropriate to the subject being studied, such as a farm, factory, or clinic), or at another location, such as a hotel conference room.

Instruction

Methods of instruction are listed first; these may include discussion groups or seminars, lectures, computer-assisted instruction, audiovisual media, independent study or tutorials, and a variety of other techniques.

The types of instructors who will be involved in teaching the courses are listed next. "Faculty" indicates regular or adjunct faculty of the host organization; they may be professors, instructors, teaching aides, or other types of teachers. "Guest speakers/lecturers" will usually mean professionals in the field being studied, who have been invited to discuss their particular work operations or techniques. The language of instruction is assumed to be English in all programs; if instruction is available in another language, this is stated *in italics* at the end of this section.

Highlights

The first item of information given here is the year the sponsor first offered this program. If the program is new, we have indicated when the sponsor first offered other short-term programs.

Next, we have indicated whether a certificate, diploma, degree, or other written documentation is awarded upon completion of the program.

If on-the-job training or internship is a regular part of the program, the statement "Practical training is a program component" will appear, followed by a statement as to whether participants receive payment for their work. If the internship is optional or not always available, the phrase "may be a program component" is used instead.

Then the type of certificate of eligibility issued for obtaining visas (I-20AB, I-20MN, or IAP-66) is listed, and whether foreign nationals on tourist visas are eligible to enroll.

Next, we have stated whether a foreign student counselor/adviser is available and what special support services are available to foreign nationals, if any.

The approximate number of participants or maximum enrollment in the specific program are listed next, along with the percentage of foreign enrollment in 1985.

Some sponsors will send a list of past participants if you request it, so that you may contact other students to find out what their experiences were. If such a list is available, this will be indicated as the last item in this section.

Eligibility

In this section, we have listed information regarding academic prerequisites, English language proficiency level, including any test scores specified by the sponsor, and the professional background required of applicants.

Cost

The total or partial cost of the program is given first, along with a list of the items included in the figure given: tuition, books and materials, meals, housing, local transportation, or health insurance. If all of these expenses are included, the term "inclusive" is used.

Following that, we have listed the availability of scholarships and whether they are full or partial.

Housing

If the sponsor provides housing for the participants of the program, the type of housing provided is given here. If housing is not provided, we have indicated whether the sponsor assists in locating housing or whether the student must make his own arrangements.

Application

The application deadline, if any, is given first. When a study program may be entered at virtually any time, the term "rolling" may be used; it generally means that, if eligible, you will be accepted for the next available class. The words "open" and "none" can indicate similar flexibility; they tend to mean that enrollments are accepted up to the beginning date of a course.

If a school requires an application fee, this is indicated next, along with information on whether the fee is refundable if you are not accepted into the program. Many schools also require a tuition and/or housing deposit along with the application; this information is NOT included in the listings.

Where there are scholarships available, the scholarship application deadline is also provided.

Contact

The specific person, office, or department to contact for information and application forms is the last item of information in each program listing. Telephone numbers, cable addresses, and telex numbers are supplied, if available.

IMPORTANT NOTICE

IIE does not review or evaluate the programs listed in this book. Inclusion of a program does not imply IIE approval, not does omission imply IIE disapproval.

IIE does not handle requests for information or applications on any of these programs. You must contact the sponsoring organization directly for more information.

AGRICULTURE

A1 COLORADO STATE UNIVERSITY, INTERNATIONAL SCHOOL OF FORESTRY AND NATURAL RESOURCES
Forestry and Natural Resources.
Specialization: Forestry, fishery, wildlife, range, watershed management, soil and water conservation, natural resource management.
Dates: Aug. 22–Dec. 15 and Jan. 15–May 11.
Location: Fort Collins, Colorado: on campus.
Instruction: *Methods:* lectures, discussion groups, field trips, independent study/research. *By:* faculty.
Highlights: Sponsor has offered program since 1982. Certificate. Issues I-20AB, IAP-66. Foreign nationals on tourist visas are eligible to enroll. A foreign student counselor/adviser is available. Host family and social programs. 25 total enrollment; 100% foreign enrollment in 1985.
Eligibility: *Academic:* bachelor's degree. *Language:* English proficiency on intermediate level is required. TOEFL: 450. *Professional:* management position in a natural resource agency.
Cost: $3,200 per semester for tuition, fees. *Scholarships:* none.
Housing: Not provided; sponsor assists in locating housing.
Application: *Deadline:* one month prior. *Fee:* $10; not refundable.
Contact: Dr. Julius G. Nagy, Director, International School of Forestry and Natural Resources, Colorado State University, Fort Collins, CO 80523; (303) 491-5901.

A2 CORNELL UNIVERSITY
International Agriculture Program.
Specialization: Develops, implements, and evaluates specially designed training programs responding to participant's goals and objectives.
Dates: To be arranged.
Location: Ithaca, New York: on campus.
Instruction: *Methods:* lectures. *By:* faculty.
Highlights: Not given.
Eligibility: *Academic:* bachelor's degree preferred. *Language:* English proficiency on intermediate level is required. TOEFL: 550. *Professional:* not given.
Cost: To be arranged. *Scholarships:* none.
Housing: To be arranged.
Application: *Deadline:* none. *Fee:* not given.
Contact: James E. Haldeman, International Agriculture Program, Cornell University, Roberts Hall, P.O. Box 16, Ithaca, NY 14853; (607) 255-3035.

A3 ECONOMICS INSTITUTE
American Agriculture.
Specialization: Adjusted to prior levels of professional training and individual goals. Includes visits to business and government offices and farms.
Dates: Five weeks: classes begin monthly.
Location: Boulder, Colorado: on campus.
Instruction: *Methods:* lectures, discussion groups, case studies, field trips, individualized

---

Abbreviations: ESL = English as a Second Language; TOEFL = Test of English as a Foreign Language; ALIGU = American Language Institute of Georgetown University; GPA = Grade Point Average; SAT = Scholastic Aptitude Test; GED = General Equivalency Diploma.

instruction, "hands-on" training, computer-assisted instruction, language labs, independent study/research. *By:* faculty, guest speakers/lecturers.

Highlights: Sponsor has offered program previously. Certificate supported by official course transcript. Issues I-20AB. Foreign nationals on tourist visas are eligible to enroll. A foreign student counselor/adviser is available. Over 100 total enrollment; 100% foreign enrollment in 1985.

Eligibility: *Academic:* bachelor's degree. *Language:* English proficiency is required. TOEFL: 425–500. *Professional:* 3–10 years of experience preferred.

Cost: About $2,047 for ten weeks inclusive. *Scholarships:* none.

Housing: In residence halls, dormitories, apartments, with families.

Application: *Deadline:* none. *Fee:* $50 deposit.

Contact: Economics Institute, 1030 13 Street, Boulder, CO 80302; (303) 492-8419. Cable: ECONINST. Telex: 450385.

A4 INSTITUTE OF WORLD AFFAIRS

Specialization: World hunger and agricultural development: diet, environmental problems, alternative production systems, land tenure, technology, cooperatives, and marketing.

Dates: June 29–July 26.

Location: Salisbury, Connecticut: at institute.

Instruction: *Methods:* lectures, discussion groups, field trips. *By:* guest speakers/lecturers.

Highlights: Sponsor has offered program previously. Certificate. College credit by special arrangement for additional fee. Issues IAP-66. Foreign nationals on tourist visas are eligible to enroll. A foreign student counselor/adviser is available. 25 total enrollment.

Eligibility: *Academic:* some graduate work, exceptional undergraduates. *Language:* English proficiency on intermediate level is required. *Professional:* none.

Cost: $1,200 for tuition, meals, housing. *Scholarships:* partial.

Housing: In dormitories.

Application: *Deadline:* May 1. *Fee:* not given. *Scholarship deadline:* not given.

Contact: William Schaufele, Director, Institute of World Affairs, Salisbury, CT 06068; (203) 824-5651. Cable: Institute-Salisbury.

A5 INTERNATIONAL PROGRAMS
Agriculture Management.

Specialization: Agricultural management, policy and project planning, establishing data bases and agricultural extension programs.

Dates: One year.

Location: Washington, D.C.: at professional work site.

Instruction: *Methods:* discussion groups, lectures, field trips, individualized instruction, "hands-on" training, independent study/research, science laboratories. *By:* faculty, guest speakers/lecturers.

Highlights: New program. Sponsor has offered short-term programs since 1977. Certificate. Foreign nationals on tourist visas are not eligible to enroll. A foreign student counselor/adviser is available. Homestay programs and social activities. 20 total enrollment; 100% foreign enrollment in 1985.

Eligibility: *Academic:* bachelor's degree. *Language:* English proficiency on advanced level is preferred. *Professional:* none.

Cost: $12,000 for tuition, books and materials, health insurance. *Scholarships:* none.

Housing: Not provided; sponsor assists in locating housing.

Application: *Deadline:* October. *Fee:* $300; not refundable.

Contact: Mr. Robert Mashburn, International Programs, 600 Maryland Ave., Room 134, Washington, DC 20024; (202) 447-7476.

A6 OKLAHOMA STATE UNIVERSITY

Specialization: Special programs can be arranged in this field.

Dates: To be arranged.

Location: Stillwater, Oklahoma: on campus, at professional work site.

Instruction: *Methods:* discussion groups, lectures, case studies, field trips, individualized instruction, "hands-on" training, independent study/research, computer-assisted instruction, language laboratories, science laboratories. *By:* faculty.
Highlights: Sponsor has offered short-term programs previously. Certificate. Practical training is a component of this program. Issues I-20AB, IAP-66. Foreign nationals on tourist visas are eligible to enroll. A foreign student counselor/adviser is available. Orientation programs and arranged activities. Unlimited total enrollment; 9% foreign enrollment in 1985.
Eligibility: *Academic:* bachelor's degree. *Language:* English proficiency on intermediate level is required. TOEFL: 550. *Professional:* none.
Cost: $10,237 per year for tuition, books and materials, meals, housing, health insurance, personal expenses. *Scholarships:* partial (assistantships).
Housing: In dormitories, apartments, furnished rooms.
Application: *Deadline:* Nov. 1 and June 1. *Fee:* $10; not refundable.
Contact: Director, Office of International Programs, Oklahoma State University, 221 USDA Bldg. North, Stillwater, OK 74078; (405) 624-6535. Telex: 160274 OSU UT or 709606 OSU INTL PROG.

A7 UNIVERSITY OF CALIFORNIA EXTENSION, DAVIS
International Programs.
Specialization: Customized programs in any area of agriculture.
Dates: To be arranged.
Location: Davis, California: on campus, at professional work site.
Instruction: *Methods:* discussion groups, lectures, case studies, field trips, individualized instruction, "hands-on" training, independent study/research, computer-assisted instruction, language laboratories, science laboratories. *By:* faculty, guest speakers/lecturers.
Highlights: Sponsor has offered short-term programs since 1978. Certificate. Issues I-20AB, IAP-66. Foreign nationals on tourist visas are eligible to enroll. A foreign student counselor/adviser is available. ESL program and other services. 100 total enrollment; 100% foreign enrollment in 1985.
Eligibility: *Academic:* varies. *Language:* none. *Professional:* none.
Cost: Varies. *Scholarships:* none.
Housing: In dormitories, apartments, furnished rooms, hotels, with families.
Application: *Deadline:* varies. *Fee:* not given.
Contact: Beth Greenwood, Director, International Programs, University of California Extension, Davis, CA 95616; (916) 752-7171 or 752-3093. Telex: 910-531-0785 UC DAVS.

A8 UTAH STATE UNIVERSITY, DEPARTMENT OF AGRICULTURAL EDUCATION
International Extension Option M.S. in Agricultural Education.
Specialization: A Plan B Thesis focused on preparation and implementation of a demonstration and field day provides a unique and valuable experience in this extension method. Student works with extension agent and farmer.
Dates: Rolling.
Location: Logan, Utah: on campus, at professional work site.
Instruction: *Methods:* discussion groups, lectures, case studies, field trips, individualized instruction, independent study/research. *By:* faculty, guest speakers/lecturers.
Highlights: Sponsor has offered program since 1981. Certificate upon completion of 50 graduate credits and Plan B Thesis. Practical training is a program component; participants are not paid. Issues I-20AB. Foreign nationals on tourist visas are not eligible to enroll. A foreign student counselor/adviser is available. 25 total enrollment; 92% foreign enrollment in 1985.
Eligibility: *Academic:* bachelor's degree in agriculture. *Language:* English proficiency on beginning level is required. TOEFL: 500 or Intensive English courses. *Professional:* prior work experience in Extension preferred.

Abbreviations: ESL = English as a Second Language; TOEFL = Test of English as a Foreign Language; ALIGU = American Language Institute of Georgetown University; GPA = Grade Point Average; SAT = Scholastic Aptitude Test; GED = General Equivalency Diploma.

Cost: About $9,000 per year for tuition, books and materials, meals, housing, health insurance. *Scholarships:* none.
Housing: Not provided; sponsor assists in locating housing.
Application: *Deadline:* three months prior. *Fee:* $30; not refundable.
Contact: Mr. Gilbert A. Long, Department of Agricultural Education, Utah State University, UMC 4805, Logan, UT 84322; (801) 750-2230.

AGRIBUSINESS

A9 ARTHUR D. LITTLE MANAGEMENT EDUCATION INSTITUTE
Specialization: Agribusiness management program.
Dates: May 29–July 11.
Location: Cambridge, Massachusetts: at institute.
Instruction: *Methods:* lectures, discussion groups, case studies, field trips, computer-assisted instruction. *By:* faculty, guest speakers/lecturers.
Highlights: Sponsor has offered program previously. Certificate. Issues I-20AB, IAP-66. Foreign nationals on tourist visas are not eligible to enroll. A foreign student counselor/adviser is available. Orientation program and social activities.
Eligibility: *Academic:* bachelor's degree preferred. *Language:* English proficiency on intermediate level is required. TOEFL: 500 (testing usually not required). *Professional:* 2–5 years of experience preferred.
Cost: $4,000 for tuition, books. *Scholarships:* none.
Housing: Sponsor assists in locating housing.
Application: *Deadline:* none. *Fee:* none.
Contact: Judith H. Francis, Admissions Coordinator and Registrar, Arthur D. Little Management Education Institute, 35 Acorn Park, Cambridge, MA 02140; (617) 864-5657. Telex: 921436.

AGRICULTURAL ECONOMICS

A10 ECONOMICS INSTITUTE
Agricultural Economics.
Specialization: Adjusted to prior levels of professional training and individual goals. Includes visits to businesses, government offices and farms.
Dates: Five weeks: classes begin in Jan., March, June, July, Sept., Oct., Nov.
Location: Boulder, Colorado: on campus, at professional work site.
Instruction: *Methods:* lectures, discussion groups, case studies, field trips, individualized instruction, "hands-on" training, computer-assisted instruction, language labs, independent study/research. *By:* faculty, guest speakers/lecturers.
Highlights: Sponsor has offered program previously. Certificates and diplomas supported by official course transcript. Issues I-20AB. Foreign nationals on tourist visas are eligible to enroll. A foreign student counselor/adviser is available. Over 100 total enrollment; 100% foreign enrollment in 1985. List of past participants is available.
Eligibility: *Academic:* bachelor's degree. *Language:* English proficiency is required. TOEFL: 425–500. *Professional:* 3–10 years of experience preferred.
Cost: About $2,047 for ten weeks inclusive. *Scholarships:* none.
Housing: In residence halls, dormitories, apartments, with families.
Application: *Deadline:* none. *Fee:* $50 deposit.
Contact: Economics Institute, 1030 13 Street, Boulder, CO 80302; (303) 492-8419. Cable: ECONINST. Telex: 450385.

ANIMAL SCIENCE

A11 UNIVERSITY OF MARYLAND EASTERN SHORE
Human and Animal Nutrition and Management.
Specialization: Biochemistry of protein quality of soybeans, poultry technology and management with focus on broilers and roasters (nutrition and physiology).
Dates: Vary.
Location: Princess Anne, Maryland: on campus, at professional work site.
Instruction: *Methods:* discussion groups, lectures, field trips, individualized instruction, "hands-on" training, independent study/research, science laboratories. *By:* faculty, guest speakers/lecturers.
Highlights: Sponsor has offered program since 1982. Certificate. Practical training is a program component; participants are not paid. Foreign nationals on tourist visas are eligible to enroll. A foreign student counselor/adviser is available. ESL program. 6 total enrollment; 100% foreign enrollment in 1985.
Eligibility: *Academic:* bachelor's degree, some graduate work. *Language:* English proficiency on intermediate level is required. TOEFL: passing. *Professional:* two years of work experience required.
Cost: Varies. *Scholarships:* none.
Housing: Not provided; sponsor assists in locating housing.
Application: *Deadline:* none. *Fee:* $20; not refundable.
Contact: Dr. C. Dennis Ignasias, Director of International Programs, University of Maryland Eastern Shore, Princess Anne, MD 21853; (301) 651-2200, Ext. 528. Telex: UMCP 887294, COMM UN MD UD.

CROP PRODUCTION

A12 MISSISSIPPI STATE UNIVERSITY
Seed Improvement.
Specialization: Specialized instruction, laboratory and experiential training in various aspects of seed technology, especially development, operation, and management of a comprehensive seed program.
Dates: Two months: classes begin in June.
Location: Mississippi State University (near Starkville), Mississippi: on campus, at professional work site.
Instruction: *Methods:* discussion groups, lectures, field trips, "hands-on" training. *By:* faculty.
Highlights: Sponsor has offered program since 1956. Certificate. Practical training is a program component; participants are not paid. Issues I-20AB, IAP-66. Foreign nationals on tourist visas are eligible to enroll. A foreign student counselor/adviser is available. 20 total enrollment; 100% foreign enrollment in 1985.
Eligibility: *Academic:* bachelor's degree. *Language:* English proficiency on intermediate level is preferred. *Professional:* one year of experience with seed programs or extension in home country.
Cost: $8,500 inclusive. *Scholarships:* none.
Housing: In dormitories.
Application: *Deadline:* March 1. *Fee:* none.
Contact: Mr. Ronald A. Brown, Mississippi State University, P.O. Drawer NZ, Mississippi State, MS 39762; (601) 325-3204. Telex: 53882 OIP.

A13 UNIVERSITY OF MINNESOTA
MAST International.
Specialization: Production agriculture.
Dates: One year: classes begin in March, June, Nov.

Abbreviations: ESL = English as a Second Language; TOEFL = Test of English as a Foreign Language; ALIGU = American Language Institute of Georgetown University; GPA = Grade Point Average; SAT = Scholastic Aptitude Test; GED = General Equivalency Diploma.

Location: St. Paul, Minnesota: on campus, at professional work site.
Instruction: *Methods:* discussion groups, lectures, case studies, field trips, individualized instruction, "hands-on" training, computer-assisted instruction. *By:* faculty, guest speakers/lecturers.
Highlights: Sponsor has offered program since 1949. Certificate. Practical training is a program component; participants are paid. Issues IAP-66. Foreign nationals on tourist visas are not eligible to enroll. A foreign student counselor/adviser is available. 100% foreign enrollment in 1985.
Eligibility: *Academic:* associate's degree in agriculture. *Language:* English proficiency on intermediate level is required. *Professional:* two years of farm work experience.
Cost: Varies. *Scholarships:* none.
Housing: With families.
Application: *Deadline:* three months prior. *Fee:* none.
Contact: MAST International, University of Minnesota, 405 Coffey Hall, 1420 Eckles Ave., St. Paul, MN 55112; (612) 373-0725.

EXTENSION PROGRAMS

A14 UNIVERSITY OF WISCONSIN—MADISON
Development and Operation of Agricultural Extension Programs.
Specialization: Recent developments in extension programs in various countries. Students work with extension specialists, local extension staff, and participants from other countries.
Dates: Two months: classes begin in June and Sept.
Location: Madison, Wisconsin: hotel conference rooms, at professional work site.
Instruction: *Methods:* lectures, discussion groups, case studies, field trips, individualized instruction, "hands-on" training, independent study/research. *By:* faculty, guest speakers/lecturers.
Highlights: Sponsor has offered program since 1967. Certificate. Practical training is a program component; participants are not paid. Issues I-20AB, IAP-66. Foreign nationals on tourist visas are eligible to enroll. A foreign student counselor adviser is available. Various support services available. 20 total enrollment; 100% foreign enrollment in 1985.
Eligibility: *Academic:* bachelor's degree. *Language:* English proficiency on intermediate level is required. *Professional:* none.
Cost: $2,600 for books and materials, local transportation, training fees.
Housing: In hotels.
Application: *Deadline:* none. *Fee:* not given.
Contact: Mr. Kenneth H. Shapiro, International Agricultural Programs, University of Wisconsin, 240 Agricultural Hall, 1450 Linden Drive, Madison, WI 53706; (608) 262-3673. Cable: AGRPROGRAMS. Telex: 265452 UOFWISC MDS.

FISHERIES AND AQUACULTURE

A15 CONSORTIUM FOR INTERNATIONAL FISHERIES AND AQUACULTURE DEVELOPMENT (CIFAD)
Fisheries Data Management Using Microcomputers.
Specialization: Use of microcomputers and software, data requirements, and application to fisheries and aquaculture data management systems.
Dates: Five weeks: classes begin in July.
Location: Corvallis, Oregon: at Oregon State University.
Instruction: *Methods:* lectures, case studies, field trips, "hands-on" training, computer-assisted instruction, science laboratories. *By:* faculty, guest speakers/lecturers.
Highlights: Sponsor has offered short-term programs since 1985. Certificate. Practical training is a program component; participants are not paid. Issues I-20AB, IAP-66. Foreign

nationals on tourist visas are eligible to enroll. A foreign student counselor/adviser is available. 20 total enrollment.
Eligibility: *Academic:* associate's degree. *Language:* English proficiency on intermediate level is preferred. *Professional:* individuals responsible for collection, management, and analysis of fisheries information.
Cost: $4,200 for tuition, books and materials. *Scholarships:* none.
Housing: Not provided; sponsor assists in locating housing.
Application: *Deadline:* none. *Fee:* none.
Contact: Mr. Kevin Hopkins, CIFAD Snell Hall 443, Oregon State University, Corvallis, OR 97331; (503) 754-2624. Telex: 510596 0682 OSUCOVS.

A16 CONSORTIUM FOR INTERNATIONAL FISHERIES AND AQUACULTURE DEVELOPMENT (CIFAD)
Fisheries Economics.
Specialization: Designed to improve understanding of fisheries and aquaculture economics, management, and policy; topics include fisheries supply, demand, and marketing.
Dates: Five weeks: classes begin in Aug.
Location: Corvallis, Oregon: at Oregon State University.
Instruction: *Methods:* lectures, case studies, field trips, independent study/research, computer-assisted instruction. *By:* faculty, guest speakers/lecturers.
Highlights: Sponsor has offered program since 1985. Certificate. Issues I-20AB, IAP-66. Foreign nationals on tourist visas are eligible to enroll. A foreign student counselor/adviser is available. 20 total enrollment.
Eligibility: *Academic:* associate's degree. *Language:* English proficiency on intermediate level is preferred. *Professional:* administrators or researchers with responsibilities for fisheries and aquaculture development.
Cost: $3,750 for tuition, books, and materials. *Scholarships:* none.
Housing: Not provided; sponsor assists in locating housing.
Application: *Deadline:* none. *Fee:* none.
Contact: Mr. Kevin Hopkins, CIFAD, Oregon State University, Snell Hall 443, Corvallis, OR 97331; (503) 754-2624. Telex: 510596 0682 OSUCOVS.

A17 CONSORTIUM FOR INTERNATIONAL FISHERIES AND AQUACULTURE DEVELOPMENT (CIFAD)
Water Quality and Aquatic Ecology.
Specialization: Covers theoretical bases and techniques for assessing water quality in aquaculture; topics include productivity, nutrients, hydrology, and toxicology.
Dates: Eight weeks: classes begin in June.
Location: East Lansing, Michigan: at Michigan State University.
Instruction: *Methods:* lectures, field trips, "hands-on" training, science laboratories. *By:* faculty, guest speakers/lecturers.
Highlights: Sponsor has offered program since 1985. Certificate. Practical training is a program component; participants are not paid. Issues I-20AB, IAP-66. Foreign nationals on tourist visas are eligible to enroll. A foreign student counselor/adviser is available. 25 total enrollment.
Eligibility: *Academic:* associate's degree. *Language:* English proficiency on intermediate level is preferred. *Professional:* scientists and administrators with responsibilities for aquaculture.
Cost: $4,500 for tuition, books, and materials. *Scholarships:* none.
Housing: In dormitories.
Application: *Deadline:* none. *Fee:* none.
Contact: Mr. Kevin Hopkins, CIFAD, Oregon State University, Snell Hall 443, Corvallis, OR 97331; (503) 754-2624. Telex: 510596 0682 OSUCOVS.

Abbreviations: ESL = English as a Second Language; TOEFL = Test of English as a Foreign Language; ALIGU = American Language Institute of Georgetown University; GPA = Grade Point Average; SAT = Scholastic Aptitude Test; GED = General Equivalency Diploma.

FORESTRY AND TREE CARE

A18 UNIVERSITY OF ARIZONA, SCHOOL OF RENEWABLE NATURAL RESOURCES
Forestry in Arid Environments.
Specialization: Seeding and planting techniques, silvicultural practices, range and watershed management, fuelwood management and agroforestry practices, informational services.
Dates: One month: classes begin in July.
Location: Tucson, Arizona: on campus, at professional work site.
Instruction: *Methods:* discussion groups, lectures, case studies, field trips, individualized instruction, "hands-on" training, independent study/research, computer-assisted instruction. *By:* faculty, guest speakers/lecturers.
Highlights: Sponsor has offered program since 1983. Certificate. Issues I-20AB, I-20MN, IAP-66. Foreign nationals on tourist visas are eligible to enroll. A foreign student counselor/adviser is available. 30 total enrollment; 100% foreign enrollment in 1985.
Eligibility: *Academic:* bachelor's degree. *Language:* English proficiency on intermediate level is required. *Professional:* experience preferred.
Cost: $2,078 for tuition, books and materials, local transportation, health insurance. *Scholarships:* none.
Housing: Not provided; sponsor assists in locating housing.
Application: *Deadline:* three days prior. *Fee:* none.
Contact: Mr. Peter F. Ffolliott, SRNR-College of Agriculture, University of Arizona, Tucson, AZ 85721; (602) 621-7276/7522.

A19 WASHINGTON STATE UNIVERSITY
Continuing Education in Forestry, Silviculture, and Ecology.
Specialization: Forestry.
Dates: April–May.
Location: Pullman, Washington: on campus.
Instruction: *Methods:* lectures, field trips. *By:* faculty.
Highlights: Sponsor has offered program since 1973. A foreign student counselor/adviser is available. 30 total enrollment.
Eligibility: *Academic:* bachelor's degree. *Language:* English proficiency on advanced level is required. *Professional:* five years of experience required.
Cost: Not given. *Scholarships:* none.
Housing: In furnished rooms.
Application: *Deadline:* not given. *Fee:* not given.
Contact: Dr. David Baumgartner, Dept. of Forestry and Range Management, Washington State University, Pullman, WA 99164; (509) 335-2964.

HORTICULTURE

A20 OHIO STATE UNIVERSITY
Ohio Agricultural International Intern Program A.
Specialization: Reciprocal program available to Western Europeans. Combines work/training on farms and agribusinesses with study at Ohio State University. Correspondence courses also available.
Dates: One year: classes begin in March, June.
Location: Columbus, Ohio: on campus, at professional work site.
Instruction: *Methods:* lectures, individualized instruction, "hands-on" training, independent study/research. *By:* faculty.
Highlights: Sponsor has offered program since 1980. Practical training is a program component; participants are paid. Certificate. Issues IAP-66. Foreign nationals on tourist

visas are not eligible to enroll. A foreign student counselor/adviser is available. 10–12 total enrollment.
Eligibility: *Academic:* associate's degree. *Language:* English proficiency on advanced level is preferred. TOEFL: 500. *Professional:* two years of work experience required in agriculture/horticulture.
Cost: $2,736 for tuition, meals, health insurance. *Scholarships:* none; but wages from internship pay all costs of participants.
Housing: Usually provided by trainer.
Application: *Deadline:* three months prior. *Fee:* none.
Contact: Mr. Michael R. Chrisman, Ohio Agricultural International Intern Program, Ohio State University, 2120 Fyffe Road, Room 113, Columbus, OH 43210; (614) 422-7720. Telex: 272894 OSUA UR.

A21 OHIO STATE UNIVERSITY
Ohio Agricultural International Intern Program B.
Specialization: Reciprocal program for Western Europeans. Work/training on farms and agribusinesses; no academic training.
Dates: One year: flexible.
Location: Columbus, Ohio: at professional work site.
Instruction: *Methods:* individualized instruction, "hands-on" training, independent study/research. *By:* guest speakers/lecturers.
Highlights: Sponsor has offered program since 1980. Certificate. Practical training is a program component; participants are paid. Issues IAP-66. Foreign nationals on tourist visas are not eligible to enroll. A foreign student counselor/adviser is available. 100 total enrollment; 100% foreign enrollment in 1985.
Eligibility: *Academic:* associate's degree. *Language:* English proficiency on advanced level is preferred. TOEFL: 500. *Professional:* two years of work experience required in agriculture/horticulture.
Cost: None; wages from internship pay all costs of participants. *Scholarships:* none.
Housing: In furnished rooms, with families.
Application: *Deadline:* three months prior. *Fee:* none.
Contact: Mr. Michael R. Chrisman, Ohio Agricultural International Intern Program, Ohio State University, 2120 Fyffe Road, Room 113, Columbus, OH 43210; (614) 422-7720. Telex: 272894 OSUA UR.

IRRIGATION AND WATER MANAGEMENT

A22 COLORADO STATE UNIVERSITY, INTERNATIONAL SCHOOL FOR WATER RESOURCES
Multiobjective Water Systems Engineering.
Specialization: Practical application of optimization techniques and use of water resources for irrigation and power.
Dates: 12 weeks: June–Aug.
Location: Fort Collins, Colorado: on campus.
Instruction: *Methods:* lectures, case studies, "hands-on" training. *By:* faculty, guest speakers/lecturers.
Highlights: Sponsor has offered program since 1975. Certificate. Issues I-20AB, IAP-66. A foreign student counselor/adviser is available. 50% foreign enrollment in 1985.
Eligibility: *Academic:* bachelor's degree. *Language:* English proficiency on advanced level is required. TOEFL: 500. *Professional:* five years of work experience.
Cost: $3,650 for tuition, local transportation. *Scholarships:* none.
Housing: Not provided; sponsor assists in locating housing.
Application: *Deadline:* three months prior. *Fee:* none.

Abbreviations: ESL = English as a Second Language; TOEFL = Test of English as a Foreign Language; ALIGU = American Language Institute of Georgetown University; GPA = Grade Point Average; SAT = Scholastic Aptitude Test; GED = General Equivalency Diploma.

Contact: Dr. Neil S. Grigg, Director, International School for Water Resources, Colorado State University, Fort Collins, CO 80523; (303) 491-5247. Telex: 910-930-9000. Cable: ENGR CSU FTCN.

A23 COLORADO STATE UNIVERSITY, INTERNATIONAL SCHOOL FOR WATER RESOURCES

International School for Water Resources and Associated Programs.

Specialization: Practical postgraduate training in water resources planning, management and engineering.
Dates: Classes begin in Aug.
Location: Fort Collins, Colorado: on campus.
Instruction: *Methods:* lectures, case studies, individualized training, "hands-on" training, independent study/research, computer-assisted instruction. *By:* faculty, guest speakers/lecturers.
Highlights: Sponsor has offered program since 1967. Certificate. Issues I-20AB, IAP-66. Foreign nationals on tourist visas are eligible to enroll. A foreign student counselor/adviser is available. 100% foreign enrollment in 1985.
Eligibility: *Academic:* bachelor's degree. *Language:* English proficiency on advanced level is required. TOEFL: 450. *Professional:* none.
Cost: $3,650 per semester for tuition, local transportation. *Scholarships:* none.
Housing: Not provided; sponsor assists in locating housing.
Application: *Deadline:* three months prior. *Fee:* none.
Contact: Dr. Neil S. Grigg, Director, International School for Water Resources, Colorado State University, Fort Collins, CO 80523; (303) 491-5247. Telex: 910-930-9000. Cable: ENGR CSU FTCN.

A24 UNIVERSITY OF ARIZONA, SCHOOL OF RENEWABLE NATURAL RESOURCES

Resource Development of Watershed Lands.

Specialization: Watershed management: soil and water conservation, water resource development land management, renewable natural resources.
Dates: Early June–late July.
Location: Tucson, Arizona: on campus, field site.
Instruction: *Methods:* discussion groups, lectures, case studies, field trips, "hands-on" training. *By:* faculty, guest speakers/lecturers.
Highlights: Sponsor has offered program since 1980. Certificate. Practical training is a program component; participants are not paid. Issues IAP-66. Foreign nationals on tourist visas are eligible to enroll. A foreign student counselor/adviser is available. International student office. 30 total enrollment; 100% foreign enrollment in 1985.
Eligibility: *Academic:* associate's degree. *Language:* English proficiency on advanced level is required. *Professional:* graduate level or several years of field experience preferred.
Cost: $3,200 for tuition, books, and materials. *Scholarships:* full.
Housing: Not provided; sponsor assists in locating housing.
Application: *Deadline:* not given. *Fee:* not given. *Scholarship deadline:* not given.
Contact: John Thames, School of Renewable Natural Resources, University of Arizona, 325 Biological Sciences East, Tucson, AZ 85721; (602) 621-7273.

A25 UNIVERSITY OF ARIZONA, AGRICULTURAL ENGINEERING DEPARTMENT

Water Management and Runoff Farming for Small Scale Agriculture.

Specialization: Hydrology of runoff farming/water harvesting, small scale water management, soil and topography, crop selection, design criteria, operation, and maintenance.
Dates: Mid-July–early Aug.
Location: Tucson, Arizona: on campus, at professional work site.

Instruction: *Methods:* lectures, case studies, field trips, "hands-on" training. *By:* faculty.
Highlights: Sponsor has offered program since 1982. Certificate. Practical training is a program component; participants are not paid. Issues I-20AB, I-20MN, IAP-66. Foreign nationals on tourist visas are eligible to enroll. A foreign student counselor/adviser is available. International student office. 15 total enrollment; 100% foreign enrollment in 1985.
Eligibility: *Academic:* bachelor's degree. *Language:* English proficiency on intermediate level is preferred. *Professional:* none.
Cost: $2,200 for tuition, books and materials, housing, local transportation, health insurance. *Scholarships:* none.
Housing: In dormitories.
Application: *Deadline:* July 1. *Fee:* not given.
Contact: W. G. Matlock, Agricultural Engineering Department, University of Arizona, 507 Shantz Building, Tucson, AZ 85721; (602) 621-7224.

A26 UNIVERSITY OF SOUTH FLORIDA
Certificate of Advanced Studies in Hydrogeology.
Specialization: A comprehensive program in groundwater development, pollution, and resource management.
Dates: Rolling.
Location: Tampa, Florida: on campus; off-campus study by arrangement.
Instruction: *Methods:* discussion groups, lectures, case studies, field trips, individualized instruction, "hands-on" training, independent study/research, science laboratories.
By: faculty.
Highlights: Sponsor has offered program since 1985. Certificate upon completion of 24 semester hours in hydrology and related courses. Foreign nationals on tourist visas are eligible to enroll. A foreign student counselor/adviser is available. Foreign student office and tutoring services. 30 per year total enrollment; 5% foreign enrollment in 1985.
Eligibility: *Academic:* bachelor's degree. *Language:* English proficiency on intermediate level is required. TOEFL. *Professional:* none.
Cost: Varies. *Scholarships:* none.
Housing: Not provided; sponsor assists in locating housing.
Application: *Deadline:* rolling. *Fee:* none.
Contact: Hydrogeology Certificate Program Coordinator, Dept. of Geology, University of South Florida, Tampa, FL 33620; (813) 974-2236.

A27 UTAH STATE UNIVERSITY, INTERNATIONAL IRRIGATION CENTER
Irrigation Water Production Functions.
Specialization: Experimental and economic aspects.
Dates: Three weeks: Feb.–Mar.
Location: Logan, Utah: on campus.
Instruction: *Methods:* lectures, discussion groups, case studies. *By:* faculty. *Also available in Spanish.*
Highlights: Sponsor has offered program since 1982. Certificate. Foreign nationals on tourist visas are eligible to enroll. A foreign student counselor/adviser is available. 30 total enrollment; 100% foreign enrollment in 1985.
Eligibility: *Academic:* bachelor's degree in agriculture or engineering. *Language:* not given. *Professional:* two years of professional experience.
Cost: $1,925 for tuition, books. *Scholarships:* none.
Housing: Not provided; sponsor assists in locating housing.
Application: *Deadline:* July 1. *Fee:* none.
Contact: Admission Committee, International Irrigation Center, Dept. of Agricultural and Irrigation Engineering, UMC 83, Utah State University, Logan, UT 84322; (801) 750-2800. Telex: 3789426 UTAHSTATE U LOGAN.

Abbreviations: ESL = English as a Second Language; TOEFL = Test of English as a Foreign Language; ALIGU = American Language Institute of Georgetown University; GPA = Grade Point Average; SAT = Scholastic Aptitude Test; GED = General Equivalency Diploma.

A28 UTAH STATE UNIVERSITY, INTERNATIONAL IRRIGATION CENTER
On-Farm Water Management.
Specialization: Measurement, control, and evaluation. Experimental determination of water production function and economic aspects.
Dates: Six weeks: mid-July–Aug.
Location: Logan, Utah: on campus.
Instruction: *Methods:* lecturers, discussion groups, case studies, field trips, "hands-on" training. *By:* faculty, guest speakers/lecturers. *Also available in Spanish.*
Highlights: Sponsor has offered short-term programs since 1982. Certificate. Foreign nationals on tourist visas are eligible to enroll. A foreign student counselor/adviser is available. 30 total enrollment; 100% foreign enrollment in 1985.
Eligibility: *Academic:* bachelor's degree in agriculture or engineering. *Language:* not given. *Professional:* two years of experience.
Cost: $3,575 for tuition, books, field trip transportation. *Scholarships:* none.
Housing: Not provided; sponsor assists in locating housing.
Application: *Deadline:* July 6. *Fee:* none.
Contact: Admission Committee, International Irrigation Center, Dept. of Agricultural and Irrigation Engineering, UMC 83, Utah State University, Logan, UT 84322; (801) 750-2800. Telex: 3789426 UTAHSTATE U LOGAN.

A29 UTAH STATE UNIVERSITY, INTERNATIONAL IRRIGATION CENTER
Operation, Maintenance, and Management of Irrigation Districts.
Specialization: Development of water resources and planning policies, organization and maintenance of irrigation districts; and management variables.
Dates: Six weeks: Oct.–Nov.
Location: Logan, Utah: on campus, at professional work site.
Instruction: *Methods:* lectures, discussion groups, case studies, field trips. *By:* faculty. *Also available in Spanish.*
Highlights: Sponsor has offered program since 1982. Certificate. Foreign nationals on tourist visas are eligible to enroll. A foreign student counselor/adviser is available. 30 total enrollment; 100% foreign enrollment in 1985.
Eligibility: *Academic:* bachelor's degree in engineering, agriculture. *Language:* not given. *Professional:* two years of experience in agriculture, irrigation.
Cost: $3,575 for tuition, books, local transportation. *Scholarships:* none.
Housing: In hotels.
Application: *Deadline:* Sept. 28. *Fee:* not given.
Contact: Admission Committee, International Irrigation Center, Dept. of Agricultural and Irrigation Engineering, UMC 83, Utah State University, Logan, UT 84322; (801) 750-2800. Telex: 3789426 UTAHSTATE U LOGAN.

A30 UTAH STATE UNIVERSITY, INTERNATIONAL IRRIGATION CENTER
Pumping for Irrigation and Drainage.
Specialization: Types of pumps, selection of pumps and power units, pump efficiencies, pump design and installation, wells, well drilling, and operation and maintenance.
Dates: Four weeks: Sept.–Oct.
Location: Logan, Utah: on campus, at professional work site.
Instruction: *Methods:* lectures, discussion groups, case studies, field trips, "hands-on" training. *By:* faculty, guest speakers/lecturers. *Also available in Spanish.*
Highlights: Sponsor has offered short-term programs since 1980. Certificate. Foreign nationals on tourist visas are eligible to enroll. A foreign student counselor/adviser is available. 30 total enrollment: 100% foreign enrollment in 1985.
Eligibility: *Academic:* bachelor's degree in engineering or agriculture. *Language:* not given. *Professional:* experience in irrigation and drainage.
Cost: $2,550 for tuition, books, local transportation. *Scholarships:* none.
Housing: In hotels.
Application: *Deadline:* Sept. 16. *Fee:* not given.

Contact: Admission Committee, International Irrigation Center, Dept. of Agricultural and Irrigation Engineering, UMC 83, Utah State University, Logan, UT 84322; (801) 750-2800. Telex: 3789426 UTAHSTATE U LOGAN.

A31 UTAH STATE UNIVERSITY, INTERNATIONAL IRRIGATION CENTER
Soil and Water Conservation and Management.

Specialization: Principles of surveying, precipitation characteristics, soil-water-plant relationships, small watershed hydrology, soil and water conservation and management, measurement of runoff and soil loss.
Dates: Five weeks: Aug.–Sept.
Location: Logan, Utah: on campus, at professional work site.
Instruction: *Methods:* lectures, discussion groups, case studies, field trips, "hands-on" training. *By:* faculty, guest speakers/lecturers. *Also available in Spanish.*
Highlights: Sponsor has offered program since 1981. Certificate. Practical training is a program component. Foreign nationals on tourist visas are eligible to enroll. A foreign student counselor/adviser is available. 30 total enrollment; 100% foreign enrollment in 1985.
Eligibility: *Academic:* bachelor's degree in engineering or agriculture. *Language:* not given. *Professional:* two years of experience in soil conservation management.
Cost: $2,975 for tuition, books, local transportation. *Scholarships:* none.
Housing: In hotels.
Application: *Deadline:* Aug. 18. *Fee:* not given.
Contact: Admission Committee, International Irrigation Center, Dept. of Agricultural and Irrigation Engineering, UMC 83 Utah State University, Logan UT 84322; (801) 750-2800. Telex: 3789426 UTAHSTATE U LOGAN.

A32 UTAH STATE UNIVERSITY, INTERNATIONAL IRRIGATION CENTER
Waterlogging, Drainage, and Salinity Control.

Specialization: Environmental impact of irrigation, applied soil science, hydrology, water flow through soil, drainage system design (surface and subsurface). Includes field trips to drainage centers in Utah and other states.
Dates: Mar. 23–May 3.
Location: Logan, Utah: on campus, at professional work site.
Instruction: *Methods:* lectures, discussion groups, case studies, field trips, "hands-on" training. *By:* faculty, guest speakers/lecturers. *Also in Spanish.*
Highlights: Sponsor has offered program since 1981. Certificate. Foreign nationals on tourist visas are eligible to enroll. A foreign student counselor/adviser is available. 30 total enrollment; 100% foreign enrollment in 1985.
Eligibility: *Academic:* bachelor's degree in engineering or agriculture. *Language:* English proficiency on intermediate level is required. *Professional:* experience in irrigation and drainage field.
Cost: $3,575 for tuition, books, local transportation. *Scholarships:* none.
Housing: In hotels.
Application: *Deadline:* March 12. *Fee:* none.
Contact: Admission Committee, International Irrigation Center, Dept. of Agricultural and Irrigation Engineering, UMC83, Utah State University, Logan, UT 84322; (801) 750-2800. Telex: 3789426 UTAHSTATE U LOGAN.

PLANT PATHOLOGY

A33 OHIO STATE UNIVERSITY, INTERNATIONAL PROGRAMS IN AGRICULTURE
Pesticide Strategies for a Changing World.

Specialization: Entomology: pesticide selection and application, and skills for information retrieval.

Abbreviations: ESL = English as a Second Language; TOEFL = Test of English as a Foreign Language; ALIGU = American Language Institute of Georgetown University; GPA = Grade Point Average; SAT = Scholastic Aptitude Test; GED = General Equivalency Diploma.

Dates: Six weeks: classes begin in June.
Location: Wooster, Ohio: on campus, at professional work site.
Instruction: *Methods:* discussion groups, lectures, field trips, "hands-on" training.
By: faculty.
Highlights: Sponsor has offered program since 1986. Certificate. Practical training is a
program component; participants are not paid. Issues I-20AB, IAP-66. Foreign nationals on
tourist visas are eligible to enroll. A foreign student counselor/adviser is available. 30 total
enrollment.
Eligibility: *Academic:* bachelor's degree. *Language:* English proficiency on intermediate level
is required. *Professional:* technical specialists, extension and research personnel preferred.
Cost: $6,525 for tuition, books and materials, meals, housing, local transportation.
Scholarships: none.
Housing: In dormitories.
Application: *Deadline:* Apr. 1. *Fee:* none.
Contact: Dr. Harvey R. Krueger, Dept. of Entomology, OARDC, Ohio State University,
Wooster, OH 44691; (216) 263-3735. Cable: ATI-WOOSTER. Telex: 272894 OSUA UR.

A34 UNIVERSITY OF ILLINOIS
Short Courses.
Specialization: Plant pathology; diseases caused by fungi, bacteria, viruses, nematodes.
Graduate students may do some dissertation research overseas.
Dates: Rolling.
Location: Urbana, Illinois: on campus, at professional work site.
Instruction: *Methods:* discussion groups, lectures, field trips, individualized instruction,
"hands-on" training, independent study/research, computer-assisted instruction, science
laboratories. *By:* faculty.
Highlights: Sponsor has offered program since 1976. Certificate. Practical training is a
program component; participants are not paid. Issues IAP-66. Foreign nationals on tourist
visas are eligible to enroll. A foreign student counselor/adviser is available. Various support
services are available.
Eligibility: *Academic:* doctorate. *Language:* English proficiency on advanced level is required.
TOEFL: 550. *Professional:* none.
Cost: $12,000 per year for graduate school for tuition, books and materials, meals, housing.
Scholarships: partial.
Housing: Not provided; sponsor assists in locating housing.
Application: *Deadline:* open. *Fee:* $20.
Contact: Head, Dept. of Plant Pathology, College of Agriculture, University of Illinois, 1102
S. Goodwin Ave., Urbana, IL 61801; (217) 333-3170.

A35 UNIVERSITY OF MINNESOTA
Microcomputers for Improved Plant Protection in Developing Countries.
Specialization: Use of computer technology in pest control biology. Course designed for
plant scientists from developing countries.
Dates: 16 days: Sept.
Location: St. Paul, Minnesota: on campus.
Instruction: *Methods:* discussion groups, lectures, "hands-on" training, field trips.
By: faculty, professional guest lecturers.
Highlights: Sponsor has offered program previously. Foreign nationals on tourist visas are
eligible to enroll. 25 total enrollment.
Eligibility: *Academic:* degree in related science. *Language:* English proficiency on
intermediate level is required. *Professional:* plant scientists.
Cost: $3,500 for tuition, materials, housing, meals, field trip, use of computer.
Scholarships: none.
Housing: In dormitories.
Application: *Deadline:* July 1. *Fee:* none.

All program information is subject to change without notice
and must be confirmed directly with the sponsor.

Contact: Fred Hoefer, 405 Coffey Hall, University of Minnesota, 1420 Eckles Ave., St. Paul, MN 55108; (612) 373-0725. Telex: TWX 5106013001. Or: Paul Teng, Associate Professor, Dept. of Plant Pathology, University of Minnesota, Borlaug Hall, St. Paul, MN 55108; (612) 376-8183 or 376-1482.

POSTHARVEST TECHNOLOGY

A36 UNIVERSITY OF IDAHO
Post Harvest Seminar.
Specialization: Food preservation. Course may include material related to home countries of participants.
Dates: Two weeks: July.
Location: Moscow, Idaho: on campus, at professional work site.
Instruction: *Methods:* discussion groups, lectures, case studies, field trips, individualized instruction, "hands-on" training. *By:* faculty.
Highlights: Sponsor has offered program since 1984. Certificate. Practical training is a program component; participants are not paid. Foreign nationals on tourist visas are eligible to enroll. A foreign student counselor/adviser is available. 10–15 total enrollment; 50% foreign enrollment in 1985.
Eligibility: *Academic:* bachelor's degree. *Language:* English proficiency on intermediate level is required. *Professional:* none.
Cost: $60 per credit hour for tuition. *Scholarships:* available.
Housing: Not provided; sponsor assists in locating housing.
Application: *Deadline:* none. *Fee:* none.
Contact: Ms. Doris K. Williams, Director, School of Home Economics, University of Idaho, Moscow, ID 83843; (208) 885-6332.

RANGE MANAGEMENT

A37 COLORADO STATE UNIVERSITY, DEPARTMENT OF RANGE SCIENCE
Range Management Applications.
Specialization: Range and pastoral management course designed for professional managers of range lands.
Dates: One year: classes begin in May.
Location: Fort Collins, Colorado: on campus.
Instruction: *Methods:* discussion groups, lectures, field trips, computer-assisted instruction. *By:* faculty.
Highlights: Sponsor has offered short-term programs since 1968. Master's degree upon completion of 32 semester hours with 3.0 GPA. Issues I-20AB, IAP-66. A foreign student counselor/adviser is available. ESL and tutoring services. 35 total enrollment; 20% foreign enrollment in 1985.
Eligibility: *Academic:* bachelor's degree. *Language:* English proficiency on advanced level is required. TOEFL: 550 (500 conditional admission). *Professional:* work experience in range or pastoral management preferred.
Cost: $16,000 for tuition, books and materials. *Scholarships:* none.
Housing: Not provided; sponsor assists in locating housing.
Application: *Deadline:* May 1. *Fee:* $20; not refundable.
Contact: Director, Master of Science Applications, Dept. of Range Science, Colorado State University, Fort Collins, CO 80523; (303) 491-6677.

Abbreviations: ESL = English as a Second Language; TOEFL = Test of English as a Foreign Language; ALIGU = American Language Institute of Georgetown University; GPA = Grade Point Average; SAT = Scholastic Aptitude Test; GED = General Equivalency Diploma.

A38 UTAH STATE UNIVERSITY, DEPARTMENT OF RANGE SCIENCE
International Range Management.
Specialization: For administrators of range/livestock development projects who have backgrounds in agriculture or livestock production.
Dates: Two weeks: Aug.
Location: Logan, Utah: on campus.
Instruction: *Methods:* discussion groups, lectures, case studies, field trips. *By:* faculty.
Highlights: Sponsor has offered program since 1982. Certificate. Issues I-20AB, IAP-66. Foreign nationals on tourist visas are eligible to enroll. A foreign student counselor/adviser is available. Special library facilities. 20 total enrollment; 60% foreign enrollment in 1985.
Eligibility: *Academic:* bachelor's degree. *Language:* English proficiency on intermediate level is required. TOEFL: 500. *Professional:* previous or anticipated work with range management projects preferred.
Cost: $1,800 for tuition, books and materials, meals, housing, local transportation. *Scholarships:* none.
Housing: In hotels.
Application: *Deadline:* two months prior. *Fee:* none.
Contact: B. E. Norton, Dept. of Range Science, Utah State University, UMC 5230, Logan, UT 84322-5230; (801) 750-2476. Telex: Graphnet 3789426, UTAHSTATE U LOGAN.

A39 UTAH STATE UNIVERSITY, DEPARTMENT OF RANGE SCIENCE
International Range Management and Extension.
Specialization: Range management: basic principles, technical training and "hands-on" experience in rangeland and range livestock management and extension methods.
Dates: Two months: June–July.
Location: Logan, Utah: on campus, at professional work site.
Instruction: *Methods:* discussion groups, lectures, case studies, field trips, individualized instruction, "hands-on" training. *By:* faculty. *Also available in French and Spanish.*
Highlights: Sponsor has offered program since 1982. Certificate. Practical training is a program component; participants are not paid. Issues I-20AB, IAP-66. Foreign nationals on tourist visas are eligible to enroll. A foreign student counselor/adviser is available. Special library resources. 50 total enrollment; 100% foreign enrollment in 1985.
Eligibility: *Academic:* associate's degree. *Language:* English proficiency is not required. *Professional:* none.
Cost: About $7,000 inclusive. *Scholarships:* none.
Housing: In apartments, hotels.
Application: *Deadline:* Mar. 31. *Fee:* none.
Contact: B. E. Norton, Dept. of Range Science, Utah State University, UMC 5230, Logan, UT 84322-5230; (801) 750-2476. Telex: Graphnet 3789426 UTAHSTATE U LOGAN.

RURAL DEVELOPMENT

A40 ECONOMICS INSTITUTE
Rural Development.
Specialization: Adjusted to prior levels of professional training and individual goals. Includes visits to business and government offices and farms.
Dates: Five weeks: classes begin in Jan., March, June, July, Sept., Oct., Nov.
Location: Boulder, Colorado: at institute.
Instruction: *Methods:* lectures, discussion groups, case studies, field trips, individualized instruction, "hands-on" training, computer-assisted instruction, language labs, independent study/research. *By:* faculty, guest speakers/lecturers.
Highlights: Sponsor has offered short-term programs since 1958. Certificates and diplomas supported by official course transcript. Issues I-20AB. Foreign nationals on tourist visas are

eligible to enroll. A foreign student counselor/adviser is available. Over 100 total enrollment; 100% foreign enrollment in 1985.

Eligibility: *Academic:* bachelor's degree. *Language:* English proficiency is required. TOEFL: 425–500 depending upon course study. *Professional:* 3–10 years of experience preferred.

Cost: About $2,047 for ten weeks inclusive. *Scholarships:* none.

Housing: In residence halls, dormitories, apartments, with families.

Application: *Deadline:* none. *Fee:* $50 deposit.

Contact: Economics Institute, 1030 13 Street, Boulder, CO 80302; (303) 492-8419. Cable: ECONINST. Telex: 450385.

A41 UNIVERSITY OF WISCONSIN—MADISON
Keys to Agricultural Development at the Local Level.

Specialization: Agriculture and community development. Participants analyze problems and formulate solutions for agricultural development, consult with authorities, and visit agencies and projects in local communities.

Dates: Two weeks: Aug.

Location: Madison, Wisconsin: on campus, at professional work site.

Instruction: *Methods:* discussion groups, lectures, case studies, field trips, individualized instruction, independent study/research. *By:* faculty, guest speakers/lecturers.

Highlights: Sponsor has offered program since 1971. Certificate. Issues I-20AB, IAP-66. Foreign nationals on tourist visas are eligible to enroll. A foreign student counselor/adviser is available. Homestay program. 20 total enrollment; 100% foreign enrollment in 1985.

Eligibility: *Academic:* bachelor's degree. *Language:* English proficiency on intermediate level is required. *Professional:* requires three years of work experience, full-time employment in agricultural development.

Cost: $2,352 for books and materials, local transportation, health insurance, training fee. *Scholarships:* none.

Housing: In apartments, with families.

Application: *Deadline:* not given. *Fee:* not given.

Contact: Kenneth H. Shapiro, International Agricultural Programs, 240 Agriculture Hall, University of Wisconsin, 1450 Linden Drive, Madison, WI 53706; (608) 262-1271. Cable: AGRPROGRAMS. Telex: 265452 UOFWISC MDS.

Abbreviations: ESL = English as a Second Language; TOEFL = Test of English as a Foreign Language; ALIGU = American Language Institute of Georgetown University; GPA = Grade Point Average; SAT = Scholastic Aptitude Test; GED = General Equivalency Diploma.

17

ARCHITECTURE

B1 OHIO STATE UNIVERSITY, DEPARTMENT OF ARCHITECTURE
Master of Architecture.
Specialization: Computer-aided architectural design, passive solar design, preservation, theory and design.
Dates: Nine months: classes begin in June.
Location: Columbus, Ohio: on campus.
Instruction: *Methods:* discussion groups, lectures, case studies, field trips, individualized instruction, "hands-on" training, independent study/research, computer-assisted instruction. *By:* faculty, guest speakers/lecturers.
Highlights: Sponsor has offered program since 1968. Certificate upon completion of 45 credit hours. Issues IAP-66. Foreign nationals on tourist visas are eligible to enroll. A foreign student counselor/adviser is available. 80 total enrollment; 25% foreign enrollment in 1985.
Eligibility: *Academic:* bachelor's degree. *Language:* English proficiency on intermediate level is required. TOEFL: 575. *Professional:* none.
Cost: $5,388 for tuition. *Scholarships:* full.
Housing: Not provided; sponsor assists in locating housing.
Application: *Deadline:* Feb. 1. *Fee:* $25; not refundable. *Scholarship deadline:* Apr. 1.
Contact: Prof. Paul Young, Chairperson, Graduate Studies Committee, 189 Brown Hall, 190 W. 17th Ave., The Ohio State University, Columbus, OH 43210; (614) 422-5567.

B2 UNIVERSITY OF PENNSYLVANIA
Master of Architecture as a Second Professional Degree.
Specialization: Individualized program.
Dates: Nine months: classes begin Sept. and Jan.
Location: Philadelphia, Pennsylvania: on campus.
Instruction: *Methods:* lectures, field trips, independent study/research, design studios. *By:* faculty.
Highlights: Sponsor has offered program previously. Master's degree upon completion of thesis or studio work. Issues I-20AB, IAP-66. Foreign nationals on tourist visas are not eligible to enroll. A foreign student counselor/adviser is available. Orientation programs and other services.
Eligibility: *Academic:* bachelor's degree in architecture. *Language:* English proficiency on advanced level is required. TOEFL: 560. *Professional:* none.
Cost: About $20,000 inclusive. *Scholarships:* none.
Housing: Not provided; sponsor assists in locating housing.
Application: *Deadline:* Jan. 15 for fall start, Oct. 30 for spring. *Fee:* $45; not refundable.
Contact: Prof. Adele Santos, Chairman, Admissions Committee, Dept. of Architecture, Graduate School of Fine Arts, University of Pennsylvania, 110 Meyerson Hall, Philadelphia, PA 19104; (215) 898-6520. Telex: 710-670-0328. Cable: PNSYL Phila PA.

All program information is subject to change without notice
and must be confirmed directly with the sponsor.

CITY, COMMUNITY, AND REGIONAL PLANNING

B3 BOSTON UNIVERSITY, METROPOLITAN COLLEGE
Master of Urban Affairs.
Specialization: Housing and community development, environmental management and planning, urban and regional policy analysis.
Dates: One year: classes begin in Sept. and Jan.
Location: Boston, Massachusetts: on campus.
Instruction: *Methods:* discussion groups, lectures, case studies, field trips, individualized instruction, "hands-on" training, independent study/research, computer-assisted instruction. *By:* faculty, guest speakers/lecturers.
Highlights: Sponsor has offered program since 1968. Certificate upon completion of 36 credits and special project (Plan A), or 40 graduate credits (Plan B). Issues I-20AB, IAP-66. Foreign nationals on tourist visas are not eligible to enroll. A foreign student counselor/adviser is available. Orientation and social programs. About 100 total enrollment; 16% foreign enrollment in 1985.
Eligibility: *Academic:* bachelor's degree. *Language:* English proficiency on intermediate level is required. TOEFL: 550. *Professional:* related work experience preferred.
Cost: $10,950 for tuition. *Scholarships:* partial.
Housing: In dormitories, apartments, furnished rooms, with families.
Application: *Deadline:* six months prior. *Fee:* $30; not refundable. *Scholarship deadline:* six months prior.
Contact: Prof. H.P. Henderson, Chairman, Dept. of Urban Affairs and Planning, Boston University—Metropolitan College, 755 Commonwealth Ave., Boston, MA 02215; (617) 353-3025.

B4 PRATT INSTITUTE
Waterfronts.
Specialization: Designing an elemental part of the New York shoreline; a design studio complemented by lectures by internationally-known architects.
Dates: Three weeks: July–Aug.
Location: New York, New York: on campus, at professional work site.
Instruction: *Methods:* lectures, discussion groups, case studies, field trips, individualized instruction, "hands-on" training, independent study/research. *By:* faculty, guest speakers/lecturers.
Highlights: Sponsor has offered program previously. Certificate. Issues I-20AB, IAP-66. Foreign nationals on tourist visas are eligible to enroll. A foreign student counselor/adviser is available. ESL program. 75 total enrollment; 50% foreign enrollment in 1985.
Eligibility: *Academic:* two years of architecture study. *Language:* English proficiency on intermediate level is required. *Professional:* none.
Cost: Varies. *Scholarships:* none.
Housing: In dormitories.
Application: *Deadline:* May 3. *Fee:* $250; not refundable.
Contact: Judith Glass, Director, Division of Continuing Education, Pratt Institute, 200 Willoughby Avenue, Brooklyn, NY 11205; (718) 636-3453.

B5 SAN JOSE STATE UNIVERSITY, DEPARTMENT OF URBAN & REGIONAL PLANNING
Certificate Program in Urban Planning Management.
Specialization: Urban analysis, urban and regional planning, housing and community development, environment planning, and urban design.
Dates: Classes begin in Jan. and Aug.
Location: San Jose, California: on campus.

Abbreviations: ESL = English as a Second Language; TOEFL = Test of English as a Foreign Language; ALIGU = American Language Institute of Georgetown University; GPA = Grade Point Average; SAT = Scholastic Aptitude Test; GED = General Equivalency Diploma.

Instruction: *Methods:* discussion groups, lectures, case studies, field trips, individualized instruction, "hands-on" training, independent study/research, computer-assisted instruction. *By:* faculty.

Highlights: Sponsor has offered program since 1980. Certificate upon completion of 3–5 courses. Practical training may be a program component; participants are not paid. Issues I-20AB, IAP-66. Foreign nationals on tourist visas are eligible to enroll. A foreign student counselor/adviser is available. 15 total enrollment; 20% foreign enrollment in 1985.

Eligibility: *Academic:* bachelor's degree. *Language:* English proficiency on intermediate level is preferred. TOEFL: 550. *Professional:* none.

Cost: $141 per semester unit for tuition. *Scholarships:* partial.

Housing: Not provided; sponsor assists in locating housing.

Application: *Deadline:* Feb. 1 for fall; Sept. 1 for spring. *Fee:* $35; not refundable. *Scholarship deadline:* none.

Contact: Daniel Garr, Department of Urban & Regional Planning, San Jose State University, San Jose, CA 95192; (408) 277-3410.

B6 UNIVERSITY OF PENNSYLVANIA
Post Master's Certificate in City and Regional Planning.

Specialization: Transportation planning.

Dates: Sept.–May.

Location: Philadelphia, Pennsylvania: on campus.

Instruction: *Methods:* discussion groups, lectures. *By:* faculty.

Highlights: Sponsor has offered program since 1982. Certificate. Issues I-20AB, IAP-66. Foreign nationals on tourist visas are not eligible to enroll. A foreign student counselor/adviser is available.

Eligibility: *Academic:* master's degree. *Language:* English proficiency on advanced level is required. TOEFL: 500. *Professional:* none.

Cost: $20,000 inclusive. *Scholarships:* none.

Housing: In dormitories.

Application: *Deadline:* Mar. 30. *Fee:* $50; not refundable.

Contact: Chair, Department of City and Regional Planning, Graduate School of Fine Arts, University of Pennsylvania, Philadelphia, PA 19104; (215) 898-8329. Cable: PNSYL Phila Pa. Telex: 710-670-0328.

B7 UNIVERSITY OF WISCONSIN—MADISON, DEPARTMENT OF URBAN AND REGIONAL PLANNING
Urban and Regional Planning Program.

Specialization: Accelerated master's program for students from developing countries. Land use, housing, growth management; economic and fiscal; environmental and resources; social planning.

Dates: One year: classes begin in Aug., Jan., June.

Location: Madison, Wisconsin: on campus.

Instruction: *Methods:* discussion groups, lectures, case studies, field trips, independent study/research, computer-assisted instruction, language laboratories. *By:* faculty, guest speakers/lecturers.

Highlights: Sponsor has offered program since 1980. Master's degree upon completion of 30 credit hours. Issues I-20AB, IAP-66. Foreign nationals on tourist visas are eligible to enroll. A foreign student counselor/adviser is available. 80 total enrollment; 27% foreign enrollment in 1985.

Eligibility: *Academic:* bachelor's degree. *Language:* English proficiency on intermediate level is required. TOEFL: 540. *Professional:* five years professional planning and/or related experience.

Cost: $15,360 inclusive. *Scholarships:* none.

Housing: Not provided; sponsor assists in locating housing.

Application: *Deadline:* June 30. *Fee:* $20; not refundable.

Contact: Chairman, Department of Urban and Regional Planning, 925 Bascom Mall/Old Music Hall, University of Wisconsin—Madison, Madison, WI 53706; (608) 262-1004. Telex: 265452.

HISTORIC PRESERVATION

B8 UNIVERSITY OF FLORIDA
Preservation Institute: Caribbean.
Specialization: Preservation of historic architecture and cultural values of the Caribbean. Program cosponsored by OAS and Plan CARIMOS.
Dates: Six months: classes begin in April.
Location: Gainesville, Florida: on campus; at professional work sites in Puerto Rico and Guatemala.
Instruction: *Methods:* discussion groups, lectures, case studies, field trips, "hands-on" training, independent study/research. *By:* faculty, guest speakers/lecturers. *Also in Spanish.*
Highlights: Sponsor has offered program since 1982. Certificate. Practical training is a program component; participants are not paid. Foreign nationals on tourist visas are eligible to enroll. A foreign student counselor/adviser is available. 25 per course total enrollment; 80% foreign enrollment in 1985.
Eligibility: *Academic:* two years of undergraduate work in architecture or related field. *Language:* English proficiency on intermediate level is preferred. *Professional:* none.
Cost: $1,700 per course for tuition, meals, housing, health insurance. *Scholarships:* partial (limited number paid by Organization of American States).
Housing: Not provided; sponsor assists in locating housing.
Application: *Deadline:* Mar. 31. *Fee:* none.
Contact: Mrs. Nadia Scheffer, ARCH 331, College of Architecture, University of Florida, Gainesville, FL 32611; (904) 392-4836.

B9 UNIVERSITY OF PENNSYLVANIA
Historic Preservation.
Specialization: Preservation design, planning, history (architecture, landscape, decorative arts), building conservation. Landscape preservation emphasis being developed.
Dates: Sept.–May.
Location: Philadelphia, Pennsylvania: on campus.
Instruction: *Methods:* lectures, field trips, individualized instruction, "hands-on" training, independent study/research, seminars, laboratory courses. *By:* faculty, guest speakers/lecturers.
Highlights: Sponsor has offered program since 1981. Certificate upon completion of eight required courses; master's degree upon completion of 16 course units. Issues I-20AB, IAP-66. Foreign nationals on tourist visas are not eligible to enroll. A foreign student counselor/adviser is available. Orientation program. 40 total enrollment; 10% foreign enrollment in 1985.
Eligibility: *Academic:* bachelor's degree; GRE scores. *Language:* English proficiency on advanced level is required. TOEFL suggested. *Professional:* none.
Cost: About $13,000 for tuition, fees, health insurance. *Scholarships:* partial.
Housing: Not provided; sponsor assists in locating housing.
Application: *Deadline:* March 1. *Fee:* $40; not refundable. *Scholarship deadline:* not given.
Contact: The Graduate Group in Historic Preservation, Graduate School in Fine Arts, University of Pennsylvania, 214 Myerson Hall, Philadelphia, PA 19104-6311; (215) 898-3169. Cable: PNSYL Phila PA. Telex: 710-670-0328.

Abbreviations: ESL = English as a Second Language; TOEFL = Test of English as a Foreign Language; ALIGU = American Language Institute of Georgetown University; GPA = Grade Point Average; SAT = Scholastic Aptitude Test; GED = General Equivalency Diploma.

INTERIOR DESIGN

B10 PLAZA THREE ACADEMY
Dates: One year: classes begin bimonthly.
Location: Phoenix, Arizona: on campus.
Instruction: *Methods:* lectures, discussion groups, case studies, field trips, individualized instruction, "hands-on" training, independent study/research. *By:* guest speakers/lecturers.
Highlights: Sponsor has offered program since 1981. Certificate upon completion of program with 2.0 GPA, 85% attendance. Issues I-20MN. Foreign nationals on tourist visas are not eligible to enroll. A foreign student counselor/adviser is not available. 72 total enrollment; 1% foreign enrollment in 1985.
Eligibility: *Academic:* associate's degree. *Language:* English proficiency on intermediate level is required. Reading and Language Evaluation Examination: 50%. *Professional:* none.
Cost: $6,295 for tuition, books. *Scholarships:* none.
Housing: Not provided; sponsor assists in locating housing.
Application: *Deadline:* open. *Fee:* none.
Contact: Director of Admissions, Plaza Three Academy, 4343 N. 16th Street, Phoenix, AZ 85016; (602) 264-9703.

AREA AND ETHNIC STUDIES

AFRICAN STUDIES

C1 **OHIO UNIVERSITY**
   African Studies Program.
Specialization: Multidisciplinary program leading to Master of Arts in International Affairs.
Dates: Nine months: classes begin quarterly.
Location: Athens, Ohio: on campus.
Instruction: *Methods:* discussion groups, lectures, field trips, independent study/research, computer-assisted instruction, language laboratories, science laboratories. *By:* faculty, guest speakers/lecturers.
Highlights: Sponsor has offered program since 1965. Certificate upon completion of 47 quarter hours of academic coursework from at least three disciplines, African language, comprehensive oral exam. Issues I-20AB, I-20MN, IAP-66. A foreign student counselor/adviser is available. 40 total enrollment; 60% foreign enrollment in 1985.
Eligibility: *Academic:* bachelor's degree. *Language:* English proficiency on advanced level is required. Univ. of Michigan Language Test: 80; administered when students arrive. *Professional:* none.
Cost: $12,000 inclusive. *Scholarships:* partial.
Housing: In dormitories, apartments, furnished rooms.
Application: *Deadline:* two months prior. *Fee:* $25; not refundable. *Scholarship deadline:* Mar. 1.
Contact: Dr. Gifford B. Doxsee, Director, African Studies Program, Ohio University, 56 E. Union Street, Athens, OH 45701; (614) 592-3472. Telex: 810239 2992.

AMERICAN STUDIES

C2 **CASA (THE CENTER FOR ADVANCED STUDIES OF THE AMERICAS)**
   U.S. Studies Program.
Specialization: A special program for Latin American and Caribbean students; an interdisciplinary course on U.S. society, economy, government and political system. Includes internships in government agencies, trade associations, and lobbying groups.
Dates: One year.
Location: Washington, D.C.: on campus.
Instruction: *Methods:* lectures, discussion groups, field trips. *By:* faculty, guest speakers/lecturers.
Highlights: Sponsor has offered program since 1984. Certificate. Practical training is a program component. Foreign nationals on tourist visas are not eligible to enroll. A foreign student counselor/adviser is available. Various support services are available.
Eligibility: *Academic:* bachelor's degree. *Language:* English proficiency on advanced level is required. *Professional:* none.
Cost: Not given.
Housing: Not given.

Abbreviations: ESL = English as a Second Language; TOEFL = Test of English as a Foreign Language; ALIGU = American Language Institute of Georgetown University; GPA = Grade Point Average; SAT = Scholastic Aptitude Test; GED = General Equivalency Diploma.

Application: *Deadline:* May 15. *Fee:* not given.
Contact: CASA U.S. Studies Program, The Center for Advanced Studies of the Americas, 1717 Massachusetts Ave. NW, Suite 104, Washington, DC 20036; (202) 462-3000.

C3 DUQUESNE UNIVERSITY
American History Program.

Dates: Three weeks: classes begin in early and late June.
Location: Pittsburgh, Pennsylvania: on campus.
Instruction: *Methods:* lectures. *By:* faculty.
Highlights: Sponsor has offered program since 1962. Credit. Certificate. Issues I-20. List of past participants is available.
Eligibility: *Academic:* bachelor's degree; SAT. *Language:* TOEFL: 500. *Professional:* none.
Cost: $161 per credit for tuition. *Scholarships:* none.
Housing: In dormitories.
Application: *Deadline:* Mar. 30. *Fee:* $30.
Contact: Rev. Sean Hogan, C.S.Sp., Office of International Education, Duquesne University, Pittsburgh, PA 15282; (412) 434-6113. Telex: 295 581 (RCA).

C4 INDIANA UNIVERSITY

Specialization: American Indian reservation cultural immersion practicum; campus orientation precedes six-week placement as a volunteer worker.
Dates: June–Aug.
Location: Bloomington, Indiana: on campus; on Indian reservations 2,000 miles west of campus.
Instruction: *Methods:* lectures, discussion groups, field trips, "hands-on" training, independent study/research. *By:* faculty, guest speakers/lecturers.
Highlights: Sponsor has offered program previously. Certificate. Practical training is a program component; participants are not paid. Issues I-20AB, I-20MN, IAP-66. Foreign nationals on tourist visas are eligible to enroll. A foreign student counselor/adviser is available. 36 total enrollment; 12% foreign enrollment in 1985.
Eligibility: *Academic:* associate's degree. *Language:* English proficiency on intermediate level is required. *Professional:* one year of professional experience or five years of college.
Cost: $3,100 for tuition, books. *Scholarships:* none.
Housing: In dormitories on campus; reservation housing is usually free.
Application: *Deadline:* Mar. 15. *Fee:* $75; not refundable.
Contact: Professor James Mahan, Indiana University, 321 Education Bldg., Bloomington, IN 47405; (812) 335-8579.

C5 LESLEY COLLEGE GRADUATE SCHOOL
American Studies.

Specialization: Individually designed independent-study master's degree program; requires four three-hour meetings on campus.
Dates: To be arranged.
Location: Cambridge, Massachusetts: on campus. Independent study may take place at student's home or another location.
Instruction: *Methods:* lectures, discussion groups, case studies, field trips, individualized instruction, "hands-on" training, independent study/research. *By:* faculty, guest speakers/lecturers.
Highlights: Sponsor has offered short-term programs since 1971. Master's degree. Practical training may be a program component. Issues I-20AB. A foreign student counselor/adviser is available. 5% foreign enrollment in 1985.
Eligibility: *Academic:* bachelor's degree. *Language:* English proficiency is required. TOEFL. *Professional:* none.
Cost: $7,200 for tuition. *Scholarships:* none.
Housing: Not provided.

Application: *Deadline:* open. *Fee:* $35; not refundable.
Contact: Margot Chamberlain, Program Advisor, Lesley College Graduate School, 29 Everett Street, Cambridge, MA 02238; (617) 868-9600, Ext. 426.

C6 SMITH COLLEGE
Diploma in American Studies.
Specialization: Designed primarily for present or future teachers of American culture and institutions.
Dates: Nine months: Sept.–May.
Location: Northampton, Massachusetts: on campus.
Instruction: *Methods:* discussion groups, lectures, independent study/research. *By:* faculty.
Highlights: Sponsor has offered program since 1980. Certificate upon completion of six courses and thesis. Issues I-20AB and IAP-66. Foreign nationals on tourist visas are not eligible to enroll. A foreign student counselor/adviser is available. 15 total enrollment; 100% foreign enrollment in 1985.
Eligibility: *Academic:* three years of undergraduate work. *Language:* English proficiency on intermediate level is required. TOEFL: 550. *Professional:* none.
Cost: Not given. *Scholarships:* full and partial.
Housing: In dormitories.
Application: *Deadline:* Feb. 1. *Fee:* $30; not refundable. *Scholarship deadline:* Feb. 1.
Contact: Mr. Alan L. Marvelli, Director of Graduate Study, Smith College, Northampton, MA 01063; (413) 584-2700.

C7 UNIVERSITY OF MINNESOTA
Seminar in American Studies.
Specialization: Intensive course in American studies for Swedish secondary school teachers, offered in cooperation with the In-Service Training Board of the Swedish Ministry of Education.
Dates: 3½ weeks: June–July.
Location: Minneapolis-St. Paul, Minnesota: on campus.
Instruction: *Methods:* lectures, seminars. *By:* faculty.
Highlights: Sponsor has offered program previously. Certificate. 30 total enrollment; 100% foreign enrollment in 1985.
Eligibility: *Academic:* bachelor's degree. *Language:* English proficiency on advanced level is required. *Professional:* Swedish teachers only.
Cost: Not given. *Scholarships:* none.
Housing: In dormitories.
Application: *Deadline:* Mar. 1. *Fee:* not given.
Contact: In-Service Training Board of The Ministry of Education, Stockholm, Sweden.

C8 UNIVERSITY OF MINNESOTA
American Studies Institute.
Specialization: American studies for European secondary school teachers; participants are chosen and financially sponsored by the Fulbright Commissions in their own countries.
Dates: Seven weeks: July–Aug.
Location: Minneapolis-St. Paul, Minnesota; with travel to New Mexico, Louisiana, Massachusetts, New York, and Washington, D.C.
Instruction: *Methods:* lectures, seminars, field trips. *By:* faculty, guest speakers/lecturers.
Highlights: Sponsor has offered program since 1980. Certificate. Does not help obtain visa. 40 total enrollment; 100% foreign enrollment in 1985.
Eligibility: *Academic:* bachelor's degree. *Language:* English proficiency on advanced level is required. *Professional:* secondary school teachers preferred.
Cost: None. *Scholarships:* none; all students are sponsored.
Housing: In dormitories.

Abbreviations: ESL = English as a Second Language; TOEFL = Test of English as a Foreign Language; ALIGU = American Language Institute of Georgetown University; GPA = Grade Point Average; SAT = Scholastic Aptitude Test; GED = General Equivalency Diploma.

Application: *Deadline:* Set by commission in home country. *Fee:* none.
Contact: Fulbright or binational commission in home country, USIS or USIA office in home country.

C9 WESTERN MICHIGAN UNIVERSITY
Summer Institute in English Language and American Culture.
Specialization: Group participation only.
Dates: 2–4 weeks: to be arranged.
Location: Kalamazoo, Michigan: on campus.
Instruction: *Methods:* lectures, discussion groups, field trips, language laboratories.
By: faculty.
Highlights: Sponsor has offered program previously. Certificate. Issues I-20AB, IAP-66.
Foreign nationals on tourist visas are eligible to enroll. A foreign student counselor/adviser is available. 100% foreign enrollment in 1985.
Eligibility: *Academic:* associate's degree or some undergraduate work. *Language:* English proficiency on beginning level is required. *Professional:* none.
Cost: $425–$475 for tuition. *Scholarships:* none.
Housing: In dormitories.
Application: *Deadline:* none. *Fee:* none.
Contact: Dr. Norman C. Greenberg, Dean, International Education & Programs, Western Michigan University, 2090 Friedmann Hall, Kalamazoo, MI 49008; (616) 383-0944.

EUROPEAN STUDIES

C10 WASHINGTON UNIVERSITY
Western European Studies Program.
Specialization: Interdisciplinary master's program for students from the University of Tubingen, West Germany.
Dates: Nine months: classes begin in Aug.
Location: St. Louis, Missouri: on campus.
Instruction: *Methods:* discussion groups, lectures. *By:* faculty. *German literature classes in German.*
Highlights: Sponsor has offered program since 1984. Master's degree. Issues IAP-66.
Foreign nationals on tourist visas are not eligible to enroll. A foreign student counselor/adviser is available. International house. 2 total enrollment; 100% foreign enrollment in 1985.
Eligibility: *Academic:* bachelor's degree. *Language:* English proficiency on advanced level is required. TOEFL: 550. *Professional:* certification is required. Abiturzeugnis, Zwischenprufung.
Cost: $15,000. *Scholarships:* full and partial.
Housing: Not provided; sponsor assists in locating housing in apartments.
Application: *Deadline:* Mar. 1. *Fee:* none. *Scholarship deadline:* Mar. 1.
Contact: University of Tubingen, West Germany.

RUSSIAN AND EASTERN EUROPEAN STUDIES

C11 UNIVERSITY OF ILLINOIS AT URBANA-CHAMPAIGN
Illinois Summer Research Laboratory on Russia and Eastern Europe.
Specialization: Russian and East European Studies. Participants receive library privileges and housing for 28 nights.
Dates: June–Aug.
Location: Urbana, Illinois: on campus.

Instruction: *Methods:* discussion groups, lectures, independent study/research. *By:* faculty, guest speakers/lecturers.
Highlights: Sponsor has offered program since 1973. Issues IAP-66. Foreign nationals on tourist visas are eligible to enroll. A foreign student counselor/adviser is not available. 350 total enrollment; 12% foreign enrollment in 1985.
Eligibility: *Academic:* master's degree. *Language:* English proficiency on advanced level is preferred. *Professional:* professionals or doctoral graduate students.
Cost: Not given. *Scholarships:* none.
Housing: In dormitories.
Application: *Deadline:* Apr. 1. *Fee:* $65; refundable.
Contact: Lynne Curry, Russian and East European Center, University of Illinois, 1208 West California Ave., Urbana, IL 61801; (217) 333-1244. Telex: TWX 910-245-0782 IU SLAVIC URBA.

C12 UNIVERSITY OF ILLINOIS AT URBANA-CHAMPAIGN
Independent Scholars Program.
Specialization: Russian and East European Studies. Participants receive library privileges, housing, and a small research allowance for 1–3 months.
Dates: Mid-Feb.–mid-May.
Location: Urbana, Illinois; on campus.
Instruction: *Methods:* independent study/research. *By:* faculty.
Highlights: Sponsor has offered program since 1983. Issues IAP-66. Foreign nationals on tourist visas are eligible to enroll. A foreign student counselor/adviser is not available. 4–6 total enrollment; 66% foreign enrollment in 1985.
Eligibility: *Academic:* doctorate. *Language:* English proficiency on advanced level is preferred. *Professional:* professionals.
Cost: Not given. *Scholarships:* research allowance of $10 per week.
Housing: In hotels.
Application: *Deadline:* Apr. 1. *Fee:* none.
Contact: Marianna Tax Choldin, Russian and East European Center, University of Illinois, 1208 West California Ave., Urbana, IL 61801; (217) 333-1244. Telex: TWX 910-245-0782 IU SLAVIC URBA.

BUSINESS

D1 BRENAU COLLEGE
General Business.
Specialization: General business studies.
Dates: Sept. 15–June 1.
Location: Atlanta, Georgia: on campus.
Instruction: *Methods:* discussion groups, lectures, case studies, "hands-on" training, independent study, computer-assisted instruction, science laboratories. *By:* faculty.
Highlights: Sponsor has offered program since 1981. Practical training is a program component; participants are not paid. Issues I-20AB. Foreign nationals on tourist visas are not eligible to enroll. A foreign student counselor/adviser is available. 20 total enrollment; 3% foreign enrollment in 1985.
Eligibility: *Academic:* associate's degree. *Language:* English proficiency on beginning level is required. TOEFL: 500. *Professional:* none.
Cost: $3,150 for tuition. *Scholarships:* none.
Housing: Not provided; sponsor assists in locating housing.
Application: *Deadline:* 1 month prior. *Fee:* $25; not refundable.
Contact: Dr. David Kelly, Dean of The Professional College, Brenau College, Butler Hall, Gainesville, GA 30501; (404) 534-6200.

D2 COUNCIL ON INTERNATIONAL EDUCATIONAL EXCHANGE
Business and Society in America.
Specialization: Programs in general business and management for Japanese employees of businesses in Japan.
Dates: Two months: classes begin in July.
Location: Philadelphia, Pennsylvania: on campus of Univ. of Pennsylvania.
Instruction: *Methods:* discussion groups, lectures, case studies, field trips, independent study/research, language laboratories. *By:* faculty, guest speakers/lecturers.
Highlights: Sponsor has offered program since 1973. Certificate upon completion of program and independent research. Foreign nationals on tourist visas are eligible to enroll. A foreign student counselor/adviser is available. Homestay and travel program. 40 total enrollment; 100% foreign enrollment in 1985.
Eligibility: *Academic:* bachelor's degree. *Language:* English proficiency on intermediate level is required; placement exam. *Professional:* determined by employer who sponsors participant.
Cost: About $4,500–$5,000 inclusive. *Scholarships:* none, but students sponsored by employers.
Housing: In dormitories, hotels.
Application: *Deadline:* Mar. 25. *Fee:* 5,000 yen; not refundable.
Contact: Council on International Educational Exchange, Sanno Grand Bldg., Room 205, 14-2 Nagata-cho, 2-chome, Chiyoda-ku, Tokyo 100, Japan; (03) 581-7581. Telex: 78133221. Or: Ms. Margaret Shiba, Council on International Educational Exchange, 205 E. 42nd Street, New York, NY 10017; (212) 661-1414.

D3 MASSACHUSETTS INSTITUTE OF TECHNOLOGY
Summer Session.
Specialization: Programs in decision making, operations management, policy design with microcomputers, corporate planning systems, investment and technology in China, research management, and physical resource management.
Dates: June–Aug.
Location: Cambridge, Massachusetts: on campus.
Instruction: *Methods:* discussion groups, lectures, case studies, "hands-on" training, independent study/research, computer-assisted instruction, science laboratories. *By:* faculty.
Highlights: Sponsor has offered program since 1949. Certificate. Foreign nationals on tourist visas are eligible to enroll. A foreign student counselor/adviser is not available. About 20–25 per class total enrollment; 10% foreign enrollment in 1985.
Eligibility: *Academic:* bachelor's degree. *Language:* English proficiency on intermediate level is required. *Professional:* none.
Cost: About $1,500 per week for tuition, books and materials, meals, housing.
Scholarships: none.
Housing: In dormitories, hotels.
Application: *Deadline:* depends on program. *Fee:* none.
Contact: Summer Session Office, Massachusetts Institute of Technology, 77 Massachusetts Ave., Room E19-356, Cambridge, MA 02139; (617) 253-2101. Telex: 921473 MIT CAM.

D4 MASSACHUSETTS INSTITUTE OF TECHNOLOGY
Visiting Fellows Program.
Specialization: Professional specialization on fulltime, nondegree basis for one or more semesters, may include any combination of coursework, research, and special study in fields of accounting, applied economics, strategic management, finance, health care management, human resource management, industrial relations, international management, management information systems, marketing, operations management, operations, research and statistics, organization studies, system dynamics, technological innovation.
Dates: Classes begin in Sept., Feb.
Location: Cambridge, Massachusetts: on campus.
Instruction: *Methods:* discussion groups, lectures, case studies, individualized instruction, "hands-on" training, independent study/research, computer-assisted instruction, language laboratories. *By:* faculty.
Highlights: Sponsor has offered program since 1956. Certificate. Issues I-20AB, IAP-66. Foreign nationals on tourist visas are not eligible to enroll. A foreign student counselor/adviser is available. Unlimited total enrollment; 14.3% foreign enrollment in 1985.
Eligibility: *Academic:* bachelor's degree. *Language:* English proficiency on intermediate level is required. TOEFL: 575. *Professional:* none.
Cost: $9,975 per term for tuition, health insurance. *Scholarships:* none.
Housing: Not provided; sponsor assists in locating housing.
Application: *Deadline:* about four months prior. *Fee:* $40; not refundable.
Contact: Mr. Alan F. White, Assoc. Dean for Executive Education, MIT Sloan School of Management, 50 Memorial Drive, Cambridge, MA 02139; (617) 253-7166. Cable: MIT CAM. Telex: 797961 MITSLOANUD.

D5 PACE UNIVERSITY
Specialization: Accounting, economic planning, financial management, information systems, international business, management, marketing, health care administration. Courses can be tailored to meet the needs of international students.
Dates: Classes begin in Sept., Jan., May, June, July.
Location: New York, New York: on campus, at work site.
Instruction: *Methods:* lectures, discussion groups, case studies, field trips, individualized instruction, "hands-on" training, computer-assisted instruction, language labs. *By:* faculty, guest speakers/lecturers. *Also in French, Spanish, Arabic.*

Abbreviations: ESL = English as a Second Language; TOEFL = Test of English as a Foreign Language; ALIGU = American Language Institute of Georgetown University; GPA = Grade Point Average; SAT = Scholastic Aptitude Test; GED = General Equivalency Diploma.

BUSINESS

Highlights: Sponsor has offered short-term programs since the 1940s. Certificate upon completion of program with B average. Issues I-20AB, IAP-66. Foreign nationals on tourist visas are eligible to enroll. A foreign student counselor/adviser is available. ESL program and International Student Club. Unlimited total enrollment; 2.5% total foreign enrollment in 1985.
Eligibility: *Academic:* bachelor's degree. *Language:* English proficiency on advanced level is required. TOEFL: 550. *Professional:* none.
Cost: About $7,000 per semester inclusive. *Scholarships:* partial (graduate assistantships).
Housing: In dormitories, or sponsor assists in locating housing.
Application: *Deadline:* rolling. *Fee:* $20; not refundable. *Scholarship deadline:* at time of application.
Contact: Mrs. R.I. Fennekohl, Graduate Admissions Office, Pace University, Pace Plaza, New York, NY 10038; (212) 488-1720.

D6 STATE UNIVERSITY OF NEW YORK AT BUFFALO
International Executive Program.
Specialization: Business studies for pre-MBA students and practicing managers, combined with intensive English Language Institute.
Dates: June–Aug.
Location: Buffalo, New York: on campus.
Instruction: *Methods:* lecturers, seminars, independent study, practical training. *By:* faculty, guest speakers/lecturers.
Highlights: Sponsor has offered program since 1978. Certificate. Issues I-20. Limited services for foreign nationals. ESL program. 50 total enrollment; 100% foreign enrollment in 1985.
Eligibility: *Academic:* bachelor's degree. *Language:* TOEFL: 500. *Professional:* management experience or acceptance into an MBA program.
Cost: $4,400 for tuition, meals, housing, health insurance. *Scholarships:* none.
Application: *Deadline:* May. *Fee:* $250.
Contact: Kristin Keough, International Executive Program, School of Management, SUNY at Buffalo, 108 Jacobs Management Center, Amherst, NY 14260; (716) 636-3201. Telex: 323183(SOM) ELN62852596.

D7 UNIVERSITY OF DALLAS, GRADUATE SCHOOL OF MANAGEMENT
Pre-MBA.
Specialization: Preparation for admission to U.S. MBA programs; emphasizes development of English communication skills, business terminology and methods, accounting, computers and intensive GMAT preparation.
Dates: Three months: classes begin in Sept., Feb., May.
Location: Dallas, Texas: on campus.
Instruction: *Methods:* discussion groups, lectures, case studies, field trips, individualized instruction, computer-assisted instruction, language laboratories. *By:* faculty, guest speakers/lecturers.
Highlights: Sponsor has offered program since 1985. Certificate. Issues I-20AB, IAP-66. Foreign nationals on tourist visas are eligible to enroll. A foreign student counselor/adviser is available. Orientation, recreational, and social programs. 20 total enrollment; 100% foreign enrollment in 1985.
Eligibility: *Academic:* bachelor's degree. *Language:* English proficiency on intermediate level is required. TOEFL: 475. *Professional:* none.
Cost: $4,450 for tuition, books and materials, meals, housing, health insurance. *Scholarships:* none.
Housing: In dormitories, apartments.
Application: *Deadline:* two months prior. *Fee:* $50; not refundable.
Contact: Ms. Julie Allan, Director, Pre-MBA Program, Graduate School of Management, University of Dallas, 1845 E. Northgate Drive, Irving, TX 75062-4799; (214) 721-5299. Telex: 792979 Executive.

All program information is subject to change without notice
and must be confirmed directly with the sponsor.

D8 **UNIVERSITY OF DETROIT, COLLEGE OF BUSINESS & ADMINISTRATION**
   Financial Planning.
Specialization: Programs in financial planning and management information systems.
Dates: Financial planning: Sept.–May. Information systems: June.
Location: Detroit, Michigan: on campus.
Instruction: *Methods:* discussion groups, lectures, "hands-on" training. *By:* faculty, guest speakers/lecturers.
Highlights: Sponsor has offered program previously. Certificate. Issues I-20AB, IAP-66. Foreign nationals on tourist visas are not eligible to enroll. A foreign student counselor/adviser is available. 50 total enrollment; no foreign enrollment in 1985.
Eligibility: *Academic:* associate's or bachelor's degree. *Language:* English proficiency on advanced level is required. *Professional:* none.
Cost: About $1,400 for noncredit tuition. *Scholarships:* none.
Housing: Not provided; sponsor assists in locating housing.
Application: *Deadline:* varies. *Fee:* none.
Contact: Dr. Shelia Ronis, Director, Renaissance Business Programs, University of Detroit, 651 E. Jefferson, Detroit, MI 48226; (313) 927-1501.

D9 **UNIVERSITY OF ILLINOIS AT URBANA-CHAMPAIGN**
   Training for Graduate Study in the USA.
Specialization: Business administration and accounting. Preparation for admission to U.S. MBA programs.
Dates: One year: classes begin in May.
Location: Champaign, Illinois: on campus.
Instruction: *Methods:* discussion groups, lectures, case studies, field trips, individualized instruction, independent study/research, computer-assisted instruction, language laboratories. *By:* faculty.
Highlights: Sponsor has offered program since 1977. Certificate. Issues IAP-66. Foreign nationals on tourist visas are not eligible to enroll. A foreign student counselor/adviser is available. Unlimited total enrollment; 100% foreign enrollment in 1985.
Eligibility: *Academic:* bachelor's degree. *Language:* English proficiency on intermediate level is required. *Professional:* one year of experience preferred.
Cost: $4,500 per term for tuition, books, and materials. *Scholarships:* none.
Housing: Not provided; sponsor assists in locating housing.
Application: *Deadline:* Mar. 1. *Fee:* $25; refundable.
Contact: Program Management Office, Program of Overseas University Collaboration, University of Illinois at Urbana-Champaign, Champaign, IL 61801; (217) 333-1990. Telex: 5101011969 UI Telcom URUD.

D10 **VOORHEES COLLEGE**
   Division of Business and Economics.
Specialization: Accounting, business administration, business education, office administration.
Dates: Nine months; classes begin in Aug. and Jan.
Location: Denmark, South Carolina: on campus, at professional work site.
Instruction: *Methods:* discussion groups, lectures, case studies, field trips, individualized instruction, "hands-on" training, independent study/research, computer-assisted instruction, science laboratories. *By:* faculty.
Highlights: Sponsor has offered program since 1969. Certificate. Practical training is a program component; participants are not paid. Issues I-20AB. Foreign nationals on tourist visas are not eligible to enroll. A foreign student counselor/adviser is available.
Eligibility: *Academic:* associate's degree. *Language:* English proficiency on beginning level is required. TOEFL. *Professional:* none.
Cost: $5,884 for tuition, meals, housing, health insurance. *Scholarships:* none.
Housing: In dormitories.

Abbreviations: ESL = English as a Second Language; TOEFL = Test of English as a Foreign Language; ALIGU = American Language Institute of Georgetown University; GPA = Grade Point Average; SAT = Scholastic Aptitude Test; GED = General Equivalency Diploma.

Application: *Deadline:* Aug. *Fee:* $10; not refundable.
Contact: Dr. Lucious Daily, Jr., Director of Admissions and Records, Voorhees College, Voorhees Road, Denmark, SC 29042; (803) 793-3351.

ACCOUNTING

D11 THE AMERICAN UNIVERSITY
Certificate of Advanced Professional Study in Accounting.
Specialization: Graduate-level courses in accounting.
Dates: Classes begin in Sept., Jan., May, July.
Location: Washington, D.C.: on campus.
Instruction: *Methods:* discussion groups, lectures, case studies. *By:* faculty.
Highlights: Sponsor has offered short-term programs previously. Certificate. Issues I-20AB. Foreign nationals on tourist visas are not eligible to enroll. A foreign student counselor/adviser is available. ESL and orientation programs.
Eligibility: *Academic:* master's degree; 3.0 GPA in last 60 hours; GMAT score: 400 or CPA exam. *Language:* English proficiency on advanced level is required. TOEFL: 600; or English Language Institute Placement Test. *Professional:* none.
Cost: $299 per semester hour for tuition. *Scholarships:* none.
Housing: Not provided; sponsor assists in locating housing.
Application: *Deadline:* none. *Fee:* none.
Contact: Programs Advisement Center, The American University, 4400 Massachusetts Ave. NW, Room 153 McKinley Bldg., Washington, DC 20016; (202) 885-2500.

D12 GUILFORD COLLEGE
Specialization: Accounting.
Dates: Aug.–late July.
Location: Greensboro, North Carolina: on campus.
Instruction: *Methods:* lectures, discussion groups. *By:* faculty.
Highlights: Sponsor has offered program since 1983. Certificate upon completion of 4–6 courses. Issues I-20AB, I-20MN. Foreign nationals on tourist visas are not eligible to enroll. A foreign student counselor/adviser is available. ESL program and International Relations Club.
Eligibility: *Academic:* bachelor's degree. *Language:* English proficiency on intermediate level is required. TOEFL: 500. *Professional:* none.
Cost: $112 per credit hour for tuition. *Scholarships:* none.
Housing: Not provided; student makes own arrangements.
Application: *Deadline:* none. *Fee:* $20; not refundable.
Contact: Dean of Admissions and Financial Aid, Guilford College, 5800 West Friendly Ave., Greensboro, NC 27410; (919) 292-5511.

D13 KELLER GRADUATE SCHOOL OF MANAGEMENT
Master of Business Administration in Accounting.
Specialization: Accounting.
Dates: One year: classes begin in Sept., Nov., Feb., April, and June.
Location: Chicago, Illinois: on campus.
Instruction: *Methods:* lectures, discussion groups, case studies. *By:* faculty, guest speakers/lecturers.
Highlights: Sponsor has offered program previously. Master's degree upon completion of program with 2.5 GPA. Issues I-20AB. Foreign nationals on tourist visas are not eligible to enroll. A foreign student counselor/adviser is available. 5% foreign enrollment in 1985.
Eligibility: *Academic:* bachelor's degree; GMAT: 34 + . *Language:* English proficiency on advanced level is required. TOEFL: 550. *Professional:* none.
Cost: $7,360 for tuition. *Scholarships:* none.

All program information is subject to change without notice
and must be confirmed directly with the sponsor.

Housing: Not provided; sponsor assists in locating housing.
Application: *Deadline:* none. *Fee:* none.
Contact: Director of Admission, Keller Graduate School of Management, 10 S. Riverside Plaza, Suite 2124, Chicago, IL 60606; (312) 454-0880.

D14 UNIVERSITY OF BALTIMORE
Certificate Program in Accounting.

Specialization: Accounting.
Dates: Rolling: fall, spring, and summer sessions.
Location: Baltimore, Maryland: on campus.
Instruction: *Methods:* discussion groups, lectures, case studies, "hands-on" training, computer-assisted instruction. *By:* faculty.
Highlights: Sponsor has offered program previously. Certificate. Issues I-20AB. Foreign nationals on tourist visas are eligible to enroll. A foreign student counselor/adviser is available. Tutoring program. Unlimited total enrollment; 3–4% foreign enrollment in 1985.
Eligibility: *Academic:* completion of 56 college credits or more. *Language:* English proficiency on advanced level is required. TOEFL: 550. *Professional:* none.
Cost: $3,000–$4,000 per year for tuition, fees. *Scholarships:* full; few available.
Housing: Not provided; sponsor assists in locating housing.
Application: *Deadline:* June 1 for fall, Nov. 1 for spring. *Fee:* $20; not refundable. *Scholarship deadline:* Apr. 1 for fall, Nov. 1 for spring.
Contact: Ms. Wendy Burgess, International Student Advisor, University of Baltimore, 1420 N. Charles Street, Baltimore, MD 21201; (301) 625-3157.

D15 U.S. DEPARTMENT OF AGRICULTURE, GRADUATE SCHOOL
Financial Auditor Training Program.

Specialization: Auditor training for government and the private sector, including EDP for auditors.
Dates: One year: classes begin in Jan.
Location: Washington, D.C.: on campus, at professional work site.
Instruction: *Methods:* lectures, case studies, field trips, individualized instruction, "hands-on" training. *By:* faculty, guest speakers/lecturers.
Highlights: Sponsor has offered program since 1985. Certificate. Issues I-20AB. Foreign nationals on tourist visas are eligible to enroll. A foreign student counselor/adviser is available. Orientation, tutoring, and social activities. 20 total enrollment; 100% foreign enrollment in 1985.
Eligibility: *Academic:* bachelor's degree. *Language:* English proficiency on advanced level is preferred. *Professional:* none.
Cost: $12,000 for tuition, books and materials, health insurance. *Scholarships:* none.
Housing: Not provided; sponsor assists in locating housing.
Application: *Deadline:* Oct. *Fee:* $300; not refundable.
Contact: Ms. Judy Jenkins, USDA International Programs, Graduate School, 600 Maryland Ave. SW, Suite 134, Washington, DC 20024; (202) 447-7476.

BANKING AND FINANCE

D16 ADELPHI UNIVERSITY
The Summer Graduate Institute in Bank Management.

Specialization: Develops a broad perspective of the banking profession and improves the management skills of bank personnel.
Dates: Two weeks: June.
Location: Garden City, New York: on campus.
Instruction: *Methods:* discussion groups, lectures, case studies, individualized instruction, computer-assisted instruction. *By:* faculty, guest speakers/lecturers.

Abbreviations: ESL = English as a Second Language; TOEFL = Test of English as a Foreign Language; ALIGU = American Language Institute of Georgetown University; GPA = Grade Point Average; SAT = Scholastic Aptitude Test; GED = General Equivalency Diploma.

Highlights: Sponsor has offered program since 1980. Certificate. Foreign nationals on tourist visas are eligible to enroll. A foreign student counselor/adviser is available. 30 total enrollment; no foreign enrollment in 1985.
Eligibility: *Academic:* bachelor's degree. *Language:* English proficiency on advanced level is required. *Professional:* five years of experience in banking or business preferred.
Cost: $1,550 for tuition, books and materials, meals, housing. *Scholarships:* none.
Housing: In dormitories.
Application: *Deadline:* June 1. *Fee:* $100; not refundable.
Contact: Dr. Carol H. Schwartz, School of Banking and Money Management, Adelphi University, Garden City, NY 11530; (516) 663-1176.

D17 COUNCIL ON INTERNATIONAL EDUCATIONAL EXCHANGE
Banking and Society in America.
Specialization: Programs in general business/management and banking for Japanese employees of businesses and regional banks in Japan.
Dates: Two months: classes begin in July.
Location: Pittsburgh, Pennsylvania, and Seattle, Washington: on campus of participating institutions.
Instruction: *Methods:* discussion groups, lectures, case studies, field trips, independent study/research, language laboratories. *By:* faculty, guest speakers/lecturers.
Highlights: Sponsor has offered program since 1973. Certificate upon completion of independent research program. Foreign nationals on tourist visas are eligible to enroll. A foreign student counselor/adviser is available. Homestay and travel program. 40 per campus total enrollment; 100% foreign enrollment in 1985.
Eligibility: *Academic:* bachelor's degree. *Language:* English proficiency on intermediate level is required; placement exam. *Professional:* determined by employer who sponsors participant.
Cost: About $4,500–$5,000 for tuition, books and materials, meals, housing, local transportation, health insurance, homestay and group travel programs. *Scholarships:* none; students sponsored by employers.
Housing: In dormitories, hotels.
Application: *Deadline:* Mar. 25. *Fee:* 5,000 yen; not refundable.
Contact: Council on International Educational Exchange, Sanno Grand Bldg., Room 205, 14-2 Nagata-cho, 2-chome, Chiyoda-ku, Tokyo 100, Japan; (03) 581-7581; Telex: 78133221. Or: Ms. Margaret Shiba, Council on International Educational Exchange, 205 E. 42nd Street, New York, NY 10017; (212) 661-1414.

D18 GRADUATE SCHOOL OF BANKING, INC.
Banking.
Specialization: Condensed banking program for bank officers.
Dates: Two weeks: Aug.
Location: Madison, Wisconsin: on campus.
Instruction: *Methods:* discussion groups, lectures, case studies, "hands-on" training, computer-assisted instruction. *By:* faculty, guest speakers/lecturers.
Highlights: Sponsor has offered program since 1945. Certificate. A foreign student counselor/adviser is not available. 1,000 total enrollment; no foreign enrollment in 1985.
Eligibility: *Academic:* bachelor's degree; knowledge of banking fundamentals.
Language: English proficiency on advanced level is required. *Professional:* five years of experience as officer of financial institution required.
Cost: $1,250 for tuition, books and materials, meals, housing. *Scholarships:* none.
Housing: In dormitories.
Application: *Deadline:* Mar. 1. *Fee:* $50; not refundable.
Contact: Mr. Richard I. Doolittle, Exec. Vice President, Graduate School of Banking, Inc., 122 W. Washington Ave., Madison, WI 53703; (608) 256-7021.

D19 INSTITUTE OF WORLD AFFAIRS
International Financial Institutions.
Specialization: History, present-day operations, and world role of major financial institutions: the World Bank, IMF, regional development banks, major private commercial banks, OPEC, UNCTAD, others. Course intended for professionals and graduate students from a variety of fields and occupations.
Dates: Four weeks: August.
Location: Salisbury, Connecticut: at institute.
Instruction: *Methods:* lectures, discussion groups, case studies. *By:* faculty, guest speakers/lecturers.
Highlights: Sponsor has offered program since 1924. Credit. Certificate. Helps obtain visa. Extensive services for foreign nationals. 25 total enrollment; 66% foreign enrollment in 1985.
Eligibility: *Academic:* graduates or exceptional undergraduates. *Language:* competency. *Professional:* none.
Cost: $1,200 inclusive. *Scholarships:* partial.
Housing: In furnished rooms.
Application: *Deadline:* June 1. *Fee:* none. *Scholarship deadline:* June 1.
Contact: William E. Schaufele, Jr., Director, Institute of World Affairs, Salisbury, CT 06068.

D20 KELLER GRADUATE SCHOOL OF MANAGEMENT
Master's of Business Administration in Finance.
Dates: One year: classes begin Sept., Nov., Feb., April, June.
Location: Chicago, Illinois: on campus.
Instruction: *Methods:* lectures, discussion groups, case studies. *By:* faculty, guest speakers/lecturers.
Highlights: Sponsor has offered short-term programs since 1973. Master's degree upon completion of program with 2.5 GPA. Issues I-20AB. Foreign nationals on tourist visas are not eligible to enroll. A foreign student counselor/adviser is available. 5% foreign enrollment in 1985.
Eligibility: *Academic:* bachelor's degree; GMAT: 24 + . *Language:* English proficiency on advanced level is required. TOEFL: 550. *Professional:* none.
Cost: $8,960 for tuition. *Scholarships:* none.
Highlights: Not provided; sponsor assists in locating housing.
Application: *Deadline:* none. *Fee:* none.
Contact: Director of Admission, Keller Graduate School of Management, 10 S. Riverside Plaza, Suite 2124, Chicago, IL 60606; (312) 454-0880.

D21 UNIVERSITY OF HAWAII AT MANOA, PACIFIC ASIAN MANAGEMENT INSTITUTE
International Banking and Finance Program.
Specialization: Intensive training in theory and practice of international banking and finance: concepts, institutions, transactions associated with offshore banking and multinational corporations, focusing on Asia and the Pacific Basin.
Dates: Three weeks: early July–Aug. Optional fourth week in California.
Location: Honolulu, Hawaii: on campus, at professional work site.
Instruction: *Methods:* discussion groups, lectures, case studies, field trips, individualized instruction. *By:* faculty, guest speakers/lecturers.
Highlights: Sponsor has offered program since 1981. Certificate. Issues I-20AB, IAP-66. A foreign student counselor/adviser is available. Social and cultural programs. 25 total enrollment; 80% foreign enrollment in 1985. List of past participants is available.
Eligibility: *Academic:* bachelor's degree preferred. *Language:* English proficiency on intermediate level is required. *Professional:* 3–5 years of work experience in managerial position in banking or financial institution.

Abbreviations: ESL = English as a Second Language; TOEFL = Test of English as a Foreign Language; ALIGU = American Language Institute of Georgetown University; GPA = Grade Point Average; SAT = Scholastic Aptitude Test; GED = General Equivalency Diploma.

BUSINESS

Cost: About $3,575 for tuition, some meals, housing, some local transportation.
Scholarships: none.
Housing: In dormitories, hotels.
Application: *Deadline:* May 20. *Fee:* $50; not refundable.
Contact: Virginia Crockett, Assistant Director, PAMI, College of Business Administration, University of Hawaii, Manoa, 2404 Maile Way, Honolulu, HI 96822; (808) 948-7564. Cable: UNIHAW. Telex: (723) 8022 PAMI HR.

D22 UNIVERSITY OF NEBRASKA AT OMAHA
Senior Bankers and Financial Executives Course.
Specialization: Courses in banking and finance for senior bankers and financial executives.
Dates: Three weeks: June–Aug.
Location: Omaha, Nebraska: on campus, at professional work site.
Instruction: *Methods:* discussion groups, lectures, case studies, field trips, "hands-on" training. *By:* faculty, guest speakers/lecturers.
Highlights: Sponsor has offered program since 1983. Certificate. Issues I-20AB, IAP-66. Foreign nationals on tourist visas are eligible to enroll. A foreign student counselor/adviser is available. Orientation and cultural programs. 20 per course total enrollment; 100% foreign enrollment in 1985.
Eligibility: *Academic:* associate's degree. *Language:* English proficiency on intermediate level is required. *Professional:* five years of work experience required.
Cost: $4,000 per course for tuition, books and materials, local transportation.
Scholarships: none.
Housing: Not provided; sponsor assists in locating housing.
Application: *Deadline:* four weeks prior. *Fee:* none.
Contact: Mr. Thomas E. Gouttierre, Director, International Studies & Programs, University of Nebraska at Omaha, Omaha, NE 68182; (402) 554-2376. Telex: 484340 UNL COMM LCN.

EXECUTIVE DEVELOPMENT

D23 CORNELL UNIVERSITY
Executive Development Program.
Specialization: General management; participants are upper-level executives from many countries and organizations.
Dates: June 16–July 18.
Location: Ithaca, New York: on campus.
Instruction: *Methods:* lectures, seminars, case studies. *By:* faculty, guest speakers/lecturers.
Highlights: Sponsor has offered program since 1953. Credit. Certificate. Does not help obtain visa. No services for foreign nationals. 100 total enrollment; 30% foreign enrollment in 1985.
Eligibility: *Academic:* bachelor's degree. *Language:* not given. *Professional:* five years of experience.
Cost: $7,500 for tuition, books, meals, housing. *Scholarships:* none.
Housing: In dormitories.
Application: *Deadline:* Apr. 1. *Fee:* none.
Contact: L. Joseph Thomas, Director, Cornell University, 503 Malott Hall, Ithaca, NY 14853; (607) 255-4854. Telex: 6713054.

D24 DARTMOUTH COLLEGE
Tuck Executive Program.
Specialization: Exposure to senior management of U.S. corporations and government agencies.
Dates: Four weeks: classes begin in July.

Location: Hanover, New Hampshire: on campus.
Instruction: *Methods:* discussion groups, lectures, case studies, computer-assisted instruction. *By:* faculty.
Highlights: Sponsor has offered program since 1974. Certificate. Issues I-20AB, IAP-66. Foreign nationals on tourist visas are eligible to enroll. A foreign student counselor/adviser is not available. 96 total enrollment; 15% foreign enrollment in 1985.
Eligibility: *Academic:* bachelor's degree. *Language:* English proficiency on advanced level is required. *Professional:* 15 years of experience required; background in general management or senior functional management.
Cost: $9,000 for tuition, books and materials, meals, housing. *Scholarships:* none.
Housing: In dormitories.
Application: *Deadline:* Apr. 1. *Fee:* none; not refundable.
Contact: Mr. Paul F. Doscher, Amos Tuck School, Dartmouth College, Hanover, NH 03755; (603) 646-2839.

D25 ECONOMICS INSTITUTE
Professional Development Program.
Specialization: Negotiations and cross-cultural communication.
Dates: Five weeks: classes begin about monthly.
Location: Boulder, Colorado: on campus, at professional work site.
Instruction: *Methods:* discussion groups, lectures, case studies, field trips, individualized instruction, "hands-on" training, independent study/research, computer-assisted instruction, language laboratories. *By:* faculty, guest speakers/lecturers.
Highlights: Sponsor has offered program since 1958. Certificate. Practical training may be a program component. Issues I-20AB. Foreign nationals on tourist visas are eligible to enroll. A foreign student counselor/adviser is available. 1,000 per year total enrollment; 100% foreign enrollment in 1985.
Eligibility: *Academic:* bachelor's degree. *Language:* English proficiency on intermediate level is preferred. TOEFL: 425. *Professional:* 3–10 years of work experience preferred.
Cost: About $2,047 inclusive. *Scholarships:* partial.
Housing: In dormitories, apartments, furnished rooms, hotels, with families, international residence halls.
Application: *Deadline:* none. *Fee:* $50; refundable. *Scholarship deadline:* none.
Contact: Admissions Office, Economics Institute, 1030 13th Street, Boulder, CO 80302; (303) 492-8419. Telex: 450385 ECONINST BDR.

D26 MURRAY STATE UNIVERSITY
Building Excellence through Executive Communication.
Specialization: Organizational communication: listening skills, conflict management, problem solving, and human resource development.
Dates: May 10–29.
Location: Murray, Kentucky: on campus.
Instruction: *Methods:* discussion groups, lectures, case studies, field trips. *By:* faculty, guest speakers/lecturers.
Highlights: New program. Certificate. Issues I-20AB, IAP-66. Foreign nationals on tourist visas are not eligible to enroll. A foreign student counselor/adviser is available. Various support services are available. 20 total enrollment.
Eligibility: *Academic:* bachelor's degree. *Language:* English proficiency on advanced level is required. *Professional:* two years of work experience required.
Cost: $2,000 for tuition, books and materials, local transportation. *Scholarships:* none.
Housing: Not provided; sponsor assists in locating housing.
Application: *Deadline:* Mar. 16. *Fee:* $25; refundable.
Contact: Vernon W. Gantt, Speech Communication & Theatre, Murray State University, P.O. Box 2014 Univ. Station, Murray, KY 42071-3316; (502) 762-4465.

Abbreviations: ESL = English as a Second Language; TOEFL = Test of English as a Foreign Language; ALIGU = American Language Institute of Georgetown University; GPA = Grade Point Average; SAT = Scholastic Aptitude Test; GED = General Equivalency Diploma.

BUSINESS

D27 NORTHEASTERN UNIVERSITY, CENTER FOR MANAGEMENT DEVELOPMENT
Management Development Program.
Specialization: Graduate-level program designed to improve overall performance of experienced managers.
Dates: Six weeks over a five-month period: classes begin in Oct. and Jan.
Location: Andover, Massachusetts: at Phillips Andover Academy.
Instruction: *Methods:* discussion groups, lectures, case studies, field trips, "hands-on" training, independent study/research. *By:* faculty, professional guest speakers.
Highlights: Sponsor has offered program since 1960. Certificate. Issues I-20AB, IAP-66. Foreign nationals on tourist visas are eligible to enroll. A foreign student counselor/adviser is available. International Student Office. 35 total enrollment; 14% foreign enrollment in 1985.
Eligibility: *Academic:* graduate-level program, but no specific requirement.
Language: English proficiency on advanced level is required. *Professional:* ten years of work experience and eight years of managerial experience required.
Cost: $9,000 for tuition, books and materials, meals, housing. *Scholarships:* none.
Housing: In Andover Inn.
Application: *Deadline:* one month prior. *Fee:* none.
Contact: Dean Richard J. Santos, Center for Management Development, Northeastern University, 208 HU, Boston, MA 02115; (617) 437-3272.

D28 TEXAS A&M UNIVERSITY
Advanced Management Program.
Specialization: Strategy-focused management and related contemporary issues.
Dates: One month: classes begin in June.
Location: College Station, Texas: on campus.
Instruction: *Methods:* discussion groups, lectures, case studies. *By:* faculty, guest speakers/lecturers.
Highlights: Sponsor has offered program since 1982. Certificate. Issues I-20AB, IAP-66. Foreign nationals on tourist visas are eligible to enroll. A foreign student counselor/adviser is available. 40 total enrollment; 15% foreign enrollment in 1985.
Eligibility: *Academic:* bachelor's degree or demonstrated executive ability. *Language:* English proficiency on advanced level is required. *Professional:* ten years of managerial experience preferred.
Cost: $5,200 for tuition, books and materials, some meals, social events, campus recreational facilities. *Scholarships:* none.
Housing: Not provided; sponsor assists in locating housing.
Application: *Deadline:* one month prior. *Fee:* none.
Contact: Twyla Nevitt, Assistant Director, Center for Executive Development, Texas A&M University, 449 John R. Blocker Bldg., College Station, TX 77843; (409) 845-1684 or 845-1216. Telex: 510 892 7689.

D29 TEXAS A&M UNIVERSITY
International Managers Program.
Specialization: For non-American managers; American business origins, culture, managerial concepts and practices.
Dates: One year: classes begin in June.
Location: College Station, Texas: on campus.
Instruction: *Methods:* discussion groups, lectures, case studies, field trips, individualized instruction, optional independent study/research, optional computer-assisted instruction, language laboratories. *By:* faculty, guest speakers/lecturers.
Highlights: Sponsor has offered program since 1985. Certificate. Issues I-20AB, IAP-66. Foreign nationals on tourist visas are not eligible to enroll. A foreign student counselor/adviser is available. 20 total enrollment; 100% foreign enrollment in 1985.
Eligibility: *Academic:* bachelor's degree. *Language:* English proficiency on advanced level is

All program information is subject to change without notice and must be confirmed directly with the sponsor.

38

required. TOEFL: 520; University test: 550 TOEFL equivalent. *Professional:* three years of experience; first level managers preferred.
Cost: $13,950 for tuition, health insurance, some meals, fees, field trips. *Scholarships:* none.
Housing: Not provided; sponsor assists in locating housing. For summer term, provided in dormitories.
Application: *Deadline:* Mar. 15. *Fee:* $2,050; all but $50 refundable if not accepted.
Contact: Mr. Robert H. Nelson, Director, Center for Executive Development, Texas A&M University, 440 John R. Blocker Bldg., College Station, TX 77843; (409) 845-4057. Telex: 510-892-7689.

D30 UNIVERSITY OF HOUSTON—UNIVERSITY PARK
Executive Development Program.
Specialization: For high potential upper middle managers, or newly appointed general managers.
Dates: Three weeks: classes begin in Sept.
Location: Houston, Texas: on campus.
Instruction: *Methods:* discussion groups, lectures, case studies, field trips, "hands-on" training, independent study/research, computer-assisted instruction. *By:* faculty, guest speakers/lecturers.
Highlights: Sponsor has offered program since 1953. Certificate. Issues I-20AB, IAP-66. Foreign nationals on tourist visas are not eligible to enroll. A foreign student counselor/adviser is available. Various support services are available. 45 total enrollment; 40% foreign enrollment in 1985.
Eligibility: *Academic:* bachelor's degree. *Language:* English proficiency on advanced level is required. *Professional:* 5–10 years of work experience required.
Cost: $4,800 for tuition, books, and materials. *Scholarships:* none.
Housing: In hotels.
Application: *Deadline:* Aug. 1. *Fee:* none.
Contact: Mr. Roger N. Blakeney, Director, Executive Development Program, College of Business Administration, University of Houston, University Park, Houston, TX 77005; (713) 749-1441. Telex: 762878.

D31 UNIVERSITY OF NEBRASKA AT OMAHA
Executive Development.
Specialization: Courses for directors and senior executives.
Dates: Three weeks: June–August.
Location: Omaha, Nebraska: on campus, at professional work site.
Instruction: *Methods:* discussion groups, lectures, case studies, field trips, "hands-on" training. *By:* faculty, guest speakers/lecturers.
Highlights: Sponsor has offered program since 1983. Certificate. Issues I-20AB, IAP-66. Foreign nationals on tourist visas are eligible to enroll. A foreign student counselor/adviser is available. Orientation and cultural programs. 20 per course total enrollment; 100% foreign enrollment in 1985.
Eligibility: *Academic:* associate's degree. *Language:* English proficiency on intermediate level is required. *Professional:* five years of work experience required.
Cost: $4,000 per course for tuition, books and materials, local transportation. *Scholarships:* none.
Housing: Not provided; sponsor assists in locating housing.
Application: *Deadline:* four weeks prior. *Fee:* none.
Contact: Mr. Thomas E. Gouttierre, Director, International Studies & Programs, University of Nebraska at Omaha, Omaha, NE 68182; (402) 554-2376. Telex: 484340 UNL COMM LCN.

Abbreviations: ESL = English as a Second Language; TOEFL = Test of English as a Foreign Language; ALIGU = American Language Institute of Georgetown University; GPA = Grade Point Average; SAT = Scholastic Aptitude Test; GED = General Equivalency Diploma.

D32 UNIVERSITY OF PITTSBURGH
Management for Executives.
Specialization: Accounting, finance, economics, marketing, planning, international business, behavioral science, and management science for upper middle-level executives.
Dates: Five weeks: classes begin in April, Sept.
Location: Pittsburgh, Pennsylvania: on campus.
Instruction: *Methods:* lectures, discussion groups, case studies, field trips, "hands-on" training. *By:* faculty, guest speakers/lecturers.
Highlights: Sponsor has offered short-term programs since 1949. Certificate. Foreign nationals on tourist visas are eligible to enroll. A foreign student counselor/adviser is not available. 40 total enrollment; 40% foreign enrollment in 1985.
Eligibility: *Academic:* bachelor's degree preferred. *Language:* English proficiency on intermediate level is required. *Professional:* ten years of managerial experience.
Cost: $9,200 inclusive. *Scholarships:* none.
Housing: In hotels.
Application: *Deadline:* 10 weeks prior. *Fee:* $1,000; refundable.
Contact: P. J. Hickey, University of Pittsburgh, 301 Mervis Hall, Pittsburgh, PA 15260; (412) 648-1603. Telex: 812466.

D33 WASHINGTON AND LEE UNIVERSITY
Institute for Executives.
Specialization: Humanities and business ethics: American values. New emphasis for foreign businessmen operating in the United States.
Dates: Two weeks: June.
Location: Lexington, Virginia: on campus.
Instruction: *Methods:* lectures, seminars, independent study, "hands-on" training. *By:* faculty, guest speakers/lecturers.
Highlights: Sponsor has offered program since 1981. Credit. Certificate. Does not help obtain visa. No services for foreign nationals. 30 total enrollment.
Eligibility: *Academic:* bachelor's degree. *Language:* not given. *Professional:* upper middle management.
Cost: $3,000 excluding health insurance. *Scholarships:* none.
Housing: In apartments.
Application: *Deadline:* May 15. *Fee:* none.
Contact: Robert Fure, Washington and Lee University, Lexington, VA 24450; (703) 463-8723.

D34 WILLIAMS COLLEGE
Executive Program.
Specialization: For executives; expands their knowledge of the American cultural, social, and political environment.
Dates: Five weeks: classes begin in June.
Location: Williamstown, Massachusetts: on campus.
Instruction: *Methods:* discussion groups, lectures, field trips, "hands-on" training, independent study/research. *By:* faculty.
Highlights: Sponsor has offered program since 1956. Certificate. Foreign nationals on tourist visas are eligible to enroll. A foreign student counselor/adviser is not available. Various support services are available. 30 total enrollment.
Eligibility: *Academic:* some undergraduate work. *Language:* English proficiency on intermediate level is required. *Professional:* ten years of experience required.
Cost: $6,400 for tuition, meals, housing. *Scholarships:* none.
Housing: In dormitories.
Application: *Deadline:* Apr. 15. *Fee:* none.
Contact: Prof. Fred Greene, Director, Williams College Executive Program, P.O. Box 116, Williamstown, MA 01267; (413) 597-2544.

All program information is subject to change without notice
and must be confirmed directly with the sponsor.

FASHION MERCHANDISING

D35 FASHION INSTITUTE OF DESIGN AND MERCHANDISING
Specialization: Fashion merchandising and marketing.
Dates: One year: classes begin in Sept.
Location: San Francisco, Los Angeles, Orange County, San Diego, and Sherman Oaks, California: on campus.
Instruction: *Methods:* discussion groups, lectures, case studies, field trips, individualized instruction, "hands-on" training, independent study/research, computer-assisted instruction, language laboratories. *By:* school faculty, guest speakers/lecturers.
Highlights: Sponsor has offered program since 1968. Certificate. Practical training is a program component; participants are paid. Issues I-20AB. Foreign nationals on tourist visas are eligible to enroll. A foreign student counselor/adviser is available. ESL program. 15% foreign enrollment in 1985.
Eligibility: *Academic:* bachelor's degree. *Language:* English proficiency on intermediate level is required. TOEFL: 500. *Professional:* none.
Cost: $7,000–$9,000 per year for tuition, books, and materials. *Scholarships:* none.
Housing: In hotels, residence clubs.
Application: *Deadline:* none. *Fee:* $25; not refundable.
Contact: Francesca Brucia, Fashion Institute of Design and Merchandising, 790 Market Street, San Francisco, CA 94102; (415) 433-6691.

D36 FASHION INSTITUTE OF TECHNOLOGY
Fashion Buying and Merchandising.
Specialization: Preparation for careers in fashion and related professions at a specialized college of art and design, business and technology.
Dates: Nine months: classes begin in Aug.
Location: New York, New York: on campus.
Instruction: *Methods:* discussion groups, lectures, case studies, field trips, "hands-on" training, computer-assisted instruction. *By:* faculty, guest speakers/lecturers.
Highlights: Sponsor has offered program previously. Certificate. Issues I-20AB. Foreign nationals on tourist visas are not eligible to enroll. A foreign student counselor/adviser is available. Orientation and student activities. 5% foreign enrollment in 1985.
Eligibility: *Academic:* bachelor's degree or some undergraduate work. *Language:* English proficiency on intermediate level is required. TOEFL: 500. *Professional:* none.
Cost: $11,875 inclusive. *Scholarships:* none.
Housing: In dormitories if space available; or sponsor assists in locating housing.
Application: *Deadline:* Mar. 15. *Fee:* $10; not refundable.
Contact: Admissions Office, Fashion Institute of Technology, 227 W. 27th Street, New York, NY 10001; (212) 760-7675.

D37 PLAZA THREE ACADEMY
Specialization: Fashion merchandising.
Dates: One year: classes begin every month.
Location: Phoenix or Tucson, Arizona: at school.
Instruction: *Methods:* lectures, discussion groups, case studies, field trips, individualized instruction, "hands-on" training. *By:* guest speakers/lecturers.
Highlights: Sponsor has offered program since 1974. Certificate upon completion of program with 2.0 GPA, 85% attendance. Issues I-20MN. Foreign nationals on tourist visas are not eligible to enroll. A foreign student counselor/adviser is not available. 140 total enrollment; 1% foreign enrollment in 1985.
Eligibility: *Academic:* associate's degree. *Language:* English proficiency on intermediate level is required. Reading and Language Evaluation Exam: 50%. *Professional:* none.
Cost: $6,295 for tuition, books. *Scholarships:* none.

Abbreviations: ESL = English as a Second Language; TOEFL = Test of English as a Foreign Language; ALIGU = American Language Institute of Georgetown University; GPA = Grade Point Average; SAT = Scholastic Aptitude Test; GED = General Equivalency Diploma.

Housing: Not provided; sponsor assists in locating housing.
Application: *Deadline:* one month prior. *Fee:* none.
Contact: Director of Admissions, Plaza Three Academy, 4343 N. 16 Street, Phoenix, AZ 85016; (602) 264-9703.

FINANCIAL MANAGEMENT

D38 DUQUESNE UNIVERSITY
Continuing Education.
Specialization: Intensive program in financial analysis.
Dates: Nine months: classes begin in Aug.
Location: Pittsburgh, Pennsylvania: on campus.
Instruction: *Methods:* discussion groups, lectures, case studies, field trips, computer-assisted instruction. *By:* faculty, guest speakers/lecturers.
Highlights: Sponsor has offered program since 1983. Certificate. Issues I-20AB, IAP-66. Foreign nationals on tourist visas are eligible to enroll. A foreign student counselor/adviser is available. ESL program and international student organization. 3% foreign enrollment in 1985.
Eligibility: *Academic:* associate's degree. *Language:* English proficiency on advanced level is preferred. TOEFL: 500. *Professional:* none.
Cost: About $11,500 per year inclusive. *Scholarships:* none.
Housing: In dormitories, or sponsor assists in locating housing.
Application: *Deadline:* July 1. *Fee:* $30; not refundable.
Contact: Rev. Sean Hogan, C.S.Sp., Director, Office of International Education, Duquesne University, Pittsburgh, PA 15282; (412) 434-6113. Telex: 295 581 (RCA).

HOTEL AND RESTAURANT MANAGEMENT

D39 NEW YORK UNIVERSITY, SCHOOL OF CONTINUING EDUCATION
Diploma Program in Hospitality Management.
Specialization: Intensive series of courses for current supervisory and middle-management hotel personnel.
Dates: Sept.–May; classes begin in Sept. and Feb.
Location: New York, New York: on campus.
Instruction: *Methods:* discussion groups, lectures, case studies, field trips, independent study/research. *By:* faculty, guest speakers/lecturers.
Highlights: Sponsor has offered program since 1982. Certificate upon completion of program with C average. Issues I-20AB. Foreign nationals on tourist visas are eligible to enroll. A foreign student counselor/adviser is available. 80 total enrollment; 5% foreign enrollment in 1985.
Eligibility: *Academic:* associate's degree. *Language:* English proficiency on advanced level is required. *Professional:* requires two years of hotel work experience on supervisory level.
Cost: About $5,000 for tuition, books, and materials. *Scholarships:* none.
Housing: Not provided.
Application: *Deadline:* none. *Fee:* $15; not refundable.
Contact: Program Director, Diploma Program in Hospitality Management, School of Continuing Education, New York University, 11 West 42nd Street, Room 400, New York, NY 10036; (212) 790-1300. Cable: 235128 NYU UR. Telex: 127587.

HUMAN RESOURCES AND PERSONNEL MANAGEMENT

D40 ARTHUR D. LITTLE MANAGEMENT EDUCATION INSTITUTE
Human Resources/Personnel Management Program.
Dates: Six weeks: classes begin in mid-Sept.
Location: Cambridge, Massachusetts: at institute.
Instruction: *Methods:* lectures, discussion groups, case studies, field trips, computer-assisted instruction. *By:* guest speakers/lecturers.
Highlights: Sponsor has offered program previously. Certificate of professional studies. Issues I-20AB, IAP-66. A foreign student counselor/adviser is available.
Eligibility: *Academic:* bachelor's degree preferred. *Language:* English proficiency on the intermediate level is preferred. *Professional:* 2–5 years of experience.
Cost: $4,000 for tuition, books. *Scholarships:* none.
Housing: Not provided; sponsor assists in locating housing.
Application: *Deadline:* none. *Fee:* none.
Contact: Judith Francis, Admissions Coordinator, Arthur D. Little Management Education Institute, 35 Acorn Park, Cambridge, MA 02140; (617) 864-5657. Telex: 921436.

D41 UNIVERSITY OF NEBRASKA AT OMAHA
Senior Personnel Management Course.
Specialization: Courses for senior personnel management.
Dates: Three weeks: June–August.
Location: Omaha, Nebraska: on campus, at professional work site.
Instruction: *Methods:* discussion groups, lectures, case studies, field trips, "hands-on" training. *By:* faculty, guest speakers/lecturers.
Highlights: Sponsor has offered program since 1983. Certificate. Issues I-20AB, IAP-66. Foreign nationals on tourist visas are eligible to enroll. A foreign student counselor/adviser is available. Orientation and cultural programs. 20 per course total enrollment; 100% foreign enrollment in 1985.
Eligibility: *Academic:* associate's degree. *Language:* English proficiency on intermediate level is required. *Professional:* five years of work experience required.
Cost: $4,000 per course for tuition, books and materials, local transportation. *Scholarships:* none.
Housing: Not provided; sponsor assists in locating housing.
Application: *Deadline:* four weeks prior. *Fee:* none.
Contact: Mr. Thomas E. Gouttierre, Director, International Studies & Programs, University of Nebraska at Omaha, Omaha, NE 68182; (402) 554-2376. Telex: 484340 UNL COMM LCN.

INDUSTRIAL MANAGEMENT

D42 PURDUE UNIVERSITY
Industrial Administration.
Specialization: Broad management training for participants with a strong technical background.
Dates: One year: classes begin in Aug.
Location: West Lafayette, Indiana: on campus.
Instruction: *Methods:* discussion groups, lectures, case studies, independent study/research, computer-assisted instruction. *By:* faculty, guest speakers/lecturers.
Highlights: Sponsor has offered program since 1957. Certificate. Issues I-20AB, IAP-66. Foreign nationals on tourist visas are eligible to enroll. A foreign student counselor/adviser is available. Foreign student office. 50 total enrollment; 17% foreign enrollment in 1985.

Eligibility: *Academic:* bachelor's degree. *Language:* English proficiency on advanced level is required. TOEFL: 550. *Professional:* one year of work experience is required.
Cost: $6,408 for tuition. *Scholarships:* none.
Housing: In dormitories, or sponsor assists in locating housing.
Application: *Deadline:* Mar. 1 for fall. *Fee:* none.
Contact: Associate Director, Professional Master's Program, Purdue University, Krannert Center, W. Lafayette, IN 47907; (317) 494-4365.

D43 UNIVERSITY OF ROCHESTER
Manufacturing or Operations Management.
Specialization: Master of Science in Business Administration with a major in either manufacturing management or operations management.
Dates: One year: classes begin in Sept.
Location: Rochester, New York: on campus.
Instruction: *Methods:* discussion groups, lectures, case studies. *By:* faculty.
Highlights: Sponsor has offered program since 1985. Certificate upon completion of 38 credit hours. Issues I-20AB, I-20MN, IAP-66. Foreign nationals on tourist visas are not eligible to enroll. A foreign student counselor/adviser is available. 20 total enrollment; no foreign enrollment in 1985.
Eligibility: *Academic:* bachelor's degree; GMAT: 550. *Language:* English proficiency on advanced level is required. TOEFL: 580. *Professional:* none.
Cost: $13,300 for tuition. *Scholarships:* none.
Housing: In dormitories, apartments, furnished rooms.
Application: *Deadline:* Aug. 1. *Fee:* $35; not refundable.
Contact: Mr. John G. Baker, or Uday Karmarkar, Graduate School of Management, University of Rochester, Rochester, NY 14627; (716) 275-3533 or 275-3065.

INSURANCE

D44 THE COLLEGE OF INSURANCE
Professional Diploma in Risk and Insurance.
Specialization: Basic course in property-liability insurance designed for recent college graduates.
Dates: Sept.–May.
Location: New York, New York: at school.
Instruction: *Methods:* lectures, discussion groups. *By:* faculty, guest speakers/lecturers.
Highlights: Sponsor has offered program since 1968. Certificate. Issues I-20AB. Foreign nationals on tourist visas are eligible to enroll. A foreign student counselor/adviser is available. 35 total enrollment; 80% foreign enrollment in 1985.
Eligibility: *Academic:* bachelor's degree. *Language:* English proficiency on intermediate level is required. TOEFL: 500. *Professional:* none.
Cost: $7,000 for tuition. *Scholarships:* none.
Housing: In dormitories.
Application: *Deadline:* July 1. *Fee:* $25; not refundable.
Contact: Camille Lazar, Asst. V.P./Foreign Student Advisor, The College of Insurance, 101 Murray Street, New York, NY 10007; (212) 962-4111.

INTERNATIONAL BUSINESS

D45 AMERICAN GRADUATE SCHOOL OF INTERNATIONAL MANAGEMENT
Specialization: International management, language, international studies.
Dates: June–Aug.
Location: Glendale, Arizona: on campus.

Instruction: *Methods:* lectures, seminars, independent study, practical training. *By:* faculty, guest speakers/lecturers.
Highlights: Sponsor has offered program previously. Credit. Certificate. Issues I-20. Extensive services for foreign nationals. 25% foreign enrollment in 1985.
Eligibility: *Academic:* bachelor's degree; GMAT. *Language:* TOEFL: 450. *Professional:* none.
Cost: $2,700 for tuition, books, and materials. *Scholarships:* partial.
Housing: In furnished rooms.
Application: *Deadline:* open. *Fee:* $40; not refundable. *Scholarship deadline:* not given.
Contact: Dean John Arthur, AGSIM Thunderbird Campus, Glendale, AZ 85306; (602) 978-7210.

D46 ARTHUR D. LITTLE MANAGEMENT EDUCATION INSTITUTE
Master of Science in Management.
Specialization: Concentrations in international business and economic and industrial development.
Dates: 11 months: classes begin in late Aug.
Location: Cambridge, Massachusetts: at institute.
Instruction: *Methods:* discussion groups, lectures, case studies, field trips, computer-assisted instruction. *By:* faculty, guest speakers/lecturers.
Highlights: Sponsor has offered program since 1964. Master's degree upon completion of program with 2.7 GPA. Issues I-20AB, IAP-66. Foreign nationals on tourist visas are eligible to enroll. A foreign student counselor/adviser is available. Orientation, host family program, and social activities.
Eligibility: *Academic:* bachelor's degree. *Language:* English proficiency on intermediate level is required. TOEFL: 500. *Professional:* 3–5 years of managerial experience preferred.
Cost: $14,350–$15,250 for tuition, books, field trips, fees. *Scholarships:* partial.
Housing: Not provided; sponsor assists in locating housing.
Application: *Deadline:* none. *Fee:* none. *Scholarship deadline:* May 15.
Contact: Judith H. Francis, Admissions Coordinator & Registrar, Arthur D. Little Management Education Institute, 35 Acorn Park, Cambridge, MA 02140; (617) 864-5657. Telex: 921436.

D47 COLUMBIA UNIVERSITY
Executive Program in International Management.
Specialization: Examines the international dimensions of business management, strategy, finance and economics.
Dates: Four weeks: classes begin in Sept.
Location: Harriman, New York: on campus.
Instruction: *Methods:* discussion groups, lectures, case studies, computer-assisted instruction, films. *By:* faculty, guest speakers/lecturers.
Highlights: Sponsor has offered program previously. Certificate. Foreign nationals on tourist visas are eligible to enroll. A foreign student counselor/adviser is available. 50 total enrollment; 80% foreign enrollment in 1985.
Eligibility: *Academic:* none. *Language:* English proficiency on intermediate level is required. *Professional:* general managers.
Cost: $9,000 for tuition, books and materials, meals, housing. *Scholarships:* none.
Housing: Arden House on campus.
Application: *Deadline:* Aug. 15. *Fee:* none.
Contact: Dr. James A. Kennelley, Graduate School of Business, Columbia University, 807 Uris Hall, New York, NY 10027; (212) 280-3395. Telex: 968862 EXECPROG NYK.

Abbreviations: ESL = English as a Second Language; TOEFL = Test of English as a Foreign Language; ALIGU = American Language Institute of Georgetown University; GPA = Grade Point Average; SAT = Scholastic Aptitude Test; GED = General Equivalency Diploma.

D48 FLORIDA INTERNATIONAL UNIVERSITY, SCHOOL OF BUSINESS
Certificate in International Business.

Specialization: Specialized, graduate-level program of in-depth academic preparation in international business.
Dates: Four months: classes begin in Jan., May, Aug.
Location: Miami, Florida: on campus.
Instruction: *Methods:* lectures, case studies, field trips. *By:* faculty.
Highlights: Sponsor has offered program since 1984. Certificate. Issues I-20AB, IAP-66. Foreign nationals on tourist visas are not eligible to enroll. A foreign student counselor/adviser is available. 10 total enrollment; 20% foreign enrollment in 1985.
Eligibility: *Academic:* bachelor's degree; GMAT score. *Language:* English proficiency on advanced level is required. TOEFL: 500. *Professional:* none.
Cost: About $3,200 for tuition, books and materials, housing. *Scholarships:* none.
Housing: In dormitories.
Application: *Deadline:* none. *Fee:* $15; not refundable.
Contact: Dr. William Renforth, School of Business, Florida International University, 151 Street and Biscayne, North Miami, FL 33181; (305) 940-5508.

D49 LAREDO STATE UNIVERSITY
M.B.A. in International Trade.

Specialization: Emphasis on the role of trade in development with balance between theory and practical application.
Dates: One year: classes begin in Aug., Jan., May.
Location: Laredo, Texas: on campus.
Instruction: *Methods:* discussion groups, lectures, case studies, field trips, independent study/research, computer-assisted instruction. *By:* faculty, guest speakers/lecturers.
Highlights: Sponsor has offered program since 1977. Master's degree upon completion of 36 semester hours. Practical training may be a program component; participants are not paid. Issues I-20AB. Foreign nationals on tourist visas are not eligible to enroll. A foreign student counselor/adviser is available. Unlimited total enrollment; 51% foreign enrollment in 1985.
Eligibility: *Academic:* bachelor's degree in business administration or equivalent.
Language: English proficiency on intermediate level is required. TOEFL: 500.
Professional: none.
Cost: $4,320 for 36 semester hours for tuition. *Scholarships:* partial.
Housing: In dormitories, apartments.
Application: *Deadline:* six weeks prior. *Fee:* none.
Contact: Ms. Sandra Richard, Ph.D., Chair, Division of Business Administration, Laredo State University, Laredo, TX 78040; (512) 722-8001, Ext. 312 or 308.

D50 NICHOLLS STATE UNIVERSITY
Seminar for International Students.

Specialization: American business, political and social environment.
Dates: One month: classes begin in July.
Location: Thibodaux, Louisiana: on campus.
Instruction: *Methods:* discussion groups, lectures, case studies, field trips, independent study/research, computer-assisted instruction. *By:* faculty, guest speakers/lecturers.
Highlights: Sponsor has offered program since 1977. Certificate. Issues I-20AB, IAP-66. Foreign nationals on tourist visas are eligible to enroll. A foreign student counselor/adviser is available. Host family program. 30 total enrollment; 100% foreign enrollment.
Eligibility: *Academic:* associate's degree. *Language:* English proficiency on intermediate level is required. TOEFL: 500. *Professional:* none.
Cost: $650 for tuition, books and materials, meals, housing, some local transportation.
Scholarships: none.
Housing: In dormitories.
Application: *Deadline:* not given. *Fee:* $50; not refundable.

All program information is subject to change without notice and must be confirmed directly with the sponsor.

46

Contact: Michele R. Bailliet, Director of Exchange Programs, P.O. Box 2015, Nicholls State University, Thibodaux, LA 70310; (504) 446-8111, Ext. 1624.

D51 PACE UNIVERSITY
International Marketing.
Specialization: International marketing.
Dates: Semesters begin Sept. 4 and Jan. 4; summer sessions begin May 6, June 17, and July 28.
Location: White Plains and Pleasantville, New York: on campus, at professional work site.
Instruction: *Methods:* discussion groups, lectures, case studies, individualized instruction, "hands-on" training, computer-assisted instruction. *By:* faculty, guest speakers/lecturers.
Highlights: Sponsor has offered short-term programs since the 1940s. Certificate upon completion of program with C average. Issues I-20AB, IAP-66. Foreign nationals on tourist visas are eligible to enroll. A foreign student counselor/adviser is available. ESL program, international student club, host-home program. Unlimited total enrollment; 2.5% foreign enrollment in 1985.
Eligibility: *Academic:* some undergraduate work: 64 semester hours. *Language:* English proficiency on advanced level is required. TOEFL: 500. *Professional:* none.
Cost: $7,200 per semester inclusive. *Scholarships:* none.
Housing: Not provided; sponsor assists in locating housing.
Application: *Deadline:* rolling. *Fee:* $20; not refundable.
Contact: Ms. F. I. Tiger-Sussman, Undergraduate Admissions, Pace University, Pace Plaza, New York, NY 10038; (212) 488-1323.

D52 PACE UNIVERSITY
International Marketing Management.
Specialization: International marketing management.
Dates: Semesters begin Sept. 4 and Jan. 4; summer sessions begin May 6, June 17, and July 28.
Location: New York, New York: on campus, at professional work site.
Instruction: *Methods:* discussion groups, lectures, case studies, individualized instruction, "hands-on" training, computer-assisted instruction. *By:* faculty, guest speakers/lecturers.
Highlights: Sponsor has offered short-term programs since the 1940s. Certificate upon completion of program with C average. Issues I-20AB, IAP-66. Foreign nationals on tourist visas are eligible to enroll. A foreign student counselor/adviser is available. ESL program, international student club, host-home program. Unlimited total enrollment; 2.5% foreign enrollment in 1985.
Eligibility: *Academic:* some undergraduate work: 64 semester hours. *Language:* English proficiency on advanced level is required. TOEFL: 500. *Professional:* none.
Cost: $7,200 per semester inclusive. *Scholarships:* none.
Housing: Not provided; sponsor assists in locating housing.
Application: *Deadline:* rolling. *Fee:* $20; not refundable.
Contact: Ms. F. I. Tiger-Sussman, Undergraduate Admissions, Pace University, Pace Plaza, New York, NY 10038; (212) 488-1323.

D53 SAINT MARY'S COLLEGE OF CALIFORNIA
Master of Science in International Business.
Specialization: A comprehensive overview of problems and opportunities in doing business internationally.
Dates: One year: classes begin in Oct.
Location: Moraga, California: on campus.
Instruction: *Methods:* discussion groups, lectures, case studies, individualized instruction, independent study/research, computer-assisted instruction. *By:* faculty, guest speakers/lecturers.
Highlights: Sponsor has offered program since 1979. Certificate upon completion of 36

Abbreviations: ESL = English as a Second Language; TOEFL = Test of English as a Foreign Language; ALIGU = American Language Institute of Georgetown University; GPA = Grade Point Average; SAT = Scholastic Aptitude Test; GED = General Equivalency Diploma.

quarter units with 3.0 GPA. Issues I-20AB. Foreign nationals on tourist visas are not eligible to enroll. A foreign student counselor/adviser is available. International student groups. 40 total enrollment; 50% foreign enrollment in 1985.
Eligibility: *Academic:* bachelor's degree. *Language:* English proficiency on advanced level is required. TOEFL: 550. *Professional:* some business experience preferred.
Cost: $6,000 for tuition, fees. *Scholarships:* none.
Housing: Not provided; sponsor assists in locating housing.
Application: *Deadline:* ten days prior. *Fee:* $30; not refundable.
Contact: Mr. Nelson Shelton, Director of Admissions, P.O. Box M, Saint Mary's College, Moraga, CA 94575; (415) 376-3840.

D54 SOUTHEAST MISSOURI STATE UNIVERSITY
International Business Institute.
Specialization: For foreign nationals employed by foreign firms doing business in the U.S.; promotes understanding of American business practices and culture, plus fluency in English. Includes management, marketing, finance, internship with a U.S. business.
Dates: Nine months: classes begin in Sept.
Location: Cape Girardeau, Missouri: on campus, at professional work site.
Instruction: *Methods:* discussion groups, lectures, case studies, field trips, independent study/research, language laboratories. *By:* faculty, guest speakers/lecturers.
Highlights: Sponsor has offered program since 1985. Certificate upon completion of program and a special project. Practical training is a program component; participants are not paid. Issues I-20AB, IAP-66. Foreign nationals on tourist visas are eligible to enroll. A foreign student counselor/adviser is available. 20 total enrollment; 100% foreign enrollment in 1985.
Eligibility: *Academic:* associate's degree. *Language:* English proficiency on intermediate level is required. TOEFL: 500. *Professional:* two years of work experience required.
Cost: $14,500 for tuition. *Scholarships:* none.
Housing: Not provided; sponsor assists in locating housing.
Application: *Deadline:* June 1. *Fee:* none.
Contact: Director, International Business Institute, Southeast Missouri State University, 900 Normal, Cape Girardeau, MO 63701; (314) 651-2562.

D55 UNIVERSITY OF HAWAII AT MANOA, PACIFIC ASIAN MANAGEMENT INSTITUTE
Summer PAMI Program.
Specialization: International business—management, finance, marketing, trade—focusing on Asia and the Pacific Basin. Intensive Asian language courses available.
Dates: Six weeks: classes begin in May, July.
Location: Honolulu, Hawaii: on campus.
Instruction: *Methods:* lectures, seminars, independent study, case studies, forums. *By:* faculty, guest speakers/lecturers.
Highlights: Sponsor has offered program since 1978. Certificate. Issues I-20, IAP-66. 50% foreign enrollment. List of past participants is available.
Eligibility: *Academic:* undergraduate and graduate programs. *Language:* TOEFL or equivalent. *Professional:* varies.
Cost: $1,330 for three courses for tuition, meals, housing. *Scholarships:* PAMI award (open to foreign nationals).
Housing: In dormitories.
Application: *Deadline:* Apr. 1 for May term, May 1 for July. *Fee:* $50. *Scholarship deadline:* Feb. 15 and Mar. 15.
Contact: Ms. Virginia R. Crockett, Assistant Director, Pacific Asian Management Institute, College of Business Administration, University of Hawaii at Manoa, 2404 Maile Way, Honolulu, HI 96822; (808) 948-7564. Cable: UNIHAW. Telex: 7238022 PAMI HR.

All program information is subject to change without notice
and must be confirmed directly with the sponsor.

D56 UNIVERSITY OF HAWAII AT MANOA, PACIFIC ASIAN MANAGEMENT INSTITUTE
Visiting Colleagues Program.
Specialization: Assists professors in business and related fields to develop international business courses; participants have choice of PAMI executive and graduate courses plus special seminar for faculty.
Dates: Six weeks: classes begin in July.
Location: Honolulu, Hawaii: on campus, at professional work site.
Instruction: *Methods:* discussion groups, lectures, case studies, field trips, individualized instruction, independent study/research. *By:* faculty, guest speakers/lecturers.
Highlights: Sponsor has offered program since 1978. Certificate. Issues I-20AB, IAP-66. Foreign nationals on tourist visas are not eligible to enroll. A foreign student counselor/adviser is available. Various support services are available. 20 total enrollment; 80% foreign enrollment in 1985. List of past participants is available.
Eligibility: *Academic:* master's degree preferred. *Language:* English proficiency on intermediate level is required. *Professional:* three years of work experience, current status as faculty member.
Cost: $1,875 for tuition, books and materials, some meals, housing, some local transportation, special events/excursions. *Scholarships:* partial may be available.
Housing: In dormitories.
Application: *Deadline:* seven weeks prior. *Fee:* $50; not refundable.
Contact: Virginia Crockett, Assistant Director, PAMI, College of Business Administration, University of Hawaii, 2404 Maile Way, C303, Honolulu, HI 96822; (808) 948-7564. Cable: UNIHAW. Telex: (723) 8022 PAMI HR.

D57 UNIVERSITY OF ILLINOIS
PEATA-Illinois Business School.
Specialization: International business program for managers and economists from Japan. Courses in accountancy, finance, business administration, and economics combined with business and industry field trips, special seminars, and cultural activities.
Dates: One year: classes begin in June.
Location: Urbana, Illinois: on campus.
Instruction: *Methods:* lectures, discussion groups, case studies, field trips, individualized instruction, computer-assisted instruction, language labs. *By:* faculty, guest speakers/lecturers.
Highlights: Sponsor has offered program since 1977. Certificate. Issues I-20AB, I-20MN, IAP-66. Foreign nationals on tourist visas are eligible to enroll. A foreign student counselor/adviser is available. 25 total enrollment; 100% foreign enrollment in 1985.
Eligibility: *Academic:* bachelor's degree with B average. *Language:* English proficiency is required. TOEFL: 500. *Professional:* five years of experience.
Cost: $14,700 for tuition, health insurance (includes meals and housing in summer only).
Housing: In dormitories (summer only). Sponsor assists in locating housing for fall and spring.
Application: *Deadline:* May. 1. *Fee:* not given.
Contact: Carolyn M. Pribble, Executive Development Center, University of Illinois, 205 David Kinley Hall, 1407 W. Gregory Drive, Urbana, IL 61801; (217) 333-4552. Telex: 510-101-1969, Attn: EDC, 205 DKH.

D58 UNIVERSITY OF ILLINOIS
International Managers Program in American Commerce Technology.
Specialization: Program for non-U.S. businessmen, emphasizing technology used in U.S. business. Combines classroom study with field trips and special seminars.
Dates: 2–3 semesters: classes begin in June, Aug., Jan.
Location: Urbana, Illinois: on campus.

Abbreviations: ESL = English as a Second Language; TOEFL = Test of English as a Foreign Language; ALIGU = American Language Institute of Georgetown University; GPA = Grade Point Average; SAT = Scholastic Aptitude Test; GED = General Equivalency Diploma.

Instruction: *Methods:* lectures, discussion groups, case studies, field trips, individualized instruction, computer-assisted instruction. *By:* faculty, guest speakers/lecturers.
Highlights: Sponsor has offered program since 1985. Certificate. Issues I-20AB, I-20MN, IAP-66. Foreign nationals on tourist visas are eligible to enroll. A foreign student counselor/adviser is available for counseling. 20 total enrollment; 100% foreign enrollment in 1985.
Eligibility: *Academic:* bachelor's degree. *Language:* English proficiency is required. TOEFL: 490. *Professional:* three years of business experience.
Cost: $5,150 per semester for tuition, health insurance, housing.
Housing: In apartments.
Application: *Deadline:* May. 1, July 1, or Dec. 1. *Fee:* none.
Contact: Carolyn M. Pribble, Executive Development Center, University of Illinois, 205 David Kinley Hall, 1407 W. Gregory Drive, Urbana, IL 61801; (217) 333-4552. Telex: 510-101-1969, Attn: EDC, 205 DKH.

D59 UNIVERSITY OF ILLINOIS
Program for International Managers.
Specialization: Management development program for managers from abroad. Courses in accountancy, finance, business administration, and economics, combined with business and industry field trips and cultural activities.
Dates: June–May (June 1–Aug. 3 optional ESL program).
Location: Urbana, Illinois: on campus.
Instruction: *Methods:* lectures, discussion groups, case studies, field trips, individualized instruction, language labs. Independent study/research, computer-assisted instruction are optional. *By:* faculty, guest speakers/lecturers.
Highlights: Sponsor has offered program since 1982. Certificate. Issues I-20AB, I-20MN, IAP-66. Foreign nationals on tourist visas are eligible to enroll. A foreign student counselor/adviser is available for counseling. 25 total enrollment; 100% foreign enrollment in 1985.
Eligibility: *Academic:* bachelor's degree with B average. *Language:* English proficiency is required. TOEFL: 520. *Professional:* business experience.
Cost: About $13,600 for tuition, health insurance; meals and housing included for summer only.
Housing: In dormitories (summer only). Sponsor assists in locating housing for fall and spring.
Application: *Deadline:* May. 1. *Fee:*
Contact: Carolyn M. Pribble, Executive Development Center, University of Illinois, 205 David Kinley Hall, 1407 W. Gregory Drive, Urbana, IL 61801; (217) 333-4552. Telex: 510-101-1969, Attn: EDC, 205 DKH.

D60 UNIVERSITY OF SOUTHERN CALIFORNIA, INTERNATIONAL BUSINESS EDUCATION AND RESEARCH PROGRAM (IBEAR)
IBEAR MBA Program.
Specialization: Intensive general management master's programs, emphasizing international and Pacific Rim business concerns. Participants complete a research paper relevant to their sponsoring firm or government agency. Field trips to industry and financial institutions.
Dates: One year: classes begin in Aug.
Location: Los Angeles, California: on campus.
Instruction: *Methods:* lectures, discussion groups, case studies, field trips, computer-assisted instruction, language labs, independent study/research, computer laboratories. *By:* faculty, guest speakers/lecturers.
Highlights: Sponsor has offered program since 1978. Master's degree upon completion of 56 units with 2.85 GPA. Practical training may be a program component; participants may be paid. Issues I-20AB, IAP-66. Foreign nationals on tourist visas are not eligible to enroll. A

foreign student counselor/adviser is available. 40 total enrollment; 85% foreign enrollment in 1985. List of past participants is available.

Eligibility: *Academic:* bachelor's degree, GMAT. *Language:* English proficiency on advanced level is required. TOEFL: 550. *Professional:* three years of experience and company sponsorship preferred.

Cost: $22,500 for tuition, books and materials, health insurance, special activities. *Scholarships:* partial.

Housing: In dormitories if application received by June 1; or sponsor assists in locating housing.

Application: *Deadline:* July 1. *Fee:* $40; not refundable. *Scholarship deadline:* July 1.

Contact: Ms. Fujiko Terayama, Admissions Coordinator, IBEAR MBA Program, Graduate School of Business Administration, University of Southern California, Bridge Hall, Room 200, Los Angeles, CA 90089-1421; (213) 743-2272. Telex: 4720490 USC LSA.

D61 WESTERN MICHIGAN UNIVERSITY
Seminar in Business and American Society.
Specialization: U.S. business and society; program tailored to needs of specific groups.

Dates: 2–4 weeks: to be arranged by group.

Location: Kalamazoo, Michigan: on campus.

Instruction: *Methods:* discussion groups, lectures, case studies, field trips, language laboratories. *By:* faculty, guest speakers/lecturers.

Highlights: Sponsor has offered short-term programs since 1983. Certificate. Issues I-20AB, IAP-66. Foreign nationals on tourist visas are eligible to enroll. A foreign student counselor/adviser is available. Program director will be fluent in group's language. 100% foreign enrollment in 1985.

Eligibility: *Academic:* associate's degree or some undergraduate work. *Language:* English proficiency on beginning level is required. *Professional:* none.

Cost: $425–$475 weekly for tuition, books and materials, some meals, housing, local transportation, health insurance, field trips. *Scholarships:* none.

Housing: In dormitories.

Application: *Deadline:* none. *Fee:* none.

Contact: Dr. Norman C. Greenberg, Dean, International Education and Programs, Western Michigan University, 2090 Freidmann Hall, Kalamazoo, MI 49008-3819; (616) 383-0944. Telex: 6877099 WestMichUniv.

D62 WORLD TRADE EDUCATION CENTER
Specialization: Exporting, international trade. Programs tailored for foreign business professors and government export promotion officials; how international business is practiced and taught in the U.S.

Dates: Six weeks: to be arranged.

Location: Cleveland, Ohio: on campus.

Instruction: *Methods:* individualized instruction, "hands-on" training. *By:* faculty.

Highlights: Sponsor has offered program since 1982. Certificate. Issues I-20AB, I-20MN, IAP-66. Foreign nationals on tourist visas are eligible to enroll. A foreign student counselor/adviser is available. 20 per year total enrollment; 100% foreign enrollment in 1985.

Eligibility: *Academic:* bachelor's degree. *Language:* English proficiency on intermediate level is required. *Professional:* 2–5 years of work experience required.

Cost: About $4,000 per six-week session for tuition, books and materials, meals, housing, local transportation. *Scholarships:* none.

Housing: In apartments, furnished rooms, with families.

Application: *Deadline:* none. *Fee:* none.

Contact: Ivan R. Vernon, Director, World Trade Education Center, Cleveland State University, Cleveland, OH 44115; (216) 687-3733. Telex: 810-410-8520.

Abbreviations: ESL = English as a Second Language; TOEFL = Test of English as a Foreign Language; ALIGU = American Language Institute of Georgetown University; GPA = Grade Point Average; SAT = Scholastic Aptitude Test; GED = General Equivalency Diploma.

LABOR RELATIONS

D63 **PACE UNIVERSITY**
   Labor-Management Relations.
Specialization: Labor relations.
Dates: Semesters begin Sept. 4 and Jan. 4; summer sessions begin May 6, June 17, and July 28.
Location: New York, New York: on campus, at professional work site.
Instruction: *Methods:* discussion groups, lectures, case studies, individualized instruction, "hands-on" training, computer-assisted instruction. *By:* faculty, guest speakers/lecturers.
Highlights: Sponsor has offered short-term programs since the 1940s. Certificate upon completion of program with C average. Issues I-20AB, IAP-66. Foreign nationals on tourist visas are eligible to enroll. A foreign student counselor/adviser is available. ESL program, international student club. Unlimited total enrollment; 2.5% foreign enrollment in 1985.
Eligibility: *Academic:* some undergraduate work: 64 semester hours. *Language:* English proficiency on advanced level is required. TOEFL: 500. *Professional:* none.
Cost: $7,200 per semester inclusive. *Scholarships:* none.
Housing: Not provided; sponsor assists in locating housing.
Application: *Deadline:* rolling. *Fee:* $20; not refundable.
Contact: Ms. F. I. Tiger-Sussman, Undergraduate Admissions, Pace University, Pace Plaza, New York, NY 10038; (212) 488-1323.

MANAGEMENT

D64 **ADELPHI UNIVERSITY**
   Management for Non-Business Majors.
Specialization: Courses in management, marketing, accounting, quantitative methods, organizational behavior, microeconomics, finance; optional field internship.
Dates: Classes begin in Sept., Jan., June.
Location: Garden City, New York: on campus, at professional work site.
Instruction: *Methods:* discussion groups, lectures, case studies. *By:* faculty.
Highlights: Sponsor has offered program since 1974. Certificate. Practical training may be a program component; participants may be paid. Issues I-20AB, IAP-66. Foreign nationals on tourist visas are not eligible to enroll. A foreign student counselor/adviser is available. Orientation program and Center for International Studies. About 119 total enrollment; 2% foreign enrollment in 1985.
Eligibility: *Academic:* bachelor's degree. *Language:* English proficiency on intermediate level is required. TOEFL: 500; ELTI Diagnostic Test given upon arrival. *Professional:* none.
Cost: $5,016 for tuition. *Scholarships:* none.
Housing: Not provided; student makes own arrangements.
Application: *Deadline:* Aug. 22. *Fee:* $25; not refundable.
Contact: Pat Marcellino, Adelphi University, School of Business, Management Programs, Room 113, Garden City, NY 11530; (516) 663-1184.

D65 **ADELPHI UNIVERSITY**
   Management for Women.
Specialization: Courses in management, marketing, accounting, quantitative methods, organizational behavior, microeconomics, finance; optional field internship.
Dates: Classes begin in Sept., Jan., June.
Location: Garden City, New York: on campus, at professional work site.
Instruction: *Methods:* discussion groups, lectures, case studies. *By:* faculty.
Highlights: Sponsor has offered program since 1974. Certificate. Practical training may be a program component; participants may be paid. Issues I-20AB, IAP-66. Foreign nationals on

All program information is subject to change without notice
and must be confirmed directly with the sponsor.

52

tourist visas are not eligible to enroll. A foreign student counselor/adviser is available. Orientation program and Center for International Studies. About 119 total enrollment; 2% foreign enrollment in 1985.
Eligibility: *Academic:* bachelor's degree. *Language:* English proficiency on intermediate level is required. TOEFL: 500; ELTI Diagnostic Test given upon arrival. *Professional:* none.
Cost: $5,016 for tuition. *Scholarships:* none.
Housing: Not provided; student makes own arrangements.
Application: *Deadline:* Aug. 22. *Fee:* $25; not refundable.
Contact: Pat Marcellino, Adelphi University, School of Business, Management Programs, Room 113, Garden City, NY 11530; (516) 663-1184.

D66 THE AMERICAN UNIVERSITY
Graduate Certificate in Business Management.
Specialization: Business management.
Dates: Classes begin in Sept., Jan., May, July.
Location: Washington, D.C.: on campus, at professional work site.
Instruction: *Methods:* discussion groups, lectures, case studies, independent study/research, computer-assisted instruction. *By:* faculty.
Highlights: Sponsor has offered program previously. Certificate. Issues I-20AB. Foreign nationals on tourist visas are not eligible to enroll. A foreign student counselor/adviser is available. Orientation programs.
Eligibility: *Academic:* bachelor's degree with 3.0 GPA; GMAT score: 400. *Language:* English proficiency on advanced level is required. TOEFL: 600; English Language Institute Placement Test. *Professional:* none.
Cost: $299 per credit hour for tuition. *Scholarships:* none.
Housing: Not provided; sponsor assists in locating housing.
Application: *Deadline:* none. *Fee:* none.
Contact: Programs Advisement Center, The American University, 4400 Massachusetts Ave. NW, Room 153 McKinley Bldg., Washington, DC 20016; (202) 885-2500.

D67 BATTELLE
Battelle Program in R&D Management.
Specialization: Philosophy of management, including planning, organizing, staffing and staff development, directing and leading, and control of research and development.
Dates: Three weeks: Aug.
Location: Columbus, Ohio: at school.
Instruction: *Methods:* lectures, case studies. *By:* guest speakers/lecturers.
Highlights: Sponsor has offered program since 1982. Certificate. Foreign nationals on tourist visas are eligible to enroll. A foreign student counselor/adviser is not available. 30 total enrollment; 95% foreign enrollment in 1985.
Eligibility: *Academic:* bachelor's degree. *Language:* English proficiency on advanced level is required. *Professional:* prior experience preferred.
Cost: $2,500 includes tuition, materials, group activities. *Scholarships:* none.
Housing: In hotels.
Application: *Deadline:* July 1. *Fee:* none.
Contact: Dr. William Hitt, Battelle, 505 King Ave., Columbus, OH 43201; (614) 424-7176. Cable: BATMIN. Telex: 245454.

D68 CENTRAL MICHIGAN UNIVERSITY—ATLANTIC REGION
Master of Science in Administration.
Specialization: General administration, human resources administration.
Dates: Rolling: one-month classes.
Location: Washington, D.C.; Baltimore, Maryland; Philadelphia, Pennsylvania; New York, New York: at professional work site.
Instruction: *Methods:* discussion groups, lectures, case studies, individualized instruction,

---

Abbreviations: ESL = English as a Second Language; TOEFL = Test of English as a Foreign Language; ALIGU = American Language Institute of Georgetown University; GPA = Grade Point Average; SAT = Scholastic Aptitude Test; GED = General Equivalency Diploma.

independent study/research, computer-assisted instruction. *By:* faculty, guest speakers/lecturers.

Highlights: Sponsor has offered program since 1974. Certificate. A foreign student counselor/adviser is available. 5–10% foreign enrollment in 1985.

Eligibility: *Academic:* bachelor's degree. *Language:* English proficiency on intermediate level is required. TOEFL: 525; Univ. of Michigan Language Test; ALIGU. *Professional:* none.

Cost: $4,788 for tuition. *Scholarships:* none.

Housing: Not provided; sponsor assists in locating housing.

Application: *Deadline:* rolling. *Fee:* $25; not refundable.

Contact: Dr. Charles N. Somers, Regional Director, Central Michigan University, 8550 Lee Highway, Suite 125, Fairfax, VA 22031; (703) 849-8218.

D69 DUQUESNE UNIVERSITY
Business Administration.

Specialization: Management and administration.

Dates: Six weeks: classes begin in May, June.

Location: Pittsburgh, Pennsylvania.

Instruction: *Methods:* lectures, seminars, independent study. *By:* faculty.

Highlights: Sponsor has offered program since 1965. Credit. Issues I-20. No services for foreign nationals. 50 total enrollment; 5% foreign enrollment in 1985.

Eligibility: *Academic:* bachelor's degree; GMAT. *Language:* TOEFL: 550. *Professional:* none.

Cost: $195 per credit for tuition. *Scholarships:* none.

Housing: Not provided; sponsor assists in locating housing.

Application: *Deadline:* Mar. 1. *Fee:* $30; not refundable.

Contact: Rev. Sean Hogan, C.S.Sp., Office of International Education, Duquesne University, Pittsburgh, PA 15282; (412) 434-6113.

D70 ECONOMICS INSTITUTE

Specialization: Extensive intercultural program in business management.

Dates: Year-round program.

Location: Boulder, Colorado: at institute.

Instruction: *Methods:* lectures, seminars, independent study, practical training. *By:* faculty, guest speakers/lecturers.

Highlights: Sponsor has offered program since 1958. Credit. Certificate. Issues I-20. Extensive services for foreign nationals. 100% foreign enrollment. List of past participants is available.

Eligibility: *Academic:* bachelor's degree. *Language:* TOEFL. *Professional:* none.

Cost: Varies. *Scholarships:* partial.

Housing: In dormitories, apartments, furnished rooms, with families.

Application: *Deadline:* none. *Fee:* $50. *Scholarship deadline:* not given.

Contact: Admissions Office, Economics Institute, 1030 13th Street, Boulder, CO 80302; (303) 492-7337. Telex: 450385 ECONINST BLDR.

D71 GUILFORD COLLEGE

Specialization: Programs available in management, democratic management, and sports management.

Dates: Aug.–late July.

Location: Greensboro, North Carolina: on campus.

Instruction: *Methods:* lectures, discussion groups. *By:* faculty.

Highlights: Sponsor has offered short-term programs since 1983. Certificate upon completion of 4–6 courses. Issues I-20AB, I-20MN. Foreign nationals on tourist visas are not eligible to enroll. A foreign student counselor/adviser is available. International Relations Club.

Eligibility: *Academic:* bachelor's degree. *Language:* English proficiency on advanced level is required. TOEFL: 500. *Professional:* none.

Cost: $112 per credit hour for tuition. *Scholarships:* none.
Housing: Not provided; student makes own arrangements.
Application: *Deadline:* open. *Fee:* $20; not refundable.
Contact: Dean of Admissions and Financial Aid, Guilford College, 5800 West Friendly Ave., Greensboro, NC 27410; (919) 292-5511.

D72 KELLER GRADUATE SCHOOL OF MANAGEMENT
Master of Business Administration.
Specialization: General management and management information systems.
Dates: One year: classes begin Sept., Nov., Feb., April, and June.
Location: Chicago, Illinois: on campus.
Instruction: *Methods:* lectures, discussion groups, case studies. *By:* faculty, guest speakers/lecturers.
Highlights: Sponsor has offered short-term programs since 1973. Master's degree upon completion of 16 courses with 2.5 GPA. Issues I-20AB. Foreign nationals on tourist visas are not eligible to enroll. A foreign student counselor/adviser is available. 5% foreign enrollment in 1985.
Eligibility: *Academic:* bachelor's degree; GMAT: 24 + . *Language:* English proficiency on advanced level is required. TOEFL: 550. *Professional:* none.
Housing: Not provided; sponsor assists in locating housing.
Application: *Deadline:* none. *Fee:* none.
Contact: Director of Admissions, Keller Graduate School of Management, 10 S. Riverside Plaza, Suite 2124, Chicago, IL 60606; (312) 454-0880.

D73 MASSACHUSETTS INSTITUTE OF TECHNOLOGY
Alfred P. Sloan Fellows Program.
Specialization: Comprehensive general management education program, leading to master of science degree in management.
Dates: One year: classes begin in June.
Location: Cambridge, Massachusetts: on campus.
Instruction: *Methods:* discussion groups, lectures, case studies, field trips, individualized instruction, "hands-on" training, independent study/research, computer-assisted instruction, science laboratories. *By:* faculty, guest speakers/lecturers.
Highlights: Sponsor has offered program since 1931. Certificate. Issues IAP-66. Foreign nationals on tourist visas are not eligible to enroll. A foreign student counselor/adviser is available. 55 total enrollment; about 33% foreign enrollment in 1985.
Eligibility: *Academic:* associate's degree. *Language:* English proficiency on intermediate level is required. TOEFL. *Professional:* ten years of work experience required; potential for senior general management assignments.
Cost: $26,000 for tuition. *Scholarships:* none.
Housing: Not provided; sponsor assists in locating housing.
Application: *Deadline:* Feb. 1. *Fee:* none.
Contact: Mr. Alan F. White, Assoc. Dean for Executive Education, MIT Sloan School of Management, 50 Memorial Drive, Cambridge, MA 02139; (617) 253-7166. Cable: MIT CAM. Telex: 797961 SLOAN UD.

D74 NEW YORK UNIVERSITY, GRADUATE SCHOOL OF BUSINESS ADMINISTRATION
Advanced Professional Certificate Program.
Specialization: Accounting, computer applications, economics, finance, international business, management, marketing, statistics. Concentrated study for managers moving to a new field or needing familiarity with current developments in their own field.
Dates: Classes begin in Sept., Feb., June, July.
Location: New York, New York: on campus.
Instruction: *Methods:* lectures, case studies. *By:* faculty.

Abbreviations: ESL = English as a Second Language; TOEFL = Test of English as a Foreign Language; ALIGU = American Language Institute of Georgetown University; GPA = Grade Point Average; SAT = Scholastic Aptitude Test; GED = General Equivalency Diploma.

Highlights: Sponsor has offered program since 1965. Certificate upon completion of six courses. Issues I-20AB, IAP-66. Foreign nationals on tourist visas are eligible to enroll. A foreign student counselor/adviser is available. Unlimited total enrollment; 25% of full-time students foreign enrollment in 1985.
Eligibility: *Academic:* master's degree. *Language:* English proficiency on advanced level is required. TOEFL: 550. *Professional:* demonstrated professional competence and career advancement.
Cost: $6,042 for tuition. *Scholarships:* none.
Housing: Not provided; student makes own arrangements.
Application: *Deadline:* Apr. 15 for fall, Oct. 15 for spring, Mar. 16 for summer. *Fee:* $50; not refundable.
Contact: Mr. Jason Sedine, Graduate School of Business, New York University, 100 Trinity Place, New York, NY 10006; (212) 285-6250. Telex: 235128.

D75 PACE UNIVERSITY
Management.

Specialization: Business management.
Dates: Semesters begin Sept. 4 and Jan. 4; summer sessions begin May 6, June 17, and July 28.
Location: Pleasantville and White Plains, New York: on campus, at professional work site.
Instruction: *Methods:* discussion groups, lectures, case studies, individualized instruction, "hands-on" training, computer-assisted instruction. *By:* faculty, guest speakers/lecturers.
Highlights: Sponsor has offered short-term programs since the 1940s. Certificate upon completion of program with C average. Issues I-20AB, IAP-66. Foreign nationals on tourist visas are eligible to enroll. A foreign student counselor/adviser is available. ESL program, international students club, host-home program. Unlimited total enrollment; 2.5% foreign enrollment in 1985.
Eligibility: *Academic:* some undergraduate work: 64 semester hours. *Language:* English proficiency on advanced level is required. TOEFL: 500. *Professional:* none.
Cost: $7,200 per semester inclusive. *Scholarships:* none.
Housing: Not provided; sponsor assists in locating housing.
Application: *Deadline:* rolling. *Fee:* $20; not refundable.
Contact: Ms. F. I. Tiger-Sussman, Undergraduate Admissions, Pace University, Pace Plaza, New York, NY 10038; (212) 488-1323.

D76 SAINT MARTIN'S COLLEGE
Master's of Business Administration.

Specialization: Accounting, marketing, international management, information systems; may be combined with ESL classes.
Dates: Not given.
Location: Lacey, Washington: on campus.
Instruction: *Methods:* discussion groups, lectures, case studies, language laboratories. *By:* faculty.
Highlights: Sponsor has offered program since 1980. Practical training may be a program component. Foreign nationals on tourist visas are not usually eligible to enroll. A foreign student counselor/adviser is available. Unlimited total enrollment; about 25% foreign enrollment in 1985.
Eligibility: *Academic:* bachelor's degree. *Language:* English proficiency on intermediate level is required. TOEFL: 525. *Professional:* none.
Cost: $6,000 for tuition. *Scholarships:* none.
Housing: In dormitories, or sponsor assists in locating housing.
Application: *Deadline:* none. *Fee:* $15; not refundable.
Contact: Director of Admissions, Saint Martin's College, Lacey, WA 98503; (206) 491-4700.

D77 SMITH COLLEGE
Smith Management Program.
Specialization: Management program comprising two summer sessions plus internship project during the year.
Dates: One year: classes begin in July.
Location: Northampton, Massachusetts: on campus, at professional work site.
Instruction: *Methods:* discussion groups, lectures, case studies, field trips, individualized instruction, "hands-on" training, independent study/research, computer-assisted instruction. *By:* faculty, guest speakers/lecturers.
Highlights: Sponsor has offered program since 1980. Certificate upon completion of two summer sessions plus integrative project. Practical training is a program component; participants are paid. Foreign nationals on tourist visas are eligible to enroll. A foreign student counselor/adviser is available. Translation assistance. 48 total enrollment; 7% foreign enrollment in 1985.
Eligibility: *Academic:* bachelor's degree. *Language:* English proficiency on intermediate level is preferred. *Professional:* 3–5 years of work experience required.
Cost: $10,500 for tuition, books and materials, meals, housing. *Scholarships:* none.
Housing: In dormitories.
Application: *Deadline:* Mar. 31. *Fee:* none.
Contact: Ms. Susan C. Lowance, Director, Smith Management Program, Smith College, Tilly Hall, Northampton, MA 01063; (413) 584-6660.

D78 SYRACUSE UNIVERSITY
Specialization: Independent-study master's degree program in business administration. Must be in residence for the first week of each semester. Bachelor's degree program also available.
Dates: Semesters begin Aug., Jan., and May.
Location: Syracuse, New York: on campus.
Instruction: *Methods:* lectures, discussion groups, case studies, "hands-on" training, independent study/research. *By:* faculty.
Highlights: Sponsor has offered program previously. Master's degree. Foreign nationals on tourist visas are eligible to enroll. A foreign student counselor/adviser is not available. 20% foreign enrollment in 1985. List of past participants is available.
Eligibility: *Academic:* bachelor's degree. *Language:* English proficiency is required. TOEFL: 550. *Professional:* none.
Cost: $246 per credit hour for tuition. *Scholarships:* none.
Housing: In apartments.
Application: *Deadline:* open. *Fee:* $30; not refundable.
Contact: Mary Lou Bagdovitz, Syracuse University, 302 Reid Hall, 610 E. Fayette Street, Syracuse, NY 13202; (315) 423-3269.

D79 WAKE FOREST UNIVERSITY
MBA.
Specialization: Integrated general management master's program using experiential teaching approach; emphasis on international business.
Dates: Classes begin in Aug., Jan.
Location: Winston-Salem, North Carolina: on campus, at professional work site.
Instruction: *Methods:* discussion groups, lectures, case studies, field trips, "hands-on" training, independent study/research. *By:* faculty, guest speakers/lecturers.
Highlights: Sponsor has offered program since 1969. Certificate. Practical training is a program component; participants are not paid. Issues I-20AB, IAP-66. Foreign nationals on tourist visas are not eligible to enroll. A foreign student counselor/adviser is available. Foreign student association. 11 total enrollment; 11% foreign enrollment in 1985.
Eligibility: *Academic:* bachelor's degree. *Language:* English proficiency on advanced level is required. TOEFL: 580. *Professional:* manager or management trainee with two years of work experience preferred.

Abbreviations: ESL = English as a Second Language; TOEFL = Test of English as a Foreign Language; ALIGU = American Language Institute of Georgetown University; GPA = Grade Point Average; SAT = Scholastic Aptitude Test; GED = General Equivalency Diploma.

Cost: $15,000 inclusive. *Scholarships:* partial.
Housing: Not provided; sponsor assists in locating housing.
Application: *Deadline:* May 1. *Fee:* $30; not refundable. *Scholarship deadline:* Apr. 1.
Contact: Mr. James G. Ptaszynski, Wake Forest University, 7659 Reynolda Station, Winston-Salem, NC 27109; (919) 761-5422.

D80 XAVIER UNIVERSITY
Master's of Business Administration Program.
Specialization: Accounting, economics, management, management information systems, industrial management, marketing, taxation, quantitative methods, multinational business, entrepreneurship, finance.
Dates: Classes begin in Sept., Jan., May, July.
Location: Cincinnati, Ohio: on campus.
Instruction: *Methods:* discussion groups, lectures, case studies, independent study/research. *By:* faculty, guest speakers/lecturers.
Highlights: Sponsor has offered program since 1952. Master's degree. Issues I-20AB. Foreign nationals on tourist visas are not eligible to enroll. A foreign student counselor/adviser is available.
Eligibility: *Academic:* bachelor's degree. *Language:* English proficiency on advanced level is required. TOEFL: 550; Univ. of Michigan Language Test: 80–85. *Professional:* 1–2 years of experience preferred.
Cost: $5,214 for tuition. *Scholarships:* none.
Housing: Not provided; sponsor assists in locating housing.
Application: *Deadline:* six weeks prior. *Fee:* $15; not refundable. *Scholarship deadline:* Mar. 31.
Contact: Ms. Nancy S. Tom, Director of Admissions, Xavier University, CBA-204, 3800 Victory Parkway, Cincinnati, OH 45207; (513) 745-3525.

MARKETING AND SALES

D81 KELLER GRADUATE SCHOOL OF MANAGEMENT
Master of Business Administration in Marketing.
Specialization: Marketing.
Dates: One year: classes begin in Sept.
Location: Chicago, Illinois: on campus.
Instruction: *Methods:* lectures, discussion groups, case studies. *By:* faculty, guest speakers/lecturers.
Highlights: Sponsor has offered short-term programs since 1973. Master's degree upon completion of program with 2.5 GPA. Issues I-20AB, I-20MN. Foreign nationals on tourist visas are eligible to enroll. A foreign student counselor/adviser is available. 5% foreign enrollment in 1985.
Eligibility: *Academic:* bachelor's degree; GMAT: 24+. *Language:* English proficiency on advanced level is required. TOEFL: 550. *Professional:* none.
Cost: $8,960 for tuition. *Scholarships:* none.
Housing: Not provided; sponsor assists in locating housing.
Application: *Deadline:* none. *Fee:* none.
Contact: Director of Admissions, Keller Graduate School of Management, 10 S. Riverside Plaza, Suite 2124, Chicago, IL 60606; (312) 454-0880.

D82 NEW YORK UNIVERSITY, SCHOOL OF CONTINUING EDUCATION
Direct Marketing Diploma Program.
Specialization: Direct marketing.
Dates: Two semesters: classes begin in Sept. and Feb.
Location: New York, New York: on campus.

All program information is subject to change without notice and must be confirmed directly with the sponsor.

58

Instruction: *Methods:* discussion groups, lectures, case studies, independent study/research, computer-assisted instruction. *By:* guest speakers/lecturers.
Highlights: Sponsor has offered program since 1983. Certificate. Issues I-20AB. Foreign nationals on tourist visas are eligible to enroll. A foreign student counselor/adviser is available. 360 total enrollment; less than 1% foreign enrollment in 1985.
Eligibility: *Academic:* bachelor's degree. *Language:* English proficiency on advanced level is required. *Professional:* marketing experience required.
Cost: $258 per credit for tuition. *Scholarships:* none.
Housing: Not provided.
Application: *Deadline:* July/Aug. for Sept., Nov./Dec: for Feb. *Fee:* $15; not refundable.
Contact: Ronald W. Janoff, Director, Center for Direct Marketing, School of Continuing Education, New York University, 2 University Place, Room 21, New York, NY 10003; (212) 598-2101. Cable: 235128 NYU/UR. Telex: 127587.

PROJECT MANAGEMENT

D83 ARTHUR D. LITTLE MANAGEMENT EDUCATION INSTITUTE
Specialization: Project analysis and project management; programs may be taken separately or in sequence.
Dates: May 29–July 11 (Project Analysis) and July 7–Aug. 15 (Project Management).
Location: Cambridge, Massachusetts: at institute.
Instruction: *Methods:* lectures, discussion groups, case studies, field trips, computer-assisted instruction. *By:* guest speakers/lecturers.
Highlights: Sponsor has offered program previously. Certificate. Issues I-20AB, IAP-66. Foreign nationals on tourist visas are eligible to enroll. A foreign student counselor/adviser is available.
Eligibility: *Academic:* bachelor's degree preferred. *Language:* TOEFL: 500 (testing usually not required). *Professional:* 2–5 years of managerial experience.
Cost: $4,000 per program, $6,500 combined for tuition, books.
Housing: Not provided; sponsor assists in locating housing.
Application: *Deadline:* May 15. *Fee:* none.
Contact: Judith Francis, Admissions Coordinator, Arthur D. Little Management Education Institute, 35 Acorn Park, Cambridge, MA 02140; (617) 864-5657. Telex: 921436.

PUBLIC RELATIONS

D84 THE AMERICAN UNIVERSITY
Graduate Certificate in Public Relations Management.
Specialization: Graduate-level courses in public relations management.
Dates: Classes begin in Sept., Jan., May, July.
Location: Washington, D.C.: on campus.
Instruction: *Methods:* discussion groups, lectures, case studies. *By:* faculty.
Highlights: Sponsor has offered program previously. Certificate upon completion of five courses. Issues I-20AB. Foreign nationals on tourist visas are not eligible to enroll. A foreign student counselor/adviser is available. Orientation and ESL programs.
Eligibility: *Academic:* bachelor's degree, 3.0 GPA, GMAT score: 400. *Language:* English proficiency on advanced level is required. TOEFL: 600; English Language Institute Placement Test. *Professional:* none.
Cost: $299 per semester hour for tuition. *Scholarships:* none.
Housing: Not provided; sponsor assists in locating housing.
Application: *Deadline:* none. *Fee:* none.
Contact: Programs Advisement Center, The American University, 4400 Massachusetts Ave. NW, Room 153 McKinley Bldg., Washington, DC 20016; (202) 885-2500.

Abbreviations: ESL = English as a Second Language; TOEFL = Test of English as a Foreign Language; ALIGU = American Language Institute of Georgetown University; GPA = Grade Point Average; SAT = Scholastic Aptitude Test; GED = General Equivalency Diploma.

59

PURCHASING

D85 **THE AMERICAN UNIVERSITY**
   Procurement Management.
Specialization: Graduate-level program in procurement management.
Dates: Classes begin in Sept., Jan., May, July.
Location: Washington, D.C.: on campus.
Instruction: *Methods:* discussion groups, lectures, case studies. *By:* faculty.
Highlights: Sponsor has offered program previously. Certificate. Issues I-20AB. Foreign nationals on tourist visas are not eligible to enroll. A foreign student counselor/adviser is available. Orientation and ESL programs.
Eligibility: *Academic:* bachelor's degree; 3.0 GPA in last 60 hours; GMAT score: 400.
Language: English proficiency on advanced level is required. TOEFL: 600; English Language Institute Placement Test. *Professional:* none.
Cost: $299 per semester hour for tuition. *Scholarships:* none.
Housing: Not provided; sponsor assists in locating housing.
Application: *Deadline:* none. *Fee:* none.
Contact: Programs Advisement Center, The American University, 4400 Massachusetts Ave. NW, Room 153 McKinley Bldg., Washington, DC 20016; (202) 885-2500.

TECHNOLOGY MANAGEMENT

D86 **MASSACHUSETTS INSTITUTE OF TECHNOLOGY**
   The Management of Technology Program.
Dates: One year: classes begin in June.
Location: Cambridge, Massachusetts: on campus.
Instruction: *Methods:* discussion groups, lectures, case studies, independent study/research. *By:* faculty, guest speakers/lecturers.
Highlights: Sponsor has offered program since 1981. Certificate. International student office. 30 total enrollment; 12% foreign enrollment in 1985.
Eligibility: *Academic:* bachelor's degree in technical field. *Language:* English proficiency on advanced level is required. TOEFL: 575. *Professional:* five years of technical work experience required.
Cost: $23,300 for tuition. *Scholarships:* none.
Housing: Not provided; sponsor assists in locating housing.
Application: *Deadline:* Feb. 1. *Fee:* $40; not refundable.
Contact: Management of Technology Program Office, MIT, 50 Memorial Drive, E52-125, Cambridge, MA 02139; (617) 253-3733. Cable: MIT CAM. Telex: 921473 MIT CAM.

TELECOMMUNICATIONS MANAGEMENT

D87 **GOLDEN GATE UNIVERSITY**
   Certificate Program in Telecommunications Management.
Specialization: Telecommunications management.
Dates: Classes begin in May, Sept., Jan.
Location: San Francisco, California: on campus.
Instruction: *Methods:* discussion groups, lectures, case studies, field trips. *By:* faculty, guest speakers/lecturers.
Highlights: Sponsor has offered program since 1980. Certificate upon completion of 18 units. Issues I-20AB, IAP-66. Foreign nationals on tourist visas are eligible to enroll. A foreign student counselor/adviser is available. Unlimited total enrollment; 4% foreign enrollment in 1985.

Eligibility: *Academic:* bachelor's degree. *Language:* English proficiency on advanced level is required. TOEFL: 525; Univ. of Michigan Language Test: 85. *Professional:* none.
Cost: $3,024 for tuition. *Scholarships:* none.
Housing: Not provided; sponsor assists in locating housing.
Application: *Deadline:* two months prior. *Fee:* $30; not refundable.
Contact: Ms. Beth Coggins, Foreign Student Advisor, Golden Gate University, 536 Mission Street, San Francisco, CA 94105; (415) 442-7237. Telex: 650 275 4174.

TRAVEL AND TOURISM

D88 GEORGE WASHINGTON UNIVERSITY
Travel and Tourism Program.
Specialization: Intensive master's degree program in travel and tourism.
Dates: Two-week intensive sessions in Jan., May, Aug.
Location: Washington, D.C.: on campus, at professional work site.
Instruction: *Methods:* discussion groups, lectures, case studies, field trips, individualized instruction, "hands-on" training, independent study/research, computer-assisted instruction, language laboratories. *By:* faculty, guest speakers/lecturers.
Highlights: Sponsor has offered program since 1975. Certificate. Practical training may be a program component. Issues I-20AB, I-20MN. Foreign nationals on tourist visas are not eligible to enroll. A foreign student counselor/adviser is available. ESL program. Unlimited total enrollment; 50% foreign enrollment in 1985.
Eligibility: *Academic:* bachelor's degree. *Language:* English proficiency on intermediate level is required. TOEFL: 550. *Professional:* three months of related work experience preferred.
Cost: About $1,800 per two-course session for tuition. *Scholarships:* none.
Housing: In dormitories, hotels.
Application: *Deadline:* two weeks prior. *Fee:* $25; applied to tuition.
Contact: Dr. John D. Hunt, Director, Travel and Tourism Program, George Washington University, 817 23rd Street NW, Washington, DC 20052; (202) 676-7071.

D89 UNIVERSITY OF HAWAII AT MANOA, SCHOOL OF TRAVEL INDUSTRY MANAGEMENT
Executive Development Institute for Tourism (EDIT).
Specialization: Tourism education and training, international tourism. Designed to serve educational needs of executive and professionals in public and private sectors of international tourism.
Dates: Five weeks; classes begin in May.
Location: Honolulu, Hawaii: on campus.
Instruction: *Methods:* lectures, discussion groups, case studies, field trips, computer-assisted instruction, independent study/research. *By:* faculty, guest speakers/lecturers.
Highlights: Sponsor has offered program since 1979. Certificate. Practical training is a program component; participants are not paid. A foreign student counselor/adviser is available. Various support services are available. 25 total enrollment; 100% foreign enrollment in 1985.
Eligibility: *Academic:* bachelor's degree preferred. *Language:* English proficiency on advanced level is required. *Professional:* manager in tourism industry.
Cost: $2,800 for tuition, materials, housing, local transportation. *Scholarships:* partial.
Housing: In hotels.
Application: *Deadline:* 6–7 weeks prior. *Fee:* $200; applied to tuition. *Scholarship deadline:* Feb. 1.
Contact: Ms. Steffi San Buenaventura, Director of Professional Programs, School of Travel Industry Management, University of Hawaii at Manoa, George Hall, 2560 Campus Road, Honolulu, HI 96822; (808) 948-8934. Cable: UNIHAW. Telex: 7431701.

D90 WASHINGTON STATE UNIVERSITY, HOTEL AND RESTAURANT ADMINISTRATION
Certificate in Hospitality and Tourism Administration.

Specialization: Introduction to the field of hospitality and tourism, plus some advanced interdisciplinary studies.

Dates: One year: classes begin in Aug., Jan.

Location: Pullman, Washington: on campus.

Instruction: *Methods:* discussion groups, lectures, case studies, individualized instruction, independent study/research, computer-assisted instruction. *By:* faculty, guest speakers/lecturers.

Highlights: Sponsor has offered program since 1932. Certificate upon completion of ten courses. Issues I-20AB, IAP-66. Foreign nationals on tourist visas are not eligible to enroll. A foreign student counselor/adviser is available. 30 total enrollment; 15% foreign enrollment in 1985.

Eligibility: *Academic:* bachelor's degree. *Language:* English proficiency on intermediate level is required. TOEFL: 520. *Professional:* hospitality/tourism industry or government experience required.

Cost: $6,962 for tuition, meals, housing. *Scholarships:* partial.

Housing: In dormitories.

Application: *Deadline:* May 1 and Oct. 1. *Fee:* $25; not refundable.

Contact: W. Terry Umbreit, Director, Hotel and Restaurant Administration, Washington State University, 245D Todd Hall, Pullman, WA 99164-4724; (509) 335-5766.

All program information is subject to change without notice
and must be confirmed directly with the sponsor.

62

COMMUNICATIONS

E1 BOSTON UNIVERSITY
Public Communication Institute.
Specialization: Development of communication skills for print and audiovisual media.
Dates: Four weeks: classes begin in July.
Location: Boston, Massachusetts: on campus.
Instruction: *Methods:* lectures, field trips, "hands-on" training. *By:* faculty, guest speakers/lecturers.
Highlights: Sponsor has offered program since 1975. Certificate. Issues I-20AB, IAP-66. Foreign nationals on tourist visas are eligible to enroll. A foreign student counselor/adviser is available. International Student Office. 60 total enrollment; 20% foreign enrollment in 1985.
Eligibility: *Academic:* associate's degree or at least two years of undergraduate study or experience in the field. *Language:* English proficiency on advanced level is required. *Professional:* none.
Cost: $1,350 for tuition. *Scholarships:* none.
Housing: In dormitories.
Application: *Deadline:* Apr. 30. *Fee:* $15; not refundable.
Contact: Ms. Susan McCarthy, Public Communication Institute, Boston University, 640 Commonwealth Ave., Boston, MA 02215; (617) 353-3447.

E2 GUILFORD COLLEGE
Specialization: Communications.
Dates: Aug.–July.
Location: Greensboro, North Carolina: on campus.
Instruction: *Methods:* lectures, discussion groups. *By:* faculty.
Highlights: Sponsor has offered program previously. Certificate upon completion of 4–6 courses. Issues I-20AB, I-20MN. Foreign nationals on tourist visas are not eligible to enroll. A foreign student counselor/adviser is available. International Relations Club.
Eligibility: *Academic:* bachelor's degree. *Language:* English proficiency on advanced level is required. TOEFL: 500. *Professional:* none.
Cost: $112 per credit hour for tuition. *Scholarships:* none.
Housing: Not provided; student makes own arrangements.
Application: *Deadline:* open. *Fee:* $20; not refundable.
Contact: Dean of Admissions and Financial Aid, Guilford College, 5800 West Friendly Ave., Greensboro, NC 27410; (919) 292-5511.

ADVERTISING

E3 FASHION INSTITUTE OF TECHNOLOGY
Advertising & Communications.
Specialization: AAS degree program in fashion advertising and communications.
Dates: Nine months: classes begin in late Aug.
Location: New York, New York: on campus.
Instruction: *Methods:* discussion groups, lectures, case studies, field trips, individualized

---

Abbreviations: ESL = English as a Second Language; TOEFL = Test of English as a Foreign Language
ALIGU = American Language Institute of Georgetown University; GPA = Grade Point Average;
SAT = Scholastic Aptitude Test; GED = General Equivalency Diploma.

instruction, "hands-on" training, independent study/research, computer-assisted instruction.
By: faculty, guest speakers/lecturers.
Highlights: Sponsor has offered program previously. Associate's degree. Issues I-20AB.
Foreign nationals on tourist visas are not eligible to enroll. A foreign student
counselor/adviser is available. Various support services are available.
Eligibility: *Academic:* bachelor's degree or some undergraduate work. *Language:* English
proficiency on intermediate level is required. TOEFL: 550. *Professional:* none.
Cost: $11,875 inclusive. *Scholarships:* none.
Housing: In dormitories if available; or sponsor assists in locating housing.
Application: *Deadline:* Mar. 15 for fall; Oct. 15 for spring. *Fee:* $10; not refundable.
Contact: Ms. Sally White, Foreign Student Advisor, Fashion Institute of Technology, 227
W. 27th Street, New York, NY 10001; (212) 760-7675.

E4 SOUTHERN ILLINOIS UNIVERSITY, SCHOOL OF JOURNALISM
Special Foreign Non-Degree Program.
Specialization: Advertising.
Dates: Classes begin in Aug., Jan., and June.
Location: Carbondale, Illinois: on campus.
Instruction: *Methods:* discussion groups, lectures, case studies, field trips, individualized
instruction, "hands-on" training, independent study/research, computer-assisted instruction.
By: faculty.
Highlights: Sponsor has offered program since 1983. Practical training may be a program
component. Issues I-20AB, I-20MN, IAP-66. Foreign nationals on tourist visas are not
eligible to enroll. A foreign student counselor/adviser is available. ESL program and
international student office. 20% foreign enrollment in 1985.
Eligibility: *Academic:* bachelor's degree. *Language:* English proficiency on intermediate level
is required. TOEFL: 600. *Professional:* two years of work experience required.
Cost: $2,000 per semester for tuition, health insurance. *Scholarships:* partial.
Housing: Not provided; sponsor assists in locating housing.
Application: *Deadline:* four months prior. *Fee:* none.
Contact: Graduate Studies Director, School of Journalism, Southern Illinois University,
Carbondale, IL 62901; (618) 536-3361.

FILM AND VIDEO

E5 MARQUETTE UNIVERSITY, INSTITUTE FOR CATHOLIC MEDIA
Intermediate Television Production Workshop in Religious Communication.
Specialization: Fundamentals of scripting, shooting, editing, and sound mixing; for
broadcast and nonbroadcast productions.
Dates: Two weeks: classes begin in June.
Location: Milwaukee, Wisconsin: on campus.
Instruction: *Methods:* lectures, field trips, individualized instruction, "hands-on" training.
By: faculty, guest speakers/lecturers.
Highlights: Sponsor has offered program since 1985. Certificate upon completion of four
group video projects. Foreign nationals on tourist visas are eligible to enroll. A foreign
student counselor/adviser is available. 20 total enrollment; no foreign enrollment in 1985.
Eligibility: *Academic:* associate's degree or some undergraduate work. *Language:* English
proficiency on intermediate level is required. TOEFL. *Professional:* six months of experience
in audio/video related field.
Cost: $150 for tuition, housing. *Scholarships:* partial.
Housing: In dormitories.
Application: *Deadline:* Apr. 1. *Fee:* none. *Scholarship deadline:* Apr. 1.
Contact: Dr. William Thorn, College of Journalism, 1131 W. Wisconsin Ave., Milwaukee,
WI 53233; (414) 224-7132.

E6 UNIVERSITY OF TEXAS AT DALLAS
Cinema Study.
Specialization: Cinema.
Dates: Not given.
Location: Richardson, Texas: on campus, at professional work site.
Instruction: *Methods:* discussion groups, lectures, case studies, field trips, individualized instruction, "hands-on" training, independent study/research, computer-assisted instruction, language laboratories, science laboratories. *By:* faculty, guest speakers/lecturers.
Highlights: A foreign student counselor/adviser is available. Unlimited total enrollment; about 15% foreign enrollment in 1985.
Eligibility: *Academic:* associate's or bachelor's degree. *Language:* English proficiency on advanced level is required. *Professional:* none.
Cost: Not given. *Scholarships:* none.
Housing: Not provided; sponsor assists in locating housing.
Application: *Deadline:* not given. *Fee:* not given.
Contact: Mr. Robert Corrigan, Cinema/Arts and Humanities, University of Texas at Dallas, Box 688, Mail Stop J03.1, Richardson, TX 75080; (214) 690-2985.

JOURNALISM

E7 OHIO UNIVERSITY, E. W. SCRIPPS SCHOOL OF JOURNALISM
Master's Degree Program in Journalism.
Specialization: Newspaper, magazine, or broadcast journalism, or public relations.
Dates: One year: classes begin quarterly; summer or fall entry preferred.
Location: Athens, Ohio: on campus.
Instruction: *Methods:* discussion groups, lectures, case studies, field trips, individualized instruction, "hands-on" training, independent study/research, computer-assisted instruction. *By:* faculty.
Highlights: Sponsor has offered program since 1946. Certificate upon completion of 49 quarter hours. Practical training is a program component; participants may be paid. Issues I-20AB, I-20MN, IAP-66. A foreign student counselor/adviser is available. 25% foreign enrollment in 1985.
Eligibility: *Academic:* bachelor's degree. *Language:* English proficiency on advanced level is required. TOEFL: 600; Univ. of Michigan Language Test. *Professional:* none.
Cost: $7,000 for tuition, books and materials, meals, housing, health insurance. *Scholarships:* full.
Housing: In dormitories, apartments.
Application: *Deadline:* 45 days prior. *Fee:* $25; not refundable. *Scholarship deadline:* 45 days prior.
Contact: Mr. Guido H. Stempel III, E.W. Scripps School of Journalism, Ohio University, Athens, OH 45701; (614) 593-2609.

E8 SOUTHERN ILLINOIS UNIVERSITY, SCHOOL OF JOURNALISM
Special Foreign Non-Degree Program.
Specialization: News-editorial.
Dates: Classes begin in Aug., Jan., and June.
Location: Carbondale, Illinois: on campus.
Instruction: *Methods:* discussion groups, lectures, case studies, field trips, individualized instruction, "hands-on" training, independent study/research, computer-assisted instruction. *By:* faculty.
Highlights: Sponsor has offered program since 1983. Transcript. Practical training may be a program component; participants may be paid. Issues I-20AB, I-20MN, IAP-66. Foreign nationals on tourist visas are not eligible to enroll. A foreign student counselor/adviser is available. International student office. 20% foreign enrollment in 1985.

Abbreviations: ESL = English as a Second Language; TOEFL = Test of English as a Foreign Language; ALIGU = American Language Institute of Georgetown University; GPA = Grade Point Average; SAT = Scholastic Aptitude Test; GED = General Equivalency Diploma.

COMMUNICATIONS

Eligibility: *Academic:* bachelor's degree. *Language:* English proficiency on intermediate level is required. TOEFL: 600. *Professional:* two years of work experience required.
Cost: $2,000 per semester for tuition, health insurance. *Scholarships:* partial.
Housing: Not provided; sponsor assists in locating housing.
Application: *Deadline:* four months prior. *Fee:* none.
Contact: Graduate Studies Director, School of Journalism, Southern Illinois University, Carbondale, IL 62901; (618) 536-3361.

E9 UNIVERSITY OF CALIFORNIA, LOS ANGELES EXTENSION
Certificate Program in Journalism.
Specialization: Political and investigative reporting, writing for newspapers and magazines, sportswriting, restaurant reviewing, travel journalism, broadcast and photojournalism.
Dates: 9–12 months: classes begin in June, Sept., Jan., and April.
Location: Los Angeles, California: on campus.
Instruction: *Methods:* discussion groups, lectures. *By:* faculty, guest speakers/lecturers.
Highlights: Sponsor has offered program previously. Certificate upon completion of nine courses. Issues I-20AB. Foreign nationals on tourist visas are eligible to enroll. A foreign student counselor/adviser is available. ESL program. Unlimited total enrollment; about 10% foreign enrollment in 1985.
Eligibility: *Academic:* some undergraduate work, bachelor's degree, or equivalent experience. *Language:* English proficiency on advanced level is required. Placement exam. *Professional:* none.
Cost: About $3,300 per quarter for tuition. *Scholarships:* none.
Housing: Not provided; student makes own arrangements.
Application: *Deadline:* three months to one year prior. *Fee:* $275; not refundable.
Contact: Foreign Student Advisor, UCLA Extension Advisory Service, 10995 Le Conte Avenue, Los Angeles, CA 90024; (213) 825-9351 or 206-6201. Cable: 9103427597. Telex: 9103427597.

PUBLISHING

E10 HOWARD UNIVERSITY PRESS BOOK PUBLISHING INSTITUTE
Specialization: Editorial, design and production, marketing, and business.
Dates: May 27–July 2.
Location: Washington, D.C.: on campus.
Instruction: *Methods:* lectures, work groups, field trips, "hands-on" training. *By:* guest speakers/lecturers.
Highlights: Sponsor has offered program previously. Certificate. Foreign nationals on tourist visas are eligible to enroll. A foreign student counselor/adviser is available. 30 total enrollment; 3% foreign enrollment in 1985. List of past participants is available.
Eligibility: *Academic:* three years of college. *Language:* English proficiency on advanced level is required. *Professional:* none.
Cost: $1,500 for tuition. *Scholarships:* none.
Housing: In dormitories.
Application: *Deadline:* April 9. *Fee:* $35; not refundable.
Contact: Program Administrator, Howard University Press Book Publishing Institute, 2900 Van Ness Street NW, Washington, DC 20008; (202) 686-6498.

E11 NEW YORK UNIVERSITY, SCHOOL OF CONTINUING EDUCATION
Magazine Publishing Diploma.
Specialization: All aspects of magazine publishing.
Dates: Nine months: classes begin in Sept., Feb.
Location: New York, New York: on campus, at professional work site.

All program information is subject to change without notice
and must be confirmed directly with the sponsor.

66

Instruction: *Methods:* discussion groups, lectures, field trips, "hands-on" training, independent study/research. *By:* faculty, guest speakers/lecturers.
Highlights: Sponsor has offered program since 1979. Certificate. Issues I-20AB. Foreign nationals on tourist visas are eligible to enroll. A foreign student counselor/adviser is available. ESL program and social activities. 75 total enrollment; 4% foreign enrollment in 1985.
Eligibility: *Academic:* bachelor's degree. *Language:* English proficiency on advanced level is preferred. NYU American Language Institute. *Professional:* related business experience preferred.
Cost: $158 per unit for tuition. *Scholarships:* none.
Housing: Not provided; sponsor assists in locating housing.
Application: *Deadline:* rolling. *Fee:* none.
Contact: Mr. Ronald W. Janoff, Director, Management Institute, School of Continuing Education, New York University, 2 University Place, Room 21, New York, NY 10003; (212) 598-2101. Cable: 235128 NYU UL. Telex: 127587.

E12 NEW YORK UNIVERSITY, SCHOOL OF CONTINUING EDUCATION
Summer Publishing Institute.
Specialization: Book and magazine publishing.
Dates: Six weeks: classes begin in mid-June.
Location: New York, New York: on campus, at professional work site.
Instruction: *Methods:* discussion groups, lectures, field trips, "hands-on" training, independent study/research. *By:* faculty, guest speakers/lecturers.
Highlights: Sponsor has offered program since 1979. Certificate. Issues I-20AB. Foreign nationals on tourist visas are eligible to enroll. A foreign student counselor/adviser is available. 75 total enrollment; 4% foreign enrollment in 1985.
Eligibility: *Academic:* bachelor's degree; proficiency in writing and typing.
Language: English proficiency on advanced level is preferred. NYU American Language Institute. *Professional:* related business experience preferred.
Cost: $2,400 for tuition. *Scholarships:* none.
Housing: In dormitories, apartments.
Application: *Deadline:* Mar. 31. *Fee:* $35; not refundable.
Contact: Mr. Ronald W. Janoff, Director, Management Institute, School of Continuing Education, New York University, 2 University Place, Room 21, New York, NY 10003; (212) 598-2101. Cable: 235128 NYU UL. Telex: 127587.

E13 PACE UNIVERSITY
Graduate Program in Publishing.
Specialization: Principles of publishing, including marketing, information systems, editing, book and magazine production, legal and ethical issues, financial aspects, distribution methods.
Dates: Two semesters: classes begin in Sept. and Jan.
Location: New York, New York: on campus.
Instruction: *Methods:* discussion groups, lectures, case studies, "hands-on" training.
By: faculty, guest lecturers.
Highlights: Sponsor has offered program since 1985. Master's degree upon completion of 36 credits. Practical training is a program component. Issues I-20AB, IAP-66. Foreign nationals on tourist visas are not eligible to enroll. A foreign student counselor/adviser is available. ESL program and international student club. 40–50 total enrollment; 5% foreign enrollment in 1985.
Eligibility: *Academic:* bachelor's degree or GRE. *Language:* English proficiency on advanced level is required. TOEFL: 550. *Professional:* none.
Cost: $240 per credit for tuition. *Scholarships:* none.
Housing: Not provided; sponsor assists in locating housing.
Application: *Deadline:* Aug. 15. *Fee:* not given.

Contact: Ms. Jonell Carter, Graduate Admissions, Pace University, Pace Plaza, New York, NY 10038; (212) 488-1531.

E14 RADCLIFFE COLLEGE
Radcliffe Publishing Procedures Course.
Specialization: Overview of book and magazine publishing.
Dates: Six weeks: classes begin in June.
Location: Cambridge, Massachusetts: on campus.
Instruction: *Methods:* discussion groups, lectures, case studies, field trips, individualized instruction, "hands-on" training, independent study/research, computer-assisted instruction. *By:* guest speakers/lecturers.
Highlights: Sponsor has offered program since 1947. Certificate. Practical training is a program component; participants are not paid. Issues I-20AB. Foreign nationals on tourist visas are not eligible to enroll. A foreign student counselor/adviser is available. International student office. 85 total enrollment; 10% foreign enrollment in 1985.
Eligibility: *Academic:* bachelor's degree. *Language:* English proficiency on advanced level is required. *Professional:* none.
Cost: $3,150 for tuition, meals, housing. *Scholarships:* partial.
Housing: In dormitories.
Application: *Deadline:* three months prior. *Fee:* $25; not refundable. *Scholarship deadline:* three months prior.
Contact: Mr. Frank Collins, Radcliffe Publishing Procedures Course, Radcliffe College, 6 Ash Street, Cambridge, MA 02138; (617) 495-8678.

E15 STANFORD ALUMNI ASSOCIATION
Stanford Publishing Course.
Specialization: Book and magazine publishing for publishing professionals; editing, design, production, new technology, marketing, sales, advertising, finance.
Dates: Two weeks: July.
Location: Stanford, California: on campus.
Instruction: *Methods:* discussion groups, lectures, case studies. *By:* faculty, guest speakers/lecturers.
Highlights: Sponsor has offered program previously. Foreign nationals on tourist visas are eligible to enroll. 150 total enrollment.
Eligibility: *Academic:* none. *Language:* English proficiency on intermediate level is preferred. *Professional:* professionals in the publishing industry.
Cost: $1,350 for tuition, books and materials. *Scholarships:* none.
Housing: In campus residence.
Application: *Deadline:* Apr. 25. *Fee:* $20; not refundable.
Contact: Justin O'Brien, Dept. PB, Stanford Alumni Association, Bowman Alumni House, Stanford, CA 94305-1618; (415) 723-2021 or 725-1083. Telex: 348 402 STANFRD STNU.

COMPUTER SCIENCES

F1 THE AMERICAN UNIVERSITY
Graduate Certificate in Computer Systems Applications.
Specialization: Graduate-level courses in computer systems applications.
Dates: Classes begin in Sept., Jan., May, July.
Location: Washington, D.C.: on campus.
Instruction: *Methods:* discussion groups, lectures, case studies. *By:* faculty.
Highlights: Sponsor has offered program previously. Certificate upon completion of five courses. Issues I-20AB. Foreign nationals on tourist visas are not eligible to enroll. A foreign student counselor/adviser is available. Orientation programs.
Eligibility: *Academic:* bachelor's degree; courses in statistics and programming.
Language: English proficiency on advanced level is required. TOEFL: 600; or English Language Institute Placement Test. *Professional:* none.
Cost: $299 per semester hour for tuition. *Scholarships:* none.
Housing: Not provided; sponsor assists in locating housing.
Application: *Deadline:* none. *Fee:* none.
Contact: Programs Advisement Center, The American University, 4400 Massachusetts Ave. NW, Room 153 McKinley Bldg., Washington, DC 20016; (202) 885-2500.

F2 DePAUL UNIVERSITY
Computer Career Program.
Specialization: COBOL programming, systems analysis and design, microcomputing on DBASE III and Lotus. Final project is a group design effort utilizing COBOL/CICS for on-line batch business system.
Dates: Seven months: classes begin in July, Oct., Feb., and April.
Location: Chicago, Illinois: on campus.
Instruction: *Methods:* discussion groups, lectures, "hands-on" training, independent study/research, computer-assisted instruction, computer laboratories. *By:* faculty, guest speakers/lecturers.
Highlights: Sponsor has offered program since 1982. Certificate. Issues I-20AB, I-20MN. Foreign nationals on tourist visas are not eligible to enroll. A foreign student counselor/adviser is available. 300 total enrollment; about 2% foreign enrollment in 1985.
Eligibility: *Academic:* bachelor's degree; qualifying exam. *Language:* English proficiency on intermediate level is required. *Professional:* none.
Cost: $2,970 for tuition, books, and materials. *Scholarships:* none.
Housing: In dormitories.
Application: *Deadline:* Sept. 12 for fall start. *Fee:* $20; not refundable.
Contact: Stephen Samuels, Director, Computer Career Program, DePaul University, 243 S. Wabash, Chicago, IL 60126; (312) 341-8735.

F3 GUILFORD COLLEGE
Specialization: Computer science.
Dates: Aug.–late July.
Location: Greensboro, North Carolina: on campus.
Instruction: *Methods:* lectures, discussion groups. *By:* faculty.

Abbreviations: ESL = English as a Second Language; TOEFL = Test of English as a Foreign Language; ALIGU = American Language Institute of Georgetown University; GPA = Grade Point Average; SAT = Scholastic Aptitude Test; GED = General Equivalency Diploma.

Highlights: Sponsor has offered short-term programs since 1983. Certificate upon completion of 4–6 courses. Issues I-20AB, I-20MN. Foreign nationals on tourist visas are not eligible to enroll. A foreign student counselor/adviser is available. International Relations Club.
Eligibility: *Academic:* bachelor's degree. *Language:* English proficiency on intermediate level is required. TOEFL: 500. *Professional:* none.
Cost: $112 per credit hour for tuition. *Scholarships:* none.
Housing: Not provided; student makes own arrangements.
Application: *Deadline:* rolling admissions. *Fee:* $20; not refundable.
Contact: Dean of Admissions and Financial Aid, Guilford College, 5800 W. Friendly Ave., Greensboro, NC 27410; (919) 292-5511.

F4 MASSACHUSETTS INSTITUTE OF TECHNOLOGY
Summer Session.
Specialization: Various computer-related programs, including computer-aided experimentation, structure and interpretation of computer programs, data communication networks, planning system security, robotics, and artificial intelligence.
Dates: June–Aug.
Location: Cambridge, Massachusetts: on campus.
Instruction: *Methods:* discussion groups, lectures, case studies, "hands-on" training, independent study/research, computer-assisted instruction, science laboratories. *By:* faculty.
Highlights: Sponsor has offered program since 1949. Certificate. Foreign nationals on tourist visas are eligible to enroll. A foreign student counselor/adviser is not available. About 20–25 per class total enrollment; 10% foreign enrollment in 1985.
Eligibility: *Academic:* bachelor's degree. *Language:* English proficiency on intermediate level is required. *Professional:* none.
Cost: About $1,500 per week for tuition, books and materials, meals, housing. *Scholarships:* none.
Housing: In dormitories, hotels.
Application: *Deadline:* depends on program. *Fee:* none.
Contact: Summer Session Office, Massachusetts Institute of Technology, 77 Massachusetts Ave., Room E19-356, Cambridge, MA 02139; (617) 253-2101. Telex: 921473 MIT CAM.

F5 UNIVERSITY OF CALIFORNIA, SANTA CRUZ
16th Annual Computer Institute.
Specialization: Compiler construction, graphics, artificial intelligence, parallel processing, images, Ada, expert systems, and others.
Dates: July 7–Aug. 25.
Location: Santa Cruz, California: on campus.
Instruction: *Methods:* lectures, seminars, "hands-on" training. *By:* faculty, guest speakers/lecturers.
Highlights: Sponsor has offered program since 1970. Credit. 25 total enrollment.
Eligibility: *Academic:* bachelor's degree. *Language:* not given. *Professional:* strong familiarity or experience with subject.
Cost: $395–$1,300 for tuition, books, and materials. *Scholarships:* limited corporate discounts available.
Housing: In dormitories, campus apartments, or off-campus housing.
Application: *Deadline:* not given. *Fee:* not given.
Contact: R. Smith, University of California Extension, Santa Cruz, CA 95064; (408) 429-2386.

F6 VOORHEES COLLEGE
Computer/Information Science.
Specialization: Computer and information sciences.
Dates: Aug.–May; classes begin in Aug. and Jan.
Location: Denmark, South Carolina: on campus, at professional work site.

Instruction: *Methods:* discussion groups, lectures, case studies, field trips, individualized instruction, "hands-on" training, independent study/research, computer-assisted instruction, science laboratories. *By:* faculty.

Highlights: Sponsor has offered program since 1969. Certificate. Practical training is a program component; participants are not paid. Issues I-20AB. Foreign nationals on tourist visas are not eligible to enroll. A foreign student counselor/adviser is available.

Eligibility: *Academic:* associate's degree. *Language:* English proficiency on beginning level is required. TOEFL. *Professional:* none.

Cost: $5,884 for tuition, meals, housing, health insurance. *Scholarships:* none.

Housing: In dormitories.

Application: *Deadline:* Aug. *Fee:* $10; not refundable.

Contact: Dr. Lucious Daily, Jr., Director of Admissions and Records, Voorhees College, Voorhees Road, Denmark, SC 29042; (803) 793-3351.

COMPUTER USE IN DEVELOPING COUNTRIES

F7 STANFORD UNIVERSITY, FOOD RESEARCH INSTITUTE
Microcomputers in Development.

Specialization: Annual workshop on the use of microcomputers in decision-making and data analysis problems of developing countries. Provides a broad overview of the technology and develops skills in use of selected commercial software packages.

Dates: Four weeks: Aug.

Location: Stanford, California: on campus.

Instruction: *Methods:* discussion groups, lectures, individualized instruction, "hands-on" training. *By:* faculty. *Also in French and Spanish.*

Highlights: Sponsor has offered program since 1983. Foreign nationals on tourist visas are eligible to enroll. A foreign student counselor/adviser is available. 30 total enrollment.

Eligibility: *Academic:* bachelor's degree. *Language:* English proficiency on advanced level is preferred. *Professional:* none.

Cost: $2,700 for tuition, full-time use of computer. *Scholarships:* none.

Housing: In dormitories, apartments.

Application: *Deadline:* June 30. *Fee:* none.

Contact: Prof. Carl H. Gotsch, Food Research Institute, Stanford University, Stanford, CA 94305; (415) 723-0693. Telex: 348402 STANFORD STN. Cable: FOODRES.

F8 UNIVERSITY OF CONNECTICUT, INSTITUTE OF PUBLIC SERVICE INTERNATIONAL
Computers in Management and Development.

Specialization: System development, project and information management. Computer applications in planning, management, and operation functions of government. Focuses on technical and managerial skills for public managers in developing countries.

Dates: Two months: classes begin in May.

Location: West Hartford, Connecticut: on campus.

Instruction: *Methods:* discussion groups, lectures, case studies, field trips. *By:* faculty, guest speakers/lecturers.

Highlights: Sponsor has offered program since 1980. Certificate. Issues IAP-66. Foreign nationals on tourist visas are not eligible to enroll. A foreign student counselor/adviser is available. Social and cultural activities. 100% foreign enrollment in 1985.

Eligibility: *Academic:* bachelor's degree, or equivalent experience and recommendations. *Language:* English proficiency on intermediate level is required. TOEFL: 500; ALIGU: 80. *Professional:* two years of experience required.

Cost: $4,700 for tuition, books, and materials. *Scholarships:* none.

Housing: Not provided; sponsor assists in locating housing.

Application: *Deadline:* six weeks prior. *Fee:* none.

Abbreviations: ESL = English as a Second Language; TOEFL = Test of English as a Foreign Language; ALIGU = American Language Institute of Georgetown University; GPA = Grade Point Average; SAT = Scholastic Aptitude Test; GED = General Equivalency Diploma.

Contact: Mrs. Josephine Mavromatis, IPS International, University of Connecticut, 1800 Asylum Ave., West Hartford, CT 06117; (203) 241-4924. Cable: IPSUCONN. Telex: 883997 (IPS INTL).

MANAGEMENT INFORMATION SYSTEMS

F9 THE AMERICAN UNIVERSITY
Graduate Certificate in Management Information Systems.
Specialization: Graduate-level courses in management information systems.
Dates: Classes begin in Sept., Jan., May, July.
Location: Washington, D.C.: on campus.
Instruction: *Methods:* discussion groups, lectures, case studies. *By:* faculty.
Highlights: Sponsor has offered program previously. Certificate. Issues I-20AB. Foreign nationals on tourist visas are not eligible to enroll. A foreign student counselor/adviser is available. Orientation programs.
Eligibility: *Academic:* bachelor's degree. *Language:* English proficiency on advanced level is required. TOEFL: 600; or English Language Institute Placement Test. *Professional:* none.
Cost: $299 per semester hour for tuition. *Scholarships:* none.
Housing: Not provided; sponsor assists in locating housing.
Application: *Deadline:* none. *Fee:* none.
Contact: Programs Advisement Center, The American University, 4400 Massachusetts Ave. NW, Room 153 McKinley Bldg., Washington, DC 20016; (202) 885-2500.

OPERATIONS

F10 ASSOCIATED TECHNICAL INSTITUTE
Data Entry/Computer Operations.
Specialization: Intensive course in computer operations.
Dates: Three months: late June–late Sept.
Location: Woburn and Boston, Massachusetts: at institute.
Instruction: *Methods:* lectures, independent study, "hands-on" training. *By:* faculty.
Highlights: Sponsor has offered program since 1982. Certificate. Does not help obtain visa. Limited services for foreign nationals. 20 total enrollment. List of past participants is available.
Eligibility: *Academic:* bachelor's degree; entrance exam. *Language:* not given.
Professional: none.
Cost: $2,500 for tuition, books. *Scholarships:* none.
Housing: Not provided: sponsor assists in locating housing.
Application: *Deadline: Fee:* $160.
Contact: Admissions, Associated Technical Institute, 234 W. Cummings Park, Woburn, MA 01801; (617) 935-3838.

F11 COMPUTER LEARNING CENTER OF LOS ANGELES
Computer Operations and Management.
Specialization: Operations and management of mainframe computers. Includes special training in data processing terminology.
Dates: Six months: classes begin monthly.
Location: Los Angeles, California: on campus.
Instruction: *Methods:* lectures, case studies, individualized instruction, "hands-on" training. *By:* faculty.
Highlights: Sponsor has offered program since 1957. Certificate upon completion of program with 2.0 GPA. Issues I-20MN. Foreign nationals on tourist visas are eligible to enroll. A

foreign student counselor/adviser is available. 10 per class total enrollment; 10% foreign enrollment in 1985.
Eligibility: *Academic:* bachelor's degree or some undergraduate work preferred.
Language: personal interview. *Professional:* business experience or familiarity with accounting preferred.
Cost: $5,350 for tuition. *Scholarships:* none.
Housing: Not provided; sponsor assists in locating housing.
Application: *Deadline:* 30 days prior. *Fee:* $45; not refundable.
Contact: Mr. Floyd M. Haugen, Director, Computer Learning Center of Los Angeles, 3130 Wilshire Blvd., Los Angeles, CA 90010; (213) 386-6311.

PROGRAMMING

F12 AIRCO COMPUTER LEARNING CENTER
   Computer Programming.
Specialization: COBOL and Assembler.
Dates: Four months: classes begin monthly.
Location: Somerville, Massachusetts: at school.
Instruction: *Methods:* lectures, individualized instruction, "hands-on" training, science labs.
By: faculty.
Highlights: Sponsor has offered program since 1967. Certificate upon completion of program with 70 grade average. Practical training is a program component; participants are not paid.
A foreign student counselor/adviser is available. Tutoring program. 50 total enrollment; 10% foreign enrollment in 1985.
Eligibility: *Academic:* undergraduate degree; IBM aptitude test. *Language:* English proficiency on intermediate level is required. *Professional:* none.
Cost: $3,595 for tuition, books. *Scholarships:* none.
Housing: Not provided; student makes own arrangments.
Application: *Deadline:* none. *Fee:* $25; not refundable.
Contact: Janet Gailun, Director, Computer Learning Center, 5 Middlesex Ave., Somerville, MA 02145; (617) 776-3500.

F13 COMPUTER LEARNING CENTER OF LOS ANGELES
   Computer Systems and Programming.
Specialization: Business application programming. Includes special training in data processing terminology.
Dates: Six months: classes begin monthly.
Location: Los Angeles, California: on campus.
Instruction: *Methods:* lectures, case studies, individualized instruction, "hands-on" training.
By: faculty.
Highlights: Sponsor has offered program since 1957. Certificate upon completion of program with 2.0 GPA. Issues I-20MN. Foreign nationals on tourist visas are eligible to enroll. A foreign student counselor/adviser is available. 10 per program total enrollment; 10% foreign enrollment in 1985.
Eligibility: *Academic:* bachelor's degree or some undergraduate work preferred.
Language: English proficiency on intermediate level is required. Personal interview.
Professional: business or accounting experience preferred.
Cost: $5,350 for tuition. *Scholarships:* none.
Housing: Not provided; sponsor assists in locating housing.
Application: *Deadline:* one month prior. *Fee:* $45; not refundable.
Contact: Mr. Floyd M. Haugen, Director, Computer Learning Center of Los Angeles, 3130 Wilshire Blvd., Los Angeles, CA 90010; (213) 386-6311.

Abbreviations: ESL = English as a Second Language; TOEFL = Test of English as a Foreign Language;
ALIGU = American Language Institute of Georgetown University; GPA = Grade Point Average;
SAT = Scholastic Aptitude Test; GED = General Equivalency Diploma.

REPAIR AND MAINTENANCE

F14 COMPUTER LEARNING CENTER OF LOS ANGELES
Computer Electronics and Technology.
Specialization: Repair and maintenance of microcomputers and microcomputer drive apparatus.
Dates: Nine months: classes begin monthly.
Location: Los Angeles, California: on campus.
Instruction: *Methods:* lectures, case studies, individualized instruction, "hands-on" training. *By:* faculty.
Highlights: Sponsor has offered program since 1985. Certificate upon completion of program with 2.0 GPA. Issues I-20MN. Foreign nationals on tourist visas are eligible to enroll. A foreign student counselor/adviser is available. 10 per program total enrollment; 10% foreign enrollment in 1985.
Eligibility: *Academic:* bachelor's degree or some undergraduate work preferred.
Language: English proficiency on intermediate level is required. Personal interview.
Professional: none.
Cost: $5,950 for tuition. *Scholarships:* none.
Housing: Not provided; sponsor assists in locating housing.
Application: *Deadline:* one month prior. *Fee:* $45; not refundable.
Contact: Mr. Floyd M. Haugen, Director, Computer Learning Center of Los Angeles, 3130 Wilshire Blvd., Los Angeles, CA 90010; (213) 386-6311.

F15 WESTARK COMMUNITY COLLEGE
Microprocessor/Computer Technology.
Specialization: Servicing and maintaining computers.
Dates: Aug.–May.
Location: Fort Smith, Arkansas: on campus.
Instruction: *Methods:* lectures, discussion groups, case studies, field trips, individualized instruction, "hands-on" training, computer-assisted instruction, independent study/research. *By:* faculty.
Highlights: Sponsor has offered program previously. Certificate. Issues I-20AB, I-20MN. Foreign nationals on tourist visas are not eligible to enroll. A foreign student counselor/adviser is available. 16 total enrollment; 33% foreign enrollment in 1985.
Eligibility: *Academic:* associate's degree in electronic technology. *Language:* English proficiency on intermediate level is required. TOEFL: 475. *Professional:* prior electronic technology experience helpful.
Cost: About $7,740 inclusive. *Scholarships:* none.
Housing: Not provided; sponsor assists in locating housing.
Application: *Deadline:* July 1. *Fee:* none.
Contact: Jane Pryor, Westark Community College, P.O. Box 3649, Fort Smith, AR 72913; (501) 785-4241.

SYSTEMS ANALYSIS

F16 GRUMMAN DATA SYSTEMS INSTITUTE
Systems Analysis.
Dates: Rolling.
Location: Woodbury, New York: on campus.
Instruction: *Methods:* discussion groups, lectures, case studies, "hands-on" training. *By:* faculty.
Highlights: Sponsor has offered program since 1970. Certificate upon completion of program with 70 grade average. Practical training is a program component; participants are not paid.

Issues I-20MN. Foreign nationals on tourist visas are not eligible to enroll. A foreign student counselor/adviser is available. 30 per class total enrollment; 5% foreign enrollment in 1985.
Eligibility: *Academic:* bachelor's degree. *Language:* English proficiency on advanced level is required; verbal evaluation. *Professional:* none.
Cost: $4,895 for tuition, books and materials. *Scholarships:* none.
Housing: Not provided; student makes own arrangements.
Application: *Deadline:* none. *Fee:* none.
Contact: Mr. Philip Cincotta, Grumman Data Systems Institute, 250 Crossways Park Drive, Woodbury, NY 11797; (516) 364-2055.

EDUCATION

G1 CALIFORNIA STATE UNIVERSITY, LONG BEACH
Global Education Institute.
Specialization: For elementary and secondary school teachers.
Dates: Three weeks: classes begin in June.
Location: Long Beach, California: on campus.
Instruction: *Methods:* discussion groups, lectures, case studies. *By:* faculty.
Highlights: Sponsor has offered program since 1985. Issues I-20AB, IAP-66. Foreign nationals on tourist visas are not eligible to enroll. A foreign student counselor/adviser is available. 30 total enrollment.
Eligibility: *Academic:* bachelor's degree. *Language:* English proficiency on intermediate level is required. *Professional:* none.
Cost: $216 for tuition, books, and materials. *Scholarships:* none.
Housing: Not provided; sponsor assists in locating housing.
Application: *Deadline:* none. *Fee:* none.
Contact: Center for International Education, CSULB, 1250 Bellflower Blvd., Long Beach, CA 90840; (213) 498-4106. Cable: CSULB. Telex: 887377.

G2 CALVIN COLLEGE
Master of Arts in Teaching.
Specialization: For certified and experienced teachers and administrators who want further professional training at a Christian college.
Dates: One year: classes begin in Sept.
Location: Grand Rapids, Michigan: on campus.
Instruction: *Methods:* lectures, independent study/research. *By:* faculty.
Highlights: Sponsor has offered program since 1976. Certificate upon completion of nine course units. Issues I-20AB. Foreign nationals on tourist visas are eligible to enroll. A foreign student counselor/adviser is available. ESL and tutoring programs. Unlimited total enrollment; 15% foreign enrollment in 1985.
Eligibility: *Academic:* bachelor's degree. *Language:* English proficiency on intermediate level is required. TOEFL: 550. *Professional:* teacher certification is required.
Cost: $8,600 for tuition, books and materials, meals, housing, local transportation. *Scholarships:* none.
Housing: In dormitories, apartments.
Application: *Deadline:* Aug. 1 for fall. *Fee:* none.
Contact: Dean for Academic Administration, Calvin College, Grand Rapids, MI 49506; (616) 957-6112.

G3 CLEVELAND STATE UNIVERSITY, COLLEGE OF EDUCATION
Master of Education Degree.
Specialization: Master's programs in most specializations.
Dates: One year: dates vary.
Location: Cleveland, Ohio: on campus.
Instruction: *Methods:* discussion groups, lectures, case studies, field trips, independent study/research, computer-assisted instruction. *By:* faculty.

Highlights: Sponsor has offered program previously. A foreign student counselor/adviser is available. Unlimited total enrollment; 1–2% foreign enrollment in 1985.
Eligibility: *Academic:* bachelor's degree. *Language:* English proficiency on intermediate level is required. TOEFL. *Professional:* none.
Cost: $57 per credit hour for tuition. *Scholarships:* none.
Housing: Not provided; sponsor assists in locating housing.
Application: *Deadline:* rolling. *Fee:* $25; refundable.
Contact: Dr. Lewis E. Patterson, Associate Dean, College of Education, Cleveland State University, East 24 and Euclid, Cleveland, OH 44115; (216) 687-3737.

G4 CONSORTIUM FOR INTERNATIONAL COOPERATION IN HIGHER EDUCATION
CICHE Administrative Fellowship Program.
Specialization: Individualized programs for professionals in all educational fields, with field-based training and observation related to each Fellow's professional interests. International educators paired with upper-level American counterparts.
Dates: Usually three months: classes begin in Sept., Nov., Jan., March.
Location: At host institutions across U.S.: on campus, at professional work site, conferences.
Instruction: *Methods:* discussion groups, lectures, case studies, field trips, individualized instruction, "hands-on" training, independent study/research, computer-assisted instruction. *By:* faculty, guest speakers/lecturers, deans of colleges of education.
Highlights: Sponsor has offered program since 1980. Certificate upon completion of final research project. Practical training is a program component; participants are not paid. Foreign nationals on tourist visas are eligible to enroll. A foreign student counselor/adviser is available. Orientation programs. Unlimited total enrollment; 100% foreign enrollment in 1985.
Eligibility: *Academic:* no requirement, but most applicants have graduate degrees. *Language:* English proficiency on intermediate level is preferred. *Professional:* midcareer professionals in education with demonstrated administrative and managerial potential.
Cost: $8,000 inclusive. *Scholarships:* none.
Housing: In dormitories, apartments, furnished rooms, hotels, with families; all housing logistics arranged by CICHE.
Application: *Deadline:* three months prior. *Fee:* none.
Contact: Consortium for International Cooperation in Higher Education, Office of International Training, One Dupont Circle, Suite 616, Washington, DC 20036; (202) 857-1833. Cable: CICHE. Telex: 5101007008.

G5 GUILFORD COLLEGE
Specialization: Programs available in education and foreign languages.
Dates: Aug.–end July.
Location: Greensboro, North Carolina: on campus.
Instruction: *Methods:* lectures, discussion groups. *By:* faculty.
Highlights: Sponsor has offered program since 1983. Certificate upon completion of 4–6 courses. Issues I-20AB, I-20MN. Foreign nationals on tourist visas are not eligible to enroll. A foreign student counselor/adviser is available. International Relations Club.
Eligibility: *Academic:* bachelor's degree. *Language:* English proficiency on advanced level is required. TOEFL: 500. *Professional:* none.
Cost: $112 per credit hour for tuition. *Scholarships:* none.
Housing: Not provided; student makes own arrangements.
Application: *Deadline:* open. *Fee:* $20; not refundable.
Contact: Dean of Admissions and Financial Aid, Guilford College, 5800 West Friendly Ave., Greensboro, NC 27410; (919) 292-5511.

Abbreviations: ESL = English as a Second Language; TOEFL = Test of English as a Foreign Language; ALIGU = American Language Institute of Georgetown University; GPA = Grade Point Average; SAT = Scholastic Aptitude Test; GED = General Equivalency Diploma.

G6 INTERNATIONAL COUNCIL ON EDUCATION FOR TEACHING
ICET Administrative Fellowship Program.
Specialization: Individualized programs for professionals in all educational fields, with field-based training and observation related to each Fellow's professional interests. International educators paired with upper-level American counterparts.
Dates: Usually three months: classes begin in Sept., Nov., Jan., March.
Location: At host institutions across U.S.: on campus, at professional work site, conferences.
Instruction: *Methods:* discussion groups, lectures, case studies, field trips, individualized instruction, "hands-on" training, independent study/research, computer-assisted instruction. *By:* faculty, guest speakers/lecturers, deans of colleges of education.
Highlights: Sponsor has offered program since 1963. Certificate upon completion of final research project. Practical training is a program component; participants are not paid. Foreign nationals on tourist visas are eligible to enroll. A foreign student counselor/adviser is available. Orientation programs. Unlimited total enrollment; 100% foreign enrollment in 1985.
Eligibility: *Academic:* no requirement, but most applicants have graduate degrees. *Language:* English proficiency on intermediate level is required. *Professional:* midcareer professionals in education with demonstrated administrative and managerial potential.
Cost: $8,000 inclusive. *Scholarships:* none, but participants funded by nominating or other agency.
Housing: In dormitories, apartments, furnished rooms, hotels, with families; all housing logistics arranged by ICET.
Application: *Deadline:* three months prior. *Fee:* none.
Contact: International Council on Education for Teaching, Office of International Training, One Dupont Circle, Suite 616, Washington, DC 20036; (202) 857-1830. Cable: ICETED. Telex: 5101007008.

G7 LESLEY COLLEGE GRADUATE SCHOOL
Specialization: Individually designed independent study degree programs conducted by faculty and professionals in the field of study. Requires four three-hour meetings on campus.
Dates: One year: to be arranged.
Location: Cambridge, Massachusetts: on campus.
Instruction: *Methods:* lectures, discussion groups, case studies, field trips, individualized instruction, "hands-on" training, independent study/research. *By:* faculty.
Highlights: Sponsor has offered short-term programs since 1971. Master's degree. Practical training may be a program component. Issues I-20AB. A foreign student counselor/adviser is available. 5% foreign enrollment in 1985.
Eligibility: *Academic:* bachelor's degree. *Language:* English proficiency is required. TOEFL. *Professional:* none.
Cost: $7,200 for tuition. *Scholarships:* none.
Housing: Not provided.
Application: *Deadline:* open. *Fee:* $35; not refundable.
Contact: Margot Chamberlain, Program Advisor, Lesley College Graduate School, 29 Everett Street, Cambridge, MA 02238; (617) 868-9600, Ext. 426.

G8 LESLEY COLLEGE GRADUATE SCHOOL
Specialization: Creative arts in learning from a cross-cultural prospective. M.A. in Expressive Therapies.
Dates: Aug.–May. Summer institute also available.
Location: Cambridge, Massachusetts: on campus.
Instruction: *Methods:* lectures, discussion groups, individualized instruction, "hands-on" training, independent study/research. *By:* faculty.
Highlights: Sponsor has offered program since 1974. Master's degree. Practical training is a program component; participants are not paid. Issues I-20AB. Foreign nationals on tourist

visas are not eligible to enroll. A foreign student counselor/adviser is available. Orientation program and International Club.

Eligibility: *Academic:* bachelor's degree. *Language:* TOEFL: 550. *Professional:* background in arts and human services experience, teaching, or museum experience.

Cost: About $17,000 inclusive. *Scholarships:* none.

Housing: In dormitories

Application: *Deadline:* open; application period begins in Jan. *Fee:* $35; not refundable.

Contact: Joanna Fabris, Program Advisor, Arts Institute, Lesley College Graduate School, 29 Everett Street, Cambridge, MA 02238; (617) 868-9600, Ext. 480.

G9 NORTHWEST REGIONAL EDUCATIONAL LABORATORY
Externship Program.

Specialization: Individually tailored, supervised training program in management techniques, program evaluation, computer applications, staff development.

Dates: To be arranged.

Location: Portland, Oregon: in NWREL offices.

Instruction: *Methods:* discussion groups, case studies, field trips, individualized instruction, "hands-on" training, independent study/research. *By:* faculty, guest speakers/lecturers.

Highlights: Sponsor has offered program since 1984. Foreign nationals on tourist visas are eligible to enroll. A foreign student counselor/adviser is not available. Five per season total enrollment; 100% foreign enrollment in 1985.

Eligibility: *Academic:* bachelor's degree. *Language:* English proficiency on intermediate level is required. *Professional:* two years of experience in selected topic of extern study.

Cost: $1,000 per month for tuition, books, and materials. *Scholarships:* none.

Housing: Not provided; sponsor assists in locating housing.

Application: *Deadline:* none. *Fee:* none.

Contact: Dr. John Mahaffy, Center for Professional Development, Northwest Regional Educational Laboratory, 300 SW Sixth Ave., Portland, OR 97204; (503) 248-6800. Cable: NWREL. Telex: 701716.

G10 STATE UNIVERSITY COLLEGE AT GENESEO, COLLEGE OF ARTS & SCIENCES
Master of Science in Education.

Specialization: Elementary education, secondary education, special education.

Dates: One year: classes begin in Sept.

Location: Geneseo, New York: on campus.

Instruction: *Methods:* discussion groups, lectures, case studies, field trips, individualized instruction, independent study/research, computer-assisted instruction, language laboratories, science laboratories. *By:* faculty.

Highlights: Sponsor has offered program previously. Certificate. A foreign student counselor/adviser is available. No foreign enrollment in 1985.

Eligibility: *Academic:* bachelor's degree. *Language:* English proficiency on advanced level is required. *Professional:* none.

Cost: $6,280 for tuition, meals, housing, college fee. *Scholarships:* none.

Housing: In dormitories.

Application: *Deadline:* none. *Fee:* $20; not refundable.

Contact: Dr. John Youngers, College of Arts and Science, SUC at Geneseo, Blake C 105, Geneseo, NY 14454; (716) 245-5558.

G11 UNIVERSITY OF ROCHESTER

Specialization: Master's degree programs available in administration, counseling, curriculum, psychological development, adult learning, and health professions education.

Dates: Sept.–Aug.

Location: Rochester, New York: on campus.

Abbreviations: ESL = English as a Second Language; TOEFL = Test of English as a Foreign Language; ALIGU = American Language Institute of Georgetown University; GPA = Grade Point Average; SAT = Scholastic Aptitude Test; GED = General Equivalency Diploma.

Instruction: *Methods:* lectures, discussion groups, individualized instruction, independent study/research. *By:* faculty.
Highlights: Sponsor has offered program since 1954. Master's degree. Practical training may be a program component. Foreign nationals on tourist visas are not eligible to enroll. A foreign student counselor/adviser is available. ESL and tutoring programs. 10% foreign enrollment in 1985.
Eligibility: *Academic:* bachelor's degree. *Language:* English proficiency on beginning level is required. TOEFL: 550. *Professional:* experienced educators preferred.
Cost: About $10,330 for tuition. *Scholarships:* partial.
Housing: Not provided; sponsor assists in locating housing.
Application: *Deadline:* May 1. *Fee:* $30; not refundable. *Scholarship deadline:* Feb. 1.
Contact: Office of Graduate Studies, University of Rochester, 304 Lattimore Hall, GSEHD, Rochester, NY 14627; (716) 275-3950.

G12 VOORHEES COLLEGE

Specialization: Early childhood, elementary, and secondary education.
Dates: Aug.–May; classes begin in Aug. and Jan.
Location: Denmark, South Carolina: on campus, at professional work site.
Instruction: *Methods:* discussion groups, lectures, case studies, field trips, individualized instruction, "hands-on" training, independent study/research, computer-assisted instruction, science laboratories. *By:* faculty.
Highlights: Sponsor has offered program since 1969. Certificate. Practical training is a program component; participants are not paid. Issues I-20AB. Foreign nationals on tourist visas are not eligible to enroll. A foreign student counselor/adviser is available.
Eligibility: *Academic:* associate's degree. *Language:* English proficiency on beginning level is required. TOEFL. *Professional:* none.
Cost: $5,884 for tuition, meals, housing, health insurance. *Scholarships:* none.
Housing: In dormitories.
Application: *Deadline:* Aug. *Fee:* $10; not refundable.
Contact: Dr. Lucious Daily, Jr., Director of Admissions and Records, Voorhees College, Voorhees Road, Denmark, SC 29042; (803) 793-3351.

G13 WESTERN MONTANA COLLEGE

Specialization: Master of education.
Dates: One year: classes begin in Aug.
Location: Dillon, Montana: on campus.
Instruction: *Methods:* discussion groups, lectures, individualized instruction, independent study/research, computer-assisted instruction, science laboratories. *By:* faculty.
Highlights: Sponsor has offered program since 1956. Certificate. Practical training may be a program component; participants are not paid. Issues I-20AB. Foreign nationals on tourist visas are not eligible to enroll. A foreign student counselor/adviser is not available. Unlimited total enrollment; no foreign enrollment in 1985.
Eligibility: *Academic:* bachelor's degree. *Language:* English proficiency on advanced level is required. TOEFL: 500. *Professional:* elementary or secondary teaching experience.
Cost: Not given. *Scholarships:* none.
Housing: In dormitories.
Application: *Deadline:* June 1. *Fee:* $20; not refundable.
Contact: Dr. Henry N. Worrest, Vice President for Academic Affairs/Director of Graduate Studies, Western Montana College, 710 S. Atlantic, Dillon, MT 59725; (406) 683-7300.

ADMINISTRATION

G14 UNIVERSITY OF NEW MEXICO, COLLEGE OF EDUCATION
MA Program in Educational Administration for Latin American Educators.
Specialization: Program in educational administration designed specifically for Latin American educators and professional administrators.
Dates: One year: classes begin in Aug., Jan., June.
Location: Albuquerque, New Mexico: on campus.
Instruction: *Methods:* discussion groups, lectures, field trips, independent study/research, computer-assisted instruction, language laboratories. *By:* faculty. *In Spanish only.*
Highlights: Sponsor has offered short-term programs previously. Certificate. Practical training is a program component; participants are not paid. Issues I-20AB, IAP-66. Foreign nationals on tourist visas are not eligible to enroll. A foreign student counselor/adviser is available. 40 total enrollment; 100% foreign enrollment in 1985.
Eligibility: *Academic:* bachelor's degree or equivalent. *Language:* English proficiency not required; classes taught in Spanish. *Professional:* five years of experience required.
Cost: $10,000 inclusive. *Scholarships:* none.
Housing: In dormitories, apartments.
Application: *Deadline:* about one month prior. *Fee:* $25; not refundable.
Contact: Mr. Ronald E. Blood, Director, LAPE/OITEC, College of Education 121, University of New Mexico, Albuquerque, NM 87131; (505) 277-2202. Telex: 660461.

ADULT AND PROFESSIONAL EDUCATION

G15 HARVARD GRADUATE SCHOOL OF EDUCATION
Institute for the Management of Lifelong Education.
Specialization: Lifelong education, adult education, continuing education. Program provides interaction with U.S. practitioners and insights into adult education programs in the U.S.
Dates: Two weeks: June.
Location: Cambridge, Massachusetts: on campus.
Instruction: *Methods:* discussion groups, lectures, case studies. *By:* faculty, guest speakers/lecturers.
Highlights: Sponsor has offered program since 1979. Certificate. Foreign nationals on tourist visas are eligible to enroll. A foreign student counselor/adviser is available. 85 total enrollment; 4% foreign enrollment in 1985.
Eligibility: *Academic:* master's degree. *Language:* English proficiency on advanced level is required. *Professional:* five years of work experience; administrative experience in adult education.
Cost: $2,200 for tuition, books and materials, meals, housing. *Scholarships:* none.
Housing: In dormitories.
Application: *Deadline:* Apr. 15. *Fee:* none.
Contact: Mr. Clifford Baden, Director, MLE, Harvard Graduate School of Education, 339 Gutman Library, Cambridge, MA 02138; (617) 495-3572.

G16 SCHOOL FOR INTERNATIONAL TRAINING
Skills for Managing Effective Training Organizations.
Specialization: Training and human resource development.
Dates: Early June–late July.
Location: Boston, Massachusetts; Brattleboro, Vermont: on campus.
Instruction: *Methods:* discussion groups, lectures, case studies, field trips, "hands-on" training, independent study/research, computer-assisted instruction. *By:* faculty, guest speakers/lecturers.
Highlights: Sponsor has offered program since 1985. Certificate. Issues I-20AB, IAP-66.

Abbreviations: ESL = English as a Second Language; TOEFL = Test of English as a Foreign Language; ALIGU = American Language Institute of Georgetown University; GPA = Grade Point Average; SAT = Scholastic Aptitude Test; GED = General Equivalency Diploma.

Foreign nationals on tourist visas are eligible to enroll. A foreign student counselor/adviser is available. ESL and homestay programs. 25 total enrollment; 100% foreign enrollment in 1985.
Eligibility: *Academic:* bachelor's degree or equivalent preferred. *Language:* English proficiency on intermediate level is required. *Professional:* current or prospective managers of training units with two years of work experience.
Cost: $5,800 for tuition, books and materials, local transportation, health insurance. *Scholarships:* none.
Housing: In dormitories.
Application: *Deadline:* April. *Fee:* none.
Contact: Mr. Leslie Long, Manager, Participant Training Programs, School for International Training, Kipling Road, Brattleboro, VT 05301; (802) 254-5935. Telex: 6817462 EXPER UW.

G17 UNIVERSITY OF CONNECTICUT HEALTH CENTER
Master Trainer Program.
Specialization: Focus on critical training, management, and administrative concepts and skills needed by managers of the training function and master trainers; development of organization, community, and national training programs.
Dates: Feb. 16–Apr. 3.
Location: Farmington, Connecticut: on campus; or on-site abroad.
Instruction: *Methods:* discussion groups, lectures, case studies, field trips, individualized instruction, independent study/research. *By:* faculty, guest speakers/lecturers.
Highlights: Sponsor has offered program previously. Certificate. Issues I-20AB, IAP-66. Foreign nationals on tourist visas are eligible to enroll. A foreign student counselor/adviser is available. Social and cultural activities, host family program. 20 total enrollment.
Eligibility: *Academic:* bachelor's degree. *Language:* English proficiency on advanced level is required. TOEFL: 500; ALIGU: 80. *Professional:* directors of training, medical school directors, curricula development specialists, and managers responsible for recruitment and development of staff.
Cost: $5,200 for tuition, books and materials, health insurance, local transportation, field trip, use of computer. *Scholarships:* none.
Housing: Not provided; sponsor assists in locating housing.
Application: *Deadline:* apply early. *Fee:* none.
Contact: Dr. Stephen L. Schensul, Director, International Health, Population, Social Service Training Programs, University of Connecticut Health Center, Room AG073, Farmington, CT 06032; (203) 674-3302. Telex: 710-423-5521/U Conn HC Lib.

ART EDUCATION

G18 MARYLAND INSTITUTE
Master of Arts in Teaching.
Specialization: Certification in elementary or secondary art education for those with a noneducation undergraduate degree.
Dates: Nine months: classes begin in Sept.
Location: Baltimore, Maryland: on campus.
Instruction: *Methods:* discussion groups, lectures, case studies, field trips, individualized instruction, "hands-on" training, independent study/research. *By:* faculty.
Highlights: Sponsor has offered program since 1984. Certificate. Practical training is a program component; participants are not paid. Issues I-20AB. Foreign nationals on tourist visas are not eligible to enroll. A foreign student counselor/adviser is available. ESL program. 15 total enrollment; 25% foreign enrollment in 1985.
Eligibility: *Academic:* bachelor's degree in Studio Art. *Language:* English proficiency on advanced level is required. TOEFL: 550; interview. *Professional:* none.

Cost: $12,500 inclusive. *Scholarships:* none.
Housing: Not provided; sponsor assists in locating housing.
Application: *Deadline:* May 1. *Fee:* $20; not refundable.
Contact: Dr. Leslie King Hammond, College of Art, Maryland Institute, 1300 West Mount Royal Ave., Baltimore, MD 21217; (301) 669-9200.

COMPUTERS IN EDUCATION

G19 LESLEY COLLEGE GRADUATE SCHOOL
Computers in Education: Computer Coordinator Specialization.
Specialization: Master's program in computer coordination in education.
Dates: Program can be completed in 2–3 summers: classes begin in June, July, Aug.
Location: Cambridge, Massachusetts: on campus.
Instruction: *Methods:* lectures, discussion groups, "hands-on" training, computer-assisted instruction. *By:* faculty.
Highlights: Program has been offered previously. Master's degree. Issues I-20AB, I-20MN, IAP-66. Foreign nationals on tourist visas are eligible to enroll. A foreign student counselor/adviser is available.
Eligibility: *Academic:* bachelor's degree. *Language:* English proficiency on intermediate level is required. TOEFL: 550. *Professional:* education or special education experience preferred.
Cost: $210 per credit for tuition. *Scholarships:* none.
Housing: In dormitories.
Application: *Deadline:* Feb. 1. *Fee:* $35; not refundable.
Contact: Ms. Beverly Faison, Lesley College Graduate School, 29 Everett Street, Cambridge, MA 02238; (617) 868-9600, Ext. 362.

G20 SPALDING UNIVERSITY
M.A. with Specialization in Computerized Instruction.
Specialization: Use of computers in the classroom.
Dates: One year: classes begin in Aug.
Location: Louisville, Kentucky: on campus, at professional work site.
Instruction: *Methods:* lectures, "hands-on" training, independent study/research, computer-assisted instruction. *By:* faculty.
Highlights: Sponsor has offered program since 1983. Master's degree with 30–36 semester hours of graduate credit. Practical training is a program component; participants are not paid. Issues I-20AB. Foreign nationals on tourist visas are not eligible to enroll. A foreign student counselor/adviser is available. English language assistance. 20 per course total enrollment.
Eligibility: *Academic:* bachelor's degree. *Language:* English proficiency on intermediate level is required. *Professional:* teaching certificate preferred.
Cost: $12,000–$14,400 inclusive. *Scholarships:* none.
Housing: In dormitories.
Application: *Deadline:* Apr. 15; July 15 if credentials from U.S. college. *Fee:* $15; not refundable.
Contact: Dr. Mary Burns, Spalding University, 851 South Fourth Street, Louisville, KY 40203; (502) 585-9911.

G21 UNIVERSITY OF SOUTHERN COLORADO
Computer-Based Education.
Dates: Three weeks: late June–mid-July.
Location: Pueblo, Colorado: on campus.
Instruction: *Methods:* lectures, "hands-on" training. *By:* faculty.
Highlights: Sponsor has offered program previously. Credit. Helps obtain visa. A foreign student counselor/adviser is available. Extensive services for foreign nationals.

Abbreviations: ESL = English as a Second Language; TOEFL = Test of English as a Foreign Language; ALIGU = American Language Institute of Georgetown University; GPA = Grade Point Average; SAT = Scholastic Aptitude Test; GED = General Equivalency Diploma.

83

Eligibility: *Academic:* bachelor's degree. *Language:* TOEFL: 500; Univ. of Michigan Language Test: 80. *Professional:* none.
Cost: $190 per credit for tuition. *Scholarships:* none.
Housing: Not provided; student makes own arrangements.
Application: *Deadline:* none. *Fee:* $10.
Contact: Dr. James Kashner, University of Southern Colorado, 2200 Bonforte Blvd., Pueblo, CO 81001; (303) 549-2313.

EARLY CHILDHOOD

G22 WHEELOCK COLLEGE GRADUATE SCHOOL
Specialization: Early childhood education.
Dates: Six weeks: late June–early Aug.
Location: Boston, Massachusetts: at school.
Instruction: *Methods:* lectures, seminars, independent study, practical training. *By:* faculty, outside lecturers, industry resources.
Highlights: Sponsor has offered program since 1974. Credit. Certificate. Issues I-20. No services for foreign nationals. List of past participants is available.
Eligibility: *Academic:* bachelor's degree. *Language:* TOEFL. *Professional:* none.
Cost: $215 per credit for tuition. *Scholarships:* none.
Housing: In dormitories.
Application: *Deadline:* open. *Fee:* $30.
Contact: Linda Brown, Acting Director, Graduate Admissions, Wheelock College Graduate School, 200 The Riverway, Boston, MA 02215; (617) 734-5200.

EDUCATIONAL TESTING

G23 EDUCATIONAL TESTING SERVICE
Computer Applications in the Analysis of Tests.
Dates: Two weeks: July–Aug.
Location: Princeton, New Jersey: at ETS.
Instruction: *Methods:* lectures, discussion groups, individualized instruction, computer-assisted instruction. *By:* faculty.
Highlights: Sponsor has offered program since 1985. Certificate. Issues IAP-66. A foreign student counselor/adviser is available. 20 total enrollment; 100% foreign enrollment in 1985. List of past participants is available.
Eligibility: *Academic:* bachelor's degree. *Language:* intermediate English proficiency. *Professional:* knowledge of test construction and basic courses in statistics.
Cost: $2,450 for tuition, books. *Scholarships:* none.
Housing: In apartments.
Application: *Deadline:* first come first served basis. *Fee:* $50; not refundable.
Contact: Frances Ottobre, Educational Testing Service, Princeton, NJ 08541; (609) 734-5076.

G24 EDUCATIONAL TESTING SERVICE
Educational Testing.
Specialization: Individual consultation on specific projects or interests, as well as group instruction.
Dates: Four weeks: June–July.
Location: Princeton, New Jersey: at ETS.
Instruction: *Methods:* lectures, discussion groups, individualized instruction, "hands-on" training. *By:* faculty.
Highlights: Sponsor has offered program since 1961. Certificate. Issues IAP-66. Foreign

---

All program information is subject to change without notice
and must be confirmed directly with the sponsor.

84

nationals on tourist visas are eligible to enroll. A foreign student counselor/adviser is available. 35 total enrollment; 100% foreign enrollment in 1985. List of past participants is available.
Eligibility: *Academic:* bachelor's degree. *Language:* English proficiency on intermediate level is required. *Professional:* basic knowledge of test construction.
Cost: $1,950 for tuition, books. *Scholarships:* none.
Housing: In apartments.
Application: *Deadline:* first come first served basis. *Fee:* $50; not refundable.
Contact: Frances Ottobre, Educational Testing Service, Princeton, NJ 08541; (609) 734-5076.

ELEMENTARY EDUCATION

G25 UNIVERSITY OF SOUTHERN COLORADO
Concepts in Elementary School Mathematics.
Specialization: Elementary school mathematics.
Dates: Two weeks: July.
Location: Pueblo, Colorado: on campus.
Instruction: *Methods:* lectures. *By:* faculty.
Highlights: New program. A foreign student counselor/adviser is available. 40 total enrollment; about 5% foreign enrollment in 1985.
Eligibility: *Academic:* bachelor's degree. *Language:* English proficiency on advanced level is preferred. TOEFL: 500; Univ. of Michigan Language Test: 80. *Professional:* teachers only.
Cost: About $190 per credit hour. *Scholarships:* none.
Housing: Not provided; student makes own arrangements.
Application: *Deadline:* June. *Fee:* $10; not refundable.
Contact: Dr. Ernest Allen, University of Southern Colorado, 2200 Bonforte Blvd., Pueblo, CO 81001; (303) 549-2693.

FOREIGN LANGUAGE TEACHING

G26 MONTEREY INSTITUTE OF INTERNATIONAL STUDIES
Master of Arts in Teaching Foreign Language.
Specialization: Master's program designed for professionals already teaching and graduate students with strong language backgrounds. Combines coursework in teaching methods and applied linguistics with advanced work in Chinese, French, German, Japanese, Russian, and Spanish.
Dates: One year: classes begin in Aug.
Location: Monterey, California: on campus.
Instruction: *Methods:* lectures, individualized instruction, independent study/research, language laboratories. *By:* faculty.
Highlights: Sponsor has offered program since 1963. Master's degree. Practical training is a program component; participants are not paid. Issues I-20AB, IAP-66. Foreign nationals on tourist visas are eligible to enroll. A foreign student counselor/adviser is available. Various support services available. About 20% foreign enrollment in 1985.
Eligibility: *Academic:* bachelor's degree with 3.0 GPA; GRE; self-administered language placement test. *Language:* TOEFL: 600. *Professional:* none.
Cost: About $3,125 per semester for tuition. *Scholarships:* none.
Housing: Not provided; sponsor assists in locating housing.
Application: *Deadline:* Aug. 1. *Fee:* $35; not refundable.
Contact: Dr. Jon Strolle, Dean of the Languages and Humanities Division, Monterey Institute of International Studies, 425 Van Buren, Monterey, CA 93940; (408) 649-3113.

Abbreviations: ESL = English as a Second Language; TOEFL = Test of English as a Foreign Language; ALIGU = American Language Institute of Georgetown University; GPA = Grade Point Average; SAT = Scholastic Aptitude Test; GED = General Equivalency Diploma.

INSTRUCTIONAL SYSTEM DESIGN AND MANAGEMENT

G27 U.S. DEPARTMENT OF AGRICULTURE GRADUATE SCHOOL
Instructional System Design.
Specialization: A "training of trainers" course on development of training systems and techniques for professional trainers.
Dates: On request.
Location: Washington, D.C.: on campus, at professional work site.
Instruction: *Methods:* discussion groups, lectures, case studies, field trips, individualized instruction. *By:* faculty, guest speakers/lecturers.
Highlights: Sponsor has offered program since 1985. Certificate. Issues I-20AB. Foreign nationals on tourist visas are not eligible to enroll. A foreign student counselor/adviser is available. Cultural programs. 10 total enrollment; 100% foreign enrollment in 1985.
Eligibility: *Academic:* associate's or bachelor's degree. *Language:* English proficiency on advanced level is required. *Professional:* some teaching experience preferred.
Cost: $7,000 for ten weeks for tuition, books, and materials. *Scholarships:* none.
Housing: Not provided; sponsor assists in locating housing.
Application: *Deadline:* none. *Fee:* none.
Contact: Ms. Elizabeth Lee, Graduate School, USDA, 600 Maryland Ave. SW, Room 134, Washington, DC 20024; (202) 447-7476.

G28 UNIVERSITY OF CONNECTICUT
Systematic Design & Management of Training (TREND).
Specialization: Training management, instructional system design. Program designed for faculty, professional staff, and managers of national or regional administrative staff colleges, institutes of management, or staff development centers.
Dates: Late May–early Aug.
Location: Hartford, Connecticut: on campus.
Instruction: *Methods:* lectures, case studies, discussion groups, field trips. *By:* faculty, guest speakers/lecturers.
Highlights: Sponsor has offered program since 1961. Certificate. Issues IAP-66. Foreign nationals on a tourist visas are not eligible to enroll. A foreign student counselor/adviser is available. Social and cultural activities. 100% foreign enrollment in 1985.
Eligibility: *Academic:* bachelor's degree is preferred. *Language:* TOEFL: 500; ALIGU: 80. *Professional:* two years of work experience.
Cost: $4,900 for tuition, books, and materials. *Scholarships:* none.
Housing: Not provided: sponsor assists in locating housing.
Application: *Deadline:* six weeks prior. *Fee:* none.
Contact: Mrs. Josephine Mavromatis, Coordinator, Hartford-based Programs, IPS International, University of Connecticut, 1800 Asylum Ave., Hartford, CT 06117; (203) 241-4924. Cable: IPSUCONN. Telex: 883997 (IPS INTL).

INTERNATIONAL EDUCATION

G29 GEORGE WASHINGTON UNIVERSITY
International Education and Higher Education.
Specialization: Short-term seminars developed to meet specific educational needs.
Dates: Classes begin in Jan., July, Dec.
Location: Washington, D.C.: on campus.
Instruction: *Methods:* discussion groups, lectures, case studies, field trips, individualized instruction, "hands-on" training, independent study/research. *By:* faculty. *Translators are available.*

All program information is subject to change without notice
and must be confirmed directly with the sponsor.

Highlights: Sponsor has offered program since 1984. Certificate. A foreign student counselor/adviser is available. 15 total enrollment; 100% foreign enrollment in 1985.
Eligibility: *Academic:* bachelor's degree. *Language:* English proficiency not required; translator available. *Professional:* none.
Cost: Varies. *Scholarships:* none.
Housing: Not provided; student makes own arrangements.
Application: *Deadline:* none. *Fee:* none.
Contact: Dr. Dorothy A. Moore, School of Education and Human Development, George Washington University, Washington, DC 20052; (202) 676-7138.

G30 LESLEY COLLEGE
International Education and Service.
Specialization: Foreign student advising, international education, intercultural management, international development.
Dates: Classes begin in Sept., Jan., Feb., June.
Location: Cambridge, Massachusetts: on campus.
Instruction: *Methods:* discussion groups, lectures, case studies, field trips, independent study/research. *By:* faculty, guest speakers/lecturers.
Highlights: Sponsor has offered program since 1981. Certificate. Practical training may be a program component. Issues I-20AB, IAP-66. Foreign nationals on tourist visas are eligible to enroll. A foreign student counselor/adviser is available. Orientation, host family program and international groups. 100 total enrollment; 10–20% foreign enrollment in 1985.
Eligibility: *Academic:* bachelor's degree. *Language:* English proficiency on advanced level is required. TOEFL: 550. *Professional:* none.
Cost: $220 per credit for tuition. *Scholarships:* partial.
Housing: In dormitories, apartments.
Application: *Deadline:* rolling. *Fee:* $35; not refundable. *Scholarship deadline:* not given.
Contact: Dr. Zareen Karani Lam, International Studies Dept., Lesley College, 29 Everett Street, Cambridge, MA 02238; (617) 868-9600, Ext. 163.

MUSIC EDUCATION

G31 HOLY NAMES COLLEGE
Kodaly Program.
Specialization: Kodaly method of music education.
Dates: Three weeks: late June–July.
Location: Oakland, California: on campus.
Instruction: *Methods:* lectures, discussion groups, "hands-on" training, demonstrations. *By:* faculty, guest speakers/lecturers.
Highlights: Sponsor has offered short-term programs since 1969. Issues I-20AB. Foreign nationals on tourist visas are eligible to enroll. A foreign student counselor/adviser is available. 80 total enrollment; 12% foreign enrollment in 1985.
Eligibility: *Academic:* bachelor's degree or degree candidate. *Language:* TOEFL: 550. *Professional:* music teaching experience.
Cost: $828–$1,268 for tuition, housing, and meals.
Housing: In dormitories.
Application: *Deadline:* June 9. *Fee:* $50; refundable up June 9.
Contact: Director, Kodaly Program, Holy Names College, 3500 Mountain Blvd., Oakland, CA 94619; (415) 436-0111.

Abbreviations: ESL = English as a Second Language; TOEFL = Test of English as a Foreign Language; ALIGU = American Language Institute of Georgetown University; GPA = Grade Point Average; SAT = Scholastic Aptitude Test; GED = General Equivalency Diploma.

NONFORMAL EDUCATION

G32 MICHIGAN STATE UNIVERSITY, SPECIAL INSTITUTE FOR STUDIES OF NONFORMAL EDUCATION
Institute for Studies of Nonformal Education.
Specialization: Participants explore concepts of participation, development, and change in the field of nonformal education.
Dates: Three weeks: June.
Location: East Lansing, Michigan: on campus.
Instruction: *Methods:* discussion groups, lectures, field trips. *By:* faculty.
Highlights: Sponsor has offered program since 1979. Certificate. Foreign nationals on tourist visas are eligible to enroll. A foreign student counselor/adviser is available. 30–40 total enrollment; 75% foreign enrollment in 1985.
Eligibility: *Academic:* bachelor's degree. *Language:* English proficiency on advanced level is required. *Professional:* none.
Cost: About $1,050 for tuition, materials, meals, housing, local transportation. *Scholarships:* none.
Housing: In dormitories.
Application: *Deadline:* May 1. *Fee:* $50; not refundable, but applied to tuition.
Contact: Prof. S. Joseph Levine, Director, Special Institute for Studies of Nonformal Education, Michigan State University, 421 Erickson Hall, East Lansing, MI 48824; (517) 355-2395. Cable: MSUINTPRO ELSG. Telex: 810 251 0737; ATTN: S.J. Levine.

PROGRAM EVALUATION

G33 EDUCATIONAL TESTING SERVICE
Specialization: Evaluation of education programs.
Dates: Three weeks: July–Aug.
Location: Princeton, New Jersey: at ETS.
Instruction: *Methods:* lectures, discussions groups, case studies, individualized instruction. *By:* faculty.
Highlights: Sponsor has offered short-term programs since 1978. Certificate. Issues IAP-66. Foreign nationals on tourist visas are eligible to enroll. A foreign student counselor/adviser is available. 35 total enrollment; 100% foreign enrollment in 1985. List of past participants is available.
Eligibility: *Academic:* bachelor's degree. *Language:* English proficiency on intermediate level is required. *Professional:* responsibility for evaluating educational programs.
Cost: $1,450 for tuition, books. *Scholarships:* none.
Housing: In apartments.
Application: *Deadline:* space-available basis. *Fee:* $50; not refundable.
Contact: Frances Ottobre, Educational Testing Service, Princeton, NJ 08541; (609) 734-5076.

SPECIAL EDUCATION

G34 MARYWOOD COLLEGE
Specialization: Education in the mainstream, art and music for the mentally/physically handicapped, adaptive physical education, characteristics of the gifted.
Dates: Five weeks: classes begin in June.
Location: Scranton, Pennsylvania: on campus.
Instruction: *Methods:* discussion groups, lectures, "hands-on" training. *By:* faculty.
Highlights: Sponsor has offered short-term programs previously. Certificate. Foreign

All program information is subject to change without notice
and must be confirmed directly with the sponsor.

88

nationals on tourist visas are eligible to enroll. A foreign student counselor/adviser is available. 4% foreign enrollment in 1985.
Eligibility: *Academic:* bachelor's degree. *Language:* English proficiency on intermediate level is required. TOEFL: 550. *Professional:* none.
Cost: $175 for tuition. *Scholarships:* none.
Housing: In apartments, or sponsor assists in locating housing.
Application: *Deadline:* not given. *Fee:* none.
Contact: Sister M. Eamon O'Neill, Marywood College, 2300 Adams Ave., Scranton, PA 18509; (717) 348-6230.

G35 UNIVERSITY OF ARKANSAS AT LITTLE ROCK
Mobility Training Teaching.
Specialization: Rehabilitation for the blind: intensive program in teaching mobility training for the blind and partially sighted.
Dates: One year: classes begin in Aug.
Location: Little Rock, Arkansas: on campus, trip to New York.
Instruction: *Methods:* lectures, field trips, individualized instruction, "hands-on" training. *By:* faculty.
Highlights: Sponsor has offered program since 1982. Certificate. Practical training is a program component; participants are not paid. Issues I-20AB. Foreign nationals on tourist visas are not eligible to enroll. A foreign student counselor/adviser is available. 15 per year total enrollment; 2% foreign enrollment in 1985.
Eligibility: *Academic:* bachelor's degree with 2.5 GPA. *Language:* English proficiency on intermediate level is required. TOEFL: 525. *Professional:* some experience with the blind required.
Cost: $3,600 for tuition. *Scholarships:* partial.
Housing: Not provided; sponsor assists in locating housing.
Application: *Deadline:* May 31. *Fee:* $25; not refundable. *Scholarship deadline:* May 31.
Contact: Dr. William Jacobson, Dept. of Rehabilitation and Special Education, University of Arkansas at Little Rock, 33rd and University Ave., Little Rock, AR 72204; (501) 569-3206.

TEACHING ENGLISH AS A FOREIGN LANGUAGE

G36 THE AMERICAN UNIVERSITY
Graduate Certificate in Teaching English to Speakers of Other Languages.
Specialization: Graduate-level course in linguistics and theory and practice of ELT.
Dates: Classes begin in Sept., Jan., May, July.
Location: Washington, D.C.: on campus.
Instruction: *Methods:* discussion groups, lectures, case studies. *By:* faculty.
Highlights: Sponsor has offered program previously. Certificate. Issues I-20AB. Foreign nationals on tourist visas are not eligible to enroll. A foreign student counselor/adviser is available. Orientation programs.
Eligibility: *Academic:* bachelor's degree. *Language:* English proficiency on advanced level is required. TOEFL: 600; English Language Institute Placement Test. *Professional:* none.
Cost: $299 per semester hour for tuition. *Scholarships:* none.
Housing: Not provided; sponsor assists in locating housing.
Application: *Deadline:* none. *Fee:* none.
Contact: Programs Advisement Center, The American University, 4400 Massachusetts Ave. NW, Room 153 McKinley Bldg., Washington, DC 20016; (202) 885-2500.

G37 HOLY NAMES COLLEGE
Teaching English as a Foreign Language.
Specialization: Program designed for international students.
Dates: Aug. 25–May 23.

Abbreviations: ESL = English as a Second Language; TOEFL = Test of English as a Foreign Language; ALIGU = American Language Institute of Georgetown University; GPA = Grade Point Average; SAT = Scholastic Aptitude Test; GED = General Equivalency Diploma.

Location: Oakland, California: on campus.
Instruction: *Methods:* lectures, discussion groups, individualized instruction, "hands-on" training, language labs, independent study/research. *By:* faculty.
Highlights: Sponsor has offered program since 1970s. Certificate upon completion of program with 2.64 GPA. Issues I-20AB. Foreign nationals on tourist visas are not eligible to enroll. A foreign student counselor/adviser is available. 20 total enrollment; 100% foreign enrollment in 1985.
Eligibility: *Academic:* French baccalaureate, British sixth form, Latin American preparatorio, or equivalent. *Language:* English proficiency on advanced level is preferred. TOEFL: 500; ESL level 107 completed. *Professional:* none.
Cost: $9,970 for tuition, meals, housing. *Scholarships:* none.
Housing: In dormitories.
Application: *Deadline:* Aug. 1. *Fee:* $25; not refundable.
Contact: Director of Admissions, Holy Names College, 3500 Mountain Blvd., Oakland, CA 94619; (415) 436-1321.

G38 MARYVILLE COLLEGE—ST. LOUIS
Summer Institute For TEFL/TESL.
Specialization: Intensive practical and theoretical training in TEFL/TESL.
Dates: Six weeks: classes begin in June.
Location: St. Louis, Missouri: on campus.
Instruction: *Methods:* discussion groups, lectures, field trips, "hands-on" training, independent study/research. *By:* faculty.
Highlights: Sponsor has offered program since 1982. Certificate upon completion of 4 courses. Issues I-20AB. A foreign student counselor/adviser is available. ESL program and Office of International Programs. 30 total enrollment; about 50% foreign enrollment in 1985.
Eligibility: *Academic:* bachelor's degree. *Language:* English proficiency on advanced level is required. TOEFL: 500; writing proficiency. *Professional:* none.
Cost: $2,716 for tuition, books and materials, meals, housing, health insurance.
Scholarships: partial tuition remission may be available to practicing teachers.
Housing: In dormitories, or sponsor assists in locating housing.
Application: *Deadline:* June 1. *Fee:* $10; not refundable.
Contact: Prof. Liga Abolins, Maryville College—St. Louis, International Programs, 13550 Conway Road, St. Louis, MO 63141; (314) 576-9503.

G39 MONTEREY INSTITUTE OF INTERNATIONAL STUDIES
Master of Arts in Teaching English to Speakers of Other Languages (TESOL).
Specialization: Master's program designed for people interested in teaching English to non-English-speaking students. Combines studies in linguistics and teaching methods with original projects and practical teaching experience.
Dates: Nine months: classes begin in Aug.
Location: Monterey, California: on campus.
Instruction: *Methods:* lectures, individualized instruction, independent study/research, language laboratories. *By:* faculty.
Highlights: Sponsor has offered program since 1963. Master's degree. Practical training is a program component; participants are not paid. Issues I-20AB, IAP-66. Foreign nationals on tourist visas are eligible to enroll. A foreign student counselor/adviser is available. Various support services available. About 20% foreign enrollment in 1985.
Eligibility: *Academic:* bachelor's degree with 3.0 GPA; GRE. *Language:* TOEFL: 600. *Professional:* none.
Cost: About $3,125 per semester for tuition. *Scholarships:* none.
Housing: Not provided; sponsor assists in locating housing.
Application: *Deadline:* Aug. 1. *Fee:* $35; not refundable.
Contact: Dr. Jon Strolle, Dean of the Languages and Humanities Division, Monterey Institute of International Studies, 425 Van Buren, Monterey, CA 93940; (408) 649-3113.

G40 STATE UNIVERSITY OF NEW YORK AT BUFFALO
Certificate Program in TEFL.
Dates: Six weeks: early July–Aug.
Location: Buffalo, New York: on campus.
Instruction: *Methods:* lectures, seminars, practical training. *By:* faculty.
Highlights: Sponsor has offered program since 1973. Certificate. Issues I-20. Extensive services for foreign nationals. 25 total enrollment, 100% foreign enrollment in 1985. List of past participants is available.
Eligibility: *Academic:* bachelor's degree. *Language:* TOEFL: 500. *Professional:* none.
Cost: $1,465 for tuition, housing, meals, fees, health insurance. *Scholarships:* partial.
Housing: In dormitories.
Application: *Deadline:* Apr. 31. *Fee:* $50 deposit. *Scholarship deadline:* Apr. 31.
Contact: Dr. Stephen C. Dunnett, Director, Intensive English Language Institute, SUNY at Buffalo, 320 Baldy Hall, Buffalo, NY 14260; (716) 636-2077.

G41 U.S. DEPARTMENT OF AGRICULTURE GRADUATE SCHOOL
EFL/ESL Teacher Training.
Specialization: Focus on communications skills, American culture, language learning theory, and methodology. Participants observe and participate in ESL classes in local school.
Dates: Eight weeks: to be arranged.
Location: Washington, D.C.: on campus.
Instruction: *Methods:* discussion groups, lectures, field trips, "hands-on" training. *By:* faculty.
Highlights: Sponsor has offered program since 1983. Certificate. Practical training is a program component; participants are not paid. Issues I-20AB. Foreign nationals on tourist visas are eligible to enroll. A foreign student counselor/adviser is available. 50 total enrollment; 100% foreign enrollment in 1985.
Eligibility: *Academic:* bachelor's degree. *Language:* English proficiency on advanced level is preferred. *Professional:* secondary school EFL teachers.
Cost: $2,250 for tuition, books and materials, housing, health insurance. *Scholarships:* none.
Housing: Not provided; sponsor assists in locating housing.
Application: *Deadline:* two months prior. *Fee:* none.
Contact: Ms. Judy Jenkins, International Programs, Graduate School, U.S. Department of Agriculture, 600 Maryland Ave. SW, Room 134, Washington, DC 20024; (202) 447-7476.

G42 UNIVERSITY OF CALIFORNIA—BERKELEY EXTENSION
Basic Course for English Teachers.
Specialization: Methods for developing communicative competence, specialized topics in TEFL and American culture.
Dates: One month: August.
Location: San Francisco, California: at professional work site.
Instruction: *Methods:* discussion groups, lectures, field trips, "hands-on" training. *By:* faculty, guest speakers/lecturers.
Highlights: Sponsor has offered program since 1983. Certificate. Issues I-20AB. Foreign nationals on tourist visas are eligible to enroll. A foreign student counselor/adviser is available. Cultural and recreational activities. 20 total enrollment; 100% foreign enrollment in 1985.
Eligibility: *Academic:* bachelor's degree or training in TEFL. *Language:* English proficiency on intermediate level is required for oral skills, on advanced level for reading and grammar. *Professional:* one year of experience required, or training in TEFL.
Cost: $615 for tuition, books and materials, application fee. *Scholarships:* none.
Housing: In residence clubs.
Application: *Deadline:* June. *Fee:* $50; not refundable.
Contact: Ms. Judith Hoyem, UC Extension Center, 55 Laguna Street, San Francisco, CA 94102; (415) 552-3016. Telex: 910 366 7114. UC BERK BERK.

Abbreviations: ESL = English as a Second Language; TOEFL = Test of English as a Foreign Language; ALIGU = American Language Institute of Georgetown University; GPA = Grade Point Average; SAT = Scholastic Aptitude Test; GED = General Equivalency Diploma.

UNIVERSITY PLANNING

G43 UNIVERSITY OF WISCONSIN—MADISON
Short Course on University Planning.
Specialization: Strengthens ability to analyze existing programs and resources of a university and develop strategies for future development of academic and campus plans.
Dates: Mid-June–early Aug.
Location: Madison, Wisconsin: on campus. Also available abroad.
Instruction: *Methods:* discussion groups, lectures, case studies, field trips, individualized instruction, "hands-on" training, independent study/research, computer-assisted instruction. *By:* faculty. *Also available in Indonesian.*
Highlights: New program. Certificate. Issues I-20AB, IAP-66. Foreign nationals on tourist visas are eligible to enroll. A foreign student counselor/adviser is available. Various support services are available. 20 total enrollment.
Eligibility: *Academic:* bachelor's degree. *Language:* English proficiency on intermediate level is required. *Professional:* involvement in university planning preferred.
Cost: $3,100 for books and materials, local transportation, health insurance, some fees. *Scholarships:* none.
Housing: In apartments.
Application: *Deadline:* Feb. 1. *Fee:* $200; not refundable.
Contact: Mr. John T. Murdock, University of Wisconsin—Madison, 240 Agriculture Hall, 1450 Linden Drive, Madison, WI 53706; (608) 262-3673. AGRPROGRAMS. Telex: 265452 UFOWISC MDS.

VOCATIONAL EDUCATION

G44 OHIO STATE UNIVERSITY
Specialization: Special programs designed to meet individual needs within the field of vocational education. Topics include institutional building, instructor or administrator training, leadership development, and curriculum development and evaluation.
Dates: To be arranged.
Location: Columbus, Ohio: on campus, at professional work site.
Instruction: *Methods:* lectures discussion groups, field trips, individualized instruction, "hands-on" training, independent study/research. *By:* faculty, guest speakers/lecturers.
Highlights: Sponsor has offered program since 1979. Certificate. Practical training may be a program component; participants are not paid. Issues I-20AB, I-20MN, IAP-66. Foreign nationals on tourist visas are eligible to enroll. A foreign student counselor/adviser is available.
Eligibility: *Academic:* associate's degree. *Language:* English proficiency on intermediate level is required. TOEFL: 500; Univ. of Michigan Language Test: 80. *Professional:* experience preferred.
Cost: Varies.
Housing: Not provided; host institution assists in locating housing.
Application: *Deadline:* two months prior to preferred starting date. *Fee:* none.
Contact: Coordinator, International In-Residents Program, National Center for Research in Vocational Education, Ohio State University, 1960 Kenny Road, Columbus, OH 43210; (614) 486-3655. Cable: CTVOCEDOSU Columbus, OH. Telex: 8104821894.

ENGINEERING

H1 COLORADO SCHOOL OF MINES
Executive Management Program in Mineral Economics.
Specialization: Engineering: minerals, energy, and materials.
Dates: Classes begin in Aug.
Location: Golden, Colorado: on campus.
Instruction: *Methods:* discussion groups, lectures, case studies, field trips, individualized instruction, "hands-on" training, independent study/research, computer-assisted instruction, language laboratories, science laboratories. *By:* faculty, guest speakers/lecturers.
Highlights: Sponsor has offered program previously. Certificate. Issues I-20AB, IAP-66. Foreign nationals on tourist visas are eligible to enroll. A foreign student counselor/adviser is available. 20% foreign enrollment in 1985.
Eligibility: *Academic:* bachelor's degree. *Language:* English proficiency on intermediate level is required. *Professional:* none.
Cost: Not given. *Scholarships:* none.
Housing: In dormitories, hotels, with families.
Application: *Deadline:* none. *Fee:* none.
Contact: Janice C. Hepworth, Director, Special Programs and Continuing Education, Colorado School of Mines, Golden, CO 80401; (303) 273-3321.

H2 COLORADO SCHOOL OF MINES
Professional Degree Program.
Specialization: A final, practically oriented degree program beyond the bachelor of science degree, preparing the student for an industrial career. Specializations include mineral economics and geophysics, engineering, chemical engineering and petroleum refining, geological engineering, geophysical engineering, metallurgical engineering, mining engineering, and petroleum engineering.
Dates: Two semesters: classes begin in Aug., Jan.
Location: Golden, Colorado: on campus.
Instruction: *Methods:* discussion groups, lectures, case studies, field trips, individualized instruction, "hands-on" training, independent study/research, computer-assisted instruction, language laboratories, science laboratories. *By:* faculty, guest speakers/lecturers.
Highlights: Sponsor has offered program since 1985. Degree upon completion of 25 hours of coursework. Issues I-20AB, IAP-66. Foreign nationals on tourist visas are eligible to enroll. A foreign student counselor/adviser is available. 20% foreign enrollment in 1985.
Eligibility: *Academic:* bachelor's degree, or upper-level undergraduates. *Language:* English proficiency on intermediate level is required. *Professional:* none.
Cost: About $3,736 per semester for tuition. *Scholarships:* none.
Housing: In dormitories, hotels, with families.
Application: *Deadline:* none. *Fee:* none.
Contact: Janice C. Hepworth, Director, Special Programs and Continuing Education, Colorado School of Mines, Golden, CO 80401; (303) 273-3321.

Abbreviations: ESL = English as a Second Language; TOEFL = Test of English as a Foreign Language; ALIGU = American Language Institute of Georgetown University; GPA = Grade Point Average; SAT = Scholastic Aptitude Test; GED = General Equivalency Diploma.

H3 ENGINEERING FOUNDATION OF THE UNITED ENGINEERING TRUSTEES, INC.

Specialization: Engineering.
Dates: Ongoing.
Location: Varies.
Instruction: *Methods:* lectures, seminars, practical training. *By:* faculty, guest speakers/lecturers.
Highlights: Sponsor has offered programs since 1962. Does not help obtain visa. No services for foreign nationals.
Eligibility: *Academic:* engineering degree. *Language:* English proficiency on intermediate level is required. *Professional:* leadership in specific fields.
Cost: Varies. *Scholarships:* none.
Housing: In dormitories, hotels.
Application: *Deadline:* varies. *Fee:* varies.
Contact: Harold Comerer, Director, Engineering Foundation, 345 E. 47th Street, New York, NY 10017; (212) 705-7836.

H4 MASSACHUSETTS INSTITUTE OF TECHNOLOGY
Advanced Study Program.

Specialization: Program is tailored to the background and objectives of the participant; activities include regular graduate courses, special courses, seminars, independent study or research.
Dates: Classes begin in Feb., Sept.
Location: Cambridge, Massachusetts: on campus.
Instruction: *Methods:* discussion groups, lectures, individualized instruction, independent study/research. *By:* faculty.
Highlights: Sponsor has offered program since 1965. Certificate. Issues I-20AB, IAP-66. Foreign nationals on tourist visas are not eligible to enroll. A foreign student counselor/adviser is available. Foreign student activities. 50 total enrollment; 50% foreign enrollment in 1985.
Eligibility: *Academic:* bachelor's degree. *Language:* English proficiency on advanced level is required. TOEFL: 575. *Professional:* five years of experience in area of interest.
Cost: $8,850 per semester for tuition. *Scholarships:* none.
Housing: Not provided; sponsor assists in locating housing.
Application: *Deadline:* April for fall; Dec. for spring. *Fee:* none.
Contact: Dr. Paul E. Brown, Director, Advanced Study Programs, Room 9-435, Center for Advanced Engineering Study, MIT, Cambridge, MA 02139; (617) 253-6161. Cable: MIT CAM. Telex: 92-1473.

H5 OKLAHOMA STATE UNIVERSITY

Specialization: Special graduate-level programs can be arranged in various engineering fields.
Dates: To be arranged.
Location: Stillwater, Oklahoma: on campus, at professional work site.
Instruction: *Methods:* discussion groups, lectures, case studies, field trips, individualized instruction, "hands-on" training, independent study/research, computer-assisted instruction, language laboratories, science laboratories. *By:* faculty.
Highlights: Sponsor has offered short-term programs previously. Certificate. Practical training is a program component. Issues I-20AB, IAP-66. Foreign nationals on tourist visas are eligible to enroll. A foreign student counselor/adviser is available. Orientation programs and arranged activities. Unlimited total enrollment; 9% foreign enrollment in 1985.
Eligibility: *Academic:* depends on program; at least bachelor's degree. *Language:* English proficiency on intermediate level is required. TOEFL: 550. *Professional:* none.
Cost: $10,237 per year inclusive. *Scholarships:* partial (assistantships).
Housing: In dormitories, apartments, furnished rooms.

Application: *Deadline:* Nov. 1 and June 1. *Fee:* $10; not refundable.
Contact: Director, Office of International Programs, Oklahoma State University, 221 USDA Bldg. North, Stillwater, OK 74078; (405) 624-6535. Telex: 160274 OSU UT or 709606 OSU INTL PROG.

H6 SAINT MARTIN'S COLLEGE
Master's of Engineering Management.
Specialization: Engineering management.
Dates: Vary.
Location: Lacey, Washington: on campus.
Instruction: *Methods:* discussion groups, lectures, case studies, language laboratories. *By:* faculty.
Highlights: Sponsor has offered program since 1980. Practical training may be a program component. Foreign nationals on tourist visas are not eligible to enroll. A foreign student counselor/adviser is available. Unlimited total enrollment; about 25% foreign enrollment in 1985.
Eligibility: *Academic:* bachelor's degree. *Language:* English proficiency on intermediate level is required. TOEFL: 525. *Professional:* none.
Cost: $7,000 for tuition. *Scholarships:* none.
Housing: In dormitories.
Application: *Deadline:* none. *Fee:* $15; not refundable.
Contact: Director of Admissions, Saint Martin's College, Lacey, WA 98503; (206) 491-4700.

H7 UNION COLLEGE
Technical Institutes.
Specialization: Mechanical, electrical, and civil engineering, with emphasis on the latest information and practice in emerging and developed special areas.
Dates: July–Aug.: two courses weekly.
Location: Schenectady, New York: at college.
Instruction: *Methods:* lectures. *By:* faculty, guest speakers/lecturers.
Highlights: Sponsor has offered program since 1967. Certificate. Issues I-20, IAP-66. No services for foreign nationals. 5% foreign enrollment in 1985.
Eligibility: *Academic:* bachelor's degree. *Language:* none. *Professional:* none.
Cost: $795–$995 for tuition, books. *Scholarships:* none.
Housing: Not provided: sponsor assists in locating housing.
Application: *Deadline:* two weeks prior. *Fee:* none.
Contact: Rae D'Amelio, Office of Graduate and Continuing Studies, Union College, 1 Union Ave., Schenectady, NY 12308; (518) 370-6288.

H8 UNIVERSITY OF CALIFORNIA, LOS ANGELES EXTENSION
Certificate Programs in Engineering.
Specialization: Programs in construction management, computer science, fire protection, manufacturing engineering, microprocessor hardware/software.
Dates: One year: classes begin in June, Sept., Jan., and April.
Location: Los Angeles, California: on campus.
Instruction: *Methods:* discussion groups, lectures, science laboratories. *By:* faculty, guest speakers/lecturers.
Highlights: Sponsor has offered program previously. Certificate. Issues I-20AB. Foreign nationals on tourist visas are eligible to enroll. A foreign student counselor/adviser is available. ESL program. Unlimited total enrollment; about 10% foreign enrollment in 1985.
Eligibility: *Academic:* bachelor's degree. *Language:* English proficiency on intermediate level is required. Placement exam. *Professional:* none.
Cost: About $3,300 per quarter for tuition. *Scholarships:* none.
Housing: Not provided; student makes own arrangements.
Application: *Deadline:* three months to one year prior. *Fee:* $275; not refundable.

Abbreviations: ESL = English as a Second Language; TOEFL = Test of English as a Foreign Language; ALIGU = American Language Institute of Georgetown University; GPA = Grade Point Average; SAT = Scholastic Aptitude Test; GED = General Equivalency Diploma.

Contact: Foreign Student Advisor, UCLA Extension Advisory Service, 10995 Le Conte Avenue, Los Angeles, CA 90024; (213) 825-9351 or 206-6201. Cable: 9103427597. Telex: 9103427597.

ELECTRICAL ENGINEERING

H9 MASSACHUSETTS INSTITUTE OF TECHNOLOGY
Summer Courses in Electrical Engineering.
Specialization: Topics include electronic devices and circuits, introduction to electronics, power electronics, power systems planning, optical propagation, speech communication, and speech spectrogram reading.
Dates: June–Aug.
Location: Cambridge, Massachusetts: on campus.
Instruction: *Methods:* discussion groups, lectures, case studies, "hands-on" training, independent study/research, computer-assisted instruction, science laboratories. *By:* faculty.
Highlights: Sponsor has offered program since 1949. Certificate. Foreign nationals on tourist visas are eligible to enroll. A foreign student counselor/adviser is not available. About 20–25 per class total enrollment; 10% foreign enrollment in 1985.
Eligibility: *Academic:* bachelor's degree. *Language:* English proficiency on intermediate level is required. *Professional:* none.
Cost: About $1,500 per week for tuition, books and materials, meals, housing.
Scholarships: none.
Housing: In dormitories, hotels.
Application: *Deadline:* depends on program. *Fee:* none.
Contact: Summer Session Office, Massachusetts Institute of Technology, 77 Massachusetts Ave., Room E19-356, Cambridge, MA 02139; (617) 253-2101. Telex: 921473 MIT CAM.

MANUFACTURING ENGINEERING

H10 CARNEGIE MELLON UNIVERSITY
Master of Manufacturing Engineering.
Specialization: Provides a tightly focused curriculum that allows qualified engineers and other with technical training to acquire an understanding of modern manufacturing operations and the skills to solve related problems.
Dates: One year: classes begin in Sept.
Location: Pittsburgh, Pennsylvania: on campus.
Instruction: *Methods:* discussion groups, lectures, independent study/research, computer-assisted instruction. *By:* faculty, guest speakers/lecturers.
Highlights: Sponsor has offered program since 1984. Certificate. Issues I-20AB, IAP-66. Foreign nationals on tourist visas are not eligible to enroll. A foreign student counselor/adviser is available. Coordinator of International Education and foreign student organizations. Unlimited total enrollment; 8% foreign enrollment in 1985.
Eligibility: *Academic:* bachelor's degree in engineering or science. *Language:* English proficiency on advanced level is required. TOEFL: 600. *Professional:* two years of experience required; some industrial experience.
Cost: $30,300 for tuition, activity fee, meals, housing, local transportation, health insurance.
Scholarships: none.
Housing: Not provided; sponsor assists in locating housing.
Application: *Deadline:* May 1. *Fee:* $25; not refundable.
Contact: Ms. Peg Faulkner, Program in Manufacturing Engineering, Carnegie Institute of Technology, Pittsburgh, PA 15213; (412) 268-2480.

All program information is subject to change without notice
and must be confirmed directly with the sponsor.

MATERIALS ENGINEERING

H11 MASSACHUSETTS INSTITUTE OF TECHNOLOGY
Materials Science and Engineering.
Specialization: Summer session courses in electron microscopy, science and control of welding and joining processes, corrosion.
Dates: June–Aug.
Location: Cambridge, Massachusetts: on campus.
Instruction: *Methods:* discussion groups, lectures, case studies, "hands-on" training, independent study/research, computer-assisted instruction, science laboratories. *By:* faculty.
Highlights: Sponsor has offered program since 1949. Certificate. Foreign nationals on tourist visas are eligible to enroll. A foreign student counselor/adviser is not available. About 20–25 per class total enrollment; 10% foreign enrollment in 1985.
Eligibility: *Academic:* bachelor's degree. *Language:* English proficiency on intermediate level is required. *Professional:* none.
Cost: About $1,500 per week for tuition, books and materials, meals, housing.
Scholarships: none.
Housing: In dormitories, hotels.
Application: *Deadline:* depends on program. *Fee:* none.
Contact: Summer Session Office, Massachusetts Institute of Technology, 77 Massachusetts Ave., Room E19-356, Cambridge, MA 02139; (617) 253-2101. Telex: 921473 MIT CAM.

NUCLEAR ENGINEERING

H12 MASSACHUSETTS INSTITUTE OF TECHNOLOGY
Nuclear Power Reactor Safety.
Specialization: Summer courses in reactor safety: thermal power reactors, and general safety issues.
Dates: Two weeks: July.
Location: Cambridge, Massachusetts: on campus.
Instruction: *Methods:* discussion groups, lectures, case studies, "hands-on" training, independent study/research, computer-assisted instruction, science laboratories. *By:* faculty.
Highlights: Sponsor has offered program previously. Certificate. Foreign nationals on tourist visas are eligible to enroll. A foreign student counselor/adviser is not available. About 20–25 per class total enrollment; 10% foreign enrollment in 1985.
Eligibility: *Academic:* bachelor's degree. *Language:* English proficiency on intermediate level is required. *Professional:* none.
Cost: About $1,500 per week for tuition, books and materials, meals, housing.
Scholarships: none.
Housing: In dormitories, hotels.
Application: *Deadline:* depends on program. *Fee:* none.
Contact: Summer Session Office, Massachusetts Institute of Technology, 77 Massachusetts Ave., Room E19-356, Cambridge, MA 02139; (617) 253-2101. Telex: 921473 MIT CAM.

REVIEW PROGRAMS

H13 COLORADO SCHOOL OF MINES, SPECIAL PROGRAMS AND CONTINUING EDUCATION
E.I.T. Review.
Specialization: Review sessions covering math, chemistry, computer science, dynamics, economic analysis, electrical theory, fluid mechanics, mechanics of materials, statics, systems theory, and thermodynamics.

Abbreviations: ESL = English as a Second Language; TOEFL = Test of English as a Foreign Language; ALIGU = American Language Institute of Georgetown University; GPA = Grade Point Average; SAT = Scholastic Aptitude Test; GED = General Equivalency Diploma.

Dates: Late Jan.–early April, late Aug.–late Oct.
Location: Golden, Colorado: on campus.
Instruction: *Methods:* discussion groups, lectures, case studies, field trips, individualized instruction, "hands-on" training, independent study/research, computer-assisted instruction, language laboratories, science laboratories. *By:* faculty, guest speakers/lecturers.
Highlights: Sponsor has offered program previously. Certificate. Issues I-20AB, IAP-66. Foreign nationals on tourist visas are eligible to enroll. A foreign student counselor/adviser is available. Special programs for foreign students and International Student Office. 20% foreign enrollment in 1985.
Eligibility: *Academic:* engineering degree. *Language:* English proficiency on intermediate level is required. *Professional:* none.
Cost: $125 for tuition. *Scholarships:* none.
Housing: In dormitories, hotels, with families.
Application: *Deadline:* first day of course. *Fee:* none.
Contact: Janice C. Hepworth, Director, Office of Special Programs and Continuing Education, Colorado School of Mines, Golden, CO 80401; (303) 273-3321.

SYSTEMS SAFETY

H14 **UNIVERSITY OF WASHINGTON, COLLEGE OF ENGINEERING**
Systems Safety and Reliability Analysis.
Specialization: Systems safety.
Dates: Two weeks: classes begin in June, July.
Location: Seattle, Washington: on campus.
Instruction: *Methods:* discussion groups, lectures, case studies, "hands-on" training. *By:* faculty, guest speakers/lecturers.
Highlights: Sponsor has offered program since 1965. Certificate. A foreign student counselor/adviser is available. 30 total enrollment; no foreign enrollment in 1985.
Eligibility: *Academic:* bachelor's degree. *Language:* English proficiency on advanced level is required. *Professional:* none.
Cost: $775 for tuition, books and materials, local transportation. *Scholarships:* none.
Housing: In dormitories.
Application: *Deadline:* two weeks prior. *Fee:* none.
Contact: Ms. Joan O'Brien, Engineering Continuing Education, College of Engineering, University of Washington, FH-19, Seattle, WA 98195; (206) 543-5539.

HOME ECONOMICS

I1 CALIFORNIA STATE UNIVERSITY, CHICO
Home Economics.

Specialization: Programs in interior design, fashion merchandising, apparel design, textiles, dietetics.
Dates: Nine months: classes begin in Aug.
Location: Chico, California: on campus.
Instruction: *Methods:* discussion groups, lectures, field trips, "hands-on" training, independent study/research, computer-assisted instruction, science laboratories. *By:* faculty.
Highlights: Sponsor has offered program previously. Certificate. Practical training is a program component; participants are not paid. A foreign student counselor/adviser is available. Center for International Studies. 450 total enrollment; less than 1% foreign enrollment in 1985.
Eligibility: *Academic:* bachelor's degree. *Language:* English proficiency on intermediate level is required. TOEFL. *Professional:* none.
Cost: Not given. *Scholarships:* none.
Housing: Not provided; sponsor assists in locating housing.
Application: *Deadline:* rolling. *Fee:* $25; not refundable.
Contact: Dr. Marilyn D. Ambrose or Dean Lucas Calpouzos, College of Agriculture and Home Economics, California State University, Chico, CA 95929; (916) 895-5131 or 895-6805.

FAMILY SERVICES

I2 VIRGINIA POLYTECHNIC INSTITUTE & STATE UNIVERSITY
Summer Study Opportunities.

Specialization: Graduate-level courses in family and child development.
Dates: Late June–late Aug.
Location: Blacksburg, Virginia: on campus, at professional work site.
Instruction: *Methods:* discussion groups, lectures, field trips, independent study/research. *By:* faculty, guest speakers/lecturers.
Highlights: Sponsor has offered program previously. A foreign student counselor/adviser is available.
Eligibility: *Academic:* bachelor's degree. *Language:* English proficiency on advanced level is required. TOEFL: 600. *Professional:* none.
Cost: Varies. *Scholarships:* none.
Housing: Not provided; student makes own arrangements.
Application: *Deadline:* three weeks prior. *Fee:* $10; not refundable.
Contact: Dr. Vera J. Wall, College of Human Resources, Virginia Polytechnic Institute & State University, Blacksburg, VA 24061-8397; (703) 961-5380.

FASHION ARTS

13 THE CLARISSA SCHOOL OF FASHION DESIGN, INC.
Apparel Technology.
Specialization: Dressmaking, patternmaking, tailoring, design.
Dates: Classes begin Apr., Sept., and Jan.
Location: Pittsburgh, Pennsylvania: on campus.
Instruction: *Methods:* discussion groups, lectures, individualized instruction, "hands-on" training. *By:* faculty.
Highlights: Sponsor has offered program since 1951. Certificate. Practical training is a program component; participants are not paid. Issues I-20AB. Foreign nationals on tourist visas are not eligible to enroll. A foreign student counselor/adviser is not available. 100 total enrollment; 2% foreign enrollment in 1985.
Eligibility: *Academic:* associate's degree. *Language:* English proficiency on advanced level is required. *Professional:* none.
Cost: $1,700 per semester for tuition. *Scholarships:* none.
Housing: In dormitories.
Application: *Deadline:* rolling. *Fee:* $25; not refundable.
Contact: The Clarissa School of Fashion Design, Inc., 107 Sixth Street, Fulton Bldg., Pittsburgh, PA 15222; (412) 471-4414.

14 FASHION INSTITUTE OF DESIGN AND MERCHANDISING
Specialization: Fashion design.
Dates: One year: classes begin in Sept.
Location: San Francisco, Los Angeles, Orange County, San Diego, and Sherman Oaks, California: on campus.
Instruction: *Methods:* discussion groups, lectures, case studies, field trips, individualized instruction, "hands-on" training, independent study/research, computer-assisted instruction, language laboratories. *By:* school faculty, guest speakers/lecturers.
Highlights: Sponsor has offered program since 1968. Certificate. Practical training is a program component; participants are paid. Issues I-20AB. Foreign nationals on tourist visas are eligible to enroll. A foreign student counselor/adviser is available. ESL program. 15% foreign enrollment in 1985.
Eligibility: *Academic:* bachelor's degree. *Language:* English proficiency on intermediate level is required. TOEFL: 500. *Professional:* none.
Cost: $7,000–$9,000 per year for tuition, books, and materials. *Scholarships:* none.
Housing: In hotels, residence clubs.
Application: *Deadline:* none. *Fee:* $25; not refundable.
Contact: Francesca Brucia, Fashion Institute of Design and Merchandising, 790 Market Street, San Francisco, CA 94102; (415) 433-6691.

15 FASHION INSTITUTE OF TECHNOLOGY
Apparel Production Management.
Specialization: Preparation for careers in fashion and related professions at a specialized college of art and design.
Dates: Nine months: classes begin in late Aug.
Location: New York, New York: on campus.
Instruction: *Methods:* discussion groups, lectures, case studies, field trips, individualized instruction, "hands-on" training, independent study/research, computer-assisted instruction. *By:* faculty, guest speakers/lecturers.
Highlights: Sponsor has offered program previously. Certificate. Practical training is a program component; participants are not paid. Issues I-20AB. Foreign nationals on tourist visas are not eligible to enroll. A foreign student counselor/adviser is available. Various support services are available.

All program information is subject to change without notice and must be confirmed directly with the sponsor.

Eligibility: *Academic:* associate's degree or some undergraduate work. *Language:* English proficiency on intermediate level is required. TOEFL: 550. *Professional:* none.
Cost: $2,400 for tuition. *Scholarships:* none.
Housing: In dormitories if room available, or sponsor assists in locating housing.
Application: *Deadline:* rolling. *Fee:* $10; not refundable.
Contact: Ms. Sally White, Foreign Student Advisor, Fashion Institute of Technology, 227 W. 27th Street, New York, NY 10001; (212) 760-7675.

16 **FASHION INSTITUTE OF TECHNOLOGY**
Fashion Design.
Specialization: Preparation for careers in fashion and related professions at a specialized college of art and design.
Dates: Nine months: classes begin in late Aug.
Location: New York, New York: on campus.
Instruction: *Methods:* discussion groups, lectures, case studies, field trips, individualized instruction, "hands-on" training, independent study/research, computer-assisted instruction. *By:* faculty, guest speakers/lecturers.
Highlights: Sponsor has offered program previously. Certificate. Practical training is a program component; participants are not paid. Issues I-20AB. Foreign nationals on tourist visas are not eligible to enroll. A foreign student counselor/adviser is available. Various support services are available.
Eligibility: *Academic:* associate's degree or some undergraduate work. *Language:* English proficiency on intermediate level is required. TOEFL: 550. *Professional:* none.
Cost: $2,400 for tuition. *Scholarships:* none.
Housing: In dormitories if room available, or sponsor assists in locating housing.
Application: *Deadline:* Rolling. *Fee:* $10; not refundable.
Contact: Ms. Sally White, Foreign Student Advisor, Fashion Institute of Technology, 227 W. 27th Street, New York, NY 10001; (212) 760-7675.

17 **FASHION INSTITUTE OF TECHNOLOGY**
Textile/Surface Design.
Specialization: Preparation for careers in fashion and related professions at a specialized college of art and design.
Dates: Nine months: classes begin in late Aug.
Location: New York, New York: on campus.
Instruction: *Methods:* discussion groups, lectures, case studies, field trips, individualized instruction, "hands-on" training, independent study/research, computer-assisted instruction. *By:* faculty, guest speakers/lecturers.
Highlights: Sponsor has offered program previously. Certificate. Practical training is a program component; participants are not paid. Issues I-20AB. Foreign nationals on tourist visas are not eligible to enroll. A foreign student counselor/adviser is available. Various support services are available.
Eligibility: *Academic:* associate's degree or some undergraduate work. *Language:* English proficiency on intermediate level is required. TOEFL: 550. *Professional:* none.
Cost: $2,400 for tuition. *Scholarships:* none.
Housing: In dormitories if room available, or sponsor assists in locating housing.
Application: *Deadline:* Rolling. *Fee:* $10; not refundable.
Contact: Ms. Sally White, Foreign Student Advisor, Fashion Institute of Technology, 227 W. 27th Street, New York, NY 10001; (212) 760-7675.

18 **FASHION INSTITUTE OF TECHNOLOGY**
Textile Technology.
Specialization: Preparation for careers in fashion and related professions at a specialized college of art and design.
Dates: Nine months: classes begin in late Aug.

Abbreviations: ESL = English as a Second Language; TOEFL = Test of English as a Foreign Language; ALIGU = American Language Institute of Georgetown University; GPA = Grade Point Average; SAT = Scholastic Aptitude Test; GED = General Equivalency Diploma.

101

Location: New York, New York: on campus.
Instruction: *Methods:* discussion groups, lectures, case studies, field trips, individualized instruction, "hands-on" training, independent study/research, computer-assisted instruction. *By:* faculty, guest speakers/lecturers.
Highlights: Sponsor has offered program previously. Certificate. Practical training is a program component; participants are not paid. Issues I-20AB. Foreign nationals on tourist visas are not eligible to enroll. A foreign student counselor/adviser is available. Various support services are available.
Eligibility: *Academic:* associate's degree or some undergraduate work. *Language:* English proficiency on intermediate level is required. TOEFL: 550. *Professional:* none.
Cost: $2,400 for tuition. *Scholarships:* none.
Housing: In dormitories if room available, or sponsor assists in locating housing.
Application: *Deadline:* Rolling. *Fee:* $10; not refundable.
Contact: Ms. Sally White, Foreign Student Advisor, Fashion Institute of Technology, 227 W. 27th Street, New York, NY 10001; (212) 760-7675.

HOUSING MANAGEMENT

I9 VIRGINIA POLYTECHNIC INSTITUTE & STATE UNIVERSITY
Summer Study Opportunities.
Specialization: Graduate-level courses in housing management.
Dates: Late June–late August.
Location: Blacksburg, Virginia: on campus, at professional work site.
Instruction: *Methods:* discussion groups, lectures, field trips, independent study/research. *By:* faculty, guest speakers/lecturers.
Highlights: Sponsor has offered program previously. A foreign student counselor/adviser is available.
Eligibility: *Academic:* bachelor's degree. *Language:* English proficiency on advanced level is required. TOEFL: 600. *Professional:* none.
Cost: Varies. *Scholarships:* none.
Housing: Not provided; student makes own arrangements.
Application: *Deadline:* three weeks prior. *Fee:* $10; not refundable.
Contact: Dr. Vera J. Wall, College of Human Resources, Virginia Polytechnic Institute & State University, Blacksburg, VA 24061-8397; (703) 961-5380.

NUTRITION

I10 UNIVERSITY OF MARYLAND
Graduate Program in Nutritional Sciences.
Specialization: Research, seminars, and colloquium.
Dates: Not given: classes begin in fall and spring.
Location: College Park, Maryland: on campus, at professional work site.
Instruction: *Methods:* lectures, individualized instruction, "hands-on" training, independent study/research, computer-assisted instruction, science laboratories. *By:* faculty.
Highlights: Sponsor has offered program since 1967. Issues IAP-66. Foreign nationals on tourist visas are not eligible to enroll. A foreign student counselor/adviser is available. 15 total enrollment; 35% foreign enrollment in 1985.
Eligibility: *Academic:* bachelor's degree. *Language:* English proficiency on advanced level is required. TOEFL: 600. *Professional:* none.
Cost: Not given. *Scholarships:* partial.
Housing: Not given.
Application: *Deadline:* Feb. 1 for fall, Aug. 1 for spring. *Fee:* $20; not refundable. *Scholarship deadline:* not given.

All program information is subject to change without notice and must be confirmed directly with the sponsor.

102

Contact: Nutritional Sciences Program Office, University of Maryland, 2145 Animal Science Bldg., College Park, MD 20742; (301) 454-7838.

111 UNIVERSITY OF MEDICINE AND DENTISTRY OF NEW JERSEY, SCHOOL OF HEALTH RELATED PROFESSIONS
Dietetic Internship.
Specialization: Dietetics.
Dates: Classes begin in Sept., Jan.
Location: Newark, New Jersey: on campus, at professional work site.
Instruction: *Methods:* lectures, case studies, "hands-on" training. *By:* faculty, guest speakers/lecturers.
Highlights: Sponsor has offered program since 1974. Certificate upon completion of 30 semester hours of coursework. Practical training is a program component; participants are not paid. Issues I-20AB. Foreign nationals on tourist visas are not eligible to enroll. A foreign student counselor/adviser is not available. 8 total enrollment.
Eligibility: *Academic:* bachelor's degree. *Language:* English proficiency on advanced level is required. TOEFL. *Professional:* none.
Cost: $1,184 per year for tuition. *Scholarships:* none.
Housing: Not provided; student makes own arrangements.
Application: *Deadline:* Feb. 20. *Fee:* $15; not refundable.
Contact: Office of Academic and Student Services, School of Health Related Professions, University of Medicine and Dentistry of New Jersey, 100 Bergen Street, Newark, NJ 07103; (202) 456-5453.

112 VIRGINIA POLYTECHNIC INSTITUTE & STATE UNIVERSITY
Summer Study Opportunities.
Specialization: Graduate-level courses in human nutrition and foods.
Dates: Late June–late August.
Location: Blacksburg, Virginia: on campus, at professional work site.
Instruction: *Methods:* discussion groups, lectures, field trips, independent study/research. *By:* faculty, guest speakers/lecturers.
Highlights: Sponsor has offered program previously. A foreign student counselor/adviser is available.
Eligibility: *Academic:* bachelor's degree. *Language:* English proficiency on advanced level is required. TOEFL: 600. *Professional:* none.
Cost: Varies. *Scholarships:* none.
Housing: Not provided; student makes own arrangements.
Application: *Deadline:* three weeks prior. *Fee:* $10; not refundable.
Contact: Dr. Vera J. Wall, College of Human Resources, Virginia Polytechnic Institute & State University, Blacksburg, VA 24061-8397; (703) 961-5380.

Abbreviations: ESL = English as a Second Language; TOEFL = Test of English as a Foreign Language; ALIGU = American Language Institute of Georgetown University; GPA = Grade Point Average; SAT = Scholastic Aptitude Test; GED = General Equivalency Diploma.

103

INDUSTRIAL ARTS AND TRADES

J1 CENTRAL CONNECTICUT STATE UNIVERSITY
Master of Science Degree in Industrial Education.
Specialization: Graduate programs of varying lengths, with options that include a comprehensive examination or thesis.
Dates: One year: classes begin in Sept.
Location: New Britain, Connecticut: on campus.
Instruction: *Methods:* discussion groups, lectures, case studies, field trips, individualized instruction, "hands-on" training, independent study/research, computer-assisted instruction, language laboratories, science laboratories. *By:* faculty.
Highlights: Sponsor has offered program previously. Certificate. Issues I-20AB, I-20MN, IAP-66. Foreign nationals on tourist visas are not eligible to enroll. A foreign student counselor/adviser is avai lable. ESL program. Unlimited total enrollment.
Eligibility: *Academic:* bachelor's degree. *Language:* English proficiency on advanced level is required. TOEFL: 550. *Professional:* none.
Cost: About $6,000 for tuition, meals, housing. *Scholarships:* partial.
Housing: In dormitories.
Application: *Deadline:* not given. *Fee:* $10; not refundable. *Scholarship deadline:* not given.
Contact: Dr. Michael J. Williams, School of Technology, Central Connecticut State University, New Britain, CT 06050; (203) 827-7379.

J2 OKLAHOMA STATE UNIVERSITY
Specialization: Special graduate-level programs can be arranged in this field.
Dates: To be arranged.
Location: Stillwater, Oklahoma: on campus, at professional work site.
Instruction: *Methods:* discussion groups, lectures, case studies, field trips, individualized instruction, "hands-on" training, independent study/research, computer-assisted instruction, language laboratories, science laboratories. *By:* faculty.
Highlights: Sponsor has offered short-term programs previously. Certificate. Practical training is a program component. Issues I-20AB, IAP-66. Foreign nationals on tourist visas are eligible to enroll. A foreign student counselor/adviser is available. Orientation programs and other activities. Unlimited total enrollment; 9% foreign enrollment in 1985.
Eligibility: *Academic:* bachelor's degree. *Language:* English proficiency on intermediate level is required. TOEFL: 550. *Professional:* none.
Cost: $10,237 per year for tuition, books and materials, meals, housing, health insurance, personal expenses. *Scholarships:* partial (assistantships).
Housing: In dormitories, apartments, furnished rooms.
Application: *Deadline:* Nov. 1 and June 1. *Fee:* $10; not refundable. *Scholarship deadline:* not given.
Contact: Director, Office of International Programs, Oklahoma State University, 221 USDA Bldg. North, Stillwater, OK 74078; (405) 624-6535. Telex: 160274 OSU UT; 709606 OSU INTL PROG.

AERONAUTICS

J3 CENTRAL MISSOURI STATE UNIVERSITY
Aviation Safety.
Specialization: Master's program in aviation safety designed to provide a professional dimension to any aviation background.
Dates: One year: classes begin in Aug., Jan., May.
Location: Warrensburg, Missouri: on campus.
Instruction: *Methods:* discussion groups, lectures, field trips, independent study/research. *By:* faculty, guest speakers/lecturers.
Highlights: Sponsor has offered program since 1975. Master's degree. Issues I-20AB, I-20MN. Foreign nationals on tourist visas are not eligible to enroll. A foreign student counselor/adviser is available. 36 total enrollment; 3% foreign enrollment in 1985.
Eligibility: *Academic:* bachelor's degree. *La nguage:* English proficiency on intermediate level is required. TOEFL: 500. *Professional:* work experience or college credits in aviation equivalent to 15 semester hours.
Cost: $7,500 for tuition, books and materials, meals, housing. *Scholarships:* none.
Housing: In dormitories, apartments.
Application: *Deadline:* one month prior. *Fee:* none.
Contact: Dr. John W. Horine, Aviation Dept. Chairman, or Mr. James Postlethwait, Assistant Director of Admissions, Central Missouri State University, Warrensburg, MO 64093; (816) 429-4975.

J4 MASSACHUSETTS INSTITUTE OF TECHNOLOGY
Advanced Study Program in Air Transportation.
Specialization: Airline economics, air traffic control, air transportation planning. Program is tailored to background and objectives of participant.
Dates: Classes begin in Feb., Sept.
Location: Cambridge, Massachusetts: on campus.
Instruction: *Methods:* discussion groups, lectures, individualized instruction, independent study/research. *By:* faculty.
Highlights: Sponsor has offered program since 1973. Certificate. Issues I-20AB, IAP-66. Foreign nationals on tourist visas are not eligible to enroll. A foreign student counselor/adviser is available. Orientation and social activities. Five total enrollment; 100% foreign enrollment in 1985.
Eligibility: *Academic:* bachelor's degree. *Language:* English proficiency on advanced level is required. TOEFL: 575. *Professional:* five years of work experience in area of interest.
Cost: $8,850 for tuition. *Scholarships:* none .
Housing: Not provided; sponsor assists in locating housing .
Application: *Deadline:* April for fall, Dec. for spring. *Fee:* none.
Contact: Dr. Paul E. Brown, Director, Advanced Study Programs, Center for Advanced Engineering Study, Massachusetts Institute of Technology, Room 9-435, Cambridge, MA 02139; (617) 253-6161. Cable: MIT CAM. Telex: 92-1473.

Abbreviations: ESL = English as a Second Language; TOEFL = Test of English as a Foreign Language; ALIGU = American Language Institute of Georgetown University; GPA = Grade Point Average; SAT = Scholastic Aptitude Test; GED = General Equivalency Diploma.

105

LANGUAGES AND LITERATURES

K1 CLEMSON UNIVERSITY
International Visitor Program.
Specialization: Personalized programs in English and other languages and literatures, combining study, research, and internships. Undergraduate, graduate, and postgraduate levels.
Dates: Rolling: semesters begin in Aug., Jan.
Location: Clemson, South Carolina: on campus.
Instruction: *Methods:* lectures, individualized instruction, "hands-on" training, independent study/research, computer-assisted instruction, laboratories. *By:* faculty.
Highlights: Sponsor has offered program previously. Certificate. Practical training may be a program component; participants are paid. Issues I-20AB, IAP-66. Foreign nationals on tourist visas are eligible to enroll. A foreign student counselor/adviser is available.
Eligibility: *Academic:* bachelor's degree or some undergraduate work. *Language:* English proficiency on the advanced level is required. TOEFL: 550. *Professional:* requires professional certification.
Cost: $815 per month for tuition, books and materials, meals, housing, health insurance. *Scholarships:* none; all participants must be sponsored by an organization.
Housing: In dormitories.
Application: *Deadline:* rolling. *Fee:* none.
Contact: International Service Office, Clemson University, Room 106 Sikes Hall, Clemson, SC 29631; (803) 656-5466.

K2 LINGUISTIC SOCIETY OF AMERICA
Linguistic Institutes.
Dates: Vary.
Location: Varies.
Instruction: *Methods:* lectures, seminars, independent study. *By:* faculty, guest speakers/lecturers.
Highlights: Sponsor has offered programs since 1928. Credit. ESL program.
Eligibility: *Academic:* graduate and undergraduate students. *Language:* English proficiency on advanced level is required. *Professional:* none.
Cost: Varies. *Scholarships:* partial.
Housing: In dormitories, apartments.
Application: *Deadline:* none. *Fee:* none. *Scholarship deadline:* Feb. 11.
Contact: Secretariat, Linguistic Society of America, 1325 18th Street, Suite 211, Washington, DC 20036-6501; (202) 835-1714.

K3 MIDDLEBURY COLLEGE
Language Schools.
Specialization: Full immersion language programs in Chinese, Arabic, French, German, Italian, Japanese, Spanish, and Russian. All courses are taught in the language of instruction—no English is used.
Dates: Six-, seven-, and nine-week courses: classes begin in June.
Location: Middlebury, Vermont: on campus.

Instruction: *Methods:* discussion groups, lectures, individualized instruction, computer-assisted instruction, language laboratories. *By:* faculty. *In foreign languages only.*
Highlights: Sponsor has offered program since 1915. Certificate. Practical training is a program component; participants are not paid. Issues I-20AB, I-20MN, IAP-66. Foreign nationals on tourist visas are not eligible to enroll. A foreign student counselor/adviser is available. 1,200 total enrollment; 3% foreign enrollment in 1985.
Eligibility: *Academic:* undergraduate degree. *Language:* English proficiency is not required. *Professional:* none.
Cost: $2,450–$3,225 for tuition, meals, housing. *Scholarships:* partial.
Housing: In dormitories, apartments.
Application: *Deadline:* May 15. *Fee:* $20; refundable. *Scholarship deadline:* May 15.
Contact: Language Center, Middlebury College, Middlebury, VT 05753; (802) 388-3711.

K4 MONTEREY INSTITUTE OF INTERNATIONAL STUDIES
Master of Arts in Language Studies.
Specialization: Master's programs in Chinese, French, German, Japanese, Russian, and Spanish, taught by native speakers of each language. Individualized programs of directed studies, including language, literature, history, media, social and political institutions.
Dates: One year: classes begin in Aug., Jan. June.
Location: Monterey, California: on campus.
Instruction: *Methods:* lectures, individualized instruction, independent study/research, language laboratories. *By:* faculty.
Available in 21 languages.
Highlights: Sponsor has offered program since 1963. Master's degree. Issues I-20AB, IAP-66. Foreign nationals on tourist visas are eligible to enroll. A foreign student counselor/adviser is available. Various support services available. About 20% foreign enrollment in 1985.
Eligibility: *Academic:* bachelor's degree with 3.0 GPA; GRE; self-administered language placement test. *Language:* TOEFL: 550. *Professional:* none.
Cost: About $3,125 per semester for tuition. *Scholarships:* none.
Housing: Not provided; sponsor assists in locating housing.
Application: *Deadline:* Aug. 1 for fall semester, Dec. 1 for spring. *Fee:* $35; not refundable.
Contact: Office of Admissions, Monterey Institute of International Studies, 425 Van Buren, Monterey, CA 93940; (408) 649-3113.

BIBLICAL LANGUAGES

K5 PRINCETON THEOLOGICAL SEMINARY
Language Program.
Specialization: New Testament Greek, Biblical Hebrew.
Dates: Seven weeks: early June–early Aug.
Location: Princeton, New Jersey: at seminary.
Instruction: *Methods:* lectures, seminars. *By:* faculty.
Highlights: Sponsor has offered program since 1971. Credit. Issues I-20. No services for foreign nationals. 5% foreign enrollment in 1985.
Eligibility: *Academic:* bachelor's degree. *Language:* none. *Professional:* none.
Cost: $1,415 per course for tuition, meals, housing. *Scholarships:* none.
Housing: In dormitories.
Application: *Deadline:* June 6. *Fee:* $25.
Contact: Mr. David H. Wall, Director, Summer School Office, Princeton Theological Seminary, 108 Stockton Street, Princeton, NJ 08540; (609) 921-8252.

Abbreviations: ESL = English as a Second Language; TOEFL = Test of English as a Foreign Language; ALIGU = American Language Institute of Georgetown University; GPA = Grade Point Average; SAT = Scholastic Aptitude Test; GED = General Equivalency Diploma.

GERMANIC LANGUAGES

K6 WASHINGTON UNIVERSITY
Master's Degree in Germanic Languages and Literature.
Specialization: For German exchange students from universities of Tubingen, Cologne, Hamburg, Berlin, Munich. Additional students accepted from University of Aachen.
Dates: Nine months: classes begin in Aug.
Location: St. Louis, Missouri: on campus.
Instruction: *Methods:* discussion groups, lectures, independent study/research, language laboratories. *By:* faculty. *In German, Swedish, and Dutch.*
Highlights: Sponsor has offered program previously. Master's degree with 30 units of credit, knowledge of additional language, oral exam or master's thesis. Issues IAP-66. Foreign nationals on tourist visas are not eligible to enroll. A foreign student counselor/adviser is available. Various support services are available. 8 total enrollment; 33% foreign enrollment in 1985.
Eligibility: *Academic:* bachelor's degree. *Language:* English proficiency is not required. *Professional:* Abiturzeugnis, Zwischenprufung.
Cost: About $15,000 inclusive. *Scholarships:* full; those from the five exchange universities in Germany also receive a stipend of $6,000.
Housing: In apartments.
Application: *Deadline:* Mar. 1. *Fee:* none.
Contact: Austauschdienst of the exchange universities in Germany.

TRANSLATION AND INTERPRETATION

K7 THE AMERICAN UNIVERSITY
Graduate Certificate in Translation.
Specialization: Graduate-level courses in language and foreign studies; emphasis is on translating into English.
Dates: Classes begin in Sept., Jan., May, July.
Location: Washington, D.C.: on campus.
Instruction: *Methods:* discussion groups, lectures, case studies. *By:* faculty.
Highlights: Sponsor has offered program previously. Certificate. Issues I-20AB. Foreign nationals on tourist visas are not eligible to enroll. A foreign student counselor/adviser is available. Orientation programs.
Eligibility: *Academic:* bachelor's degree; junior level conversation/composition course in French, German, Russian, Spanish. *Language:* English proficiency on advanced level is required. TOEFL: 600; English Language Institute Placement Test. *Professional:* none.
Cost: $299 per semester hour for tuition. *Scholarships:* none.
Housing: Not provided; sponsor assists in locating housing.
Application: *Deadline:* none. *Fee:* none.
Contact: Programs Advisement Center, The American University, 4400 Massachusetts Ave. NW, Room 153 McKinley Bldg., Washington, DC 20016; (202) 885-2500.

K8 THE AMERICAN UNIVERSITY
Undergraduate Certificate in Translation.
Specialization: Translation skills: German, French, Russian, or Spanish into English.
Dates: Sept.–Aug.
Location: Washington, D.C.: on campus.
Instruction: *Methods:* discussion groups, lectures, case studies. *By:* faculty.
Highlights: Sponsor has offered program previously. Certificate. Issues I-20AB. Foreign nationals on tourist visas are not eligible to enroll. A foreign student counselor/adviser is available. Orientation programs.

All program information is subject to change without notice
and must be confirmed directly with the sponsor.

Eligibility: *Academic:* upper division undergraduates; passing grades on conversation and composition courses in language of specialization. *Language:* English proficiency on advanced level is required. TOEFL: 600. *Professional:* none.
Cost: $299 per semester hour for tuition. *Scholarships:* none.
Housing: Not provided; sponsor assists in locating housing.
Application: *Deadline:* none. *Fee:* none.
Contact: Programs Advisement Center, The American University, 4400 Massachusetts Ave. NW, Room 153 McKinley Bldg., Washington, DC 20016; (202) 885-2500.

K9 MONTEREY INSTITUTE OF INTERNATIONAL STUDIES
Court Interpreting.
Specialization: Designed for students fluent in both Spanish and English, and those with court interpreting experience who want to improve their skills.
Dates: Four weeks: classes begin in June, July.
Location: Monterey, California: on campus.
Instruction: *Methods:* lectures, individualized instruction, independent study/research, language laboratories. *By:* guest speakers/lecturers.
Highlights: Sponsor has offered program since 1963. Issues I-20AB, IAP-66. Foreign nationals on tourist visas are eligible to enroll. A foreign student counselor/adviser is available. Various support services available. About 20% foreign enrollment in 1985.
Eligibility: *Academic:* fluency in English and Spanish. *Language:* TOEFL: 600. *Professional:* none.
Cost: Not given. *Scholarships:* none.
Housing: Not provided; sponsor assists in locating housing.
Application: *Deadline:* June 1. *Fee:* $35; not refundable.
Contact: The Summer Language Program, Monterey Institute of International Studies, 425 Van Buren, Monterey, CA 93940; (408) 649-3113.

K10 MONTEREY INSTITUTE OF INTERNATIONAL STUDIES
Master of Arts in Terminology.
Specialization: Includes courses in translation, theory of terminology, databanks, and computer aids to translation, plus internship in international organization.
Dates: One year: classes begin in Aug.
Location: Monterey, California: on campus.
Instruction: *Methods:* lectures, individualized instruction, independent study/research, language laboratories. *By:* faculty.
Highlights: Sponsor has offered program since 1963. Master's degree. Issues I-20AB, IAP-66. Foreign nationals on tourist visas are eligible to enroll. A foreign student counselor/adviser is available. Various support services available. About 20% foreign enrollment in 1985.
Eligibility: *Academic:* bachelor's degree with 3.0 GPA; GRE; fluency in English and two other languages. *Language:* TOEFL: 600. *Professional:* none.
Cost: About $3,125 per semester for tuition. *Scholarships:* none.
Housing: Not provided; sponsor assists in locating housing.
Application: *Deadline:* Aug. 1. *Fee:* $35; not refundable.
Contact: Prof. Wilhelm Weber, Dean of the Translation and Interpretation Division, Monterey Institute of International Studies, 425 Van Buren, Monterey, CA 93940; (408) 649-3113.

Abbreviations: ESL = English as a Second Language; TOEFL = Test of English as a Foreign Language; ALIGU = American Language Institute of Georgetown University; GPA = Grade Point Average; SAT = Scholastic Aptitude Test; GED = General Equivalency Diploma.

LAW

L1 HARVARD LAW SCHOOL
Program of Instruction for Lawyers.
Specialization: Administrative and regulatory law, business law, constitutional law, international and comparative law, procedural law, and tax law.
Dates: Two weeks: June.
Location: Cambridge, Massachusetts: on campus.
Instruction: *Methods:* discussion groups, lectures, case studies. *By:* faculty.
Highlights: Sponsor has offered program since 1967. Certificate. Issues I-20AB. Extensive services are available for foreign nationals. 7% foreign enrollment in 1985.
Eligibility: *Academic:* law degree. *Language:* English proficiency on advanced level is preferred. *Professional:* member of the bar or license to practice law.
Cost: $1,900 for tuition, course materials. *Scholarships:* partial.
Housing: In dormitories, hotels.
Application: *Deadline:* June 1. *Fee:* none. *Scholarship deadline:* June 1.
Contact: Program of Instruction for Lawyers, Harvard Law School, Pound Hall 207, Cambridge, MA 02138; (617) 495-3187.

L2 UNIVERSITY OF MICHIGAN LAW SCHOOL
Graduate Law Studies.
Specialization: Graduate studies leading to M.C.L. or LL.M. degree.
Dates: Aug.–May.
Location: Ann Arbor, Michigan: on campus.
Instruction: *Methods:* lectures, discussion groups, independent study/research. *By:* faculty.
Highlights: Sponsor has offered program previously. Degree upon completion of 20–24 credit hours and research paper. Issues I-20AB, IAP-66. Foreign nationals on tourist visas are not eligible to enroll. A foreign student counselor/adviser is available. 25 total enrollment; 96% foreign enrollment in 1985.
Eligibility: *Academic:* LL.B. or J.D. degree. *Language:* English proficiency on advanced level is required. TOEFL; Univ. of Michigan Language Test. *Professional:* none.
Cost: About $17,000 inclusive. *Scholarships:* Full, partial.
Housing: Not provided; student makes own arrangements.
Application: *Deadline:* Jan. 15. *Fee:* none. *Scholarship deadline:* Jan. 15.
Contact: Barbara Roble, Graduate Office, University of Michigan Law School, Ann Arbor, MI 48109-1215; (313) 764-0535.

L3 UNIVERSITY OF PENNSYLVANIA
Master of Law.
Specialization: LL.M. degree program designed to suit the needs and background of individual students.
Dates: Sept.–May.
Location: Philadelphia, Pennsylvania: on campus.
Instruction: *Methods:* lectures, discussion groups, case studies. *By:* faculty, guest speakers/lecturers.
Highlights: Sponsor has offered program previously. Degree upon completion of 20 semester

---

All program information is subject to change without notice
and must be confirmed directly with the sponsor.

hours of coursework or 13 hours of coursework and thesis. Issues I-20AB, IAP-66. Foreign nationals on tourist visas are not eligible to enroll. A foreign student counselor/adviser is available. Orientation programs. 50 total enrollment; 95% foreign enrollment in 1985.
Eligibility: *Academic:* LL.B. or J.D. degree. *Language:* English proficiency on advanced level is required. TOEFL: 580. *Professional:* none.
Cost: $19,000 inclusive. *Scholarships:* limited.
Housing: In dormitories.
Application: *Deadline:* Feb. 1. *Fee:* none. *Scholarship deadline:* Feb. 1.
Contact: Geraldine Higgs, University of Pennsylvania Law School, 3400 Chestnut Street, Philadelphia, PA 19104; (215) 898-7400. Cable: PNSYL Phila PA. Telex: 710-670-0328.

L4 UNIVERSITY OF WISCONSIN LAW SCHOOL, LAW EXTENSION
United States Law and Legal Institutions.
Specialization: U.S. law as related to international transactions.
Dates: Five weeks: mid-July–mid-Aug.
Location: Madison, Wisconsin: on campus.
Instruction: *Methods:* lectures, discussions, field trips. *By:* faculty, guest speakers/lecturers.
Highlights: Sponsor has offered program since 1983. Certificate. Issues I-20, IAP-66. Extensive services for foreign nationals. 35 total enrollment; 100% foreign enrollment in 1985.
Eligibility: *Academic:* law degree or advanced standing. *Language:* English proficiency on intermediate level is required. *Professional:* none.
Cost: $1,900 for tuition, books, meals, housing. *Scholarships:* none.
Housing: In dormitories.
Application: *Deadline:* May 1. *Fee:* $350; sometimes refundable.
Contact: Lynn Thompson, University of Wisconsin, Law Extension, 905 University Ave., Suite 309, Madison, WI 53715; (608) 262-4915. Telex: 265452.

CRIMINAL JUSTICE

L5 BOSTON UNIVERSITY, METROPOLITAN COLLEGE
Master of Criminal Justice.
Specialization: Criminal justice administration, research, and planning. Program requirements include specialization electives individually selected to match student interests; some special international courses.
Dates: One year: classes begin in Sept., Jan., May, mid-June.
Location: Boston, Massachusetts: on campus.
Instruction: *Methods:* discussion groups, lectures, case studies, field trips, individualized instruction, "hands-on" training, independent study/research, computer-assisted instruction. *By:* faculty, guest speakers/lecturers.
Highlights: Sponsor has offered program since 1971. Certificate upon completion of 36 graduate credits. Issues I-20AB, IAP-66. Foreign nationals on tourist visas are not eligible to enroll. A foreign student counselor/adviser is available. Orientation, social, and other programs. About 40 total enrollment; 10% foreign enrollment in 1985.
Eligibility: *Academic:* bachelor's degree. *Language:* English proficiency on intermediate level is required. TOEFL: 550. *Professional:* related work experience preferred.
Cost: $10,950 for tuition. *Scholarships:* partial.
Housing: In dormitories, apartments, furnished rooms, with families.
Application: *Deadline:* six weeks prior. *Fee:* $30; not refundable. *Scholarship deadline:* six weeks prior.
Contact: Prof. H.P. Henderson, Director, Criminal Justice Program, Metropolitan College, Boston University, 755 Commonwealth Ave., Boston, MA 02215; (617) 353-3025.

Abbreviations: ESL = English as a Second Language; TOEFL = Test of English as a Foreign Language; ALIGU = American Language Institute of Georgetown University; GPA = Grade Point Average; SAT = Scholastic Aptitude Test; GED = General Equivalency Diploma.

L6 GUILFORD COLLEGE
Specialization: Administration of justice.
Dates: Aug.–end of July.
Location: Greensboro, North Carolina: on campus.
Instruction: *Methods:* lectures, discussion groups. *By:* faculty.
Highlights: Sponsor has offered short-term programs since 1983. Certificate upon completing 4–6 courses. Issues I-20AB, I-20MN. Foreign nationals on tourist visas are not eligible to enroll. A foreign student counselor/adviser is available. International Relations Club.
Eligibility: *Academic:* bachelor's degree. *Language:* English proficiency on advanced level is required. TOEFL: 500. *Professional:* none.
Cost: $112 per credit hour for tuition. *Scholarships:* none.
Housing: Not provided; student makes own arrangements.
Application: *Deadline:* none. *Fee:* $20; not refundable.
Contact: Dean of Admissions and Financial Aid, Guilford College, 5800 West Friendly Ave., Greensboro, NC 27410; (919) 292-5511.

INTERNATIONAL LAW

L7 SOUTHWESTERN LEGAL FOUNDATION, ACADEMY OF AMERICAN AND INTERNATIONAL LAW
International Law.
Dates: Six weeks: early June–mid-July.
Location: Richardson, Texas: at academy.
Instruction: *Methods:* lectures, seminars. *By:* guest speakers/lecturers.
Highlights: Sponsor has offered program since 1964. Certificate. Does not help obtain visa. Limited services for foreign nationals. 60 total enrollment; 100% foreign enrollment in 1985. List of past participants is available.
Eligibility: *Academic:* bachelor's degree. *Language:* none. *Professional:* professional certification.
Cost: $4,875 inclusive. *Scholarships:* full.
Housing: In hotels.
Application: *Deadline:* Mar. 15. *Fee:* none. *Scholarship deadline:* none.
Contact: Mrs. Ina Gillespie, Southwestern Legal Foundation, P.O. Box 830707, Richardson, TX 75080; (214) 690-2370.

PARALEGAL

L8 UNIVERSITY OF CALIFORNIA—LOS ANGELES EXTENSION
Attorney Assistant Training Program.
Specialization: Litigation, corporation/litigation.
Dates: 18 weeks: classes begin quarterly.
Location: Los Angeles, California: on campus.
Instruction: *Methods:* lectures, case studies, field trips, independent study/research. *By:* guest speakers/lecturers.
Highlights: Sponsor has offered program since 1972. Certificate. Practical training is a program component; participants are not paid. Issues I-20AB. Foreign nationals on tourist visas are eligible to enroll. A foreign student counselor/adviser is available. 60 total enroll ment; 7.5% foreign enrollment in 1985.
Eligibility: *Academic:* bachelor's degree. *Language:* English proficiency on advanced level is required. *Professional:* two years of work experience required.
Cost: $2,400 for tuition, books, and materials. *Scholarships:* none.
Housing: Not provided; student makes own arrangements.
Application: *Deadline:* not given. *Fee:* $35; not refundable.
Contact: Attorney Assistant Training Program, UCLA Extension, 10995 Le Conte Avenue, Room 517, Los Angeles, CA 90024; (213) 825-0741.

All program information is subject to change without notice and must be confirmed directly with the sponsor.

LIBERAL AND INTERDISCIPLINARY STUDIES

M1 CLEMSON UNIVERSITY
International Visitor Program.
Specialization: Personalized programs in liberal arts and multidisciplinary studies, combining study, research, and internships. Undergraduate, graduate, and postgraduate levels.
Dates: Rolling: semesters begin in Aug., Jan.
Location: Clemson, South Carolina: on campus.
Instruction: *Methods:* lectures, individualized instruction, "hands-on" training, independent study/research, computer-assisted instruction, laboratories. *By:* faculty.
Highlights: Sponsor has offered program previously. Certificate. Practical training may be a program component; participants are paid. Issues I-20AB, IAP-66. Foreign nationals on tourist visas are eligible to enroll. A foreign student counselor/adviser is available.
Eligibility: *Academic:* bachelor's degree or some undergraduate work. *Language:* English proficiency on the advanced level is required. TOEFL: 550. *Professional:* requires professional certification.
Cost: $815 per month for tuition, books and materials, meals, housing, health insurance. *Scholarships:* none; all participants must be sponsored by an organization.
Housing: In dormitories.
Application: *Deadline:* rolling. *Fee:* none.
Contact: International Service Office, Clemson University, Room 106 Sikes Hall, Clemson, SC 29631; (803) 656-5466.

M2 GUILFORD COLLEGE
Specialization: Programs available in black studies, women's studies, political science, history, psychology, philosophy, and religion.
Dates: Aug.–July.
Location: Greensboro, North Carolina: on campus.
Instruction: *Methods:* lectures, discussion groups. *By:* faculty.
Highlights: Sponsor has offered short-term programs since 1983. Certificate upon completion of 4–6 courses. Issues I-20AB, I-20MN. Foreign nationals on tourist visas are not eligible to enroll. A foreign student counselor/adviser is available. International Relations Club.
Eligibility: *Academic:* bachelor's degree. *Language:* English proficiency on advanced level is required. TOEFL: 500. *Professional:* none.
Cost: $112 per credit hour for tuition. *Scholarships:* none.
Housing: Not provided; sponsor assists in locating housing.
Application: *Deadline:* open. *Fee:* $20; not refundable.
Contact: Dean of Admissions and Financial Aid, Guilford College, 5800 W. Friendly Ave., Greensboro, NC 27410; (919) 292-5511.

M3 LESLEY COLLEGE
Independent Study Degree Program.
Specialization: Student designs own program guided by faculty and professionals in his field of study.
Dates: To be arranged.

Abbreviations: ESL = English as a Second Language; TOEFL = Test of English as a Foreign Language; ALIGU = American Language Institute of Georgetown University; GPA = Grade Point Average; SAT = Scholastic Aptitude Test; GED = General Equivalency Diploma.

Location: Cambridge, Massachusetts or Zurich, Switzerland: on campus, at professional work site, other geographic area.
Instruction: *Methods:* discussion groups, lectures, case studies, field trips, individualized training, "hands-on" training, independent study/research, computer-assisted instruction, language laboratories, science laboratories. *By:* faculty. *In Zurich, French or German may be used.*
Highlights: Sponsor has offered program since 1971. Diploma. Issues I-20AB. A foreign student counselor/adviser is available. Unlimited total enrollment; 8% foreign enrollment in 1985.
Eligibility: *Academic:* bachelor's degree. *Language:* English proficiency on advanced level is required for study in U.S. TOEFL. *Professional:* none.
Cost: $7,200 per credit for tuition. *Scholarships:* none.
Housing: In dormitories, apartments.
Application: *Deadline:* open. *Fee:* $35; not refundable.
Contact: Margot Chamberlain, Program Advisor, Independent Study Degree Program, Lesley College, 29 Everett Street, Cambridge, MA 02238; (617) 868-9600, Ext. 426.

M4 PITTSBURG STATE UNIVERSITY, CONTINUING EDUCATION
Visiting International Scholars.
Specialization: Program is individually designed to meet the goals of the student; any university subject may be taken.
Dates: To be arranged.
Location: Pittsburgh, Kansas: on campus.
Instruction: *Methods:* discussion groups, lectures, field trips, individualized instruction, "hands-on" training, independent study/research, language laboratories, science laboratories. *By:* faculty.
Highlights: Sponsor has offered program since 1985. Certificate. Issues I-20AB, I-20MN, IAP-66. Foreign nationals on tourist visas are not eligible to enroll. A foreign student counselor/adviser is available. 3.75% foreign enrollment in 1985.
Eligibility: *Academic:* varies. *Language:* English proficiency on advanced level is required. TOEFL. *Professional:* none.
Cost: $700 per month for tuition. *Scholarships:* none.
Housing: In dormitories, or sponsor assists in locating housing.
Application: *Deadline:* 2–3 months prior. *Fee:* $50; not refundable.
Contact: Suzan H. Schafer, Ed.D, Pittsburg State University, Room 215 Russ Hall, Pittsburg, KS 66762; (316) 231-7000, Ext. 4175.

M5 WESLEYAN UNIVERSITY
Graduate Liberal Arts Program.
Specialization: Interdisciplinary courses in social studies, science, mathematics, humanities, arts, general studies.
Dates: Classes begin in Sept., Jan., June.
Location: Middletown, Connecticut: on campus.
Instruction: *Methods:* lectures, discussion groups, case studies, field trips, "hands-on" training, science labs, computer-assisted instruction; primarily seminar format. *By:* faculty, guest speakers/lecturers.
Highlights: Sponsor has offered short-term programs since 1953. Master's degree upon completion of 30 units of graduate study. Issues I-20AB, IAP-66. Foreign nationals on tourist visas are not eligible to enroll. A foreign student counselor/adviser is available.
Eligibility: *Academic:* bachelor's degree. *Language:* English proficiency on advanced level is required. TOEFL: 550. *Professional:* none.
Cost: $500 per three-unit course for tuition. *Scholarships:* none.
Housing: Not provided; sponsor assists in locating housing.
Application: *Deadline:* about ten weeks prior. *Fee:* $35; not refundable.

Contact: Mary E. Ferguson or Barbara MacEachern, Graduate Liberal Studies Program. Wesleyan University, Middletown, CT 06547; (203) 347-9411, Ext. 2010.

ENERGY MANAGEMENT

M6 ARTHUR D. LITTLE MANAGEMENT EDUCATION INSTITUTE
Specialization: Petroleum management.
Dates: Mid-Aug.–late Nov.
Location: Cambridge, Massachusetts: on campus, at professional work site.
Instruction: *Methods:* lectures, discussion groups, case studies, computer-assisted instruction. *By:* faculty, guest speakers/lecturers.
Highlights: Sponsor has offered program since 1970. Certificate. Issues I-20AB, IAP-66. A foreign student counselor/adviser is available. Host family and special social activities are available.
Eligibility: *Academic:* bachelor's degree preferred. *Language:* English proficiency on intermediate level is required. TOEFL: 500. *Professional:* two years of experience in energy field preferred.
Cost: $8,600 for tuition, books.
Housing: Not provided; sponsor assists in locating housing.
Application: *Deadline:* none. *Fee:* none.
Contact: Judith H. Francis, Admissions Coordinator and Registrar, Arthur D. Little Management Education Institute, 35 Acorn Park, Cambridge, MA 02140; (617) 864-5657. Telex: 921436.

M7 SONOMA STATE UNIVERSITY
Certificate in Energy Management and Design.
Dates: One year: classes begin in Sept.
Location: Rohnert Park, California: on campus, at professional work site.
Instruction: *Methods:* discussion groups, lectures, case studies, field trips, individualized instruction, "hands-on" training, computer-assisted instruction, science laboratories. *By:* faculty.
Highlights: Sponsor has offered program since 1976. Certificate. Practical training is a program component; participants are paid. A foreign student counselor/adviser is available. 20 per year total enrollment; 5% foreign enrollment in 1985.
Eligibility: *Academic:* bachelor's degree. *Language:* English proficiency on beginning level is required. *Professional:* none.
Cost: $280 per semester for tuition, health insurance. *Scholarships:* none.
Housing: Not provided; sponsor assists in locating housing.
Application: *Deadline:* Aug. 1. *Fee:* $35; not refundable.
Contact: W.J. (Rocky) Rohwedder, Asst. Professor, Energy Management and Design, Sonoma State University, Rohnert Park, CA 94928; (707) 664-2306.

M8 UNIVERSITY OF PENNSYLVANIA
Special Course in Energy.
Specialization: Energy management and policy; fully sponsored by USAID.
Dates: Jan.–Aug.
Location: Philadelphia, Pennsylvania: on campus.
Instruction: *Methods:* lectures, discussion groups, case studies, field trips, independent study/research, computer-assisted instruction. *By:* faculty, guest speakers/lecturers.
Highlights: New program. Certificate. Foreign nationals on tourist visas are not eligible to enroll. A foreign student counselor/adviser is available. 24 total enrollment; 100% foreign enrollment in 1986.
Eligibility: *Academic:* bachelor's degree. *Language:* English proficiency on advanced level is required. TOEFL: 500. *Professional:* none.

Abbreviations: ESL = English as a Second Language; TOEFL = Test of English as a Foreign Language; ALIGU = American Language Institute of Georgetown University; GPA = Grade Point Average; SAT = Scholastic Aptitude Test; GED = General Equivalency Diploma.

Cost: Not given. *Scholarships:* all students sponsored by USAID.
Housing: Provided.
Application: *Deadline:* Oct. 1. *Fee:* none.
Contact: USAID office in participant's country.

M9 UNIVERSITY OF PENNSYLVANIA
Appropriate Technology and Energy Management for Development.
Specialization: Focus on rural and urban areas in developing countries.
Dates: Sept.–Dec. or Jan.–May.
Location: Philadelphia, Pennsylvania: on campus.
Instruction: *Methods:* lectures, discussion groups. *By:* faculty.
Highlights: Sponsor has offered program since 1983. Certificate upon completion of four courses. Issues I-20AB, IAP-66. Foreign nationals on tourist visas are eligible to enroll. A foreign student counselor/adviser is available. Orientation programs.
Eligibility: *Academic:* bachelor's degree. *Language:* English proficiency on advanced level is required. TOEFL: 500. *Professional:* three years of field experience in a developing country.
Cost: About $16,000 inclusive. *Scholarships:* none.
Housing: Not provided; sponsor assists in locating housing.
Application: *Deadline:* July 1. *Fee:* $40; not refundable.
Contact: Dr. Lucy Creevey, Program in Appropriate Technology and Energy Management for Development, University of Pennsylvania, 3400 Walnut Street, Philadelphia, PA 19104; (215) 898-6445 or 898-6429. Cable: PNSYL Phila PA. Telex: 710-670-0328.

M10 UNIVERSITY OF PENNSYLVANIA
Energy Management for Development.
Specialization: Master's program emphasizes the engineering and social considerations of energy utilization.
Dates: Sept.–Aug.
Location: Philadelphia, Pennsylvania: on campus. Summer field course in developing country in Western hemisphere.
Instruction: *Methods:* lectures, discussion groups, independent study/research. *By:* faculty, guest speakers/lecturers.
Highlights: Sponsor has offered program since 1983. Master's degree upon completion of thesis and summer field course. Issues I-20AB. Foreign nationals on tourist visas are not eligible to enroll. A foreign student counselor/adviser is available. Orientation programs.
Eligibility: *Academic:* bachelor's degree; knowledge of engineering. *Language:* English proficiency on advanced level is required. TOEFL: 500. *Professional:* none.
Cost: About $21,000 inclusive. *Scholarships:* none.
Housing: Not provided; sponsor assists in locating housing.
Application: *Deadline:* July 15. *Fee:* $40; not refundable.
Contact: Dr. Lucy Creevey, Program in Appropriate Technology and Energy Management for Development, University of Pennsylvania, 3400 Walnut Street, Philadelphia, PA 19104; (215) 898-6445 or 898-6429. Cable: PNSYL Phila PA. Telex: 710-670-0328.

M11 UNIVERSITY OF PITTSBURGH, INSTITUTE OF TRAINING AND ORGANIZATIONAL DEVELOPMENT (ITOD)
Energy Management.
Specialization: Management of energy and energy resources.
Dates: Three months: classes begin in April.
Location: Pittsburgh, Pennsylvania: on campus, at professional work site.
Instruction: *Methods:* discussion groups, lectures, case studies. *By:* university faculty, industrial lecturers.
Highlights: Sponsor has offered program since 1983. Certificate. Issues IAP-66. Various support services are available. Unlimited total enrollment; 100% foreign enrollment in 1985.
Eligibility: *Academic:* associate's or bachelor's degree recommended. *Language:* English

All program information is subject to change without notice
and must be confirmed directly with the sponsor.

116

proficiency on intermediate level is required. *Professional:* course geared to executives and professionals in energy or related fields.
Cost: $4,950 for tuition, books and materials, health insurance. *Scholarships:* none.
Housing: Not provided; sponsor assists in locating housing.
Application: *Deadline:* six weeks prior. *Fee:* $200; applied to tuition.
Contact: Mr. Ron Gigliotti, ITOD, University of Pittsburgh, 3J03 Forbes Quadrangle, Pittsburgh, PA 15260; (412) 648-7430. Telex: 812466 or 199126.

GEOGRAPHIC INFORMATION SYSTEMS

M12 CENTRAL WASHINGTON UNIVERSITY
Geographic Information Systems Laboratory.
Specialization: Geographic information systems and resource management.
Dates: Vary.
Location: Ellensburg, Washington: on campus.
Instruction: *Methods:* lectures, individualized instruction, "hands-on" training, computer-assisted instruction. *By:* faculty. *Also available in Spanish.*
Highlights: Sponsor has offered program since 1985. Certificate. Issues I-20AB, I-20MN, IAP-66. Foreign nationals on tourist visas are eligible to enroll. A foreign student counselor/adviser is available. ESL program and Office of International Programs. 8 per session total enrollment; no foreign enrollment in 1985.
Eligibility: *Academic:* associate's degree; background in resource-related field.
Language: English proficiency on advanced level is required. TOEFL: 500; Univ. of Michigan Language Test: 80. *Professional:* two years of experience.
Cost: About $7,000 per year inclusive. *Scholarships:* none.
Housing: In dormitories, furnished rooms.
Application: *Deadline:* two months prior. *Fee:* $25; not refundable.
Contact: William C. Smith, GIS Laboratory, Central Washington University, Ellensburg, WA 98926; (509) 963-1188.

PROFESSIONAL DEVELOPMENT

M13 AMERICAN CULTURAL EXCHANGE
ITEP Program—Management/Personal Development.
Specialization: Management training in negotiation, report writing, multicultural training, professional counterpart matching, individualized curriculum based on needs assessment.
Dates: Classes begin monthly.
Location: Seattle and Tacoma, Washington: on campus, at professional work site.
Instruction: *Methods:* discussion groups, lectures, case studies, field trips, individualized instruction, independent study/research, computer-assisted instruction, language laboratories. *By:* faculty, guest speakers/lecturers.
Highlights: Sponsor has offered program since 1980. Certificate. Foreign nationals on tourist visas are eligible to enroll. A foreign student counselor/adviser is available. Host family program. 4 per month total enrollment; 100% foreign enrollment in 1985.
Eligibility: *Academic:* bachelor's degree. *Language:* English proficiency on intermediate level is required. *Professional:* 3–5 years of experience; middle management or professionals preferred.
Cost: $2,840–$4,025 for tuition, books and materials, meals, field trips, seminars.
Scholarships: none.
Housing: In dormitories, apartments, furnished rooms, in hotels, with families.
Application: *Deadline:* 15 days prior. *Fee:* $50; not refundable.
Contact: Burton E. Bard, Jr., American Cultural Exchange, 1107 NE 45th, Suite 315A, Seattle, WA 98105; (206) 633-3239. Telex: 329473 BURGESS SEA.

Abbreviations: ESL = English as a Second Language; TOEFL = Test of English as a Foreign Language; ALIGU = American Language Institute of Georgetown University; GPA = Grade Point Average; SAT = Scholastic Aptitude Test; GED = General Equivalency Diploma.

M14 THE AMERICAN UNIVERSITY
Graduate Certificate in Professional Development.
Specialization: Graduate-level program to assist in meeting specific personal or professional goals.
Dates: Classes begin in Sept., Jan., May, July.
Location: Washington, D.C.: on campus.
Instruction: *Methods:* discussion groups, lectures, case studies. *By:* faculty.
Highlights: Sponsor has offered program previously. Certificate. Issues I-20AB. Foreign nationals on tourist visas are not eligible to enroll. A foreign student counselor/adviser is available. Orientation and ESL programs.
Eligibility: *Academic:* bachelor's degree. *Language:* English proficiency on advanced level is required. TOEFL: 600; English Language Institute Placement Test. *Professional:* none.
Cost: $299 per semester hour for tuition. *Scholarships:* none.
Housing: Not provided; sponsor assists in locating housing.
Application: *Deadline:* none. *Fee:* none.
Contact: Programs Advisement Center, The American University, 4400 Massachusetts Ave. NW, Room 153 McKinley Bldg., Washington, DC 20016; (202) 885-2500.

M15 ECONOMICS INSTITUTE
Professional Development Program.
Specialization: Project planning, implementation, and evaluation.
Dates: Five weeks: classes begin about monthly.
Location: Boulder, Colorado: on campus, at professional work site.
Instruction: *Methods:* discussion groups, lectures, case studies, field trips, individualized instruction, "hands-on" training, independent study/research, computer-assisted instruction, language laboratories. *By:* faculty, guest speakers/lecturers.
Highlights: Sponsor has offered program since 1958. Certificate or diploma. Practical training is a program component; participants may be paid. Issues I-20AB. Foreign nationals on tourist visas are eligible to enroll. A foreign student counselor/adviser is available. 1,000 per year total enrollment; 100% foreign enrollment in 1985.
Eligibility: *Academic:* bachelor's degree. *Language:* English proficiency on intermediate level is required. TOEFL: 425. *Professional:* 3–10 years of experience preferred.
Cost: About $2,047 per month inclusive. *Scholarships:* partial.
Housing: In dormitories, apartments, furnished rooms, in hotels, with families.
Application: *Deadline:* none. *Fee:* $50; refundable to attendees. *Scholarship deadline:* none.
Contact: Admissions Office, Economics Institute, 2030 13th Street, Boulder, CO 80302; (303) 492-8419. Telex: 450385 ECONINST BDR.

REGIONAL RESOURCES MANAGEMENT

M16 WESTERN CAROLINA UNIVERSITY and THE TENNESSEE VALLEY AUTHORITY
Integrated Regional Resources Management.
Specialization: Principles and values of integrated resources management, development of programs and projects, synergistic effects of integrated management, applications to participants' own region or work. Specialists discuss water, agriculture, fertilizer and chemicals, forest, wildlife, air, and energy resources, community development, and land use.
Dates: Eight weeks: to be arranged.
Location: Cullowhee, North Carolina, and the Tennessee Valley, Tennessee: on campus, at professional work site.
Instruction: *Methods:* discussion groups, lectures, case studies, field trips, "hands-on" training, computer-assisted instruction, science laboratories. *By:* faculty, guest speakers/lecturers.
Highlights: New program. Certificate. Issues I-20AB, I-20MN, IAP-66. Foreign nationals on

All program information is subject to change without notice and must be confirmed directly with the sponsor.

118

tourist visas are not eligible to enroll. A foreign student counselor/adviser is available.
Various support services are available. 25 total enrollment.
Eligibility: *Academic:* bachelor's degree or equivalent preferred. *Language:* English
proficiency on intermediate level is required. TOEFL: 500; ALIGU: 240.
Professional: managers or potential managers of resource development projects preferred.
Cost: To be arranged. *Scholarships:* none.
Housing: In dormitories.
Application: *Deadline:* not given. *Fee:* none.
Contact: Dr. John D. McCrone, School of Arts and Sciences, Western Carolina University,
Cullowhee, NC 28723; (704) 227-7436 or 227-7495. Telex: 4946590 WCARUNV.

REMOTE SENSING

M17 MURRAY STATE UNIVERSITY, MID-AMERICA REMOTE SENSING CENTER (MARC)
Remote Sensing Technology Transfer.
Specialization: Remote sensing of natural resources, digital image processing of satellite
remote sensing data.
Dates: To be arranged.
Location: Murray, Kentucky: on campus.
Instruction: *Methods:* discussion groups, lectures, case studies, field trips, individualized
instruction, "hands-on" training, independent study/research, computer-assisted instruction,
language laboratories, science laboratories. *By:* faculty. *Also in Spanish.*
Highlights: Sponsor has offered program since 1979. Certificate. Practical training is a
program component; participants are not paid. Issues I-20AB, I-20MN, IAP-66. Foreign
nationals on tourist visas are eligible to enroll. A foreign student counselor/adviser is
available. 15 total enrollment; 35% foreign enrollment in 1985.
Eligibility: *Academic:* bachelor's degree. *Language:* English proficiency on intermediate level
is preferred. *Professional:* none.
Cost: Varies. *Scholarships:* none.
Housing: Provided.
Application: *Deadline:* two months prior. *Fee:* none.
Contact: Dr. Neil V. Weber, Director, Mid-American Remote Sensing Center, Murray State
University, Murray, KY 42071; (502) 762-2149.

M18 SOUTH DAKOTA STATE UNIVERSITY
Remote Sensing Short Courses.
Specialization: Intensive courses in remote sensing technology as applied to agriculture, land
use management, natural resources, geology, mapping, archaeology.
Dates: Two weeks: classes begin year-round.
Location: Brookings, South Dakota: on campus, at professional work site.
Instruction: *Methods:* discussion groups, lectures, case studies, field trips, individualized
instruction, "hands-on" training, independent study/research, computer-assisted instruction.
By: faculty. *Also in French.*
Highlights: Sponsor has offered program since 1982. Certificate. Practical training is a
program component; participants are not paid. Foreign nationals on tourist visas are eligible
to enroll. A foreign student counselor/adviser is available. 30 total enrollment; 50% foreign
enrollment in 1985.
Eligibility: *Academic:* associate's degree. *Language:* English proficiency on intermediate level
is preferred. *Professional:* experience in related area preferred.
Cost: $500–$700 per week for tuition, materials. *Scholarships:* none.
Housing: Not provided; sponsor assists in locating housing.
Application: *Deadline:* one month prior. *Fee:* none.

Abbreviations: ESL = English as a Second Language; TOEFL = Test of English as a Foreign Language;
ALIGU = American Language Institute of Georgetown University; GPA = Grade Point Average;
SAT = Scholastic Aptitude Test; GED = General Equivalency Diploma.

Contact: Ms. Barbara Dyer, Remote Sensing Institute, South Dakota State University, Box 507, Wenona Hall, Brookings, SD 57007-0199; (605) 688-4184. Telex: 910 668 6894. RSI SDSU BKNG.

M19 SOUTH DAKOTA STATE UNIVERSITY
Visiting International Scientist Program.
Specialization: Remote sensing research and application. Latest aspects of remote sensing technology are practicably applied to natural resources and land use management in participants' country.

Dates: To be arranged.

Location: Brookings, South Dakota: on campus, at professional work site.

Instruction: *Methods:* discussion groups, lectures, case studies, field trips, individualized instruction, "hands-on" training, independent study/research, computer-assisted instruction. *By:* faculty, guest speakers/lecturers. *Also in French.*

Highlights: Sponsor has offered program since 1979. Certificate. Practical training is a program component; participants are not paid. Foreign nationals on tourist visas are eligible to enroll. A foreign student counselor/adviser is available. 20 total enrollment; 100% foreign enrollment in 1985.

Eligibility: *Academic:* associate's degree. *Language:* English proficiency on intermediate level is preferred. *Professional:* experience in a related area.

Cost: $3,000 per month for tuition, materials, photo lab, computer time, use of in-house imagery, EROS Data Center tours, limited field trips. *Scholarships:* none.

Housing: Not provided; sponsor assists in locating housing.

Application: *Deadline:* one month prior. *Fee:* none.

Contact: Mr. K.J. Dalsted, Remote Sensing Institute, South Dakota State University, Box 507, Wenona Hall, Brookings, SD 57007-0199; (605) 688-4184. Telex: 910 668 6894 RSI SDSU BKNG.

LIBRARY AND INFORMATION SCIENCES

N1 SIMMONS COLLEGE
Graduate School of Library and Information Science.
Specialization: Master's program in school librarianship, records management, archives.
Dates: Eleven months: classes begin in Sept., Jan., June.
Location: Boston, Massachusetts: on campus.
Instruction: *Methods:* discussion groups, lectures, case studies, field trips, "hands-on" training, independent study/research, computer-assisted instruction. *By:* faculty.
Highlights: Sponsor has offered program since 1902. Certificate upon completion of 36 semester hours with B average. Issues I-20AB, IAP-66. Foreign nationals on tourist visas are not eligible to enroll. A foreign student counselor/adviser is available. 150 per year total enrollment; 5% foreign enrollment in 1985.
Eligibility: *Academic:* bachelor's degree. *Language:* English proficiency on advanced level is required. TOEFL: 550; Univ. of Michigan Language Test: 91. *Professional:* none.
Cost: $19,000 for tuition, books and materials, meals, housing, infirmary use, health insurance. *Scholarships:* none.
Housing: In dormitories for women; with families for men and women.
Application: *Deadline:* two months prior. *Fee:* $25; not refundable.
Contact: Ms. Judith B. Yenawine, Director of Admissions, Simmons College Graduate School of Library and Information Science, 300 The Fenway, Boston, MA 02115; (617) 738-2264.

N2 SAM HOUSTON STATE UNIVERSITY
Master of Library Science.
Dates: Not given.
Location: Huntsville, Edinburg, Laredo, and Corpus Christi, Texas: on campus, at professional work site.
Instruction: *Methods:* discussion groups, lectures, case studies, field trips, "hands-on" training, computer-assisted instruction. *By:* faculty.
Highlights: Sponsor has offered program since 1972. Certificate. Practical training is a program component. Issues I-20MN. Foreign nationals on tourist visas are not eligible to enroll. A foreign student counselor/adviser is not available. Unlimited total enrollment; 1% foreign enrollment in 1985.
Eligibility: *Academic:* bachelor's degree. *Language:* English proficiency on advanced level is required. TOEFL: 500. *Professional:* none.
Cost: Not given. *Scholarships:* none.
Housing: In dormitories.
Application: *Deadline:* not given. *Fee:* not given.
Contact: Dr. Bonnie Thorne, School of Library Science, Sam Houston State University, Huntsville, TX 77341; (409) 294-1153.

N3 SYRACUSE UNIVERSITY
Specialization: Master's degree in library science.
Dates: Nine months: classes begin in Sept., Jan., and May. Two-week workshops available in May, June, and July.

Abbreviations: ESL = English as a Second Language; TOEFL = Test of English as a Foreign Language; ALIGU = American Language Institute of Georgetown University; GPA = Grade Point Average; SAT = Scholastic Aptitude Test; GED = General Equivalency Diploma.

Location: Syracuse, New York: on campus, at professional work site.
Instruction: *Methods:* lectures, field trips, "hands-on" training, independent study/research. *By:* faculty, guest speakers/lecturers.
Highlights: Sponsor has offered program previously. Master's degree upon completion of 36 graduate credits. Practical training is a program component; participants are paid. Issues I-20AB. Foreign nationals on tourist visas are eligible to enroll. A foreign student counselor/adviser is available. International Living Center. 100 total enrollment; 20% foreign enrollment in 1985.
Eligibility: *Academic:* bachelor's degree. *Language:* English proficiency is required. TOEFL: 550. *Professional:* none.
Cost: $9,000 for tuition. *Scholarships:* partial.
Housing: In dormitories, furnished rooms.
Application: *Deadline:* July for fall, Nov. for spring, May for summer. *Fee:* $30; not refundable. *Scholarship deadline:* March for fall and summer, Nov. for spring
Contact: Jeffrey Katzer, Interim Dean, School of Information Studies, Syracuse University, Syracuse, NY 13244-2340; (315) 423-2911.

N4 TEXAS WOMAN'S UNIVERSITY
MLS in Library Science.
Specialization: Graduate program for men and women: information centers; corporate, academic, special, and public school librarianship; comparative librarianship.
Dates: One year: classes begin in Sept., Jan., June.
Location: Denton, Texas: on campus.
Instruction: *Methods:* discussion groups, lectures, case studies, field trips, individualized instruction, "hands-on" training, independent study/research, computer-assisted instruction, language laboratories, science laboratories. *By:* faculty, guest speakers/lecturers. *Also in Spanish.*
Highlights: Sponsor has offered program since 1929. Certificate. Practical training is a program component; participants may be paid. Issues I-20AB, IAP-66. Foreign nationals on tourist visas are eligible to enroll part-time. A foreign student counselor/adviser is available. 300 total enrollment; 4% foreign enrollment in 1985.
Eligibility: *Academic:* bachelor's degree with 3.0 GPA. *Language:* English proficiency on intermediate level is preferred. TOEFL: 550; TSE: 200. *Professional:* none.
Cost: $12,000 per year for tuition, books and materials, meals, housing, health insurance. *Scholarships:* partial after first semester of enrollment.
Housing: In dormitories, apartments.
Application: *Deadline:* five months prior. *Fee:* none. *Scholarship deadline:* five months prior.
Contact: Dr. Brooke E. Sheldon, Dean, School of Library and Information Studies, Texas Woman's University, Box 22905, Denton, TX 76204; (817) 898-2602.

N5 UNIVERSITY OF ALABAMA, GRADUATE SCHOOL OF LIBRARY SERVICE
Master of Library Science.
Specialization: Information science, book arts, educational media.
Dates: One year: classes begin in Aug., Jan., June.
Location: Tuscaloosa, Alabama: on campus.
Instruction: *Methods:* discussion groups, lectures, case studies, field trips, individualized instruction, "hands-on" training, independent study/research, computer-assisted instruction. *By:* faculty.
Highlights: Sponsor has offered program since 1970. Certificate upon completion of 36 graduate credits. Issues I-20AB, IAP-66. Foreign nationals on tourist visas are not eligible to enroll. A foreign student counselor/adviser is available. ESL program and International House. Unlimited total enrollment; 10% foreign enrollment in 1985.
Eligibility: *Academic:* bachelor's degree. *Language:* English proficiency on advanced level is required. TOEFL: 525. *Professional:* none.
Cost: $7,168 for tuition, meals, housing, health insurance. *Scholarships:* partial.

Housing: In dormitories, apartments.

Application: *Deadline:* six weeks prior. *Fee:* $15; not refundable. *Scholarship deadline:* Apr. 15.

Contact: Dean James D. Ramer, University of Alabama, P.O. Box 6242, University, AL 35486; (205) 348-4610.

N6 UNIVERSITY OF WISCONSIN—MILWAUKEE, LIBRARY & INFORMATION SCIENCE

Summer Program in Information Science.

Specialization: Technology for information storage and retrieval, information networks, automation of library archives, records services.

Dates: Three months: classes begin in May.

Location: Milwaukee, Wisconsin: on campus, at professional work site.

Instruction: *Methods:* discussion groups, lectures, case studies, field trips, individualized instruction, "hands-on" training, independent study/research. *By:* faculty, guest speakers/lecturers.

Highlights: Sponsor has offered program since 1982. Certificate upon completion of program with 3.0 GPA. Practical training is a program component; participants are not paid. Issues I-20AB, IAP-66. Foreign nationals on tourist visas are not eligible to enroll. A foreign student counselor/adviser is available. Tutoring program. 2 total enrollment; no foreign enrollment in 1985.

Eligibility: *Academic:* bachelor's degree. *Language:* English proficiency on advanced level is required. TOEFL: 500–550; Univ. of Michigan Language Test: 80–85.

Professional: experience in library or information services preferred.

Cost: $6,000 inclusive. *Scholarships:* none.

Housing: In dormitories, apartments.

Application: *Deadline:* May 1. *Fee:* $40; not refundable.

Contact: Dean Mohammed M. Aman, University of Wisconsin—Milwaukee, P.O. Box 413, Milwaukee, WI 53201; (414) 963-4707. Cable: UWM-SLIS, Milw., WI 53201. Telex: 4909991372.

Abbreviations: ESL = English as a Second Language; TOEFL = Test of English as a Foreign Language; ALIGU = American Language Institute of Georgetown University; GPA = Grade Point Average; SAT = Scholastic Aptitude Test; GED = General Equivalency Diploma.

123

LIFE SCIENCES

O1 CLEMSON UNIVERSITY
International Visitor Program.
Specialization: Personalized programs in life sciences, combining study, research, and internships. Undergraduate, graduate, and postgraduate levels.
Dates: Rolling: semesters begin in Aug., Jan.
Location: Clemson, South Carolina: on campus.
Instruction: *Methods:* lectures, individualized instruction, "hands-on" training, independent study/research, computer-assisted instruction, laboratories. *By:* faculty.
Highlights: Sponsor has offered program previously. Certificate. Practical training may be a program component; participants are paid. Issues I-20AB, IAP-66. Foreign nationals on tourist visas are eligible to enroll. A foreign student counselor/adviser is available.
Eligibility: *Academic:* bachelor's degree or some undergraduate work. *Language:* English proficiency on the advanced level is required. TOEFL: 550. *Professional:* requires professional certification.
Cost: $815 per month for tuition, books and materials, meals, housing, health insurance. *Scholarships:* none; all participants must be sponsored by an organization.
Housing: In dormitories.
Application: *Deadline:* rolling. *Fee:* none.
Contact: International Service Office, Clemson University, Room 106 Sikes Hall, Clemson, SC 29631; (803) 656-5466.

BIOLOGY

O2 GUILFORD COLLEGE
Specialization: Programs available in biology, history and philosophy of science, other sciences.
Dates: One year: classes begin in Aug.
Location: Greensboro, North Carolina: on campus.
Instruction: *Methods:* lectures, discussion groups, science labs. *By:* faculty.
Highlights: Sponsor has offered program previously. Certificate upon completion of 4–6 courses. Issues I-20AB, I-20MN. Foreign nationals on tourist visas are not eligible to enroll. A foreign student counselor/adviser is available. International student club membership.
Eligibility: *Academic:* bachelor's degree. *Language:* English proficiency on advanced level is required. TOEFL: 500. *Professional:* none.
Cost: $112 per credit hour. *Scholarships:* none.
Housing: Not provided; student makes own arrangements.
Application: *Deadline:* open. *Fee:* $20; not refundable.
Contact: Dean of Admissions and Financial Aid, Guilford College, 5800 West Friendly Ave., Greensboro, NC 27410; (919) 292-5511.

O3 SOUTHERN ILLINOIS UNIVERSITY, EDWARDSVILLE
M.S. Biology.
Specialization: Broadly based master's program in biological sciences.
Dates: Sept.–Aug.

All program information is subject to change without notice
and must be confirmed directly with the sponsor.

Location: Edwardsville, Illinois: on campus.
Instruction: *Methods:* discussion groups, lectures, field trips, individualized instruction, independent study/research, science laboratories. *By:* faculty.
Highlights: Sponsor has offered program since 1965. Certificate. Foreign nationals on tourist visas are eligible to enroll. A foreign student counselor/adviser is available. Unlimited total enrollment; 5% foreign enrollment in 1985.
Eligibility: *Academic:* bachelor's degree. *Language:* TOEFL. *Professional:* none.
Cost: Not given. *Scholarships:* none.
Housing: In apartments.
Application: *Deadline:* one month prior. *Fee:* none.
Contact: Dr. M. Levy, Biology Dept., Southern Illinois University, Box 1651, Edwardsville, IL 62026; (618) 692-3927.

O4 STATE UNIVERSITY COLLEGE AT GENESEO, COLLEGE OF ARTS AND SCIENCE
Master of Arts.
Specialization: Master's program in biology.
Dates: Sept.–Aug.
Location: Geneseo, New York: on campus.
Instruction: *Methods:* discussion groups, lectures, case studies, field trips, individualized instruction, independent study/research, computer-assisted instruction, language laboratories, science laboratories. *By:* faculty.
Highlights: Sponsor has offered program previously. Certificate. A foreign student counselor/adviser is available. No foreign enrollment in 1985.
Eligibility: *Academic:* bachelor's degree. *Language:* English proficiency on advanced level is required. *Professional:* none.
Cost: $6,280 for tuition, meals, housing, fees. *Scholarships:* none.
Housing: In dormitories.
Application: *Deadline:* not given. *Fee:* $20; not refundable.
Contact: Dr. Robert Simon, College of Arts and Science, SUC at Geneseo, Bailey 106B, Geneseo, NY 14454; (716) 245-5301.

O5 VOORHEES COLLEGE
Biology.
Dates: Aug.–May: classes begin in Aug. and Jan.
Location: Denmark, South Carolina: on campus, at professional work site.
Instruction: *Methods:* discussion groups, lectures, case studies, field trips, individualized instruction, "hands-on" training, independent study/research, computer-assisted instruction, science laboratories. *By:* faculty.
Highlights: Sponsor has offered program since 1969. Certificate. Issues I-20AB. Foreign nationals on tourist visas are not eligible to enroll. A foreign student counselor/adviser is available.
Eligibility: *Academic:* associate's degree. *Language:* English proficiency on beginning level is required. TOEFL. *Professional:* none.
Cost: $5,884 for tuition, meals, housing, health insurance. *Scholarships:* none.
Housing: In dormitories.
Application: *Deadline:* Aug. *Fee:* $10; not refundable.
Contact: Dr. Lucious Daily, Jr., Director of Admissions and Records, Voorhees College, Voorhees Road, Denmark, SC 29042; (803) 793-3351.

Abbreviations: ESL = English as a Second Language; TOEFL = Test of English as a Foreign Language; ALIGU = American Language Institute of Georgetown University; GPA = Grade Point Average; SAT = Scholastic Aptitude Test; GED = General Equivalency Diploma.

BIOPHYSICS

O6 UNIVERSITY OF MARYLAND AT BALTIMORE
Ion Transport Thru Cell Membranes.
Specialization: Biophysics.
Dates: Early Sept.–late Aug.
Location: Baltimore, Maryland: on campus.
Instruction: *Methods:* discussion groups, lectures, independent study/research. *By:* faculty.
Highlights: Sponsor has offered program since 1980. Issues IAP-66. Foreign nationals on tourist visas are eligible to enroll. A foreign student counselor/adviser is available.
Eligibility: *Academic:* bachelor's degree. *Language:* TOEFL. *Professional:* none.
Cost: Not given. *Scholarships:* none.
Housing: Not provided.
Application: *Deadline:* none. *Fee:* not given.
Contact: Department of Biophysics, University of Maryland at Baltimore, 660 W. Redwood Street, Room 455 Howard Hall, Baltimore, MD 21201; (301) 528-7940.

BIOTECHNOLOGY

O7 MASSACHUSETTS INSTITUTE OF TECHNOLOGY
Biotechnology Process Engineering Center.
Specialization: Biotechnology: microbial principles and processes for fuels, chemicals, and biologicals; downstream processing; fermentation technology.
Dates: Aug. 4–22.
Location: Cambridge, Massachusetts: on campus.
Instruction: *Methods:* discussion groups, lectures, case studies, "hands-on" training, independent study/research, computer-assisted instruction, science laboratories. *By:* faculty.
Highlights: Sponsor has offered program since 1949. Certificate. Foreign nationals on tourist visas are eligible to enroll. A foreign student counselor/adviser is not available. About 20–25 per class total enrollment; 10% foreign enrollment in 1985.
Eligibility: *Academic:* bachelor's degree. *Language:* English proficiency on intermediate level is required. *Professional:* none.
Cost: About $1,500 per week for tuition, books and materials, meals, housing. *Scholarships:* none.
Housing: In dormitories, hotels.
Application: *Deadline:* depends on program. *Fee:* none.
Contact: Summer Session Office, Massachusetts Institute of Technology, 77 Massachusetts Ave., Room E19-356, Cambridge, MA 02139; (617) 253-2101. Telex: 921473 MIT CAM.

BOTANY

O8 THE UNIVERSITY OF TENNESSEE, KNOXVILLE
Plant Cell and Tissue Culture.
Specialization: Plant propagation and production of chemicals with emphasis on the underlying science.
Dates: Two weeks: August.
Location: Knoxville, Tennessee: on campus.
Instruction: *Methods:* lectures, "hands-on" training, science laboratories. *By:* faculty.
Highlights: Sponsor has offered program since 1983. Certificate. Issues I-20AB, I-20MN, IAP-66. Foreign nationals on tourist visas are eligible to enroll. A foreign student counselor/adviser is available. International student office. 17 total enrollment; 20% foreign enrollment in 1985.

All program information is subject to change without notice
and must be confirmed directly with the sponsor.

Eligibility: *Academic:* some graduate work. *Language:* English proficiency on advanced level is required. *Professional:* none.
Cost: $1,100 for tuition, books and materials. *Scholarships:* none.
Housing: Not provided; sponsor assists in locating housing.
Application: *Deadline:* July 1. *Fee:* none.
Contact: Dr. D.K. Dougall, Botany Department, The University of Tennessee, Knoxville, TN 37996-1100; (615) 974-2256.

ENVIRONMENTAL SCIENCE

O9 COLLEGE OF THE ATLANTIC
Workshop in Environmental Studies.
Specialization: Field ecology, environmental chemistry, marine mammals.
Dates: Two weeks: July.
Location: Bar Harbor, Maine: on campus.
Instruction: *Methods:* seminars, field study. *By:* faculty.
Highlights: Sponsor has offered program since 1981. Credit. Issues I-20. Limited services for foreign nationals. 48 total enrollment. List of past participants is available.
Eligibility: *Academic:* bachelor's degree. *Language:* not given. *Professional:* not given.
Cost: $625 for tuition, meals, housing. *Scholarships:* none.
Housing: In dormitories.
Application: *Deadline:* June 15. *Fee:* none.
Contact: Director of the Summer Program, College of the Atlantic, Bar Harbor, ME 04609; (207) 288-5015.

Abbreviations: ESL = English as a Second Language; TOEFL = Test of English as a Foreign Language; ALIGU = American Language Institute of Georgetown University; GPA = Grade Point Average; SAT = Scholastic Aptitude Test; GED = General Equivalency Diploma.

MATHEMATICS

P1 CLEMSON UNIVERSITY
International Visitor Program.
Specialization: Personalized programs in mathematics, combining study, research, and internships. Undergraduate, graduate, and postgraduate levels.
Dates: Rolling: semesters begin in Aug., Jan.
Location: Clemson, South Carolina: on campus.
Instruction: *Methods:* lectures, individualized instruction, "hands-on" training, independent study/research, computer-assisted instruction, laboratories. *By:* faculty.
Highlights: Sponsor has offered program previously. Certificate. Practical training may be a program component; participants are paid. Issues I-20AB, IAP-66. Foreign nationals on tourist visas are eligible to enroll. A foreign student counselor/adviser is available.
Eligibility: *Academic:* bachelor's degree or some undergraduate work. *Language:* English proficiency on the advanced level is required. TOEFL: 550. *Professional:* requires professional certification.
Cost: $815 per month for tuition, books and materials, meals, housing, health insurance. *Scholarships:* none; all participants must be sponsored by an organization.
Housing: In dormitories.
Application: *Deadline:* rolling. *Fee:* none.
Contact: International Service Office, Clemson University, Room 106 Sikes Hall, Clemson, SC 29631; (803) 656-5466.

P2 THE AMERICAN UNIVERSITY
Graduate Certificate in Applied Statistics.
Specialization: Applied statistics.
Dates: Classes begin in Sept., Jan., May, July.
Location: Washington, D.C.: on campus.
Instruction: *Methods:* discussion groups, lectures, case studies. *By:* faculty.
Highlights: Sponsor has offered program previously. Certificate upon completion of five courses. Issues I-20AB. Foreign nationals on tourist visas are not eligible to enroll. A foreign student counselor/adviser is available. Orientation and ESL programs.
Eligibility: *Academic:* bachelor's degree; undergraduate courses in mathematics. *Language:* English proficiency on advanced level is required. TOEFL: 600; English Language Institute Placement Test. *Professional:* none.
Cost: $299 per semester hour for tuition. *Scholarships:* none.
Housing: Not provided; sponsor assists in locating housing.
Application: *Deadline:* none. *Fee:* none.
Contact: Programs Advisement Center, The American University, 4400 Massachusetts Ave. NW, Room 153 McKinley Bldg., Washington, DC 20016; (202) 885-2500.

P3 GUILFORD COLLEGE
Specialization: Programs available in mathematics, physics, and history and philosophy of science.
Dates: One year: classes begin in Aug.
Location: Greensboro, North Carolina: on campus.

Instruction: *Methods:* lectures, discussion groups, science labs. *By:* faculty.
Highlights: Sponsor has offered program previously. Certificate upon completion of 4–6 courses. Issues I-20AB, I-20MN. Foreign nationals on tourist visas are not eligible to enroll. A foreign student counselor/adviser is available. International student club membership.
Eligibility: *Academic:* bachelor's degree. *Language:* English proficiency on advanced level is required. TOEFL: 500. *Professional:* none.
Cost: $112 per credit hour. *Scholarships:* none.
Housing: Not provided; student makes own arrangements.
Application: *Deadline:* open. *Fee:* $20; not refundable.
Contact: Dean of Admissions and Financial Aid, Guilford College, 5800 West Friendly Ave., Greensboro, NC 27410; (919) 292-5511.

P4 VOORHEES COLLEGE
Mathematics.
Dates: Aug.–May; classes begin in Aug. and Jan.
Location: Denmark, South Carolina: on campus, at professional work site.
Instruction: *Methods:* discussion groups, lectures, case studies, field trips, individualized instruction, "hands-on" training, independent study/research, computer-assisted instruction, science laboratories. *By:* faculty.
Highlights: Sponsor has offered program since 1969. Certificate. Practical training is a program component; participants are not paid. Issues I-20AB. Foreign nationals on tourist visas are not eligible to enroll. A foreign student counselor/adviser is available.
Eligibility: *Academic:* associate's degree. *Language:* English proficiency on beginning level is required. TOEFL. *Professional:* none.
Cost: $5,884 for tuition, meals, housing, health insurance. *Scholarships:* none.
Housing: In dormitories.
Application: *Deadline:* Aug. *Fee:* $10; not refundable.
Contact: Dr. Lucious Daily, Jr., Director of Admissions and Records, Voorhees College, Voorhees Road, Denmark, SC 29042; (803) 793-3351.

Abbreviations: ESL = English as a Second Language; TOEFL = Test of English as a Foreign Language; ALIGU = American Language Institute of Georgetown University; GPA = Grade Point Average; SAT = Scholastic Aptitude Test; GED = General Equivalency Diploma.

129

MEDICINE AND HEALTH SERVICES

Q1 SPARTAN HEALTH SCIENCES UNIVERSITY
Clinical Clerkships for M.D. Program.
Specialization: Participants must have completed Basic Medical Sciences.
Dates: One year: classes begin in Jan., April, Sept.
Location: Detroit, Michigan: on campus, at professional work site.
Instruction: *Methods:* discussion groups, lectures, case studies, field trips, "hands-on" training, independent study/research, science laboratories. *By:* faculty, guest speakers/lecturers.
Highlights: Sponsor has offered program since 1981. Certificate. Foreign nationals on tourist visas are eligible to enroll. A foreign student counselor/adviser is available. 25–30 total enrollment; 40% foreign enrollment in 1985.
Eligibility: *Academic:* bachelor's degree or premedical studies. *Language:* English proficiency on advanced level is required. TOEFL. *Professional:* none.
Cost: $2,850 per semester for tuition. *Scholarships:* partial.
Housing: Not provided; sponsor assists in locating housing.
Application: *Deadline:* one month prior. *Fee:* $60; not refundable. *Scholarship deadline:* one month prior.
Contact: Shakil A. Khan, M.D., Associate Dean, Spartan Health Sciences University, P.O. Box 1012, Detroit, MI 48231; (313) 963-7262.

Q2 UNIVERSITY OF KENTUCKY, COLLEGE OF MEDICINE
Specialization: University of Heidelberg exchange program.
Dates: One year: classes begin in Aug.
Location: Lexington, Kentucky: on campus, at professional work site.
Instruction: *Methods:* discussion groups, lectures, case studies, individualized instruction, "hands-on" training, independent study/research, computer-assisted instruction, science laboratories. *By:* faculty.
Highlights: Sponsor has offered program since 1960. Certificate. Issues IAP-66. Foreign nationals on tourist visas are not eligible to enroll. A foreign student counselor/adviser is available. 2 total enrollment.
Eligibility: *Academic:* enrollment in medical school. *Language:* English proficiency on advanced level is required. TOEFL: 550. *Professional:* none.
Cost: Not given. *Scholarships:* none.
Housing: Not provided; sponsor assists in locating housing.
Application: *Deadline:* not given. *Fee:* not given.
Contact: Dr. David Bettez, College of Medicine, University of Kentucky, 118 Bradley Hall, Lexington, KY 40536; (606) 257-8908.

Q3 WAKE FOREST UNIVERSITY, BOWMAN GRAY SCHOOL OF MEDICINE
International Fellowships.
Specialization: Fellowships in basic research, clinical disciplines, and health administration, primarily for the development of young faculty members for service in their own countries.
Dates: Vary.
Location: Winston-Salem, North Carolina: on campus, at professional work site.

All program information is subject to change without notice
and must be confirmed directly with the sponsor.

Instruction: *Methods:* discussion groups, lectures, case studies, individualized instruction, "hands-on" training, independent study/research, computer-assisted instruction, science laboratories. *By:* faculty.

Highlights: Sponsor has offered program since 1980. Certificate. Practical training is a program component; participants may be paid. Issues IAP-66. Foreign nationals on tourist visas are eligible to enroll. A foreign student counselor/adviser is available. Less than 1% foreign enrollment in 1985.

Eligibility: *Academic:* doctorate. *Language:* English proficiency on intermediate level is required. Personal interview. *Professional:* clear commitment to return to country of origin.

Cost: Varies. *Scholarships:* none.

Housing: Not provided; sponsor assists in locating housing.

Application: *Deadline:* none. *Fee:* none.

Contact: Office of International Health Affairs, Bowman Gray School of Medicine, Wake Forest University, 300 S. Hawthorne Road, Winston-Salem, NC 27103; (919) 748-4671. Telex: 806449BGSMWSL.

AUDIOLOGY AND SPEECH PATHOLOGY

Q4 STATE UNIVERSITY COLLEGE AT GENESEO
Master of Arts.

Specialization: Audiology, speech pathology.

Dates: One year: classes begin in Sept.

Location: Geneseo, New York: on campus.

Instruction: *Methods:* discussion groups, lectures, case studies, field trips, individualized instruction, independent study/research, computer-assisted instruction, language laboratories, science laboratories. *By:* faculty.

Highlights: Sponsor has offered program previously. Certificate. A foreign student counselor/adviser is available. No foreign enrollment in 1985.

Eligibility: *Academic:* bachelor's degree. *Language:* English proficiency on advanced level is required. *Professional:* none.

Cost: $6,280 for tuition, fees, meals, housing. *Scholarships:* none.

Housing: In dormitories.

Application: *Deadline:* none. *Fee:* $20; not refundable.

Contact: Dr. Ronald Sitler, SUC at Geneseo, Sturges 218, Geneseo, NY 14454; (716) 245-5328.

CHILD HEALTH CARE

Q5 BOSTON UNIVERSITY
Management for Child Survival.

Specialization: Management of maternal and child health services in developing countries; essentials of child survival, health economics, management methods, microcomputer applications, and community participation.

Dates: Six weeks: classes begin in March.

Location: Boston, Massachusetts: on campus, at professional work site.

Instruction: *Methods:* discussion groups, lectures, case studies, field trips, "hands-on" training. *By:* faculty, guest speakers/lecturers.

Highlights: Sponsor has offered program since 1986. Certificate. Issues IAP-66. Foreign nationals on tourist visas are eligible to enroll. A foreign student counselor/adviser is available. 25 total enrollment; 100% foreign enrollment in 1985.

Eligibility: *Academic:* bachelor's degree preferred. *Language:* English proficiency on intermediate level is required. *Professional:* 4–5 years primary health care management experience preferred.

Abbreviations: ESL = English as a Second Language; TOEFL = Test of English as a Foreign Language; ALIGU = American Language Institute of Georgetown University; GPA = Grade Point Average; SAT = Scholastic Aptitude Test; GED = General Equivalency Diploma.

Cost: $5,727 inclusive. *Scholarships:* none.
Housing: In apartments.
Application: *Deadline:* six weeks prior. *Fee:* none.
Contact: Dr. William J. Bicknell, Course Director, Office of Special Projects, School of Public Health, Boston University, Boston, MA 02118; (617) 638-5234. Telex: 200191 BUHPI.

CROSS-CULTURAL ISSUES

Q6 **UNIVERSITY OF MINNESOTA, SCHOOL OF PUBLIC HEALTH**
  Cross-Cultural Health Issues in Minnesota.
Specialization: Health status and health care for Asiatics, Blacks, Native Americans, and Hispanics in Minnesota; can be directly applied to international setting.
Dates: Two months: classes begin in April.
Location: Minneapolis, Minnesota: on campus.
Instruction: *Methods:* discussion groups, lectures, independent study/research. *By:* faculty, guest speakers/lecturers.
Highlights: New program. Certificate. Credit. Issues IAP-66. Foreign nationals on tourist visas are eligible to enroll. A foreign student counselor/adviser is available. International Student Center. 16 total enrollment.
Eligibility: *Academic:* bachelor's degree. *Language:* English proficiency on intermediate level is required. TOEFL: 500. *Professional:* one year of experience in health science preferred.
Cost: $150 for tuition. *Scholarships:* partial.
Housing: Not provided; sponsor assists in locating housing.
Application: *Deadline:* Jan. 1. *Fee:* none. *Scholarship deadline:* one year prior.
Contact: Mr. Robert ten Bensel, Program Director, Dept. of Maternal and Child Health, University of Minnesota, Box 197 Mayo, 420 Delaware Street SE, Minneapolis, MN 55455; (612) 373-8066.

CYTOTECHNOLOGY

Q7 **UNIVERSITY OF MEDICINE AND DENTISTRY OF NEW JERSEY, SCHOOL OF HEALTH RELATED PROFESSIONS**
  Cytotechnology.
Dates: One year: classes begin in Sept.
Location: Newark, New Jersey: on campus, at professional work site.
Instruction: *Methods:* lectures, case studies, "hands-on" training, science laboratories. *By:* faculty, guest speakers/lecturers.
Highlights: Sponsor has offered program since 1975. Certificate. Practical training is a program component; participants are not paid. Issues I-20AB. Foreign nationals on tourist visas are not eligible to enroll. A foreign student counselor/adviser is not available. 8 total enrollment.
Eligibility: *Academic:* 60 semester hours of undergraduate work. *Language:* English proficiency on advanced level is required. TOEFL. *Professional:* none.
Cost: $1,516 per year for tuition. *Scholarships:* none.
Housing: Not provided; student makes own arrangements.
Application: *Deadline:* Mar. 15. *Fee:* $15; not refundable.
Contact: Office of Academic and Student Services, University of Medicine and Dentistry of New Jersey, 100 Bergen Street, Newark, NJ 07103; (201) 456-5453.

All program information is subject to change without notice
and must be confirmed directly with the sponsor.

Q8 UNIVERSITY OF WISCONSIN—MADISON
School of Cytotechnology.
Specialization: Differentiation of malignant from normal cells. Assists in detecting cancer in its earliest and potentially most curable stages.
Dates: One year: classes begin in Aug.
Location: Madison, Wisconsin: on campus, at professional work site.
Instruction: *Methods:* lectures, discussion groups, case studies, science labs, independent study/research. *By:* faculty.
Highlights: Sponsor has offered program since 1957. Certificate upon completion of program with 2.0 GPA. Practical training is a program component; participants are not paid. Issues I-20AB. Foreign nationals on tourist visas are not eligible to enroll. A foreign student counselor/adviser is available. 12 total enrollment; 30% foreign enrollment in 1985.
Eligibility: *Academic:* some undergraduate work: 20 credit hours in biological sciences; eight credit hours in chemistry. *Language:* English proficiency on advanced level is preferred. *Professional:* none.
Cost: About $8,900 inclusive. *Scholarships:* none.
Housing: Not provided; student makes own arrangements.
Application: *Deadline:* March 1. *Fee:* none.
Contact: Dr. S.L. Inhorn, Medical Director, State Laboratory of Hygiene, University of Wisconsin, 465 Henry Mall, Madison, WI 53706; (608) 262-3911.

DENTISTRY

Q8A UNIVERSITY OF CALIFORNIA, LOS ANGELES EXTENSION
Foreign Dental Refresher.
Specialization: Complete review of dentistry for graduates of foreign dental schools; includes oral diagnosis and treatment planning, operative dentistry, periodontics, and prosthodontics.
Dates: Three months: classes begin in Sept. and Jan.
Location: Los Angeles, California: on campus.
Instruction: *Methods:* discussion groups, lectures, science laboratories. *By:* faculty, guest speakers/lecturers.
Highlights: Sponsor has offered program previously. Certificate. Issues I-20AB. Foreign nationals on tourist visas are eligible to enroll. A foreign student counselor/adviser is available. ESL program. Unlimited total enrollment; about 10% foreign enrollment in 1985.
Eligibility: *Academic:* bachelor's degree. *Language:* English proficiency on intermediate level is required. Placement exam. *Professional:* none.
Cost: $3,300 for tuition. *Scholarships:* none.
Housing: Not provided; student makes own arrangements.
Application: *Deadline:* three months to one year prior. *Fee:* $275; not refundable.
Contact: Foreign Student Advisor, UCLA Extension Advisory Service, 10995 Le Conte Avenue, Los Angeles, CA 90024; (213) 825-9351 or 206-6201. Cable: 9103427597. Telex: 9103427597.

Q9 UNIVERSITY OF MEDICINE AND DENTISTRY OF NEW JERSEY, NEW JERSEY DENTAL SCHOOL
M.S. in Biodental Sciences.
Specialization: New techniques in modern dentistry; basic sciences and dental research.
Dates: Nine months: classes begin in Sept.
Location: Newark, New Jersey: on campus.
Instruction: *Methods:* discussion groups, lectures, case studies, individualized instruction, "hands-on" training, independent study/research, computer-assisted instruction, science laboratories. *By:* faculty, guest speakers/lecturers.
Highlights: Sponsor has offered program since 1980. Certificate. Issues I-20AB. Foreign

---

Abbreviations: ESL = English as a Second Language; TOEFL = Test of English as a Foreign Language; ALIGU = American Language Institute of Georgetown University; GPA = Grade Point Average; SAT = Scholastic Aptitude Test; GED = General Equivalency Diploma.

nationals on tourist visas are not eligible to enroll. A foreign student counselor/adviser is not available.
Eligibility: *Academic:* bachelor's degree. *Language:* English proficiency on advanced level is required. TOEFL: 600. *Professional:* none.
Cost: $10,000 inclusive. *Scholarships:* none.
Housing: Not provided; student makes own arrangements.
Application: *Deadline:* not given. *Fee:* not given.
Contact: Dr. Zia Shey, Director, Office of Advanced Educational Programs, UMDNJ—New Jersey Dental School, 100 Bergen Street, Newark, NJ 07103; (201) 456-5362.

EPIDEMIOLOGY

Q10 **JOHNS HOPKINS UNIVERSITY, SCHOOL OF PUBLIC HEALTH**
Graduate Program in Epidemiology.
Specialization: Intensive training in the basics of epidemiology and biostatistics; advanced training in infectious disease, cancer, pharmaco-epidemiology, clinical trials, and evaluation of health services.
Dates: Three weeks: classes begin in June.
Location: Baltimore, Maryland: on campus.
Instruction: *Methods:* discussion groups, lectures, case studies, individualized instruction, "hands-on" training, computer-assisted instruction. *By:* faculty.
Highlights: Sponsor has offered program since 1982. Certificate. Issues I-20AB, IAP-66. Foreign nationals on tourist visas are eligible to enroll. A foreign student counselor/adviser is available. About 150–200 total enrollment; 20–35% foreign enrollment in 1985.
Eligibility: *Academic:* some graduate work. *Language:* English proficiency on advanced level is required. TOEFL: 550. *Professional:* 2–3 years experience in a public health agency.
Cost: $400 per course for tuition. *Scholarships:* none.
Housing: In dormitories, apartments.
Application: *Deadline:* June 1. *Fee:* $50; refundable.
Contact: Mrs. Helen Walters, School of Hygiene and Public Health, Johns Hopkins University, 615 N. Wolfe Street, Baltimore, MD 21205; (301) 955-7158. Cable: PUB HYG BAL. Telex: 710 234 0022.

FAMILY PLANNING

Q11 **SAN DIEGO STATE UNIVERSITY, INTERNATIONAL POPULATION CENTER**
Family Planning, Health and Social Services Delivery Systems.
Specialization: Population and family planning; practical concepts, skills, and strategies needed for effective project management; systematic program design, planning, implementation, and evaluation.
Dates: Six weeks: classes begin in Sept.
Location: San Diego, California: on campus.
Instruction: *Methods:* discussion groups, lectures, case studies, field trips, individualized instruction, "hands-on" training, independent study/research. *By:* faculty.
Highlights: New program. Certificate. Issues I-20AB, I-20MN, IAP-66. Foreign nationals on tourist visas are eligible to enroll. A foreign student counselor/adviser is available. Social activities. 30 total enrollment.
Eligibility: *Academic:* bachelor's degree. *Language:* English proficiency on advanced level is required. TOEFL: 500. *Professional:* one year of professional involvement in family planning.

Cost: $5,000 for tuition, books and materials, health insurance, travel for field trips.
Scholarships: none.
Housing: Not provided; sponsor assists in locating housing.
Application: *Deadline:* July 15. *Fee:* none.
Contact: Dr. John R. Weeks, International Population Center, San Diego State University, San Diego, CA 92182; (619) 265-5449. Telex: 9103351733.

Q12 UNIVERSITY OF CONNECTICUT HEALTH CENTER
Family Planning Policies and Approaches.
Specialization: U.S. and international family planning policies, contraceptive technology, health education and training, identification of target population, needs, and resources, birth-spacing as a tool in child survival.
Dates: One month: April.
Location: Farmington, Connecticut: on campus; or on-site abroad.
Instruction: *Methods:* discussion groups, lectures, case studies, field trips, individualized instruction, independent study/research. *By:* faculty, guest speakers/lecturers.
Highlights: New program. Certificate. Issues I-20AB, IAP-66. Foreign nationals on tourist visas are eligible to enroll. A foreign student counselor/adviser is available. Social and cultural activities, host family program. 20 total enrollment.
Eligibility: *Academic:* bachelor's degree. *Language:* English proficiency on advanced level is required. TOEFL: 500; ALIGU: 80. *Professional:* administrators, government personnel, trainers, and organizers responsible for family planning projects.
Cost: $3,600 for tuition, books and materials, health insurance, local transportation, field trips. *Scholarships:* none.
Housing: Not provided; sponsor assists in locating housing.
Application: *Deadline:* apply early. *Fee:* none.
Contact: Dr. Stephen L. Schensul, Director, International Health, Population, Social Service Training Programs, University of Connecticut Health Center, Room AG073, Farmington, CT 06032; (203) 674-3302. Telex: 710-423-5521/U Conn HC Lib.

Q13 UNIVERSITY OF ILLINOIS AT CHICAGO
Creating Dynamic Programs in Fertility Regulation.
Specialization: Designed for participants from the Middle East; course is conducted in Arabic.
Dates: One month: classes begin in Oct.
Location: Chicago, Illinois: on campus, at professional work site.
Instruction: *Methods:* discussion groups, lectures, case studies, field trips, individualized instruction, independent study/research, science laboratories. *By:* faculty. *In Arabic only.*
Highlights: New program. Certificate. Practical training is a program component; participants are not paid. Issues I-20AB, I-20MN, IAP-66. Foreign nationals on tourist visas are eligible to enroll. A foreign student counselor/adviser is available. Cultural program. 20 total enrollment; 100% foreign enrollment in 1985.
Eligibility: *Academic:* bachelor's degree. *Language:* English proficiency is not required. *Professional:* none.
Cost: $4,000 for tuition, books and materials. *Scholarships:* none.
Housing: In hotels.
Application: *Deadline:* Aug. 15. *Fee:* none.
Contact: Dr. Charles H. Lyons, University of Illinois at Chicago, 808 S. Wood Street, Room 173, Chicago, IL 60304; (312) 996-5455. Telex: 4949064 INTL PRO.

Q14 UNIVERSITY OF ILLINOIS AT CHICAGO
Fertility Regulation: Methodologies and Health Aspects.
Specialization: Designed for participants from the Middle East; course is conducted in Arabic.
Dates: One month: classes begin in June.

Location: Chicago, Illinois: on campus, at professional work site.
Instruction: *Methods:* discussion groups, lectures, case studies, field trips, individualized instruction, independent study/research, science laboratories. *By:* faculty. *In Arabic only.*
Highlights: New program. Certificate. Issues I-20AB, I-20MN, IAP-66. Foreign nationals on tourist visas are eligible to enroll. A foreign student counselor/adviser is available. Cultural programs. 20 total enrollment; 100% foreign enrollment in 1985.
Eligibility: *Academic:* bachelor's degree. *Language:* English proficiency is not required. *Professional:* none.
Cost: $4,000 for tuition, books, and materials. *Scholarships:* none.
Housing: In hotels.
Application: *Deadline:* May 1. *Fee:* none.
Contact: Dr. Charles H. Lyons, University of Illinois at Chicago, 808 S. Wood Street, Room 173, Chicago, IL 60602; (312) 996-5455. Telex: 4949064 INTL PRO.

HEALTH CARE IN DEVELOPING COUNTRIES

Q15 BOSTON UNIVERSITY, SCHOOL OF PUBLIC HEALTH
Certificate Program in Health Care in Developing Countries.
Specialization: Effective application of epidemiological principles and methods to primary health care and impact of socioeconomic development on health status and services delivery in countries where resources are limited.
Dates: Three months: classes begin in May.
Location: Boston, Massachusetts: on campus, at professional work site.
Instruction: *Methods:* discussion groups, lectures, case studies, field trips, "hands-on" training, science laboratories. *By:* faculty, guest speakers/lecturers.
Highlights: Sponsor has offered program since 1983. Certificate. Issues IAP-66. Foreign nationals on tourist visas are eligible to enroll. A foreign student counselor/adviser is available. Orientation programs. 45 total enrollment; 85% foreign enrollment in 1985.
Eligibility: *Academic:* bachelor's degree preferred. *Language:* English proficiency on advanced level is required. *Professional:* about 4–5 years of primary health care experience preferred.
Cost: $7,490 inclusive. *Scholarships:* none.
Housing: In apartments.
Application: *Deadline:* one month prior. *Fee:* none.
Contact: Dr. William J. Bicknell, Course Director, Office of Special Projects, School of Public Health, Boston University, Boston, MA 02118; (617) 638-5234. Telex: 200191 BUHPI.

Q16 LOMA LINDA UNIVERSITY
Master's Programs in International Health.
Specialization: Certificate, M.P.H., and M.S.P.H. programs in primary health care in developing countries.
Dates: Nine months: classes begin quarterly.
Location: Loma Linda, California: on campus, field project.
Instruction: *Methods:* discussion groups, lectures, case studies, field trips, individualized instruction, independent study/research, computer-assisted instruction, science laboratories. *By:* faculty.
Highlights: Sponsor has offered program since 1970. Certificate or master's degree. Practical training is a program component; participants are not paid. Issues I-20AB, IAP-66. A foreign student counselor/adviser is available. ESL program. About 40% foreign enrollment in 1985.
Eligibility: *Academic:* bachelor's degree. *Language:* English proficiency on intermediate level is required. TOEFL: 600; Univ. of Michigan Language Test: 93. *Professional:* none.
Cost: $150 per quarter unit for tuition. *Scholarships:* none.
Housing: In dormitories, or sponsor assists in locating housing.

Application: *Deadline:* none. *Fee:* $25; not refundable.
Contact: Loma Linda University, School of Health, International Health Program, Loma Linda, CA 92350; (714) 824-4902.

Q17 UNIVERSITY OF ALABAMA AT BIRMINGHAM, SCHOOL OF PUBLIC HEALTH
International Health Training Course.
Specialization: Provides skills for resolving public health problems and issues in developing countries; nutrition and maternal and child health options.
Dates: Five months: Jan.–June.
Location: Birmingham, Alabama: on campus.
Instruction: *Methods:* discussion groups, lectures, case studies, field trips, individualized instruction, "hands-on" training, independent study/research. *By:* faculty, guest speakers/lecturers.
Highlights: New program. Certificate. Credit. Issues I-20AB, IAP-66. A foreign student counselor/adviser is available.
Eligibility: *Academic:* bachelor's degree. *Language:* English proficiency on intermediate level is required. TOEFL: 450. *Professional:* not given.
Cost: Not given. *Scholarships:* none.
Housing: Not provided; sponsor assists in locating housing.
Application: *Deadline:* none. *Fee:* $40; not refundable.
Contact: Dr. Juan Navia, School of Public Health, University of Alabama at Birmingham, Birmingham, AL 35243; (205) 934-2288.

Q18 UNIVERSITY OF ALABAMA AT BIRMINGHAM, SCHOOL OF PUBLIC HEALTH
Master of Public Health in International Public Health.
Specialization: Provides skills for resolving public health problems and issues in developing countries.
Dates: One year: classes begin in Sept., Dec., March, June.
Location: Birmingham, Alabama: on campus.
Instruction: *Methods:* discussion groups, lectures, case studies, field trips, individualized instruction, "hands-on" training, independent study/research. *By:* faculty, guest speakers/lecturers.
Highlights: Sponsor has offered program since 1984. Master's degree. Issues I-20AB, IAP-66. A foreign student counselor/adviser is available. 15 total enrollment; 30% foreign enrollment in 1985.
Eligibility: *Academic:* bachelor's degree. *Language:* English proficiency on intermediate level is required. TOEFL: 450. *Professional:* requires two years of experience and professional certification; evidence of field experience or field work preferred.
Cost: $8,000 for tuition, books and materials, meals, housing. *Scholarships:* partial.
Housing: Not provided; sponsor assists in locating housing.
Application: *Deadline:* none. *Fee:* $40; not refundable. *Scholarship deadline:* not given.
Contact: Dr. Juan Navia, School of Public Health, University of Alabama at Birmingham, Birmingham, AL 35243; (205) 934-2288.

Q19 UNIVERSITY OF ALABAMA AT BIRMINGHAM
Master of Public Health in Public Health Nutrition.
Specialization: Provides skills for resolving public health nutrition problems and issues in developing countries.
Dates: One year: classes begin quarterly.
Location: Birmingham, Alabama: on campus.
Instruction: *Methods:* discussion groups, lectures, case studies, field trips, individualized instruction, "hands-on" training, independent study/research, science laboratories.
By: faculty, guest speakers/lecturers.

Abbreviations: ESL = English as a Second Language; TOEFL = Test of English as a Foreign Language; ALIGU = American Language Institute of Georgetown University; GPA = Grade Point Average; SAT = Scholastic Aptitude Test; GED = General Equivalency Diploma.

MEDICINE

Highlights: Sponsor has offered program since 1985. Master's degree. Practical training is a program component; participants may be paid. Issues I-20AB, IAP-66. Foreign nationals on tourist visas are eligible to enroll. A foreign student counselor/adviser is available. ESL program and International Student Association. 15 total enrollment; 30% foreign enrollment in 1985.
Eligibility: *Academic:* bachelor's degree. *Language:* English proficiency on intermediate level is required. TOEFL: 500. *Professional:* two years of public health experience required.
Cost: $8,000 for tuition, books and materials, meals, housing, health insurance. *Scholarships:* partial.
Housing: In dormitories, apartments.
Application: *Deadline:* none. *Fee:* $40; not refundable. *Scholarship deadline:* not given.
Contact: Dr. Juan Navia, School of Public Health, University of Alabama at Birmingham, Birmingham, AL 352494 (205) 934-2288.

Q20 UNIVERSITY OF NORTH CAROLINA AT CHAPEL HILL, SCHOOL OF PUBLIC HEALTH
Delivery of Rural Health Services.
Specialization: Planning management systems for coordination and control of primary health care in rural areas of developing countries.
Dates: Three weeks: classes begin in June.
Location: Chapel Hill, North Carolina: at conference center.
Instruction: *Methods:* discussion groups, lectures, case studies. *By:* faculty.
Highlights: Sponsor has offered program since 1972. Certificate. Foreign nationals on tourist visas are eligible to enroll. A foreign student counselor/adviser is not available. 31 total enrollment; 100% foreign enrollment in 1985.
Eligibility: *Academic:* bachelor's degree; most participants have M.D. or Ph.D.
Language: English proficiency on intermediate level is required. *Professional:* five years of health and/or administrative experience.
Cost: $3,100 inclusive. *Scholarships:* none.
Housing: At conference center.
Application: *Deadline:* May 1. *Fee:* none.
Contact: Mr. Robert Loddengaard, Dept. of Health Policy and Administration, School of Public Health, University of North Carolina, Chapel Hill, NC 27514; (919) 966-4091.

Q21 UNIVERSITY OF SOUTH FLORIDA, COLLEGE OF PUBLIC HEALTH
Intensive Summer Program in Health Planning and Management.
Specialization: Problems in planning, organization, and management common to developing countries.
Dates: Ten weeks: classes begin in May.
Location: Tampa, Florida: on campus, at professional work site.
Instruction: *Methods:* discussion groups, lectures, case studies, field trips. *By:* faculty, guest speakers/lecturers.
Highlights: Sponsor has offered program since 1984. Certificate. Issues IAP-66. Foreign nationals on tourist visas are eligible to enroll. A foreign student counselor/adviser is available. 20 total enrollment; 100% foreign enrollment in 1985.
Eligibility: *Academic:* bachelor's degree. *Language:* English proficiency on intermediate level is required. TOEFL: 550; instruction in English at university level. *Professional:* senior clinicians and health managers/administrators preferred.
Cost: $2,594 for tuition. *Scholarships:* partial.
Housing: Not provided; sponsor assists in locating housing.
Application: *Deadline:* Mar. 31. *Fee:* $15; not refundable. *Scholarship deadline:* Mar. 31.
Contact: Robert Gerlach, DDS, College of Public Health, University of South Florida, 13301 N. 30th, MHH-104, Tampa, FL 33612; (813) 974-3623. Telex: 8108760829.

HEALTH SYSTEMS MANAGEMENT

Q22 CORNELL UNIVERSITY
Health Executives Development Program.
Specialization: Health services administration, including international development.
Dates: Two weeks: June.
Location: Ithaca, New York: on campus.
Instruction: *Methods:* discussion groups, lectures, case studies. *By:* faculty, guest speakers/lecturers.
Highlights: Sponsor has offered program since 1957. Certificate. Foreign nationals on tourist visas are eligible to enroll. A foreign student counselor/adviser is not available. 60 total enrollment; 35% foreign enrollment in 1985.
Eligibility: *Academic:* bachelor's degree. *Language:* English proficiency on intermediate level is required. *Professional:* for senior executives with strong experience in health care.
Cost: $2,600 for tuition, books and materials, meals, housing, local transportation, recreational facilities. *Scholarships:* partial.
Housing: In dormitories.
Application: *Deadline:* May 1 preferred. *Fee:* $100; refundable until June 1. *Scholarship deadline:* none.
Contact: Mr. Douglas R. Brown, Ph.D., Health Executives Development Program, Cornell University, N222 MVR Hall, Ithaca, NY 14853; (607) 255-8013.

Q23 HARVARD UNIVERSITY, SCHOOL OF PUBLIC HEALTH
Program for Health Systems Management.
Specialization: Provides a forum for hospital administrators, physician executives, health planners, and other health care managers to examine current trends in strategic, financial, and regulatory areas, and ways in which key constituencies can work together more effectively.
Dates: Two weeks: late Oct.–early Nov.
Location: Boston, Massachusetts: on campus.
Instruction: *Methods:* lectures, discussion groups, case studies, individualized instruction, films, small-group work. *By:* faculty, guest speakers/lecturers.
Highlights: Sponsor has offered program for over ten years. Certificate. Issues I-20AB, IAP-66. Foreign nationals on tourist visas are eligible to enroll. A foreign student counselor/adviser is not available. 50 total enrollment; 9% foreign enrollment in 1985.
Eligibility: *Academic:* some graduate work. *Language:* English proficiency on advanced level is required. *Professional:* experience preferred.
Cost: $1,850 for tuition, materials, some meals. *Scholarships:* none.
Housing: Not provided; sponsor provides hotel information.
Application: *Deadline:* Sept. 26. *Fee:* none.
Contact: Dade W. Moeller, Ph.D., Associate Dean for Continuing Education, School of Public Health, Harvard University, 677 Huntington Ave., Boston, MA 02115; (617) 732-1171. Cable: Harvard School of Public Health, Boston.

Q24 JOHNS HOPKINS UNIVERSITY, SCHOOL OF HYGIENE AND PUBLIC HEALTH
Senior Health Planners Program.
Specialization: Provides skills in health services planning and evaluation. Program designed for experienced administrators in public health ministries and agencies.
Dates: Two months: classes begin in Feb., April.
Location: Baltimore, Maryland: on campus.
Instruction: *Methods:* discussion groups, lectures, case studies, individualized instruction, independent study/research. *By:* faculty.
Highlights: Sponsor has offered program since the 1960s. Certificate. Issues I-20AB, IAP-66.

Abbreviations: ESL = English as a Second Language; TOEFL = Test of English as a Foreign Language; ALIGU = American Language Institute of Georgetown University; GPA = Grade Point Average; SAT = Scholastic Aptitude Test; GED = General Equivalency Diploma.

139

Foreign nationals on tourist visas are eligible to enroll. A foreign student counselor/adviser is available. Orientation program. 35 total enrollment; 100% foreign enrollment in 1985.
Eligibility: *Academic:* some graduate work; health professional degree preferred.
Language: English proficiency on advanced level is required. TOEFL: 550. *Professional:* 2–3 years of administrative experience in public health and professional certification preferred.
Cost: $3,900 inclusive. *Scholarships:* none, but many students sponsored by the World Health Organization and similar organizations.
Housing: Not provided; sponsor assists in locating housing.
Application: *Deadline:* two months prior. *Fee:* none.
Contact: Dr. Timothy Baker, School of Hygiene and Public Health, Johns Hopkins University, 615 N. Wolfe Street, Baltimore, MD 21205; (301) 955-3934/3734. Cable: PUB HYG BAL. Telex: 710 234 0022.

Q25 PACE UNIVERSITY
Specialization: Management of health care services. Courses can be tailored to meet the needs of international students.
Dates: Classes begin in Sept., Jan., May, June, July.
Location: White Plains, New York: on campus, at professional work site.
Instruction: *Methods:* lectures, discussion groups, case studies, field trips, individualized instruction, "hands-on" training, computer-assisted instruction, language labs. *By:* faculty, guest speakers/lecturers. *Also in French, Spanish, Arabic.*
Highlights: Sponsor has offered short-term programs since the 1940s. Certificate upon completion of program with B average. Issues I-20AB, IAP-66. Foreign nationals on tourist visas are eligible to enroll. A foreign student counselor/adviser is available. ESL program and International Student Club. Unlimited total enrollment; 2.5% total foreign enrollment in 1985.
Eligibility: *Academic:* bachelor's degree. *Language:* English proficiency on advanced level is required. TOEFL: 550. *Professional:* none.
Cost: About $7,000 per semester inclusive. *Scholarships:* partial (graduate assistantships).
Housing: In dormitories, or sponsor assists in locating housing.
Application: *Deadline:* rolling. *Fee:* $20; not refundable. *Scholarship deadline:* at time of application.
Contact: Mrs. R.I. Fennekohl, Graduate Admissions Office, Pace University, Pace Plaza, New York, NY 10038; (212) 488-1720.

Q26 UNIVERSITY OF ALABAMA AT BIRMINGHAM, CENTER FOR HEALTH SERVICES CONTINUING EDUCATION
Health Services Administrators Development.
Specialization: Management, human resources management, and financial management of health services.
Dates: Two weeks: March.
Location: Birmingham, Alabama: on campus.
Instruction: *Methods:* discussion groups, lectures, field trips, independent study/research, computer-assisted instruction. *By:* faculty, guest speakers/lecturers.
Highlights: Sponsor has offered program since 1965. Certificate. A foreign student counselor/adviser is not available. International student association. 30 total enrollment; 4% foreign enrollment in 1985.
Eligibility: *Academic:* associate's degree. *Language:* English proficiency on advanced level is required.*Professional:* three years of work experience required.
Cost: $2,100 for tuition, books and materials. *Scholarships:* none.
Housing: Not provided; sponsor assists in locating housing.
Application: *Deadline:* Feb. 15. *Fee:* $90; refundable.
Contact: Mr. Michael D. Laus, Ph.D., Director, Dept. of Health Services Administration, University of Alabama, #560 Susan Mott Webb Bldg., University Station, UAB, Birmingham, AL 35294; (205) 934-1671.

All program information is subject to change without notice
and must be confirmed directly with the sponsor.

HOLISTIC STUDIES

Q27 LESLEY COLLEGE GRADUATE SCHOOL
Holistic Studies and Healing Arts.
Specialization: Holistic healing methods.
Dates: Aug.–May.
Location: Cambridge, Massachusetts: on campus.
Instruction: *Methods:* lectures, discussion groups, individualized instruction, "hands-on" training, independent study/research. *By:* faculty.
Highlights: Sponsor has offered program since 1981. Master's degree. Practical training is a program component; participants are not paid. Issues I-20AB. Foreign nationals on tourist visas are not eligible to enroll. A foreign student counselor/adviser is available. Orientation program. 100 total enrollment; 35% foreign enrollment in 1985.
Eligibility: *Academic:* bachelor's degree. *Language:* English proficiency on advanced level is required. TOEFL: 550. *Professional:* experience in health/mental health field required.
Cost: About $17,000 inclusive. *Scholarships:* none.
Housing: In dormitories.
Application: *Deadline:* May 1. start. *Fee:* $35; not refundable.
Contact: Joanna Fabris, Program Advisor, Arts Institute, Lesley College Graduate School, 29 Everett Street, Cambridge, MA 02238; (617) 868-9600, Ext. 480.

INFORMATION SYSTEMS

Q28 UNIVERSITY OF CONNECTICUT HEALTH CENTER
Improving Health Information Systems with Microcomputers.
Specialization: Emphasis on developing and maintaining information processing capabilities for health, child survival, population, and social service programs.
Dates: Nov. 17–Dec. 12.
Location: Farmington, Connecticut: on campus; or on-site abroad.
Instruction: *Methods:* discussion groups, lectures, case studies, field trips, individualized instruction, independent study/research. *By:* faculty, guest speakers/lecturers.
Highlights: New program. Certificate. Issues I-20AB, IAP-66. Foreign nationals on tourist visas are eligible to enroll. A foreign student counselor/adviser is available. Social and cultural activities, host family program. 20 total enrollment.
Eligibility: *Academic:* bachelor's degree. *Language:* English proficiency on advanced level is required. TOEFL: 500; ALIGU: 80. *Professional:* program managers, data gathering personnel, evaluators and statisticians, administrators, and applied researchers.
Cost: $4,400 for tuition, books and materials, health insurance, local transportation, field trip, use of computer. *Scholarships:* none.
Housing: Not provided; sponsor assists in locating housing.
Application: *Deadline:* apply early. *Fee:* none.
Contact: Dr. Stephen L. Schensul, Director, International Health, Population, Social Service Training Programs, University of Connecticut Health Center, Room AG073, Farmington, CT 06032; (203) 674-3302. Telex: 710-423-5521/U Conn HC Lib.

MEDICAL TECHNOLOGY

Q29 INTERAMERICAN UNIVERSITY OF PUERTO RICO
Medical Technology.
Specialization: Combines classroom and laboratory instruction; instruction is in Spanish.
Dates: One year: classes begin in Aug. and Feb.
Location: Mayaguez, Puerto Rico: at Mayaguez Medical Center.

Abbreviations: ESL = English as a Second Language; TOEFL = Test of English as a Foreign Language; ALIGU = American Language Institute of Georgetown University; GPA = Grade Point Average; SAT = Scholastic Aptitude Test; GED = General Equivalency Diploma.

141

Instruction: *Methods:* lectures, discussion groups, individualized instruction, "hands-on" training, science labs. *By:* faculty, guest speakers/lecturers. *In Spanish only.*
Highlights: Sponsor has offered program since 1981. Certificate upon completion of one semester of formal instruction, one semester internship. Practical training is a program component; participants are not paid. Issues I-20AB. Foreign nationals on tourist visas are eligible to enroll. A foreign student counselor/adviser is available. No special support services for foreign nationals. 15 total enrollment; 1% foreign enrollment in 1985.
Eligibility: *Academic:* bachelor's degree. *Language:* English proficiency on intermediate level is preferred. *Professional:* none.
Cost: $4,000 for tuition. *Scholarships:* none.
Housing: In dormitories, guest houses.
Application: *Deadline:* July 15 and Dec. 15. *Fee:* none.
Contact: Lic. Annie Lugo, InterAmerican University of Puerto Rico, Box 5100, San German, PR 00753; (809) 834-6070.

MIDWIFERY

Q30 UNIVERSITY OF MEDICINE AND DENTISTRY OF NEW JERSEY, SCHOOL OF HEALTH RELATED PROFESSIONS
Nurse Midwifery.
Specialization: Midwifery.
Dates: One year: classes begin in Sept.
Location: Newark, New Jersey: on campus, at professional work site.
Instruction: *Methods:* lectures, case studies, individualized instruction, "hands-on" training. *By:* faculty, guest speakers/lecturers.
Highlights: Sponsor has offered program since 1974. Certificate upon completion of about 32 semester hours. Practical training is a program component; participants are not paid. Issues I-20AB. Foreign nationals on tourist visas are not eligible to enroll. A foreign student counselor/adviser is not available. 14 total enrollment.
Eligibility: *Academic:* degree in nursing. *Language:* English proficiency on advanced level is required. TOEFL. *Professional:* registered nurses with two years of maternal neonatal health care experience.
Cost: $1,516 per year for tuition. *Scholarships:* none.
Housing: Not provided; student makes own arrangements.
Application: *Deadline:* Dec. 31. *Fee:* $15; not refundable.
Contact: Office of Academic and Student Services, School of Health Related Professions, University of Medicine and Dentistry of New Jersey, 100 Bergen Street, Newark, NJ 07103; (201) 456-5453.

NURSING

Q31 GEORGE MASON UNIVERSITY, SCHOOL OF NURSING
International Nursing Program.
Specialization: Nursing in primary health care. Individualized program combining seminars and field observation.
Dates: To be arranged.
Location: Fairfax, Virginia: on campus, at professional work site.
Instruction: *Methods:* individualized instruction, independent study/research. *By:* faculty.
Highlights: Sponsor has offered program since 1984. Certificate. Issues IAP-66. Foreign nationals on tourist visas are eligible to enroll. A foreign student counselor/adviser is available. 15 total enrollment; 8% foreign enrollment in 1985.
Eligibility: *Academic:* bachelor's degree. *Language:* English proficiency on intermediate level is required. *Professional:* none.

Cost: $1,500 per week for four weeks or less, or $3,000 per semester for tuition.
Scholarships: none.
Housing: In hotels or dormitories.
Application: *Deadline:* none. *Fee:* none.
Contact: Dr. Yuen C. Liu, School of Nursing, George Mason University, 4400 University Drive, Fairfax, VA 22030; (703) 323-2446.

Q32 UNIVERSITY OF ALABAMA, SCHOOL OF NURSING
Advanced Clinical Nursing.
Specialization: Nursing theory, research, and advanced practice in 12 different specialty areas.
Dates: Vary.
Location: Birmingham, Alabama: on campus, at professional work site.
Instruction: *Methods:* discussion groups, lectures, case studies, individualized instruction, independent study/research, computer-assisted instruction. *By:* faculty, guest speakers/lecturers.
Highlights: Sponsor has offered program since 1974. Certificate. Practical training may be a program component; participants are not paid. A foreign student counselor/adviser is not available. ESL program. Less than 1% foreign enrollment in 1985.
Eligibility: *Academic:* bachelor's degree. *Language:* English proficiency on intermediate level is required. TOEFL; MAT. *Professional:* certification is required.
Cost: $600–$2,000 for tuition, health insurance, fees. *Scholarships:* none.
Housing: In dormitories.
Application: *Deadline:* none. *Fee:* $40; not refundable.
Contact: Continuing Education Program or Master's Program in Nursing, University of Alabama at Birmingham, University Station, Birmingham, AL 35294; (205) 934-3485.

Q33 UNIVERSITY OF ALABAMA, SCHOOL OF NURSING
Summer Doctoral Study.
Specialization: Core and elective courses offered; core courses may be completed in four summers.
Dates: Classes begin in June.
Location: Birmingham, Alabama: on campus, at professional work site.
Instruction: *Methods:* discussion groups, lectures, case studies, field trips, individualized instruction, independent study/research, computer-assisted instruction. *By:* faculty, guest speakers/lecturers, mentors.
Highlights: New program. Sponsor has offered short-term programs previously. Certificate. Practical training is a program component; participants are not paid. A foreign student counselor/adviser is not available. ESL program. Less than 1% foreign enrollment in 1985.
Eligibility: *Academic:* master's degree; GRE. *Language:* English proficiency on intermediate level is required. TOEFL. *Professional:* certification is required.
Cost: $600 for tuition, health insurance, fees. *Scholarships:* none.
Housing: In dormitories.
Application: *Deadline:* May 15. *Fee:* $40; not refundable.
Contact: Doctoral Program in Nursing, University of Alabama at Birmingham, University Station, Birmingham, AL 35294; (205) 934-3485.

Q34 UNIVERSITY OF CONNECTICUT HEALTH CENTER
Program and Curriculum Development in Public Health Nursing.
Specialization: Development of public health nursing program, including community outreach, home care visiting, school health, maternal and child health, and communicable disease follow-up.
Dates: One month: April.
Location: Farmington, Connecticut: on campus; or on-site abroad.

Instruction: *Methods:* discussion groups, lectures, case studies, field trips, individualized instruction, independent study/research. *By:* faculty, guest speakers/lecturers.

Highlights: New program. Certificate. Issues I-20AB, IAP-66. Foreign nationals on tourist visas are eligible to enroll. A foreign student counselor/adviser is available. Social and cultural activities, host family program. 20 total enrollment.

Eligibility: *Academic:* nursing degree. *Language:* English proficiency on advanced level is required. TOEFL: 500; ALIGU: 80. *Professional:* nursing supervisors, and administrators and managers of hospitals, public health departments, community centers and clinics.

Cost: $3,600 for tuition, books and materials, health insurance, local transportation, field trips. *Scholarships:* none.

Housing: Not provided; sponsor assists in locating housing.

Application: *Deadline:* apply early. *Fee:* none.

Contact: Dr. Stephen L. Schensul, Director, International Health, Population, Social Service Training Programs, University of Connecticut Health Center, Room AG073, Farmington, CT 06032; (203) 674-3302. Telex: 710-423-5521/U Conn HC Lib.

Q35 UNIVERSITY OF ILLINOIS, COLLEGE OF NURSING
International Studies.

Specialization: Clinical nursing, nursing education, administration and research; program designed to meet individual needs.

Dates: Four quarters: classes begin in Sept.

Location: Chicago, Illinois: on campus.

Instruction: *Methods:* discussion groups, lectures, case studies, field trips, seminars, "hands-on" training, independent study, computer-assisted instruction, language and science labs. *By:* faculty.

Highlights: Sponsor has offered program since 1980. Credit. Certificate. Practical training is a program component; participants are not paid. Issues I-20AB, I-20 MN, IAP-66. Foreign nationals on tourist visas are eligible to enroll. A foreign student counselor/adviser is available. ESL program.

Eligibility: *Academic:* bachelor's degree. *Language:* English proficiency on advanced level is required. TOEFL: 550. *Professional:* registered nurses.

Cost: $3,000 per quarter for tuition, books and materials, housing, health insurance. *Scholarships:* full.

Housing: In dormitories, apartments, hotels.

Application: *Deadline:* six months prior. *Fee:* $20; not refundable. *Scholarship deadline:* not given.

Contact: Jo Ann Glittenberg, RN, Ph.D., College of Nursing, University of Illinois, 845 S. Damen Ave., Chicago, IL 60612; (312) 996-0781.

PHYSICAL THERAPY

Q36 BRENAU COLLEGE
Physiological Practicum.

Dates: Sept. 15–June 1.

Location: Atlanta, Georgia: on campus.

Instruction: *Methods:* discussion groups, lectures, case studies, "hands-on" training, independent study, computer-assisted instruction, science laboratories. *By:* faculty.

Highlights: Sponsor has offered program since 1981. Practical training is a program component; participants are not paid. Issues I-20AB. Foreign nationals on tourist visas are not eligible to enroll. A foreign student counselor/adviser is available. 20 total enrollment; 3% foreign enrollment in 1985.

Eligibility: *Academic:* associate's degree. *Language:* English proficiency on beginning level is required. TOEFL: 500. *Professional:* none.

Cost: $3,150 for tuition. *Scholarships:* none.

Housing: Not provided; sponsor assists in locating housing.
Application: *Deadline:* 1 month prior. *Fee:* $25; not refundable.
Contact: Dr. David Kelly, Dean of The Professional College, Brenau College, Butler Hall, Gainesville, GA 30501; (404) 534-6200.

PUBLIC HEALTH

Q37 HARVARD UNIVERSITY, SCHOOL OF PUBLIC HEALTH
Master of Occupational Health.
Specialization: General training in public health and/or specific training in individual public health disciplines.
Dates: Sept.–June.
Location: Boston, Massachusetts: on campus.
Instruction: *Methods:* lectures, discussion groups, case studies, field trips, independent study/research, science labs. *By:* faculty, guest speakers/lecturers.
Highlights: Sponsor has offered program since the 1920s. Master's degree upon completion of 40 credit units. Issues I-20AB, IAP-66. Foreign nationals on tourist visas are not eligible to enroll. A foreign student counselor/adviser is available. 4–10 total enrollment.
Eligibility: *Academic:* bachelor's degree. *Language:* English proficiency on advanced level is required. TOEFL: 550. *Professional:* one year of experience in public health.
Cost: $20,328 inclusive. *Scholarships:* none.
Housing: In apartments.
Application: *Deadline:* none. *Fee:* $40; not refundable.
Contact: Ms. Judith Hull, Director of Admissions and Registrar, School of Public Health, Harvard University, 677 Huntington Ave., Boston, MA 02115; (617) 732-1030.

Q38 HARVARD UNIVERSITY, SCHOOL OF PUBLIC HEALTH
Master of Public Health.
Specialization: General training in public health and/or specific training in individual public health disciplines.
Dates: Sept.–June.
Location: Boston, Massachusetts: on campus.
Instruction: *Methods:* lectures, discussion groups, case studies, field trips, independent study/research, science labs. *By:* faculty, guest speakers/lecturers.
Highlights: Sponsor has offered program since the 1920s. Master's degree upon completion of 40 credit units. Issues I-20AB, IAP-66. Foreign nationals on tourist visas are not eligible to enroll. A foreign student counselor/adviser is available. 100–150 total enrollment; 30% foreign enrollment in 1985.
Eligibility: *Academic:* bachelor's degree. *Language:* English proficiency on advanced level is required. TOEFL: 550. *Professional:* one year of experience in public health.
Cost: $20,328 inclusive. *Scholarships:* none.
Housing: In apartments.
Application: *Deadline:* none. *Fee:* $40; not refundable.
Contact: Ms. Judith Hull, Director of Admissions and Registrar, School of Public Health, Harvard University, 677 Huntington Ave., Boston, MA 02115; (617) 732-1030.

Q39 HARVARD UNIVERSITY, SCHOOL OF PUBLIC HEALTH
Master of Science in Public Health.
Specialization: General training in public health and/or specific training in individual public health disciplines.
Dates: Sept.–June.
Location: Boston, Massachusetts: on campus.
Instruction: *Methods:* lectures, discussion groups, case studies, field trips, independent study/research, science labs. *By:* faculty, guest speakers/lecturers.

Abbreviations: ESL = English as a Second Language; TOEFL = Test of English as a Foreign Language; ALIGU = American Language Institute of Georgetown University; GPA = Grade Point Average; SAT = Scholastic Aptitude Test; GED = General Equivalency Diploma.

145

Highlights: Sponsor has offered program since the 1920s. Master's degree upon completion of 40 credit units. Issues I-20AB, IAP-66. Foreign nationals on tourist visas are not eligible to enroll. A foreign student counselor/adviser is available. 120–170 total enrollment; 20% foreign enrollment in 1985.
Eligibility: *Academic:* bachelor's degree. *Language:* English proficiency on advanced level is required. TOEFL: 550. *Professional:* one year of experience in public health.
Cost: $20,328 inclusive. *Scholarships:* none.
Housing: In apartments.
Application: *Deadline:* none. *Fee:* $40; not refundable.
Contact: Ms. Judith Hull, Director of Admissions and Registrar, School of Public Health, Harvard University, 677 Huntington Ave., Boston, MA 02115; (617) 732-1030.

Q40 JOHNS HOPKINS UNIVERSITY, SCHOOL OF HYGIENE AND PUBLIC HEALTH
Master of Public Health Degree.
Specialization: General public health program for health and health-related professionals, such as physicians, nurses, engineers, and health services administrators.
Dates: 11 months: classes begin in July.
Location: Baltimore, Maryland: on campus.
Instruction: *Methods:* discussion groups, lectures, case studies, field trips, individualized instruction, independent study/research, science laboratories. *By:* faculty.
Highlights: Sponsor has offered program since 1920. Master's degree upon completion of 80 academic credits. Issues I-20AB, IAP-66. Foreign nationals on tourist visas are eligible to enroll. A foreign student counselor/adviser is available. Orientation program. 165 total enrollment; about 20% foreign enrollment in 1985.
Eligibility: *Academic:* a professional degree. *Language:* English proficiency on advanced level is required. TOEFL: 550. *Professional:* 2–3 years of experience preferred.
Cost: About $16,000–$17,000 inclusive. *Scholarships:* none, but many participants are funded by the World Health Organization and similar organizations.
Housing: Not provided; sponsor assists in locating housing.
Application: *Deadline:* March. *Fee:* $40; not refundable.
Contact: Dr. David Paige, Director, MPH Program, Johns Hopkins University, 615 N. Wolfe Street, Baltimore, MD 21205; (301) 955-3804. Cable: PUB HYG BAL. Telex: 710 234 0022.

Q41 UNIVERSITY OF CONNECTICUT HEALTH CENTER
Urban Health Planning.
Specialization: Urban epidemiology, urban health resources, primary health care, high-risk populations, child survival techniques, and monitoring methods.
Dates: Oct. 14–Nov. 14.
Location: Farmington, Connecticut: on campus; or on-site abroad.
Instruction: *Methods:* discussion groups, lectures, case studies, field trips, individualized instruction, independent study/research. *By:* faculty, guest speakers/lecturers.
Highlights: New program. Certificate. Issues I-20AB, IAP-66. Foreign nationals on tourist visas are eligible to enroll. A foreign student counselor/adviser is available. Social and cultural activities, host family program. 20 total enrollment.
Eligibility: *Academic:* bachelor's degree. *Language:* English proficiency on advanced level is required. TOEFL: 500; ALIGU: 80. *Professional:* urban planners, primary health care providers, administrators and managers in health care delivery and social services.
Cost: $3,600 for tuition, books and materials, health insurance, local transportation, field trips. *Scholarships:* none.
Housing: Not provided; sponsor assists in locating housing.
Application: *Deadline:* apply early. *Fee:* none.
Contact: Dr. Stephen L. Schensul, Director, International Health, Population, Social Service Training Programs, University of Connecticut Health Center, Room AG073, Farmington, CT 06032; (203) 674-3302. Telex: 710-423-5521/U Conn HC Lib.

REVIEW COURSES

Q42 EXCELLENCE IN EDUCATION, INC.
FMGEMS Medical Review Course.
Specialization: Instruction in basic and clinical sciences.
Dates: Ten weeks: classes begin in Oct., April, Feb.
Location: Salt Lake City, Utah: on campus.
Instruction: *Methods:* discussion groups, lectures, case studies, independent study/research, language laboratories. *By:* faculty.
Highlights: New program. Sponsor has offered short-term programs since 1972. Certificate. Issues I-20AB. Foreign nationals on tourist visas are eligible to enroll. A foreign student counselor/adviser is available. ESL program, University of Utah Medical Library permit, assistance with FMGEMS exam application, National Resident Matching Program. 20 total enrollment; 100% foreign enrollment in1985.
Eligibility: *Academic:* some graduate work towards a medical degree. *Language:* English proficiency on advanced level is required. *Professional:* none.
Cost: $2,100 for tuition, books and materials, health insurance. *Scholarships:* none.
Housing: In dormitories, with families.
Application: *Deadline:* rolling. *Fee:* $100; refundable.
Contact: Mr. Robert L. Brown, EIE, 1840 S. 1300 E., Salt Lake City, UT 84105; (801) 488-4255.

Q43 INSTITUTE OF CONTINUING BIOMEDICAL EDUCATION
Comprehensive Program in Basic Medical Sciences and Clinical Disciplines.
Specialization: Specially structured for FLEX and FMGEMS examinations; fall semester covers basic medical sciences, spring semester covers clinical medicine review. Semesters may be taken separately.
Dates: Sept.–Jan., Feb.–June.
Location: New York, New York: at institute, at professional work site.
Instruction: *Methods:* discussion groups, lectures, case studies, field trips. *By:* faculty.
Highlights: Sponsor has offered program previously. Certificate. Issues I-20AB. Foreign nationals on tourist visas are eligible to enroll. A foreign student counselor/adviser is available.
Eligibility: *Academic:* bachelor's degree. *Language:* English proficiency on intermediate level is required. TOEFL. *Professional:* admission to the examination applicant is preparing for.
Cost: $3000 for tuition. *Scholarships:* partial.
Housing: Not provided; sponsor assists in locating housing.
Application: *Deadline:* one month prior. *Fee:* $50; not refundable. *Scholarship deadline:* not given.
Contact: Mr. Fabian Bertocci, Adm., Institute of Continuing Biomedical Education, 1249 Fifth Ave., New York, NY 10029; (212) 410-5246.

Q44 INSTITUTE OF CONTINUING BIOMEDICAL EDUCATION
FLEX-FMGEMS Preexamination Workshop.
Specialization: Intensive workshops in basic medical science and clinical disciplines, test-taking methodology and strategies for FLEX and FMGEMS examinations.
Dates: 100 hours: May, Nov.
Location: New York, New York: at institute, at professional work site.
Instruction: *Methods:* discussion groups, lectures, case studies, field trips. *By:* faculty.
Highlights: Sponsor has offered program previously. Certificate. Issues I-20AB. Foreign nationals on tourist visas are eligible to enroll. A foreign student counselor/adviser is available.
Eligibility: *Academic:* bachelor's degree. *Language:* English proficiency on intermediate level is required. TOEFL. *Professional:* admission to the examination applicant is preparing for.

Abbreviations: ESL = English as a Second Language; TOEFL = Test of English as a Foreign Language; ALIGU = American Language Institute of Georgetown University; GPA = Grade Point Average; SAT = Scholastic Aptitude Test; GED = General Equivalency Diploma.

Cost: $650 for tuition. *Scholarships:* partial.
Housing: Not provided; sponsor assists in locating housing.
Application: *Deadline:* one month prior. *Fee:* $50; not refundable. *Scholarship deadline:* not given.
Contact: Mr. Fabian Bertocci, Adm., Institute of Continuing Biomedical Education, 1249 Fifth Ave., New York, NY 10029; (212) 410-5246.

SPORTS MEDICINE

Q45 GUILFORD COLLEGE
Sports Medicine.
Dates: Aug.–late July.
Location: Greensboro, North Carolina: on campus.
Instruction: *Methods:* lectures, discussion groups, science labs. *By:* faculty.
Highlights: Sponsor has offered short-term programs since 1983. Certificate upon completion of 4–6 courses. Issues I-20AB, I-20MN. Foreign nationals on tourist visas are not eligible to enroll. A foreign student counselor/adviser is available.
Eligibility: *Academic:* bachelor's degree. *Language:* English proficiency on advanced level is required. TOEFL: 500. *Professional:* none.
Cost: $112 per credit hour for tuition. *Scholarships:* none.
Housing: Not provided; student makes own arrangements.
Application: *Deadline:* open. *Fee:* $20; not refundable.
Contact: Dean of Admissions and Financial Aid, Guilford College, 5800 W. Friendly Ave., Greensboro, NC 27410; (919) 292-5511.

VETERINARY SCIENCE

Q46 TEXAS A&M UNIVERSITY, COLLEGE OF VETERINARY MEDICINE
Personalized Veterinary Continuing Education.
Specialization: Individually designed programs in any discipline in the field of veterinary medicine, including embryo transfer.
Dates: 2–4 weeks: to be arranged.
Location: College Station, Texas: on campus.
Instruction: *Methods:* discussion groups, lectures, case studies, individualized instruction, "hands-on" training, independent study/research. *By:* faculty.
Highlights: Sponsor has offered program since 1982. Certificate. Practical training is a program component; participants are not paid. Foreign nationals on tourist visas are eligible to enroll. A foreign student counselor/adviser is not available. 2 total enrollment.
Eligibility: *Academic:* Doctor of Veterinary Medicine; knowledge of animal reproductive physiology. *Language:* English proficiency on intermediate level is required. *Professional:* veterinarians.
Cost: $200–$2,000 per week for tuition. *Scholarships:* none.
Housing: Not provided; student makes own arrangements.
Application: *Deadline:* none. *Fee:* none.
Contact: Walter F. Juliff, DVM, Director, Office of Continuing Education, College of Veterinary Medecine, Texas A&M University, College Station, TX 77843-4457; (409) 845-9103.

PHILOSOPHY AND RELIGION

R1 **COLGATE ROCHESTER DIVINITY SCHOOL, BEXLEY HALL, and CROZER THEOLOGICAL SEMINARY**
Ecumenical Scholar Program.
Dates: Nine months: classes begin in Sept.
Location: Rochester, New York: on campus.
Instruction: *Methods:* discussion groups, lectures, independent study/research. *By:* faculty.
Highlights: Sponsor has offered program previously. Certificate. Issues I-20AB. A foreign student counselor/adviser is available. Two total enrollment.
Eligibility: *Academic:* bachelor's degree. *Language:* English proficiency on intermediate level is required. *Professional:* none.
Cost: $10,000 inclusive. *Scholarships:* full.
Housing: In dormitories.
Application: *Deadline:* June 1. *Fee:* none. *Scholarship deadline:* not given.
Contact: John Backer, Director, Leadership Development Program, NCCC, 475 Riverside Drive, New York, NY 10115; (212) 870-2335.

R2 **COLUMBIA THEOLOGICAL SEMINARY**
Theological Education.
Specialization: Multidenominational professional degree program in theology.
Dates: Sept.–May.
Location: Decatur, Georgia: at seminary, at professional work site.
Instruction: *Methods:* lectures, discussion groups, case studies, field trips, independent study/research. *By:* faculty, guest speakers/lectures.
Highlights: Sponsor has offered program previously. Practical training is a program component; participants are paid. Foreign nationals on tourist visas are not eligible to enroll. A foreign student counselor/adviser is available. 5% foreign enrollment in 1985.
Eligibility: *Academic:* master's degree. *Language:* English proficiency on intermediate level is required. TOEFL. *Professional:* ordained minister with five years of experience.
Cost: $3,500 for tuition, meals, housing. *Scholarships:* partial and full.
Housing: In dormitories, apartments.
Application: *Deadline:* not given. *Fee:* not given. *Scholarship deadline:* not given.
Contact: Prof. T.E. Clarke, Columbia Theological Seminary, Box 520, 701 Columbia Drive, Decatur, GA 30031.

R3 **SCHOOL OF WORLD MISSION**
Specialization: Theology, religion, and anthropology.
Dates: Two weeks: classes begin in June, July, and Aug.
Location: Pasadena, California: at mission.
Instruction: *Methods:* lectures, discussion groups.
Highlights: Sponsor has offered short-term programs since 1976. Certificate. Issues I-20AB, I-20MN, IAP-66. A foreign student counselor/adviser is available. 40% foreign enrollment in 1985.
Eligibility: *Academic:* bachelor's degree. *Language:* TOEFL: 500. *Professional:* three years of experience.

Abbreviations: ESL = English as a Second Language; TOEFL = Test of English as a Foreign Language; ALIGU = American Language Institute of Georgetown University; GPA = Grade Point Average; SAT = Scholastic Aptitude Test; GED = General Equivalency Diploma.

Cost: $600 per two weeks inclusive. *Scholarships:* partial.
Housing: In dormitories, apartments.
Application: *Deadline:* June 1. *Fee:* $25. *Scholarship deadline:* June 1.
Contact: Paul Pierson, School of World Mission, 135 N. Oakland, Pasadena, CA 91101; (618) 449-1745. Cable: FULLSEM.

R4 SOUTHERN CALIFORNIA COLLEGE
Graduate Studies Program.
Specialization: Master's program prepares students, pastors, and teachers to use professional skills in ministry, teaching, and training more effectively.
Dates: Classes begin in the fall, winter, spring, summer.
Location: Costa Mesa, California: on campus.
Instruction: *Methods:* discussion groups, lectures, case studies, field trips, individualized instruction, "hands-on" training, independent study/research, computer-assisted instruction. *By:* faculty.
Highlights: Sponsor has offered program since 1983. Certificate on completion of 30–33 designated units. Issues I-20AB. Foreign nationals on tourist visas are eligible to enroll. A foreign student counselor/adviser is available. Intercultural orientation and student life program.
Eligibility: *Academic:* bachelor's degree. *Language:* English proficiency on advanced level is required. TOEFL: 550. *Professional:* none.
Cost: $12,000 for tuition, books and materials, meals, housing, health insurance. *Scholarships:* partial.
Housing: In dormitories, or sponsor assists in locating housing.
Application: *Deadline:* Apr. 15. *Fee:* $25; not refundable. *Scholarship deadline:* Apr. 15.
Contact: Faye Bowden, Graduate Studies Office, Southern California College, 55 Fair Drive, Costa Mesa, CA 92626; (714) 556-3610.

CHRISTIANITY

R5 CALVIN COLLEGE
Master of Arts in Christian Studies.
Specialization: An interdisciplinary program integrating a Christian perspective with a broad range of scholarly disciplines.
Dates: One year: classes begin in Sept., Jan., Feb., May.
Location: Grand Rapids, Michigan: on campus.
Instruction: *Methods:* lectures, independent study/research. *By:* faculty.
Highlights: Sponsor has offered program since 1980. Certificate on completion of ten course units. Issues I-20AB. Foreign nationals on tourist visas are eligible to enroll. A foreign student counselor/adviser is available. English and tutoring programs. Unlimited total enrollment; 10% foreign enrollment in 1985.
Eligibility: *Academic:* bachelor's degree. *Language:* English proficiency on intermediate level is required. TOEFL: 550. *Professional:* none.
Cost: About $8,600 for tuition, books and materials, meals, housing, local transportation, personal expenses. *Scholarships:* none.
Housing: In dormitories, apartments.
Application: *Deadline:* Aug. 1. *Fee:* none.
Contact: Dean for Academic Administration, Calvin College, Grand Rapids, MI 49506; (616) 957-6112.

R6 JESUIT SCHOOL OF THEOLOGY AT BERKELEY
Institute for Spirituality and Worship.
Specialization: Graduate-level academic study, community participation, and worship.
Dates: Aug.–May.

All program information is subject to change without notice
and must be confirmed directly with the sponsor.

Location: Berkeley, California: on campus.
Instruction: *Methods:* lectures, seminars. *By:* faculty.
Highlights: Sponsor has offered program since 1972. Certificate upon completion of eight courses. Issues I-20AB, IAP-66. A foreign student counselor/adviser is available. 45 total enrollment; 26% foreign enrollment in 1985.
Eligibility: *Academic:* bachelor's degree. *Language:* English proficiency on advanced level is required. TOEFL. *Professional:* ministerial experience.
Cost: About $10,915 inclusive. *Scholarships:* very limited.
Housing: In apartments if available, or sponsor assists in locating housing.
Application: *Deadline:* Mar. 1. *Fee:* $25; not refundable. *Scholarship deadline:* May 15.
Contact: Lorna Wallace McKeown, Asst. to the Dean, Institute for Spirituality and Worship, Jesuit School of Theology at Berkeley, 1735 LeRoy Ave., Berkeley, CA 94709; (415) 841-8804.

R7 LA SALLE UNIVERSITY
Religious Studies for the Christian Ministries.
Specialization: Theology, pastoral ministry, religious education, youth ministry, liturgical ministry, ministry to marriage and family.
Dates: Six weeks: classes begin in late June.
Location: Philadelphia, Pennsylvania: on campus.
Instruction: *Methods:* discussion groups, lectures, individualized instruction, independent study/research. *By:* faculty, guest speakers/lecturers.
Highlights: Sponsor has offered program since 1950. Certificate upon completion of 18 credits. Master's degree upon completion of 30–36 credits. Foreign nationals on tourist visas are eligible to enroll. A foreign student counselor/adviser is available. 225 total enrollment; 10% foreign enrollment in 1985.
Eligibility: *Academic:* bachelor's degree. *Language:* English proficiency on intermediate level is required. *Professional:* none.
Cost: $147 per credit for tuition. *Scholarships:* none.
Housing: In dormitories.
Application: *Deadline:* May 30. *Fee:* $25; not refundable.
Contact: Dr. Leo M. Van Everbroeck, La Salle University, Philadelphia, PA 19141; (215) 951-1350.

R8 PACIFIC SCHOOL OF RELIGION
Certificate of Special Studies.
Specialization: Flexible program in Christian religion and theology.
Dates: Nine months: classes begin in Sept.
Location: Berkeley, California: on campus.
Instruction: *Methods:* discussion groups, lectures. *By:* faculty.
Highlights: Sponsor has offered program since 1965. Certificate upon completion of 18 semester hours with 3.0 GPA. Issues I-20AB. Foreign nationals on tourist visas are not eligible to enroll. A foreign student counselor/adviser is available. International student liaison program and social activities. Unlimited total enrollment; 9% foreign enrollment in 1985.
Eligibility: *Academic:* bachelor's degree. *Language:* English proficiency on intermediate level is required. TOEFL: 550. *Professional:* none.
Cost: $10,680–$16,080 inclusive. *Scholarships:* partial.
Housing: In dormitories, apartments.
Application: *Deadline:* Mar. 1. *Fee:* $25; not refundable. *Scholarship deadline:* Mar. 15.
Contact: Alan Schut, Director of Admissions/Foreign Student Advisor, Pacific School of Religion, 1798 Scenic Ave., Berkeley, CA 94709; (415) 848-0528.

R9 PRINCETON THEOLOGICAL SEMINARY
Summer School.
Specialization: Biblical studies, theology and ethics, church history, homiletics, Christian education, church administration, evangelism, pastoral theology.
Dates: Nine weeks: classes begin in June.
Location: Princeton, New Jersey: at seminary.
Instruction: *Methods:* lectures, discussion groups. *By:* faculty.
Highlights: Sponsor has offered program since 1971. Certificate. Issues I-20AB, IAP-66. Foreign nationals on tourist visas are eligible to enroll. A foreign student counselor/advisor is not available. 9% foreign enrollment in 1985.
Eligibility: *Academic:* bachelor's degree. *Language:* English proficiency on advanced level is preferred. *Professional:* none.
Cost: $1,415 per course for tuition, meals, housing. *Scholarships:* none.
Housing: In dormitories.
Application: *Deadline:* one week prior. *Fee:* $25; not refundable.
Contact: Summer School Office, Princeton Theological Seminary, 108 Stockton Street, Princeton, NJ 08540; (609) 921-8252.

R10 ST. JOHN'S UNIVERSITY, SCHOOL OF THEOLOGY
School of Theology Summer Session.
Specialization: Religious education, liturgy, pastoral theology, taught in a university/monastic setting surrounded by woods and lakes.
Dates: Six weeks: classes begin in June.
Location: Collegeville, Minnesota: on campus.
Instruction: *Methods:* discussion groups, lectures, independent study/research. *By:* faculty.
Highlights: Sponsor has offered program previously. Foreign nationals on tourist visas are eligible to enroll. A foreign student counselor/adviser is not available. 200 total enrollment; 3% foreign enrollment in 1985.
Eligibility: *Academic:* bachelor's degree. *Language:* English proficiency on intermediate level is required. *Professional:* none.
Cost: $1,465 for tuition, meals, housing. *Scholarships:* partial.
Housing: Not provided; sponsor assists in locating housing.
Application: *Deadline:* May 16. *Fee:* $10; not refundable. *Scholarship deadline:* Mar. 31.
Contact: Sr. Elise Saggau, Assistant Dean for Students, School of Theology, St. John's University, Collegeville, MN 56321; (612) 363-2102.

R11 WADHAMS HALL SEMINARY-COLLEGE
Pre-Theologate Program.
Specialization: A flexible program of philosophy and religious courses, emphasizing preparation for the Roman Catholic priesthood.
Dates: Nine months: classes begin in late Aug.
Location: Ogdensburg, New York: on campus.
Instruction: *Methods:* discussion groups, lectures, independent study/research. *By:* faculty.
Highlights: Sponsor has offered program previously. Certificate. A foreign student counselor/adviser is not available. No foreign enrollment in 1985.
Eligibility: *Academic:* bachelor's degree. *Language:* English proficiency on intermediate level is required. *Professional:* none.
Cost: About $6,000 for tuition, books and materials, meals, housing. *Scholarships:* none; most candidates are sponsored by Canadian or U.S. dioceses.
Housing: In dormitories.
Application: *Deadline:* July. *Fee:* $50; not refundable.
Contact: Dr. Jerome L. Wyant, Academic Dean, Wadhams Hall Seminary-College, R.R. #4, Box 80, Ogdensburg, NY 13669; (315) 393-2667.

All program information is subject to change without notice
and must be confirmed directly with the sponsor.

R12 WESLEY THEOLOGICAL SEMINARY

Specialization: Broad range of courses in Bible, church history, theology, sociology of religion, Black preaching, Biblical Greek or Hebrew, pastoral counseling, and Christian education.
Dates: Six weeks: late June–early Aug.
Location: Washington, D.C.: at seminary.
Instruction: *Methods:* lectures, discussion groups, case studies, field trips, individualized instruction. *By:* faculty.
Highlights: Sponsor has offered short-term programs since 1882. Certificate upon completion of 20 semester hours of instruction. Issues I-20AB. Foreign nationals on tourist visas are not eligible to enroll. A foreign student counselor/adviser is available.
Eligibility: *Academic:* bachelor's degree. *Language:* English proficiency on advanced level is required. TOEFL: 600. *Professional:* none.
Cost: $162 per semester hour for tuition. *Scholarships:* none.
Housing: In dormitories.
Application: *Deadline:* June 13. *Fee:* $25; not refundable.
Contact: John E. Bevan, Registrar, Wesley Theological Seminary, 4500 Massachusetts Ave. NW, Washington, DC 20016; (202) 885-8650.

JUDAISM

R13 THE JEWISH THEOLOGICAL SEMINARY OF AMERICA
Graduate Summer School.

Specialization: Intensive study of Jewish tradition in the context of a Jewish community.
Dates: Classes begin in May, June.
Location: New York, New York: on campus.
Instruction: *Methods:* lectures. *By:* faculty. *Some classes conducted in Hebrew.*
Highlights: Sponsor has offered program since 1976. Issues I-20AB, IAP-66. Foreign nationals on tourist visas are eligible to enroll. A foreign student counselor/adviser is available. Unlimited total enrollment; less than 2% foreign enrollment in 1985.
Eligibility: *Academic:* bachelor's degree. *Language:* English proficiency on beginning level is required. *Professional:* none.
Cost: About $1,000 for tuition, housing, fees. *Scholarships:* partial.
Housing: In dormitories.
Application: *Deadline:* prior to start. *Fee:* $15; not refundable. *Scholarship deadline:* one month prior.
Contact: Rabbi Morris Allen, The Jewish Theological Seminary of America, 3080 Broadway, New York, NY 10027; (212) 678-8886.

Abbreviations: ESL = English as a Second Language; TOEFL = Test of English as a Foreign Language; ALIGU = American Language Institute of Georgetown University; GPA = Grade Point Average; SAT = Scholastic Aptitude Test; GED = General Equivalency Diploma.

153

PHYSICAL SCIENCES

S1 COLORADO SCHOOL OF MINES
Specialization: Petroleum, chemical engineering and petroleum refining, geology, geophysics, mining, metallurgy. Programs can be customized for groups and conducted in the U.S. or abroad.
Dates: To be arranged.
Location: Golden, Colorado: on campus, at professional work site.
Instruction: *Methods:* discussion groups, lectures, case studies, field trips, individualized instruction, "hands-on" training, independent study/research, computer-assisted instruction, language laboratories, science laboratories. *By:* faculty, guest speakers/lecturers.
Highlights: Sponsor has offered program previously. Certificate. Issues I-20AB, IAP-66. Foreign nationals on tourist visas are eligible to enroll. A foreign student counselor/adviser is available. International student office. 14% foreign enrollment in 1985.
Eligibility: *Academic:* criteria set by sponsoring agency. *Language:* English proficiency on intermediate level is required. TOEFL: 500; Univ. of Michigan Language Test: 78. *Professional:* criteria set by sponsor.
Cost: Varies. *Scholarships:* none.
Housing: In dormitories, or sponsor assists in locating housing.
Application: *Deadline:* varies. *Fee:* none.
Contact: Dr. J. Hepworth, Director of Continuing Education, Colorado School of Mines, Golden, CO 80401; (303) 273-3322. Telex: 910 934 0190.

S2 GUILFORD COLLEGE
Specialization: Programs available in biology, chemistry, history and philosophy of science, geology, mathematics, and physics.
Dates: One year: classes begin in Aug.
Location: Greensboro, North Carolina: on campus.
Instruction: *Methods:* lectures, discussion groups, science labs. *By:* faculty.
Highlights: Sponsor has offered program previously. Certificate upon completion of 4–6 courses. Issues I-20AB, I-20MN. Foreign nationals on tourist visas are not eligible to enroll. A foreign student counselor/adviser is available. International student club membership.
Eligibility: *Academic:* bachelor's degree. *Language:* English proficiency on advanced level is required. TOEFL: 500. *Professional:*
Cost: $112 per credit hour. *Scholarships:* none.
Housing: Not provided; student makes own arrangements.
Application: *Deadline:* open. *Fee:* $20; not refundable.
Contact: Dean of Admissions and Financial Aid, Guilford College, 5800 West Friendly Ave., Greensboro, NC 27410; (919) 292-5511.

S3 VOORHEES COLLEGE
Division of Natural Sciences and Mathematics.
Dates: Nine months: classes begin in Aug. and Jan.
Location: Denmark, South Carolina: on campus, at professional work site.
Instruction: *Methods:* discussion groups, lectures, case studies, field trips, individualized

---

All program information is subject to change without notice
and must be confirmed directly with the sponsor.

instruction, "hands-on" training, independent study/research, computer-assisted instruction, science laboratories. *By:* faculty.
Highlights: Sponsor has offered program since 1969. Certificate. Issues I-20AB. Foreign nationals on tourist visas are not eligible to enroll. A foreign student counselor/adviser is available.
Eligibility: *Academic:* associate's degree. *Language:* English proficiency on beginning level is required. TOEFL. *Professional:* none.
Cost: $5,884 for tuition, meals, housing, health insurance. *Scholarships:* none.
Housing: In dormitories.
Application: *Deadline:* Aug. *Fee:* $10; not refundable.
Contact: Dr. Lucious Daily, Jr., Director of Admissions and Records, Voorhees College, Voorhees Road, Denmark, SC 29042; (803) 793-3351.

CHEMISTRY

S4 MASSACHUSETTS INSTITUTE OF TECHNOLOGY
Polymer Science and Technology.
Specialization: Toughening brittle polymers, rheological behavior of polymeric fluids, electrical properties of polymers, composite materials, and physical chemistry of polymers.
Dates: June–Aug.
Location: Cambridge, Massachusetts: on campus.
Instruction: *Methods:* discussion groups, lectures, case studies, "hands-on" training, independent study/research, computer-assisted instruction, science laboratories. *By:* faculty.
Highlights: Sponsor has offered program since 1949. Certificate. Foreign nationals on tourist visas are eligible to enroll. A foreign student counselor/adviser is not available. About 20–25 per class total enrollment; 10% foreign enrollment in 1985.
Eligibility: *Academic:* bachelor's degree. *Language:* English proficiency on intermediate level is required. *Professional:* none.
Cost: About $1,500 per week for tuition, books and materials, meals, housing. *Scholarships:* none.
Housing: In dormitories, hotels.
Application: *Deadline:* depends on program. *Fee:* none.
Contact: Summer Session Office, Massachusetts Institute of Technology, 77 Massachusetts Ave., Room E19-356, Cambridge, MA 02139; (617) 253-2101. Telex: 921473 MIT CAM.

S5 NORTH DAKOTA STATE UNIVERSITY
Coatings Science.
Specialization: Topics include high solids and radiation curable coatings, film formation, resins, appearance of coatings, pigments and pigment dispersion, solvents, rheology, coatings performance and formulation.
Dates: Two weeks: June.
Location: Fargo, North Dakota: on campus.
Instruction: *Methods:* discussion groups, lectures. *By:* faculty.
Highlights: Sponsor has offered program since 1979. Certificate. Foreign nationals on tourist visas are eligible to enroll. A foreign student counselor/adviser is available. 36 total enrollment; 8% foreign enrollment in 1985.
Eligibility: *Academic:* bachelor's degree; two years of college chemistry including organic chemistry. *Language:* English proficiency on intermediate level is required. *Professional:* none.
Cost: $1,150 for tuition. *Scholarships:* none.
Housing: In dormitories.
Application: *Deadline:* Mar. 31. *Fee:* none.
Contact: Dr. Frank Jones or Dr. S. Peter Pappas, Polymers & Coatings Dept., North Dakota State University, Fargo, ND 58105; (701) 237-7633.

S6 SWARTHMORE COLLEGE
Research Participation and Supervision.
Specialization: Emphasis on undergraduate research participation with exceptionally gifted students.
Dates: Year-round.
Location: Swarthmore, Pennsylvania: on campus.
Instruction: *Methods:* discussion groups, individualized instruction, "hands-on" training, independent study/research, science laboratories. *By:* faculty.
Highlights: Sponsor has offered program previously. Practical training is a program component; participants are paid. Issues IAP-66. A foreign student counselor/adviser is available. 5–6 total enrollment.
Eligibility: *Academic:* doctorate. *Language:* English proficiency on intermediate level is required. *Professional:* none.
Cost: $15,000 for meals, housing, health insurance. *Scholarships:* some.
Housing: Not provided; sponsor assists in locating housing.
Application: *Deadline:* none. *Fee:* none. *Scholarship deadline:* not given.
Contact: Robert F. Pasternach, Professor and Chairman, Dept. of Chemistry, Swarthmore College, Swarthmore, PA 19081; (215) 447-7559.

S7 TEXAS A&M UNIVERSITY, CENTER FOR EXECUTIVE DEVELOPMENT
Chemistry for Non-Chemists.
Specialization: Fundamentals of materials and processes for nonchemists/nontechnical managers employed in chemically-related industries.
Dates: Two weeks: July.
Location: College Station, Texas: on campus.
Instruction: *Methods:* lectures, case studies, science laboratories. *By:* faculty.
Highlights: Sponsor has offered program since 1985. Certificate. Issues I-20AB, IAP-66. Foreign nationals on tourist visas are eligible to enroll. A foreign student counselor/adviser is available. 30 total enrollment; no foreign enrollment in 1985.
Eligibility: *Academic:* bachelor's degree. *Language:* English proficiency on advanced level is required. *Professional:* none.
Cost: $3,000 for tuition, books and materials, some meals, recreational facilities. *Scholarships:* none.
Housing: Not provided; sponsor assists in locating housing.
Application: *Deadline:* one month prior. *Fee:* none.
Contact: Jean Gresham, Program Manager, Center for Executive Development, Texas A&M University, 449 John R. Blocker Bldg., College Station, TX 77843; (409) 845-1216. Telex: 510 892 7689.

S8 UNIVERSITY OF WASHINGTON, DEPARTMENT OF CHEMISTRY
Nonthesis Master of Science.
Specialization: Graduate-level courses in chemistry and related areas.
Dates: Nine months: classes begin in Sept.
Location: Seattle, Washington: on campus.
Instruction: *Methods:* lectures, science laboratories. *By:* faculty, guest speakers/lecturers.
Highlights: Sponsor has offered program since 1900. Certificate upon completion of 36 quarter course credits with 3.0 GPA. Issues IAP-66. Foreign nationals on tourist visas are not eligible to enroll. A foreign student counselor/adviser is available. 2–3 per year total enrollment; 50% foreign enrollment in 1985.
Eligibility: *Academic:* bachelor's degree; Master of Science degree required from some countries. *Language:* English proficiency on advanced level is required. TOEFL: 550; Univ. of Michigan Language Test: 80. *Professional:* none.
Cost: $14,500 inclusive. *Scholarships:* none.
Housing: Not provided; student makes own arrangements.

Application: *Deadline:* Apr. 1. *Fee:* $35; not refundable.
Contact: Prof. A.G. Anderson, Jr., Dept. of Chemistry BG-10, University of Washington, Seattle, WA 98195; (206) 543-9343.

GEOLOGY

S9 COLLEGE OF THE ATLANTIC
Geological Foundations for Teachers.
Specialization: Geology.
Dates: Two weeks: Aug.
Location: Bar Harbor, Maine: on campus, at professional work site.
Instruction: *Methods:* discussion groups, field trips, individualized instruction, "hands-on" training. *By:* faculty, guest speakers/lecturers.
Highlights: Sponsor has offered short-term programs since 1981. Certificate. Issues I-20AB. Foreign nationals on tourist visas are eligible to enroll. A foreign student counselor/adviser is not available. 15 total enrollment.
Eligibility: *Academic:* bachelor's degree; some knowledge of geology. *Language:* English proficiency on advanced level is required. *Professional:* teachers.
Cost: $760 for tuition, meals, housing. *Scholarships:* none.
Housing: In dormitories, with families.
Application: *Deadline:* none. *Fee:* none.
Contact: Ted Koffman, College of the Atlantic, Eden Street, Bar Harbor, ME 04609; (207) 288-5015, Ext. 38.

S10 NEW MEXICO INSTITUTE OF MINING AND TECHNOLOGY
Mineral Exploration Short Course.
Specialization: Geoscience, including mineral exploration, methods of mineralogy, field geology, petrography, economic geology.
Dates: Three weeks: summer.
Location: Socorro, New Mexico: on campus.
Instruction: *Methods:* lectures. *By:* faculty. *Also in Spanish.*
Highlights: New program. Certificate. Issues I-20AB, I-20MN, IAP-66. Foreign nationals on tourist visas are eligible to enroll. A foreign student counselor/adviser is available. 15 total enrollment.
Eligibility: *Academic:* some undergraduate work, good background in earth science, mathematics, and chemistry. *Language:* not given. *Professional:* none.
Cost: $1,210 for tuition, books and materials, meals, housing, local transportation. *Scholarships:* none.
Housing: In dormitories.
Application: *Deadline:* not given. *Fee:* not given.
Contact: William C. Bradley, Director of Development, New Mexico Institute of Mining and Technology, Box K, Campus Station, Socorro, NM 87801; (505) 835-5525.

S11 SOUTHERN ILLINOIS UNIVERSITY
Geology/Geophysics.
Specialization: Coal geology, coal petrology, exploration geophysics; programs can be customized.
Dates: To be arranged.
Location: Carbondale, Illinois: on campus, at professional work site.
Instruction: *Methods:* discussion groups, lectures, case studies, field trips, individualized instruction, "hands-on" training, independent study/research, computer-assisted instruction, science laboratories. *By:* faculty.
Highlights: Sponsor has offered program previously. Certificate. A foreign student counselor/adviser is available. Office of International Studies.

Abbreviations: ESL = English as a Second Language; TOEFL = Test of English as a Foreign Language; ALIGU = American Language Institute of Georgetown University; GPA = Grade Point Average; SAT = Scholastic Aptitude Test; GED = General Equivalency Diploma.

157

Eligibility: *Academic:* bachelor's degree. *Language:* English proficiency on intermediate level is preferred. TOEFL. *Professional:* none.
Cost: Varies. *Scholarships:* none.
Housing: Not given.
Application: *Deadline:* not given. *Fee:* not given.
Contact: John E. Utgaard, Dept. of Geology, Southern Illinois University, Parkinson 102, Carbondale, IL 62901; (618) 453-3351.

S12 UNIVERSITY OF CINCINNATI
Master of Science in Economic Sedimentology.
Specialization: Comprehensive training in sedimentology, includes carbonate petrology, field geology, sandstone petrology, analytical methods, clay mineralogy, other courses.
Dates: Nine months: classes begin in Sept.
Location: Cincinnati, Ohio: on campus.
Instruction: *Methods:* lectures, field trips, science laboratories. *By:* faculty.
Highlights: Sponsor has offered program since 1984. Certificate. Issues I-20AB, IAP-66. Foreign nationals on tourist visas are not eligible to enroll. A foreign student counselor/adviser is available. 6 total enrollment; 100% foreign enrollment in 1985.
Eligibility: *Academic:* bachelor's degree. *Language:* English proficiency on intermediate level is required. TOEFL: 550. *Professional:* five years of experience.
Cost: $17,000–$22,000 inclusive. *Scholarships:* none.
Housing: Not provided; sponsor assists in locating housing.
Application: *Deadline:* Feb. 15. *Fee:* $20; not refundable.
Contact: I.B. Maynard, Dept. of Geology, University of Cincinnati, Cincinnati, OH 45221; (513) 475-3732.

OCEANOGRAPHY

S13 COLLEGE OF THE ATLANTIC
Teachers' Introductory Workshop to Oceanography.
Specialization: Oceanography.
Dates: Six weeks: classes begin in mid-July.
Location: Bar Harbor, Maine: on campus, at professional work site.
Instruction: *Methods:* discussion groups, field trips, individualized instruction, "hands-on" training. *By:* faculty.
Highlights: Sponsor has offered short-term programs since 1981. Certificate. Issues I-20AB. Foreign nationals on tourist visas are eligible to enroll. A foreign student counselor/adviser is not available. 15 total enrollment; 1% foreign enrollment in 1985.
Eligibility: *Academic:* bachelor's degree; some knowledge of oceanography.
Language: English proficiency on advanced level is required. *Professional:* teachers.
Cost: $860 for tuition, meals, housing, some fees. *Scholarships:* none.
Housing: In dormitories, with families.
Application: *Deadline:* none. *Fee:* none.
Contact: Ted Koffman, College of the Atlantic, Eden Street, Bar Harbor, ME 04609; (207) 288-5015, Ext. 38.

PSYCHOLOGY, PSYCHIATRY, AND PSYCHOTHERAPY

T1 CLEMSON UNIVERSITY
International Visitor Program.
Specialization: Personalized programs in psychology, combining study, research, and internships. Undergraduate, graduate, and postgraduate levels.
Dates: Rolling: semesters begin in Aug., Jan.
Location: Clemson, South Carolina: on campus.
Instruction: *Methods:* lectures, individualized instruction, "hands-on" training, independent study/research, computer-assisted instruction, laboratories. *By:* faculty.
Highlights: Sponsor has offered program previously. Certificate. Practical training may be a program component; participants are paid. Issues I-20AB, IAP-66. Foreign nationals on tourist visas are eligible to enroll. A foreign student counselor/adviser is available.
Eligibility: *Academic:* bachelor's degree or some undergraduate work. *Language:* English proficiency on the advanced level is required. TOEFL: 550. *Professional:* requires professional certification.
Cost: $815 per month for tuition, books and materials, meals, housing, health insurance. *Scholarships:* none; all participants must be sponsored by an organization.
Housing: In dormitories.
Application: *Deadline:* rolling. *Fee:* none.
Contact: International Service Office, Clemson University, Room 106 Sikes Hall, Clemson, SC 29631; (803) 656-5466.

T2 FAMILY CENTER OF THE BERKSHIRES/BERKSHIRE MEDICAL CENTER
Visiting Residency in Family Therapy.
Specialization: Provides an intensive exposure to systemic family therapy as taught and practiced in a comprehensive psychiatric service.
Dates: Four weeks: activities begin monthly.
Location: Pittsfield, Massachusetts: at medical center.
Instruction: *Methods:* observation and discussion groups, case studies, video-assisted instruction, independent study/research. *By:* faculty.
Highlights: Sponsor has offered program since 1979. Issues I-20AB. Foreign nationals on tourist visas are eligible to enroll. A foreign student counselor/adviser is available. 2 total enrollment.
Eligibility: *Academic:* master's degree or doctorate. *Language:* English proficiency on intermediate level is required. *Professional:* experience in field of mental health, psychology, psychiatry, or family therapy.
Cost: $1,000 for tuition. *Scholarships:* none.
Housing: Not provided; sponsor assists in locating housing.
Application: *Deadline:* none. *Fee:* none.
Contact: Dr. Carlos E. Sluzki, Chairman, Dept. of Psychiatry, Berkshire Medical Center, Pittsfield, MA 01201; (413) 499-4161, Ext. 2162.

Abbreviations: ESL = English as a Second Language; TOEFL = Test of English as a Foreign Language; ALIGU = American Language Institute of Georgetown University; GPA = Grade Point Average; SAT = Scholastic Aptitude Test; GED = General Equivalency Diploma.

T3 GUILFORD COLLEGE

Specialization: Programs in psychology and related disciplines.
Dates: Aug.–July.
Location: Greensboro, North Carolina: on campus.
Instruction: *Methods:* lectures, discussion groups. *By:* faculty.
Highlights: Sponsor has offered short-term programs since 1983. Certificate upon completion of 4–6 courses. Issues I-20AB, I-20MN. Foreign nationals on tourist visas are not eligible to enroll. A foreign student counselor/adviser is available. International Relations Club.
Eligibility: *Academic:* bachelor's degree. *Language:* English proficiency on advanced level is required. TOEFL: 500. *Professional:* none.
Cost: $112 per credit hour for tuition. *Scholarships:* none.
Housing: Not provided; sponsor assists in locating housing.
Application: *Deadline:* open. *Fee:* $20; not refundable.
Contact: Dean of Admissions and Financial Aid, Guilford College, 5800 W. Friendly Ave., Greensboro, NC 27410, (919) 292-5511.

T4 LESLEY COLLEGE GRADUATE SCHOOL
The Institute for the Arts in Human Development.

Specialization: Master's program in expressive therapies: art therapy, dance therapy, music therapy, psychodrama. Emphasis on cross-cultural learning, healing, mental health.
Dates: Semesters: Sept.-Dec., Feb.-May. January mini-semester. Summer intensive: July 20-Aug. 22.
Location: Cambridge, Massachusetts: on campus.
Instruction: *Methods:* lectures, discussion groups, individualized instruction, "hands-on" training, independent study/research. *By:* faculty.
Highlights: Sponsor has offered program since 1974. Master's degree. Practical training is a program component; participants may be paid. Issues I-20AB, I-20MN, IAP-66. Foreign nationals on tourist visas are not eligible to enroll. A foreign student counselor/adviser is available. Orientation program and Office of International Studies. 100 total enrollment; 35% foreign enrollment in 1985.
Eligibility: *Academic:* bachelor's degree. *Language:* English proficiency on advanced level is required. TOEFL: 550.
Professional: Background in psychology, the arts; work experience in mental health.
Cost: About $17,000 inclusive. *Scholarships:* none.
Housing: In dormitories.
Application: *Deadline:* May 1 for Aug. start. *Fee:* $35; not refundable.
Contact: Joanna Fabris, Program Advisor, Arts Institute, Lesley College Graduate School, 29 Everett Street, Cambridge, MA 02238; (617) 868-9600, Ext. 480.

T5 STATE UNIVERSITY COLLEGE AT GENESEO, COLLEGE OF ARTS AND SCIENCES
Master of Arts in Psychology.

Specialization: Psychology.
Dates: One year: classes begin in Sept.
Location: Geneseo, New York: on campus.
Instruction: *Methods:* discussion groups, lectures, case studies, field trips, individualized instruction, independent study/research, computer-assisted instruction, language laboratories, science laboratories. *By:* faculty.
Highlights: Sponsor has offered program previously. Certificate. A foreign student counselor/adviser is available. No foreign enrollment in 1985.
Eligibility: *Academic:* bachelor's degree. *Language:* English proficiency on advanced level is required. *Professional:* none.
Cost: $6,280 for tuition, meals, housing, fees. *Scholarships:* none.
Housing: In dormitories.

All program information is subject to change without notice
and must be confirmed directly with the sponsor.

160

Application: *Deadline:* none. *Fee:* $20; not refundable.
Contact: Dr. Melvyn Yessenow, College of Arts and Sciences, SUC at Geneseo, Sturges 119D, Geneseo, NY 14454; (716) 245-5206.

T6 UNIVERSITY OF NORTH CAROLINA, SCHOOL OF MEDICINE
Treatment and Education of Autistic and Related Communication Handicapped Children.

Specialization: Treatment and study of autism and developmental disorders.
Dates: Vary.
Location: Chapel Hill, North Carolina: on campus, at professional work site.
Instruction: *Methods:* discussion groups, lectures, case studies, field trips, "hands-on" training, independent study/research. *By:* faculty.
Highlights: Sponsor has offered program since 1980. Certificate. Practical training is a program component; participants are paid. Issues I-20AB, IAP-66. Foreign nationals on tourist visas are eligible to enroll. A foreign student counselor/adviser is available. 15% foreign enrollment in 1985.
Eligibility: *Academic:* bachelor's degree. *Language:* English proficiency on intermediate level is required. TOEFL: 250. *Professional:* two years of study or experience in this area.
Cost: Varies. *Scholarships:* full, through Rotary Club or other foundations.
Housing: In dormitories, furnished rooms, hotels, with families.
Application: *Deadline:* none. *Fee:* none. *Scholarship deadline:* not given.
Contact: Mr. Eric Schopler, Ph.D., Director, Division TEACCH, University of North Carolina, 310 Medical School Wing E, 222H, Chapel Hill, NC 27514; (919) 966-2173/4/5.

PUBLIC ADMINISTRATION

U1 **THE AMERICAN UNIVERSITY**
Graduate Certificate in Governmental Management.
Specialization: Governmental management.
Dates: Classes begin in Sept., Jan., May, July.
Location: Washington, D.C.: on campus.
Instruction: *Methods:* discussion groups, lectures, case studies. *By:* faculty.
Highlights: Sponsor has offered program previously. Certificate upon completion of five courses. Issues I-20AB. Foreign nationals on tourist visas are not eligible to enroll. A foreign student counselor/adviser is available. Orientation programs.
Eligibility: *Academic:* bachelor's degree. *Language:* English proficiency on advanced level is required. TOEFL: 600; English Language Institute Placement Test. *Professional:* none.
Cost: $299 per semester hour for tuition. *Scholarships:* none.
Housing: Not provided; sponsor assists in locating housing.
Application: *Deadline:* none. *Fee:* none.
Contact: Programs Advisement Center, The American University, 4400 Massachusetts Ave. NW, Room 153 McKinley Bldg., Washington, DC 20016; (202) 885-2500.

U2 **THE AMERICAN UNIVERSITY**
Graduate Certificate in Public Management.
Specialization: Graduate-level courses in the field of public management.
Dates: Classes begin in Sept., Jan., May, July.
Location: Washington, D.C.: on campus.
Instruction: *Methods:* discussion groups, lectures, case studies. *By:* faculty.
Highlights: Sponsor has offered program previously. Certificate upon completion of five courses. Issues I-20AB. Foreign nationals on tourist visas are not eligible to enroll. A foreign student counselor/adviser is available. Orientation and ESL programs.
Eligibility: *Academic:* bachelor's degree. *Language:* English proficiency on advanced level is required. TOEFL: 600; English Language Institute Placement Test. *Professional:* none.
Cost: $299 per semester hour for tuition. *Scholarships:* none.
Housing: Not provided; sponsor assists in locating housing.
Application: *Deadline:* none. *Fee:* none.
Contact: Programs Advisement Center, The American University, 4400 Massachusetts Ave. NW, Room 153 McKinley Bldg., Washington, DC 20016; (202) 885-2500.

U3 **CENTRAL MICHIGAN UNIVERSITY**
Master of Science in Administration.
Specialization: Concentrations in public administration and health services administration.
Dates: Rolling.
Location: Washington, D.C.; Baltimore, Maryland; Philadelphia, Pennsylvania; New York, New York: at professional work site.
Instruction: *Methods:* discussion groups, lectures, case studies, individualized instruction, independent study/research, computer-assisted instruction. *By:* faculty, guest speakers/lecturers.

All program information is subject to change without notice
and must be confirmed directly with the sponsor.

Highlights: Sponsor has offered program since 1974. Certificate or MSA degree. A foreign student counselor/adviser is available. About 5–10% foreign enrollment in 1985.
Eligibility: *Academic:* bachelor's degree. *Language:* English proficiency on advanced level is required. TOEFL: 525; ALIGU. *Professional:* none.
Cost: $4,788 for tuition. *Scholarships:* none.
Housing: Not provided; student makes own arrangements.
Application: *Deadline:* open. *Fee:* $25; not refundable.
Contact: Dr. Charles N. Somers, Regional Director, Central Michigan University, 8550 Lee Highway, Suite 125, Fairfax, VA 22031; (703) 849-8218.

U4 EASTERN WASHINGTON UNIVERSITY
Graduate Program in Public Administration.
Specialization: Personnel, finance, local government.
Dates: Classes begin in Sept., Jan., April, June.
Location: Spokane, Washington: at Higher Education Center.
Instruction: *Methods:* discussion groups, lectures, case studies. *By:* faculty, guest speakers/lecturers.
Highlights: Sponsor has offered program since 1975. Certificate on completion of 18 credits. Practical training is a program component; participants are not paid. A foreign student counselor/adviser is available. 5% foreign enrollment in 1985.
Eligibility: *Academic:* bachelor's degree. *Language:* English proficiency on advanced level is required. TOEFL. *Professional:* none.
Cost: $1,698 per quarter for tuition. *Scholarships:* full.
Housing: Not provided; student makes own arrangements.
Application: *Deadline:* rolling. *Fee:* $25; not refundable. *Scholarship deadline:* Apr. 1.
Contact: Larry S. Luton, MS-30 Public Administration, Eastern Washington University, Cheney, WA 99004; (509) 359-2365.

U5 HARVARD UNIVERSITY, KENNEDY SCHOOL OF GOVERNMENT
Edward S. Mason Fellows Program.
Specialization: Public policy and management; for senior public officials from developing and newly industrialized countries.
Dates: One year: classes begin in July.
Location: Cambridge, Massachusetts: on campus.
Instruction: *Methods:* discussion groups, lectures, case studies, field trips, independent study/research, computer-assisted instruction. *By:* faculty.
Highlights: Sponsor has offered program since 1957. Master's degree upon completion of eight courses with B average. Issues I-20AB, I-20MN, IAP-66. A foreign student counselor/adviser is available. ESL, social, and cultural programs. 50 total enrollment; 100% foreign enrollment in 1985.
Eligibility: *Academic:* bachelor's degree. *Language:* English proficiency on advanced level is required. TOEFL: 600 preferred. *Professional:* five years of experience.
Cost: $31,000 inclusive, plus overseas field trip. *Scholarships:* none.
Housing: In dormitories, apartments.
Application: *Deadline:* Feb. 1. *Fee:* $40; not refundable.
Contact: Dr. Nancy S. Pyle, Edward S. Mason Fellows Program, Kennedy School of Government, Harvard University, 79 Kennedy Street, Cambridge, MA 02138; (617) 495-2133 or 495-1321. Cable: HIID, Cambridge. Telex: 7103200315.

U6 HARVARD UNIVERSITY
Lucius N. Littauer Master in Public Administration Program.
Specialization: Individually designed program for midcareer professionals seeking to become leaders in their fields.
Dates: Nine months: classes begin in Sept.
Location: Cambridge, Massachusetts: on campus.

Abbreviations: ESL = English as a Second Language; TOEFL = Test of English as a Foreign Language; ALIGU = American Language Institute of Georgetown University; GPA = Grade Point Average; SAT = Scholastic Aptitude Test; GED = General Equivalency Diploma.

163

Instruction: *Methods:* discussion groups, lectures, case studies, field trips, individualized instruction. *By:* faculty, guest speakers/lecturers.

Highlights: Sponsor has offered program since 1936. Master's degree upon completion of eight courses. Issues I-20AB, I-20MN, IAP-66. A foreign student counselor/adviser is available. 250 total enrollment; 25% foreign enrollment in 1985.

Eligibility: *Academic:* bachelor's degree. *Language:* English proficiency on advanced level is required. TOEFL: 550–600. *Professional:* five years of experience in the public sector, leadership potential.

Cost: $10,300 for tuition. *Scholarships:* none.

Housing: Not provided; sponsor assists in locating housing.

Application: *Deadline:* June 15. *Fee:* $40; not refundable.

Contact: Dr. Nancy S. Pyle, Kennedy School of Government, Harvard University, 79 Kennedy Street, Cambridge, MA 02138; (617) 495-1353.

U7 NEW YORK UNIVERSITY, INSTITUTE OF PUBLIC ADMINISTRATION
Advanced Professional Certificate Program.

Specialization: Comparative and developmental administration; international administration. Program designed for professionals in the field.

Dates: One semester: classes begin in Sept., Feb., June.

Location: New York, New York: on campus.

Instruction: *Methods:* discussion groups, lectures. *By:* faculty.

Highlights: Sponsor has offered program since 1977. Certificate on completion of four graduate courses. A foreign student counselor/adviser is available. Unlimited total enrollment.

Eligibility: *Academic:* master's degree. *Language:* English proficiency on advanced level is required. *Professional:* none.

Cost: $3,696 for tuition. *Scholarships:* none.

Housing: Not provided; sponsor assists in locating housing.

Application: *Deadline:* Aug. 1, Jan. 1, May 1. *Fee:* $20; not refundable.

Contact: Admissions Office, Graduate School of Public Administration, New York University, 4 Washington Square North, New York, NY 10003; (212) 598-3244.

U8 LESLEY COLLEGE GRADUATE SCHOOL
Public Administration.

Specialization: Individually designed independent study degree program; requires four three-hour meetings on campus. Participants work with faculty and professionals in the field.

Dates: To be arranged.

Location: Cambridge, Massachusetts: on campus. Independent study at student's home or other appropriate site.

Instruction: *Methods:* lectures, discussion groups, case studies, field trips, individualized instruction, "hands-on" training, independent study/research. *By:* faculty.

Highlights: Sponsor has offered short-term programs since 1971. Master's degree. Practical training may be a program component. Issues I-20AB. A foreign student counselor/adviser is available. 5% foreign enrollment in 1985.

Eligibility: *Academic:* bachelor's degree. *Professional:* none. *Language:* English proficiency is required. TOEFL.

Cost: $7,200 for tuition. *Scholarships:* none.

Housing: Not provided.

Application: *Deadline:* open. *Fee:* $35; not refundable.

Contact: Margot Chamberlain, Program Advisor, Lesley College Graduate School, 29 Everett Street, Cambridge, MA 02238; (617) 868-9600, Ext. 426.

All program information is subject to change without notice
and must be confirmed directly with the sponsor.

164

U9 NEW YORK UNIVERSITY, GRADUATE SCHOOL OF PUBLIC ADMINISTRATION

Master of Science in Management.
Specialization: Developmental and international administration for midcareer managers and professionals with advanced degrees.
Dates: Nine months: classes begin in Sept.
Location: New York, New York: on campus.
Instruction: *Methods:* discussion groups, lectures, case studies, independent study/research, computer-assisted instruction. *By:* faculty.
Highlights: Sponsor has offered program since 1985. Master's degree upon completion of eight courses. A foreign student counselor/adviser is available. Unlimited total enrollment.
Eligibility: *Academic:* bachelor's degree. *Language:* English proficiency on advanced level is required. *Professional:* none.
Cost: $7,392 for tuition. *Scholarships:* none.
Housing: Not provided; sponsor assists in locating housing.
Application: *Deadline:* Aug. *Fee:* $20; not refundable.
Contact: Admissions Office, Graduate School of Public Administration, New York University, 4 Washington Square North, New York, NY 10003; (212) 598-3244.

U10 NORTHERN ILLINOIS UNIVERSITY, INTERNATIONAL AND SPECIAL PROGRAMS

International Seminar in Effective Management and Decision Making.
Specialization: National and local administration. Custom-designed programs for foreign government officials also available.
Dates: Six weeks: classes begin in June.
Location: DeKalb, Illinois: at university, at professional work site.
Instruction: *Methods:* individualized instruction, "hands-on" training, independent study/research, computer-assisted instruction. *By:* faculty.
Highlights: Sponsor has offered short-term programs previously. Certificate. Practical training is a program component; participants are not paid. Issues I-20, IAP-66. Foreign nationals on tourist visas are eligible to enroll. Extensive services for foreign nationals. 20 total enrollment; 100% foreign enrollment in 1985.
Eligibility: *Academic:* bachelor's degree. *Language:* TOEFL: 550 or comparable certification. *Professional:* criteria set by sponsor.
Cost: $3,500 for tuition, books and materials, meals, housing, local seminar-related transportation, receptions. *Scholarships:* none.
Housing: In dormitories.
Application: *Deadline:* May 15. *Fee:* none.
Contact: Dr. Daniel Wit, Dean, International and Special Programs, Northern Illinois University, Lowden Hall 203, DeKalb, IL 60115; (815) 753-1988. Telex: 311261 NIU DEKALB UD.

U11 NORTHERN ILLINOIS UNIVERSITY

Specialization: Public policy; development, fiscal, and human resource administration. Designed to meet the needs of foreign nationals interested in public administration training.
Dates: June 20–July 15, July 18–Aug. 12.
Location: DeKalb, Illinois: on campus.
Instruction: *Methods:* lectures, seminars, independent study, "hands-on" training. *By:* faculty.
Highlights: Sponsor has offered program since 1963. Credit. Certificate. Issues I-20, IAP-66. Extensive services for foreign nationals. 20 total enrollment; 100% foreign enrollment in 1985.
Eligibility: *Academic:* bachelor's degree. *Language:* not given. *Professional:* one year of experience in governmental agency.
Cost: Varies. *Scholarships:* none.

Abbreviations: ESL = English as a Second Language; TOEFL = Test of English as a Foreign Language; ALIGU = American Language Institute of Georgetown University; GPA = Grade Point Average; SAT = Scholastic Aptitude Test; GED = General Equivalency Diploma.

Housing: In dormitories, hotels.
Application: *Deadline:* May 1. *Fee:* none.
Contact: Dr. Daniel Wit, Dean, International and Special Programs, Northern Illinois University, Lowden Hall 203, DeKalb, IL 60115; (815) 753-1988.

U12 OHIO STATE UNIVERSITY
In-Career M.A.
Specialization: Preparation for management in the public sector; specialization options include criminal justice, fiscal, health, labor and human resources, regulation, and urban policy.
Dates: Nine months: classes begin in Sept.
Location: Columbus, Ohio: on campus.
Instruction: *Methods:* lectures. *By:* faculty.
Highlights: Sponsor has offered program since 1970. Certificate upon completion of 48 hours of coursework with 3.0 GPA. Issues I-20AB, IAP-66. Foreign nationals on tourist visas may be eligible to enroll. A foreign student counselor/adviser is available. Orientation, ESL, and social programs. Unlimited total enrollment.
Eligibility: *Academic:* bachelor's degree. *Language:* English proficiency on advanced level is required. TOEFL: 575. *Professional:* 3–5 years of administrative/analytical work experience.
Cost: $7,184 for tuition. *Scholarships:* partial.
Housing: In dormitories, apartments.
Application: *Deadline:* June 1. *Fee:* $25; not refundable. *Scholarship deadline:* Feb. 1.
Contact: Cindy Haidle, Ohio State University, School of Public Administration, 208 Hagerty Hall, 1775 College Road, Columbus, OH 43210; (614) 422-8697.

U13 PACE UNIVERSITY
Specialization: Public administration, health services administration. Courses can be tailored to meet the needs of international students.
Dates: Classes begin in Sept., Jan., May, June, July.
Location: White Plains, New York: on campus, at professional work site.
Instruction: *Methods:* lectures, discussion groups, case studies, field trips, individualized instruction, "hands-on" training, computer-assisted instruction, language labs. *By:* faculty, guest speakers/lecturers. *Also in French, Spanish, Arabic.*
Highlights: Sponsor has offered short-term programs since the 1940s. Certificate upon completion of program with B average. Issues I-20AB, IAP-66. Foreign nationals on tourist visas are eligible to enroll. A foreign student counselor/adviser is available. ESL program and International Student Club. Unlimited total enrollment; 2.5% total foreign enrollment in 1985.
Eligibility: *Academic:* bachelor's degree. *Language:* English proficiency on advanced level is required. TOEFL: 550. *Professional:* none.
Cost: About $7,000 per semester inclusive. *Scholarships:* partial (graduate assistantships).
Housing: In dormitories, or sponsor assists in locating housing.
Application: *Deadline:* rolling. *Fee:* $20; not refundable. *Scholarship deadline:* at time of application.
Contact: Mrs. R.I. Fennekohl, Graduate Admissions Office, Pace University, Pace Plaza, New York, NY 10038; (212) 488-1720.

U14 SYRACUSE UNIVERSITY, MAXWELL SCHOOL OF CITIZENSHIP & PUBLIC AFFAIRS
Maxwell Midcareer Development Certificate Program.
Specialization: Flexible program in public sector management and administration. Provides contact with U.S. government professionals from AID, the State Dept., NASA, the IRS, etc.
Dates: Classes begin in Aug., Jan.
Location: Syracuse, New York: on campus.

Instruction: *Methods:* lectures, discussion groups, case studies, individualized instruction, "hands-on" training, independent study/research. *By:* faculty.
Highlights: Sponsor has offered program since 1964. Certificate. Issues I-20AB. Foreign nationals on tourist visas are eligible to enroll. A foreign student counselor/adviser is available. International Student Office. 25 total enrollment per semester; 15% foreign enrollment in 1985.
Eligibility: *Academic:* bachelor's degree or equivalent professional certification.
Language: English proficiency on advanced level is required. *Professional:* 5–10 years of experience, middle-level manager.
Cost: $4,795 for tuition, books and materials, health insurance, application fee, student activity fee.
Housing: Not provided; sponsor assists in locating housing.
Application: *Deadline:* two months prior. *Fee:* $30; not refundable.
Contact: Deborah Coquillon, Program Administrator, Midcareer Program, Syracuse University, 206 Maxwell Hall, Syracuse, NY 13244-1090; (315) 423-3759.

U15 SYRACUSE UNIVERSITY, MAXWELL SCHOOL OF CITIZENSHIP & PUBLIC AFFAIRS
Maxwell Midcareer Master of Arts in Public Adminstration.
Specialization: Flexible master's program in public administration may be completed in two semesters of fulltime study on campus, or one semester on campus plus transfer credits, independent study, and short courses.
Dates: Classes begin in Aug., Jan.
Location: Syracuse, New York: on campus.
Instruction: *Methods:* lectures, discussion groups, case studies, individualized instruction, "hands-on" training, independent study/research. *By:* faculty.
Highlights: Sponsor has offered program since 1981. Master's degree upon completion of 30 graduate credit hours with 3.0 GPA. Issues I-20AB. Foreign nationals on tourist visas are eligible to enroll. A foreign student counselor/adviser is available. International Student Office. 25 total enrollment per semester; 15% foreign enrollment in 1985.
Eligibility: *Academic:* bachelor's degree or equivalent professional certification.
Language: English proficiency on advanced level is required. *Professional:* 5–10 years of experience, middle-level manager.
Cost: $9,360 for tuition, books and materials, health insurance, application fee, student activity fee.
Housing: Not provided; sponsor assists in locating housing.
Application: *Deadline:* two months prior. *Fee:* $30; not refundable.
Contact: Deborah Coquillon, Program Administrator, Midcareer Program, Syracuse University, 206 Maxwell Hall, Syracuse, NY 13244-1090; (315) 423-3759.

U16 UNIVERSITY OF CONNECTICUT, INSTITUTE OF PUBLIC SERVICE INTERNATIONAL
Fundamentals of Management.
Specialization: Combines essential management theory with practical skills spplications; designed for professionals lacking formal training in managerial aspects of their work.
Dates: Nine months: classes begin in Sept., Jan.
Location: West Hartford, Connecticut; on campus.
Instruction: *Methods:* discussions, lectures, case studies, field trips. *By:* faculty, guest speakers/lecturers.
Highlights: Sponsor has offered program since 1961. Certificate. Issues IAP-66. Foreign nationals on tourist visas are not eligible to enroll. Extensive services for foreign nationals. 100% foreign enrollment in 1985.
Eligibility: *Academic:* bachelor's degree or equivalent professional experience.
Language: TOEFL: 500; ALIGU: 80. *Professional:* 2–5 years of experience.
Cost: $7,200 for tuition, books. *Scholarships:* none.

Abbreviations: ESL = English as a Second Language; TOEFL = Test of English as a Foreign Language; ALIGU = American Language Institute of Georgetown University; GPA = Grade Point Average; SAT = Scholastic Aptitude Test; GED = General Equivalency Diploma.

Housing: Not provided; sponsor assists in locating housing.
Application: *Deadline:* six weeks prior. *Fee:* none.
Contact: Mrs. Josephine Mavromatis, Coordinator, Hartford-based Programs, IPS International, University of Connecticut, 1800 Asylum Ave., West Hartford, CT 06117; (203) 241-4924. Cable: IPSUCONN. Telex: 883997 IPS INTL.

U17 UNIVERSITY OF CONNECTICUT, INSTITUTE OF PUBLIC SERVICE INTERNATIONAL
Public Management Development.
Specialization: Specializations offered in financial management, local development administration, management of training, management services and computer applications, personnel management, and project analysis and implementation.
Dates: Nine months: classes begin in Sept., Jan.
Location: West Hartford, Connecticut; on campus.
Instruction: *Methods:* discussions, lectures, case studies, field trips. *By:* faculty, guest speakers/lecturers.
Highlights: Sponsor has offered program since 1961. Certificate. Issues IAP-66. Foreign nationals on tourist visas are not eligible to enroll. Extensive services for foreign nationals. 100% foreign enrollment in 1985.
Eligibility: *Academic:* bachelor's degree or equivalent professional experience.
Language: TOEFL: 500; ALIGU: 80. *Professional:* 2–5 years of experience.
Cost: $7,200 for tuition, books. *Scholarships:* none.
Housing: Not provided; sponsor assists in locating housing.
Application: *Deadline:* six weeks prior. *Fee:* none.
Contact: Mrs. Josephine Mavromatis, Coordinator, Hartford-based Programs, IPS International, University of Connecticut, 1800 Asylum Ave., West Hartford, CT 06117; (203) 241-4924. Cable: IPSUCONN. Telex: 883997 IPS INTL.

U18 UNIVERSITY OF CONNECTICUT, INSTITUTE OF PUBLIC SERVICE INTERNATIONAL
Public Management Systems and Skills.
Specialization: Management fundamentals; Part I of Public Management Development Program.
Dates: Three months: classes begin in Sept.
Location: West Hartford, Connecticut; on campus.
Instruction: *Methods:* discussions, lectures, case studies, field trips. *By:* faculty, guest speakers/lecturers.
Highlights: Sponsor has offered program since 1961. Certificate. Issues IAP-66. Foreign nationals on tourist visas are not eligible to enroll. Extensive services for foreign nationals. 100% foreign enrollment in 1985.
Eligibility: *Academic:* bachelor's degree or equivalent professional experience.
Language: TOEFL: 500; ALIGU: 80. *Professional:* 2–5 years of experience.
Cost: $4,900 for tuition, books. *Scholarships:* none.
Housing: Not provided; sponsor assists in locating housing.
Application: *Deadline:* six weeks prior. *Fee:* none.
Contact: Mrs. Josephine Mavromatis, Coordinator, Hartford-based Programs, IPS International, University of Connecticut, 1800 Asylum Ave., West Hartford, CT 06117; (203) 241-4924. Cable: IPSUCONN. Telex: 883997 IPS INTL.

U19 UNIVERSITY OF MICHIGAN, INSTITUTE OF PUBLIC POLICY STUDIES
Master of Public Administration.
Specialization: Emphasis on quantitative social science methods as applied to public administration.
Dates: Nine months: fall and spring semesters.
Location: Ann Arbor, Michigan: on campus.

All program information is subject to change without notice
and must be confirmed directly with the sponsor.

Instruction: *Methods:* discussion groups, lectures, case studies, individualized instruction, independent study/research, computer-assisted instruction. *By:* faculty.
Highlights: Sponsor has offered program since the early 1970s. Master's degree upon completion of 30 hours of coursework. Issues I-20AB, I-20MN, IAP-66. Foreign nationals on tourist visas are eligible to enroll. A foreign student counselor/adviser is available. About 6% foreign enrollment in 1985.
Eligibility: *Academic:* bachelor's degree. *Language:* English proficiency on advanced level is required. TOEFL: 650; Univ. of Michigan Language Test. *Professional:* three years of experience.
Cost: $15,934 for tuition, health insurance. *Scholarships:* none.
Housing: Not provided; student makes own arrangements.
Application: *Deadline:* Feb. 15. *Fee:* $20; not refundable.
Contact: Yolanda Lizardi Marino, Asst. Director for Student Affairs, Institute of Public Policy Studies, University of Michigan, 440 Lorch Hall, Ann Arbor, MI 48109-1220; (313) 764-9586.

U20 VIRGINIA COMMONWEALTH UNIVERSITY, DEPARTMENT OF PUBLIC ADMINISTRATION
Certificate in Public Administration.
Specialization: Executive management personnel, finance, policy analysis, human resources; designed for working professionals in public and semipublic organizations.
Dates: Classes begin in Aug., Jan., May.
Location: Richmond, Virginia: on campus, at professional work site.
Instruction: *Methods:* discussion groups, individualized instruction, "hands-on" training, independent study/research, optional computer-assisted instruction. *By:* faculty, guest speakers/lecturers.
Highlights: Sponsor has offered program since 1984. Certificate upon completion of 18 credit hours with B average. Issues I-20AB, IAP-66. Foreign nationals on tourist visas are not eligible to enroll. A foreign student counselor/adviser is available. International student program. 10 total enrollment; no foreign enrollment in 1985.
Eligibility: *Academic:* bachelor's degree. *Language:* not given. TOEFL. *Professional:* three years of experience, supervisory or professional-level work.
Cost: About $4,500 for tuition, books and materials. *Scholarships:* none.
Housing: Not provided; sponsor assists in locating housing.
Application: *Deadline:* July 1, Nov. 1, Apr. 1. *Fee:* $10; not refundable.
Contact: Gilbert W. Fairholm or F. William Heiss, Dept. of Public Administration, Virginia Commonwealth University, 816 W. Franklin Street, Richmond, VA 23284; (804) 257-1046.

U21 WEST VIRGINIA UNIVERSITY
Public Administration.
Specialization: A small, elite program combining courses, workshops, and internship.
Dates: Classes begin in Aug., Jan., May, July.
Location: Morgantown, West Virginia: on campus, at professional work site.
Instruction: *Methods:* discussion groups, lectures, case studies, field trips, individualized instruction, "hands-on" training, independent study/research. *By:* faculty.
Highlights: Sponsor has offered program since 1969. Certificate upon completion of 47 semester hours. Practical training is a program component; participants may be paid. Issues I-20AB, I-20MN, IAP-66. Foreign nationals on tourist visas are eligible to apply. A foreign student counselor/adviser is available. International student office, ESL program, and international student organization. 50 total enrollment; 30% foreign enrollment in 1985.
Eligibility: *Academic:* bachelor's degree. *Language:* English proficiency on advanced level is required. TOEFL: 550. *Professional:* two years of experience preferred.
Cost: About $13,000 for tuition, books and materials, meals, housing, local transportation, health insurance. *Scholarships:* none.
Housing: Not provided; sponsor assists in locating housing.

Abbreviations: ESL = English as a Second Language; TOEFL = Test of English as a Foreign Language; ALIGU = American Language Institute of Georgetown University; GPA = Grade Point Average; SAT = Scholastic Aptitude Test; GED = General Equivalency Diploma.

Application: *Deadline:* Mar. 1, Oct. 1. *Fee:* $20; not refundable.
Contact: Public Administration Dept., West Virginia University, 302 Woodburn Hall, Morgantown, WV 26506; (304) 293-2614. Telex: 7108210309.

CONSULTING

U22 INSTITUTE OF PUBLIC ADMINISTRATION
Developing Consulting Skills.
Specialization: Develops skills needed by professional consultants to governments and public enterprises.
Dates: Two weeks: classes begin in July.
Location: Washington, D.C.: at conference center.
Instruction: *Methods:* discussion groups, lectures, case studies, field trips. *By:* faculty, guest speakers/lecturers.
Highlights: Sponsor has offered program since 1985. Certificate. Foreign nationals on tourist visas are eligible to enroll. A foreign student counselor/adviser is available. 20 total enrollment.
Eligibility: *Academic:* bachelor's degree. *Language:* English proficiency on intermediate level is required. *Professional:* faculty or civil servants involved in consulting work, especially to their governments.
Cost: $1,250 for tuition, books and materials. *Scholarships:* none.
Housing: In dormitories.
Application: *Deadline:* June 28. *Fee:* $350; applied to tuition.
Contact: Dr. Annmarie Walsh, President, Institute of Public Administration, 55 W. 44th Street, New York, NY 10036; (212) 730-5480. Telex: 220437 IPA UR.

CULTURAL RESOURCES

U23 U.S. DEPARTMENT OF AGRICULTURE GRADUATE SCHOOL
International Program for Cultural and Museum Management.
Specialization: Improvement of museums in developing countries through effective leadership.
Dates: Nine months: classes begin in Apr.
Location: Washington, D.C.: on campus, at professional work site.
Instruction: *Methods:* discussion groups, lectures, case studies, field trips, "hands-on" training, independent study/research, science laboratories. *By:* faculty, guest speakers/lecturers.
Highlights: Sponsor has offered short-term programs previously. Certificate. Practical training is a program component; participants are not paid. Issues I-20AB. A foreign student counselor/adviser is available. 25 total enrollment.
Eligibility: *Academic:* bachelor's degree. *Language:* English proficiency on intermediate level is required. *Professional:* one year experience in some aspect of cultural administration or museum work.
Cost: $10,500 for tuition, books and materials, local transportation, health insurance. *Scholarships:* none.
Housing: Not provided; sponsor assists in locating housing.
Application: *Deadline:* Feb. 28. *Fee:* $25; not refundable.
Contact: Prentiss S. de Jesus, International Programs, USDA Graduate School, Room 134, 600 Maryland Ave. SW, Washington, DC 20024; (202) 447-7476.

DEVELOPMENT STUDIES

U24 CORNELL UNIVERSITY
Master's in Professional Studies/International Development.
Specialization: Concentrations in nutrition, population, regional planning, development policy. Interdisciplinary program for midcareer professionals with some development experience to build upon.
Dates: One year: classes begin in Aug., Jan.
Location: Ithaca, New York: on campus.
Instruction: *Methods:* lectures, independent study/research. *By:* faculty.
Highlights: Sponsor has offered program since 1974. Certificate upon completion of 30 credits and thesis. Foreign nationals on tourist visas are not eligible to enroll. A foreign student counselor/adviser is available. About 15–25 total enrollment; 50% foreign enrollment in 1985.
Eligibility: *Academic:* bachelor's degree. *Language:* English proficiency on advanced level is required. TOEFL: 550. *Professional:* two years of development work.
Cost: $11,500 for tuition. *Scholarships:* Cornell University Fellowship Competition.
Housing: Not provided; student makes own arrangements.
Application: *Deadline:* none. *Fee:* $35; not refundable. *Scholarship deadline:* Jan. 15.
Contact: Graduate Faculty Representative, International Development, Center for International Studies, Cornell University, 170 Uris Hall, Ithaca, NY 11853; (607) 255-6370. Cable: Cornell Itca. Telex: W.U.I. 6713054.

U25 FLORIDA STATE UNIVERSITY, CENTER FOR COMPARATIVE DEVELOPMENT ADMINISTRATION
Comparative/Development Administration.
Specialization: Designed for advanced graduate students from developing countries; includes field experiences, workshops, guest lectures, and social events.
Dates: Not given.
Location: Tallahassee, Florida: on campus, at professional work site.
Instruction: *Methods:* discussion groups, lectures, field trips, independent study/research. *By:* faculty, guest speakers/lecturers.
Highlights: Sponsor has offered program since 1985. A foreign student counselor/adviser is available. 20 total enrollment; 100% foreign enrollment in 1985.
Eligibility: *Academic:* master's degree. *Language:* English proficiency on advanced level is required. TOEFL. *Professional:* none.
Cost: $1,000 for tuition. *Scholarships:* none.
Housing: Not given.
Application: *Deadline:* fall. *Fee:* not given.
Contact: James A. Johnson, Program Director, Center for Development Administration, 614 BEL, Florida State University, Tallahassee, FL 32306.

U26 INDIANA UNIVERSITY, SCHOOL OF PUBLIC AND ENVIRONMENTAL AFFAIRS
Master's Program in Development Management.
Specialization: Public sector management in developing countries. Full MPA professional accreditation, international and comparative focus, internship possibilities, sectoral specializations as options, area studies options.
Dates: One year: classes begin in late Aug.
Location: Bloomington, Indiana: on campus.
Instruction: *Methods:* discussion groups, lectures, case studies, computer-assisted instruction, science laboratories. *By:* faculty, guest speakers/lecturers.
Highlights: Sponsor has offered program since 1985. Certificate. Practical training may be a program component. Issues I-20AB, I-20MN, IAP-66. Foreign nationals on tourist visas are

Abbreviations: ESL = English as a Second Language; TOEFL = Test of English as a Foreign Language; ALIGU = American Language Institute of Georgetown University; GPA = Grade Point Average; SAT = Scholastic Aptitude Test; GED = General Equivalency Diploma.

171

eligible to enroll. A foreign student counselor/adviser is available. International student center and program. 25 total enrollment; 90% foreign enrollment in 1985.
Eligibility: *Academic:* bachelor's degree. *Language:* English proficiency on advanced level is required. TOEFL: 560. *Professional:* five years of work experience in public sector.
Cost: $190.25 per credit hour for tuition. *Scholarships:* full.
Housing: Not provided; sponsor assists in locating housing.
Application: *Deadline:* none. *Fee:* $30; not refundable. *Scholarship deadline:* Mar. 1.
Contact: Dr. T. Miller, Graduate Program, Indiana University, SPEA 260, Bloomington, IN 47405; (812) 335-3107.

U27 INSTITUTE OF PUBLIC ADMINISTRATION
The Luther Gulick Workshop on Public Management for Development.
Specialization: Techniques of public sector management, especially in development.
Dates: Three weeks: July.
Location: Washington, D.C.: at conference center.
Instruction: *Methods:* discussion groups, lectures, case studies, field trips. *By:* faculty, guest speakers/lecturers.
Highlights: Sponsor has offered short-term programs since 1960. Certificate. Foreign nationals on tourist visas are eligible to enroll. A foreign student counselor/adviser is available. 20 total enrollment.
Eligibility: *Academic:* bachelor's degree. *Language:* English proficiency on intermediate level is required. *Professional:* three years of exployment in the public sector.
Cost: $1,850 for tuition, books and materials. *Scholarships:* none.
Housing: In dormitories.
Application: *Deadline:* June 7. *Fee:* $500; applied to tuition.
Contact: Dr. Annmarie Walsh, President, Institute of Public Administration, 55 W. 44th Street, New York, NY 10036; (212) 730-5480. Telex: 220437 IPA UR.

U28 LONG ISLAND UNIVERSITY, THE BROOKLYN CAMPUS
United Nations and World Faiths.
Specialization: The role of the nongovernmental organization in economic and social development in developing countries.
Dates: Sept.–Jan., Feb.–June.
Location: Brooklyn, New York: on campus, at U.N. staff or NGO member briefings, U.N. sessions.
Instruction: *Methods:* discussion groups, lectures, case studies, individualized instruction, independent study/research. *By:* faculty.
Highlights: Certificate. Issues I-20AB. Foreign nationals on tourist visas are eligible to enroll. A foreign student counselor/adviser is available. Various support services are available. 15 total enrollment.
Eligibility: *Academic:* bachelor's degree. *Language:* English proficiency on advanced level is required. TOEFL. *Professional:* none.
Cost: $2,850 for tuition. *Scholarships:* partial.
Housing: In dormitories.
Application: *Deadline:* Aug. 15, Dec. 15. *Fee:* $20; not refundable. *Scholarship deadline:* not given.
Contact: Prof. D.D. Kostich, Director ISIO/UNWF, Room M-500/501, Long Island University, Brooklyn Campus, University Plaza, Brooklyn, NY 11201; (718) 834-6000, Ext. 3587 or 3598.

U29 LONG ISLAND UNIVERSITY, THE BROOKLYN CAMPUS
United Nations Graduate Certificate Program.
Specialization: International organizations; U.N. specialized agencies and development.
Dates: Nine months: classes begin in Sept.

Location: Brooklyn and Manhattan, New York: on campus, at U.N. briefings, sessions of the General Assembly, Security Council and committees.
Instruction: *Methods:* discussion groups, lectures, case studies, individualized instruction, independent study/research. *By:* faculty, senior U.N. staff.
Highlights: Sponsor has offered program since 1972. Certificate upon completion of 24 graduate credits. Issues I-20MN. Foreign nationals on tourist visas are eligible to enroll. A foreign student counselor/adviser is available. Various support services are available. 15 in each of three sections total enrollment; 45% foreign enrollment in 1985.
Eligibility: *Academic:* bachelor's degree. *Language:* English proficiency on advanced level is required. TOEFL. *Professional:* none.
Cost: $5,000 for tuition, fees, health insurance. *Scholarships:* partial.
Housing: In dormitories.
Application: *Deadline:* Aug. *Fee:* $20; not refundable. *Scholarship deadline:* April.
Contact: Prof. D.D. Kostich, Director ISIO, Long Island University, Brooklyn Campus (M-501), University Plaza, Brooklyn, NY 11201-5372; (718) 834-6000, Ext. 3587, or (718) 403-1041.

U30 **SCHOOL FOR INTERNATIONAL TRAINING**
Master's Program in Intercultural Management.
Specialization: International development, world issues, and ESL training for those who wish to pursue careers with international development and relief organizations.
Dates: Classes begin in Sept., March.
Location: Brattleboro, Vermont: on campus.
Instruction: *Methods:* discussion groups, lectures, case studies, field trips, "hands-on" training, independent study/research, computer-assisted instruction, language laboratories. *By:* faculty. *Also in French, Spanish, Chinese.*
Highlights: Sponsor has offered program since 1964. Certificate. Practical training is a program component; participants are paid. Issues I-20AB. Foreign nationals on tourist visas are not eligible to enroll. A foreign student counselor/adviser is available. 90 per year total enrollment; 38% foreign enrollment in 1985.
Eligibility: *Academic:* bachelor's degree. *Language:* English proficiency on advanced level is required. TOEFL: 550. *Professional:* two years of experience with an international development or relief organization.
Cost: $12,000 inclusive. *Scholarships:* partial.
Housing: In dormitories.
Application: *Deadline:* two months prior. *Fee:* $35; not refundable. *Scholarship deadline:* two months prior.
Contact: Admissions Office, School for International Training, Kipling Road, Brattleboro, VT 05301; (800) 451-4510 inside U.S.; (802) 257-7751 outside U.S. Cable: EXPERIMENT BRATTLEBORO, VT. Telex: 710-3636774.

U31 **SCHOOL FOR INTERNATIONAL TRAINING**
Project Monitoring.
Specialization: Development project monitoring and evaluation. Major emphasis on back-home application and adaptation.
Dates: Early July–mid-Aug.
Location: Brattleboro, Vermont: on campus.
Instruction: *Methods:* discussion groups, lectures, case studies, field trips, "hands-on" training, independent study/research, computer-assisted instruction. *By:* faculty, guest speakers/lecturers.
Highlights: New program. Sponsor has offered short-term programs since 1984. Certificate. Issues I-20AB, IAP-66. Foreign nationals on tourist visas are eligible to enroll. A foreign student counselor/adviser is available. ESL and homestay programs. 25 total enrollment.
Eligibility: *Academic:* bachelor's degree or equivalent preferred. *Language:* English

---

Abbreviations: ESL = English as a Second Language; TOEFL = Test of English as a Foreign Language; ALIGU = American Language Institute of Georgetown University; GPA = Grade Point Average; SAT = Scholastic Aptitude Test; GED = General Equivalency Diploma.

173

proficiency on intermediate level is required. *Professional:* requires three years of work experience; participants should be current or prospective managers of development projects. **Cost:** $4,900 for tuition, books and materials, local transportation, health insurance. *Scholarships:* none.
Housing: In dormitories, hotels.
Application: *Deadline:* May. *Fee:* none.
Contact: Paul G. Ventura, Associate Manager, Participant Training, School for International Training, Kipling Road, Brattleboro, VT 05301; (802) 254-5935. Telex: 6817462 EXPER UW.

U32 UNIVERSITY OF PENNSYLVANIA
Development Planning and Analysis.
Specialization: Broad range of disciplines including housing, transportation, health, education, rural development, regional income differences, rural to urban migration, location of industries, and appropriate technologies.
Dates: Sept.–May.
Location: Philadelphia, Pennsylvania: on campus.
Instruction: *Methods:* lectures, discussion groups. *By:* faculty.
Highlights: Sponsor has offered program previously. Certificate. Issues I-20AB, IAP-66. A foreign student counselor/adviser is available.
Eligibility: *Academic:* bachelor's degree. *Language:* English proficiency on advanced level is required. *Professional:* none.
Cost: $20,000 inclusive. *Scholarships:* none.
Housing: In dormitories, off-campus housing.
Application: *Deadline:* rolling. *Fee:* none.
Contact: Certificate in Development Planning and Analysis Committee, City and Regional Planning Dept., University of Pennsylvania, 127 Graduate School of Fine Arts, Philadelphia, PA 19104; (215) 898-8329. Cable: PNSYL Phila Pa. Telex: 710-670-0328.

U33 UNIVERSITY OF PENNSYLVANIA
Master of Science in Appropriate Technology for Development.
Specialization: Combines the perspectives of economists, social scientists, engineers, and practitioners for development planning and business in developing countries. Includes energy, health, water supply, shelter, clothing, food, and industrial diversification.
Dates: Sept.–Aug.
Location: Philadelphia, Pennsylvania: on campus. Field study in developing country in Western Hemisphere.
Instruction: *Methods:* lectures, discussion groups, independent study/research. *By:* faculty.
Highlights: Sponsor has offered short-term programs since 1983. Master's degree upon completion of ten courses, field study, and thesis. Issues I-20AB, IAP-66. Foreign nationals on tourist visas are not eligible to enroll. A foreign student counselor/adviser is available. Orientation program.
Eligibility: *Academic:* bachelor's degree; knowledge of microeconomics and statistics recommended. *Language:* English proficiency on advanced level is required.
Professional: none.
Cost: $21,000 inclusive. *Scholarships:* none.
Housing: Not provided; sponsor assists in locating housing.
Application: *Deadline:* July 15. *Fee:* $40; not refundable.
Contact: Dr. Lucy Creevey, Program in Appropriate Technology, University of Pennsylvania, 3400 Walnut Street, Philadelphia, PA 19104-6208; (215) 898-6445. Cable: PNSYL Phila Pa. Telex: 710-670-0328.

ENTERPRISE MANAGEMENT

U34 UNIVERSITY OF CONNECTICUT, INSTITUTE OF PUBLIC SERVICE INTERNATIONAL
Enterprise Management for Development.
Specialization: Management of government-owned and -regulated industries: financial, operational, and supervisory problems. Designed for middle- to senior-level managers with specific functional responsibilities.
Dates: Eight weeks: classes begin in Sept.
Location: West Hartford, Connecticut: on campus.
Instruction: *Methods:* discussions, lectures, case studies, field trips. *By:* faculty, guest speakers/lecturers.
Highlights: Sponsor has offered program since 1986. Certificate. Issues IAP-66. Foreign nationals on tourist visas are not eligible to enroll. Extensive services for foreign nationals.
Eligibility: *Academic:* bachelor's degree or equivalent professional experience.
Language: TOEFL: 500; ALIGU: 80. *Professional:* 2–5 years of experience.
Cost: $4,700 for tuition, books. *Scholarships:* none.
Housing: Not provided: sponsor assists in locating housing.
Application: *Deadline:* six weeks prior. *Fee:* none.
Contact: Mrs. Josephine Mavromatis, Coordinator, Hartford-based Programs, IPS International, University of Connecticut, 1800 Asylum Ave., West Hartford, CT 06117; (203) 241-4924. Cable: IPSUCONN. Telex: 883997 IPS INTL.

FINANCIAL MANAGEMENT

U35 THE AMERICAN UNIVERSITY
Graduate Certificate in Public Financial Management.
Specialization: Public financial management.
Dates: Classes begin in Sept., Jan., May, July.
Location: Washington, D.C.: on campus.
Instruction: *Methods:* discussion groups, lectures, case studies. *By:* faculty.
Highlights: Sponsor has offered program previously. Certificate upon completion of five courses. Issues I-20AB. Foreign nationals on tourist visas are not eligible to enroll. A foreign student counselor/adviser is available. Orientation programs.
Eligibility: *Academic:* bachelor's degree. *Language:* English proficiency on advanced level is required. TOEFL: 600; English Language Institute Placement Test. *Professional:* none.
Cost: $299 per semester hour for tuition. *Scholarships:* none.
Housing: Not provided; sponsor assists in locating housing.
Application: *Deadline:* none. *Fee:* none.
Contact: Programs Advisement Center, The American University, 4400 Massachusetts Ave. NW, Room 153 McKinley Bldg., Washington, DC 20016; (202) 885-2500.

U36 U.S. DEPARTMENT OF AGRICULTURE GRADUATE SCHOOL
International Management Development Program.
Specialization: Financial management for managers and administrators from developing countries. Instructors include senior U.S. government officials.
Dates: Nine months: classes begin in Sept.
Location: Washington, D.C.: on campus.
Instruction: *Methods:* discussion groups, lectures, case studies, field trips, "hands-on" training, computer-assisted instruction. *By:* faculty, guest speakers/lecturers.
Highlights: Sponsor has offered program since 1974. Certificate. Practical training is a program component; participants are not paid. Issues I-20AB. Foreign nationals on tourist

---

Abbreviations: ESL = English as a Second Language; TOEFL = Test of English as a Foreign Language; ALIGU = American Language Institute of Georgetown University; GPA = Grade Point Average; SAT = Scholastic Aptitude Test; GED = General Equivalency Diploma.

visas are not eligible to enroll. A foreign student counselor/adviser is available. 25 total enrollment; 100% foreign enrollment in 1985.
Eligibility: *Academic:* bachelor's degree. *Language:* English proficiency on advanced level is required. TOEFL: 525. *Professional:* none.
Cost: $11,500 for tuition, books and materials. *Scholarships:* none.
Housing: Not provided; sponsor assists in locating housing.
Application: *Deadline:* July 1. *Fee:* $300; refundable.
Contact: Mr. Kenneth L. Hawkins, The Graduate School, USDA, 600 Maryland Ave. SW, Room 134, Washington, DC 20024; (202) 447-7476. Telex: 756563 GS INTL WSH.

U37 UNIVERSITY OF CONNECTICUT, INSTITUTE OF PUBLIC SERVICE INTERNATIONAL
Performance Auditing.
Specialization: Audit standards, management of audit functions.
Dates: Eight weeks: classes begin in Sept.
Location: West Hartford, Connecticut: on campus.
Instruction: *Methods:* discussions, lectures, case studies, field trips. *By:* faculty, guest speakers/lecturers.
Highlights: Sponsor has offered program since 1961. Certificate. Issues IAP-66. Foreign nationals on tourist visas are not eligible to enroll. Extensive services for foreign nationals. 100% foreign enrollment in 1985.
Eligibility: *Academic:* bachelor's degree or equivalent professional experience.
Language: TOEFL: 500; ALIGU: 80. *Professional:* 2–5 years of experience.
Cost: $4,700 for tuition, books. *Scholarships:* none.
Housing: Not provided: sponsor assists in locating housing.
Application: *Deadline:* six weeks prior. *Fee:* none.
Contact: Mrs. Josephine Mavromatis, Coordinator, Hartford-based Programs, IPS International, University of Connecticut, 1800 Asylum Ave., West Hartford, CT 06117; (203) 241-4924. Cable: IPSUCONN. Telex: 883997 IPS INTL.

U38 UNIVERSITY OF CONNECTICUT, INSTITUTE OF PUBLIC SERVICE INTERNATIONAL
Public Financial Management.
Specialization: International finance, microcomputer applications in financial management, advanced operations assessment, methods and improvement.
Dates: Three months: classes begin in Jan.
Location: West Hartford, Connecticut; on campus.
Instruction: *Methods:* discussions, lectures, case studies, field trips. *By:* faculty, guest speakers/lecturers.
Highlights: Sponsor has offered program previously. Certificate. Issues IAP-66. Foreign nationals on tourist visas are not eligible to enroll. Extensive services for foreign nationals. 100% foreign enrollment in 1985.
Eligibility: *Academic:* bachelor's degree or equivalent professional experience.
Language: TOEFL: 500; ALIGU: 80. *Professional:* 2–5 years of experience.
Cost: $4,900 for tuition, books. *Scholarships:* none.
Housing: Not provided; sponsor assists in locating housing.
Application: *Deadline:* six weeks prior. *Fee:* none.
Contact: Mrs. Josephine Mavromatis, Coordinator, Hartford-based Programs, IPS International, University of Connecticut, 1800 Asylum Ave., West Hartford, CT 06117; (203) 241-4924. Cable: IPSUCONN. Telex: 883997 IPS INTL.

All program information is subject to change without notice
and must be confirmed directly with the sponsor.

176

FUNDRAISING

U39 UNIVERSITY OF CONNECTICUT, SCHOOL OF SOCIAL WORK
The Complete Course on Securing Funding for Your Organization.
Specialization: Fundraising.
Dates: Mid-March–late April.
Location: Hartford, Connecticut: at professional work site.
Instruction: *Methods:* discussion groups, lectures, case studies, field trips, "hands-on" training. *By:* faculty, guest speakers/lecturers.
Highlights: Sponsor has offered program since 1985. Certificate. Foreign nationals on tourist visas are eligible to enroll. A foreign student counselor/adviser is not available. 30 total enrollment; no foreign enrollment in 1985.
Eligibility: *Academic:* bachelor's degree. *Language:* not given. *Professional:* current employment in nonprofit agency with development responsibilities.
Cost: $200 for tuition, books, and materials. *Scholarships:* none.
Housing: Not provided.
Application: *Deadline:* Feb. 26. *Fee:* not given.
Contact: Robin Krieber, MSW Assistant Director, STEP, School of Social Work, University of Connecticut, 1798 Asylum Ave., West Hartford, CT 06511; (203) 241-4748.

HUMAN RESOURCES AND PERSONNEL MANAGEMENT

U40 UNIVERSITY OF CONNECTICUT, INSTITUTE OF PUBLIC SERVICE INTERNATIONAL
Human Resource Management.
Specialization: Microcomputer applications in human resource management and managing the records cycle.
Dates: Jan. 3–Apr. 17.
Location: West Hartford, Connecticut: on campus.
Instruction: *Methods:* discussion groups, lectures, case studies, field trips. *By:* faculty, guest speakers/lecturers.
Highlights: Sponsor has offered program previously. Certificate. Issues IAP-66. Foreign nationals on tourist visas are not eligible to enroll. A foreign student counselor/adviser is available. Social and cultural activities. 100% foreign enrollment in 1985.
Eligibility: *Academic:* bachelor's degree preferred. *Language:* TOEFL: 500; ALIGU: 80. *Professional:* two years of work experience required.
Cost: $4,900 for tuition, books, and materials. *Scholarships:* none.
Housing: Not provided; sponsor assists in locating housing.
Application: *Deadline:* six weeks prior. *Fee:* none.
Contact: Josephine Mavromatis, Coordinator, Hartford-based Programs, IPS International, University of Connecticut, 1800 Asylum Ave., West Hartford, CT 06117; (203) 241-4924. Cable: IPSUCONN. Telex: 883997 (IPS INTL).

U41 UNIVERSITY OF CONNECTICUT, INSTITUTE OF PUBLIC SERVICE INTERNATIONAL
Personnel Management.
Specialization: Personnel policy and procedures, staff development.
Dates: Two months: classes begin in May.
Location: West Hartford, Connecticut: on campus.
Instruction: *Methods:* discussion groups, lectures, case studies, field trips. *By:* faculty, guest speakers/lecturers.
Highlights: Sponsor has offered program since 1961. Certificate. Issues IAP-66. Foreign

---

Abbreviations: ESL = English as a Second Language; TOEFL = Test of English as a Foreign Language; ALIGU = American Language Institute of Georgetown University; GPA = Grade Point Average; SAT = Scholastic Aptitude Test; GED = General Equivalency Diploma.

nationals on tourist visas are not eligible to enroll. A foreign student counselor/adviser is available. Various support services are available. 100% foreign enrollment in 1985.
Eligibility: *Academic:* bachelor's degree preferred. *Language:* TOEFL: 500; ALIGU: 80. *Professional:* two years of work experience required.
Cost: $4,700 for tuition, books, and materials. *Scholarships:* none.
Housing: Not provided; sponsor assists in locating housing.
Application: *Deadline:* six weeks prior. *Fee:* none.
Contact: Josephine Mavromatis, Coordinator, Hartford-based Programs, IPS International, University of Connecticut, 1800 Asylum Ave., West Hartford, CT 06117; (203) 241-4924. Cable: IPSUCONN. Telex: 883997 (IPS INTL).

INFORMATION SERVICES

U42 THE AMERICAN UNIVERSITY
Graduate Certificate in Government Public Information.
Specialization: Government public information.
Dates: Classes begin in Sept., Jan., May, July.
Location: Washington, D.C.: on campus.
Instruction: *Methods:* discussion groups, lectures, case studies. *By:* faculty.
Highlights: Sponsor has offered program previously. Certificate upon completion of five courses. Issues I-20AB. Foreign nationals on tourist visas are not eligible to enroll. A foreign student counselor/adviser is available. Orientation programs.
Eligibility: *Academic:* bachelor's degree, 3.0 GPA, GMAT score: 400. *Language:* English proficiency on advanced level is required. TOEFL: 600; English Language Institute Placement Test. *Professional:* none.
Cost: $299 per semester hour for tuition. *Scholarships:* none.
Housing: Not provided; sponsor assists in locating housing.
Application: *Deadline:* none. *Fee:* none.
Contact: Programs Advisement Center, The American University, 4400 Massachusetts Ave. NW, Room 153 McKinley Bldg., Washington, DC 20016; (202) 885-2500.

LAW ENFORCEMENT

U43 UNIVERSITY OF WASHINGTON, GRADUATE SCHOOL OF PUBLIC AFFAIRS
Law Enforcement Executive Management Institute.
Specialization: Law enforcement management.
Dates: Ten days: April.
Location: Seattle, Washington: at residential site.
Instruction: *Methods:* discussion groups, lectures, case studies. *By:* faculty, guest speakers/lecturers.
Highlights: Sponsor has offered program since 1985. Certificate upon completion of program with 80% attendance. Foreign nationals on tourist visas are eligible to enroll. A foreign student counselor/adviser is available. 25 total enrollment; no foreign enrollment in 1985.
Eligibility: *Academic:* bachelor's degree. *Language:* English proficiency on intermediate level is required. *Professional:* five years of experience; practicing executive in a law enforcement agency.
Cost: $1,100 for tuition, books, and materials. *Scholarships:* none.
Housing: In furnished rooms.
Application: *Deadline:* Mar. 14. *Fee:* none.
Contact: Eric Wolters, Graduate School of Public Affairs, University of Washington, Smith Hall DP-30, Seattle, WA 98195; (206) 543-4920. Cable: UWSEA. Telex: 910 474 0096.

NONPROFIT AND VOLUNTARY ORGANIZATIONS

U44 INSTITUTE OF PUBLIC ADMINISTRATION
Managing Non-Governmental and Private Voluntary Organizations.
Specialization: Development of management skills for nonprofit and voluntary organizations.
Dates: Three weeks: Aug.
Location: Arlington, Virginia: at conference center.
Instruction: *Methods:* discussion groups, field trips, independent study/research. *By:* faculty, guest speakers/lecturers.
Highlights: Sponsor has offered short-term programs since 1960. Certificate. Foreign nationals on tourist visas are eligible to enroll. A foreign student counselor/adviser is available. 20 total enrollment.
Eligibility: *Academic:* bachelor's degree. *Language:* English proficiency on advanced level is required. *Professional:* three years of experience; executive directors and senior staff members of PVOs and NGOs.
Cost: $1,850 for tuition, books and materials. *Scholarships:* none.
Housing: In dormitories.
Application: *Deadline:* July 11. *Fee:* $500; applied to tuition.
Contact: Dr. Annmarie Walsh, President, Institute of Public Administration, 55 W. 44th Street, New York, NY 10036; (212) 730-5480. Telex: 220437 IPA UR.

U45 NEW YORK UNIVERSITY, GRADUATE SCHOOL OF PUBLIC ADMINISTRATION
Summer Institute in Management of Nonprofit Organizations.
Specialization: Fundamentals of management of nonprofit organizations, applicable to the nongovernmental organizations associated with the United Nations.
Dates: Five weeks: classes begin in June.
Location: New York, New York: on campus.
Instruction: *Methods:* discussion groups, lectures, case studies. *By:* faculty, guest speakers/lecturers.
Highlights: Sponsor has offered program since 1979. Certificate on completion of two papers. Foreign nationals on tourist visas are eligible to enroll. A foreign student counselor/adviser is available. 60 total enrollment.
Eligibility: *Academic:* bachelor's degree. *Language:* English proficiency on advanced level is preferred. *Professional:* none.
Cost: $924 for tuition. *Scholarships:* none.
Housing: Not provided; sponsor assists in locating housing.
Application: *Deadline:* June 3. *Fee:* none.
Contact: Mr. Charles Nicolson, Summer Institute in Management of Nonprofit Organizations, Graduate School of Public Administration, New York University, 4 Washington Square North, New York, NY 10003; (212) 498-3133.

POLICY PLANNING AND MANAGEMENT

U46 U.S. DEPARTMENT OF AGRICULTURE GRADUATE SCHOOL
Strategic Management.
Specialization: Policy planning and management program for professionals in ministries, government-controlled corporations, and legislative and judicial branches of government.
Dates: To be arranged.
Location: Washington, D.C.: on campus.
Instruction: *Methods:* discussion groups, lectures, individualized instruction. *By:* faculty, guest speakers/lecturers.

Abbreviations: ESL = English as a Second Language; TOEFL = Test of English as a Foreign Language; ALIGU = American Language Institute of Georgetown University; GPA = Grade Point Average; SAT = Scholastic Aptitude Test; GED = General Equivalency Diploma.

Highlights: Sponsor has offered program since 1985. Certificate. Issues I-20AB. A foreign student counselor/adviser is available. 12 total enrollment; 100% foreign enrollment in 1985.
Eligibility: *Academic:* bachelor's degree. *Language:* English proficiency on advanced level is required. *Professional:* five years of work experience required.
Cost: $3,075 for tuition, books and materials, some meals. *Scholarships:* none.
Housing: Not provided; sponsor assists in locating housing.
Application: *Deadline:* Sept. 1. *Fee:* none.
Contact: Mr. Robert H. Mashburn, The Graduate School, USDA, 600 Maryland Ave. SW, Room 134, Washington, DC 20024; (202) 447-7476. Telex: 756563 GS INTL WSH.

PROJECT MANAGEMENT

U47 HARVARD UNIVERSITY, INSTITUTE FOR INTERNATIONAL DEVELOPMENT
Program on Investment Appraisal and Management.
Specialization: Topics include finance, economics, management, and computer techniques that apply to investment projects; provides expertise for people involved in planning, assessing, or executing projects.
Dates: Eight weeks: classes begin in June.
Location: Cambridge, Massachusetts: on campus.
Instruction: *Methods:* discussion groups, lectures, case studies, field trips, computer-assisted instruction. *By:* faculty.
Highlights: Sponsor has offered program since 1985. Certificate. Issues I-20AB. Foreign nationals on tourist visas are eligible to enroll. A foreign student counselor/adviser is available. International student office. 55 total enrollment; 100% foreign enrollment in 1985.
Eligibility: *Academic:* master's degree in economics or related field preferred.
Language: English proficiency on advanced level is required. *Professional:* two years of experience in economic, financial, or related work.
Cost: $7,250 for tuition, books, housing, health insurance. *Scholarships:* none.
Housing: In hotels.
Application: *Deadline:* Apr. 1. *Fee:* $20; not refundable.
Contact: Ms. Vivian Goldman, Harvard Institute for International Development, Harvard University, 1737 Cambridge Street, Cambridge, MA 02138; (617) 495-4274. Telex: 7103200315.

U48 TEXAS TECH UNIVERSITY, CENTER FOR APPLIED INTERNATIONAL DEVELOPMENT STUDIES (CAIDS)
Project Management Workshop for Administrators in Francophone Countries.
Specialization: Strategies for rural development, national planning in project development, information systems, microcomputers in project administration.
Dates: Three weeks: classes begin in July.
Location: Lubbock, Texas: on campus, at professional work site.
Instruction: *Methods:* discussion groups, lectures, case studies, field trips, independent study/research. *By:* faculty, guest speakers/lecturers. *In French only.*
Highlights: Sponsor has offered program since 1984. Certificate; three hours graduate credit. Foreign nationals on tourist visas are eligible to enroll. A foreign student counselor/adviser is available. International Programs Office and international student organizations. 30 total enrollment; 100% foreign enrollment in 1985.
Eligibility: *Academic:* bachelor's degree, or comparable professional experience.
Language: English proficiency on beginning level is preferred. *Professional:* one year of experience, national or local government officials, post-secondary or adult educators, international organization officials.
Cost: $3,350 inclusive. *Scholarships:* none.
Housing: In dormitories, apartments.

Application: *Deadline:* June 15. *Fee:* none.
Contact: Center for Applied International Development Studies, Texas Tech University, P.O. Box 4290, Lubbock, TX 79409; (806) 742-3878. Cable: TTUCIDLBK. Telex: 910 896 4398.

U49 UNIVERSITY OF CONNECTICUT HEALTH CENTER
   Project Management Program.
Specialization: Provides skills, strategies, and practical concepts for effective project management and administration: planning, scheduling, implementing, monitoring, and evaluating projects, as well as development, training, and appraisal of staff.
Dates: Apr. 29–June 17. One-month program in Arabic also available.
Location: Farmington, Connecticut: on campus; or on-site abroad.
Instruction: *Methods:* discussion groups, lectures, case studies, field trips, individualized instruction, independent study/research. *By:* faculty, guest speakers/lecturers. *Also available in Arabic.*
Highlights: Sponsor has offered program previously. Certificate. Issues I-20AB, IAP-66. Foreign nationals on tourist visas are eligible to enroll. A foreign student counselor/adviser is available. Social and cultural activities, host family program. 20 total enrollment.
Eligibility: *Academic:* bachelor's degree. *Language:* English proficiency on advanced level is required. TOEFL: 500; ALIGU: 80. *Professional:* planners, managers, and administrators responsible for project development and management, managers of training or of women's income-generating projects.
Cost: $5,200 for tuition, books and materials, health insurance, local transportation, field trip, use of computer. *Scholarships:* none.
Housing: Not provided; sponsor assists in locating housing.
Application: *Deadline:* apply early. *Fee:* none.
Contact: Dr. Stephen L. Schensul, Director, International Health, Population, Social Service Training Programs, University of Connecticut Health Center, Room AG073, Farmington, CT 06032; (203) 674-3302. Telex: 710-423-5521/U Conn HC Lib).

U50 UNIVERSITY OF CONNECTICUT, INSTITUTE OF PUBLIC SERVICE INTERNATIONAL
   Project Management and Local Development.
Specialization: Cost-effectiveness analysis, community development, investment decision-making techniques, and managing integrated rural development. Includes project workshop where practical skills are applied.
Dates: Three months: classes begin in Jan.
Location: West Hartford, Connecticut; on campus.
Instruction: *Methods:* discussions, lectures, case studies, field trips. *By:* faculty, guest speakers/lecturers.
Highlights: Sponsor has offered program since 1961. Certificate. Issues IAP-66. Foreign nationals on tourist visas are not eligible to enroll. Extensive services for foreign nationals. 100% foreign enrollment in 1985.
Eligibility: *Academic:* bachelor's degree or equivalent professional experience.
Language: TOEFL: 500; ALIGU: 80. *Professional:* 2–5 years of experience.
Cost: $4,900 for tuition, books. *Scholarships:* none.
Housing: Not provided; sponsor assists in locating housing.
Application: *Deadline:* six weeks prior. *Fee:* none.
Contact: Mrs. Josephine Mavromatis, Coordinator, Hartford-based Programs, University of Connecticut, IPS International, 1800 Asylum Ave., West Hartford, CT 06117; (203) 241-4924. Cable: IPSUCONN. Telex: 883997 IPS INTL.

Abbreviations: ESL = English as a Second Language; TOEFL = Test of English as a Foreign Language; ALIGU = American Language Institute of Georgetown University; GPA = Grade Point Average; SAT = Scholastic Aptitude Test; GED = General Equivalency Diploma.

U51 UNIVERSITY OF CONNECTICUT, INSTITUTE OF PUBLIC SERVICE INTERNATIONAL
Project Management for Local Development.

Specialization: Project planning and implementation, local development. Designed for officials of national government organizations dealing with local or rural development and for regional, provincial, and municipal government officials.

Dates: Ten weeks: classes begin in May.

Location: West Hartford, Connecticut; on campus.

Instruction: *Methods:* discussions, lectures, case studies, field trips. *By:* faculty, guest speakers/lecturers.

Highlights: Sponsor has offered program since 1961. Certificate. Issues IAP-66. Foreign nationals on tourist visas are not eligible to enroll. Extensive services for foreign nationals. 100% foreign enrollment in 1985.

Eligibility: *Academic:* bachelor's degree or equivalent professional experience. *Language:* TOEFL: 500; ALIGU: 80. *Professional:* 2–5 years of experience.

Cost: $4,900 for tuition, books. *Scholarships:* none.

Housing: Not provided; sponsor assists in locating housing.

Application: *Deadline:* six weeks prior. *Fee:* none.

Contact: Mrs. Josephine Mavromatis, Coordinator, Hartford-based Programs, IPS International, University of Connecticut, 1800 Asylum Ave., West Hartford, CT 06117; (203) 241-4924. Cable: IPSUCONN. Telex: 883997 IPS INTL.

U52 UNIVERSITY OF PITTSBURGH, INSTITUTE OF TRAINING AND ORGANIZATIONAL DEVELOPMENT (ITOD)
Advanced Program on Project Evaluation.

Specialization: Modern project management and evaluation techniques.

Dates: Four weeks: July.

Location: Pittsburgh, Pennsylvania: on campus.

Instruction: *Methods:* discussion groups, lectures, case studies. *By:* faculty, guest speakers/lecturers.

Highlights: Sponsor has offered program since 1974. Certificate. Issues IAP-66. Foreign nationals on tourist visas are eligible to enroll. A foreign student counselor/adviser is available. Unlimited total enrollment; 100% foreign enrollment in 1985.

Eligibility: *Academic:* bachelor's degree. *Language:* English proficiency on intermediate level is preferred. *Professional:* five years of experience in the project area, or graduate degree and three years of experience.

Cost: $3,000 for tuition, books and materials, health insurance. *Scholarships:* none.

Housing: Not provided; sponsor assists in locating housing.

Application: *Deadline:* May 25. *Fee:* $200; applied to tuition.

Contact: Mr. Ron Gigliotti, Program Administrator, ITOD, University of Pittsburgh, 3J03 Forbes Quadrangle, Pittsburgh, PA 15260; (412) 648-7430. Telex: 812466 or 199126.

RECREATION RESOURCES

U53 CLEMSON UNIVERSITY
International Visitor Program.

Specialization: Personalized programs in parks and recreation, combining study, research, and internships. Undergraduate, graduate, and postgraduate levels.

Dates: Rolling: semesters begin in Aug., Jan.

Location: Clemson, South Carolina: on campus.

Instruction: *Methods:* lectures, individualized instruction, "hands-on" training, independent study/research, computer-assisted instruction, laboratories. *By:* faculty.

Highlights: Sponsor has offered program previously. Certificate. Practical training may be a

---

program component; participants are paid. Issues I-20AB, IAP-66. Foreign nationals on tourist visas are eligible to enroll. A foreign student counselor/adviser is available.
Eligibility: *Academic:* bachelor's degree or some undergraduate work. *Language:* English proficiency on the advanced level is required. TOEFL: 550. *Professional:* requires professional certification.
Cost: $815 per month for tuition, books and materials, meals, housing, health insurance. *Scholarships:* none; all participants must be sponsored by an organization.
Housing: In dormitories.
Application: *Deadline:* rolling. *Fee:* none.
Contact: International Service Office, Clemson University, Room 106 Sikes Hall, Clemson, SC 29631; (803) 656-5466.

U54 UNIVERSITY OF GEORGIA
Recreation and Leisure Studies.
Specialization: Administration of leisure services.
Dates: Classes begin in Sept., Jan., April, June.
Location: Athens, Georgia: on campus.
Instruction: *Methods:* discussion groups, lectures, case studies, field trips, individualized instruction, "hands-on" training, independent study/research, computer-assisted instruction. *By:* faculty, guest speakers/lecturers.
Highlights: Sponsor has offered program since 1966. Certificate upon completion of 55–60 quarter hours of credit. Foreign nationals on tourist visas are eligible to enroll. A foreign student counselor/adviser is available. 20 total enrollment; no foreign enrollment in 1985.
Eligibility: *Academic:* bachelor's degree. *Language:* English proficiency on beginning level is required. TOEFL. *Professional:* none.
Cost: $6,000 for tuition. *Scholarships:* none.
Housing: In dormitories, or sponsor assists in locating housing.
Application: *Deadline:* Aug. 15. *Fee:* $10; not refundable.
Contact: Mrs. Janet Schrock, Graduate Director, Physical Education Bldg., University of Georgia, Athens, GA 30602; (404) 542-2674.

SYSTEMS ANALYSIS AND DESIGN

U55 UNIVERSITY OF CONNECTICUT, INSTITUTE OF PUBLIC SERVICE INTERNATIONAL
Management Analysis and Computer Applications.
Specialization: Scientific analysis, design, and evaluation of management and operational systems, and the appropriate use of manual and automated technologies.
Dates: Three months: classes begin in Jan.
Location: West Hartford, Connecticut: on campus.
Instruction: *Methods:* discussions, lectures, case studies, field trips. *By:* faculty, guest speakers/lecturers.
Highlights: Sponsor has offered program previously. Certificate. Issues IAP-66. Foreign nationals on tourist visas are not eligible to enroll. Extensive services for foreign nationals. 100% foreign enrollment in 1985.
Eligibility: *Academic:* bachelor's degree or equivalent professional experience.
Language: TOEFL: 500; ALIGU: 80. *Professional:* 2–5 years of experience.
Cost: $4,900 for tuition, books. *Scholarships:* none.
Housing: Not provided; sponsor assists in locating housing.
Application: *Deadline:* six weeks prior. *Fee:* none.
Contact: Mrs. Josephine Mavromatis, Coordinator, Hartford-based Programs, University of Connecticut, IPS International, 1800 Asylum Ave., West Hartford, CT 06117; (203) 241-4924. Cable: IPSUCONN. Telex: 883997 IPS INTL.

Abbreviations: ESL = English as a Second Language; TOEFL = Test of English as a Foreign Language; ALIGU = American Language Institute of Georgetown University; GPA = Grade Point Average; SAT = Scholastic Aptitude Test; GED = General Equivalency Diploma.

TAXATION

U56 THE AMERICAN UNIVERSITY
Certificate of Graduate Professional Study in Taxation.
Specialization: Graduate-level program in taxation.
Dates: Classes begin in Sept., Jan., May, July.
Location: Washington, D.C.: on campus.
Instruction: *Methods:* discussion groups, lectures, case studies. *By:* faculty.
Highlights: Sponsor has offered program previously. Certificate upon completion of five courses. Issues I-20AB. Foreign nationals on tourist visas are not eligible to enroll. A foreign student counselor/adviser is available. Orientation programs.
Eligibility: *Academic:* master's degree; 3.0 GPA in last 60 hours; GMAT score: 400, or CPA exam. *Language:* English proficiency on advanced level is required. TOEFL: 600; English Language Institute Placement Test. *Professional:* none.
Cost: $299 per semester hour for tuition. *Scholarships:* none.
Housing: Not provided; sponsor assists in locating housing.
Application: *Deadline:* none. *Fee:* none.
Contact: Programs Advisement Center, The American University, 4400 Massachusetts Ave. NW, Room 153 McKinley Bldg., Washington, DC 20016; (202) 885-2500.

UNIVERSITY MANAGEMENT

U57 HARVARD UNIVERSITY
Institute for Educational Management.
Specialization: Professional development for senior-level administrators of colleges and universities; focuses on marketing, law and higher education, finance and control, politics, strategic planning, management of professional and personal life, cultural diversity, human resources management, and the future of higher education.
Dates: One month: July–Aug.
Location: Cambridge, Massachusetts: on campus.
Instruction: *Methods:* discussion groups, lectures, case studies. *By:* faculty, guest speakers/lecturers.
Highlights: Sponsor has offered program since 1970. Certificate. Foreign nationals on tourist visas are eligible to enroll. A foreign student counselor/adviser is not available. 92 total enrollment; 5% foreign enrollment in 1985.
Eligibility: *Academic:* doctorate. *Language:* English proficiency on advanced level is required. *Professional:* 15 years of work experience.
Cost: $5,850 for tuition, books and supplies, meals, housing. *Scholarships:* none.
Housing: In hotels.
Application: *Deadline:* April 1. *Fee:* none.
Contact: Sharon A. McDade, Program Director, Institute for Educational Management, Harvard University, 339 Gutman Library, Cambridge, MA 02138; (617) 495-2655.

U58 UNIVERSITY OF ILLINOIS AT URBANA-CHAMPAIGN
Management Training Programs.
Specialization: Management of universities and closely related organizations in developing countries.
Dates: One year: classes begin in May.
Location: Champaign, Illinois: on campus.
Instruction: *Methods:* discussion groups, lectures, case studies, field trips, "hands-on" training, individualized instruction, independent study/research, computer-assisted instruction, language laboratories. *By:* faculty.
Highlights: Sponsor has offered program since 1977. Certificate. Issues IAP-66. Foreign

All program information is subject to change without notice
and must be confirmed directly with the sponsor.

nationals on tourist visas are not eligible to enroll. A foreign student counselor/adviser is available. Unlimited total enrollment; 100% foreign enrollment in 1985.
Eligibility: *Academic:* bachelor's degree. *Language:* English proficiency on intermediate level is required. *Professional:* one year of work experience preferred.
Cost: $4,500 per term for tuition, books, and materials. *Scholarships:* none.
Housing: Not provided; sponsor assists in locating housing.
Application: *Deadline:* Mar. 1. *Fee:* $25; refundable.
Contact: Program Management Office, Program of Overseas University Collaboration, University of Illinois at Urbana-Champaign, 310 Coble Hall, 801 S. Wright Street, Champaign, IL 61820; (217) 333-1990. Telex: 5101011969 UI Telecom URUD.

Abbreviations: ESL = English as a Second Language; TOEFL = Test of English as a Foreign Language; ALIGU = American Language Institute of Georgetown University; GPA = Grade Point Average; SAT = Scholastic Aptitude Test; GED = General Equivalency Diploma.

185

SOCIAL SCIENCES

V1 CLEMSON UNIVERSITY
International Visitor Program.
Specialization: Personalized programs in the social sciences, combining study, research, and internships. Undergraduate, graduate, and postgraduate levels.
Dates: Rolling: semesters begin in Aug., Jan.
Location: Clemson, South Carolina: on campus.
Instruction: *Methods:* lectures, individualized instruction, "hands-on" training, independent study/research, computer-assisted instruction, laboratories. *By:* faculty.
Highlights: Sponsor has offered program previously. Certificate. Practical training may be a program component; participants are paid. Issues I-20AB, IAP-66. Foreign nationals on tourist visas are eligible to enroll. A foreign student counselor/adviser is available.
Eligibility: *Academic:* bachelor's degree or some undergraduate work. *Language:* English proficiency on the advanced level is required. TOEFL: 550. *Professional:* requires professional certification.
Cost: $815 per month for tuition, books and materials, meals, housing, health insurance. *Scholarships:* none; all participants must be sponsored by an organization.
Housing: In dormitories.
Application: *Deadline:* rolling. *Fee:* none.
Contact: International Service Office, Clemson University, Room 106 Sikes Hall, Clemson, SC 29631; (803) 656-5466.

V2 LESLEY COLLEGE GRADUATE SCHOOL
Social Science.
Specialization: Individually designed independent study degree programs available in the social sciences. Four three-hour meetings on campus required.
Dates: One year: to be arranged.
Location: Cambridge, Massachusetts: on campus. Independent study at student's home or other work site.
Instruction: *Methods:* lectures, discussion groups, case studies, field trips, individualized instruction, "hands-on" training, independent study/research. *By:* faculty.
Highlights: Sponsor has offered program previously. Master's degree. Practical training may be a program component. Issues I-20AB. A foreign student counselor/adviser is available. 5% foreign enrollment in 1985.
Eligibility: *Academic:* bachelor's degree. *Language:* English proficiency is required. TOEFL. *Professional:* none.
Cost: $7,200 for tuition. *Scholarships:* none.
Housing: Not provided.
Application: *Deadline:* open. *Fee:* $35; not refundable.
Contact: Margot Chamberlain, Program Advisor, Lesley College Graduate School, 29 Everett Street, Cambridge, MA 02238; (617) 868-9600, Ext. 426.

V3 LONG ISLAND UNIVERSITY, THE BROOKLYN CAMPUS
Master of Science in Social Science.
Specialization: Any discipline within social sciences or international organizations; may be combined with graduate programs on the U.N.
Dates: Sept.–June.
Location: Brooklyn, New York: on campus.
Instruction: *Methods:* lectures, case studies, individualized instruction, independent study/research. *By:* faculty.
Highlights: Sponsor has offered program since 1972. Master's degree. Issues I-20AB, I-20MN. Foreign nationals on tourist visas are eligible to enroll. A foreign student counselor/adviser is available. ESL and tutoring services. 30% foreign enrollment in 1985.
Eligibility: *Academic:* bachelor's degree. *Language:* English proficiency on advanced level is required. TOEFL. *Professional:* none.
Cost: $6,840 for tuition. *Scholarships:* partial.
Housing: In dormitories.
Application: *Deadline:* Aug. 15. *Fee:* $20; not refundable. *Scholarship deadline:* Mar. 15.
Contact: Prof. D.D. Kostich, Director ISIO/MScSS, Room M-500/501, Long Island University, The Brooklyn Campus, University Plaza, Brooklyn, NY 11201; (718) 834-6000, Ext. 3587 or 3598.

V4 SYRACUSE UNIVERSITY
Master of Social Science.
Specialization: Independent study programs in history, political science, or international relations, require two weeks of residency in July, two summer sessions.
Dates: To be arranged.
Location: Syracuse, New York: on campus.
Instruction: *Methods:* lectures, discussions groups, independent study/research. *By:* faculty.
Highlights: Sponsor has offered program since 1975. Master's degree upon completion of 30 credit hours with B average. Foreign nationals on tourist visas are eligible to enroll. A foreign student counselor/adviser is not available. 7–15 per class total enrollment; 20% foreign enrollment in 1985.
Eligibility: *Academic:* bachelor's degree. *Language:* English proficiency is required. TOEFL. *Professional:* none.
Cost: $7,380 for tuition. *Scholarships:* none.
Housing: In apartments.
Application: *Deadline:* open. *Fee:* $30; not refundable.
Contact: Mary Lou Bagdovitz, ISDP, Syracuse University, 302 Reid Hall, 610 E. Fayette Street, Syracuse, NY 13202; (315) 423-3269. Telex: 937430.

V5 VOORHEES COLLEGE
Specialization: Sociology, social work, political science, criminal justice.
Dates: Aug.–May: classes begin in Aug. and Jan.
Location: Denmark, South Carolina: on campus, at professional work site.
Instruction: *Methods:* discussion groups, lectures, case studies, field trips, individualized instruction, "hands-on" training, independent study/research, computer-assisted instruction, science laboratories. *By:* faculty.
Highlights: Sponsor has offered program since 1969. Certificate. Practical training is a program component; participants are not paid. Issues I-20AB. Foreign nationals on tourist visas are not eligible to enroll. A foreign student counselor/adviser is available.
Eligibility: *Academic:* associate's degree. *Language:* English proficiency on beginning level is required. TOEFL. *Professional:* none.
Cost: $5,884 for tuition, meals, housing, health insurance. *Scholarships:* none.
Housing: In dormitories.
Application: *Deadline:* Aug. *Fee:* $10; not refundable.
Contact: Dr. Lucious Daily, Jr., Director of Admissions and Records, Voorhees College, Voorhees Road, Denmark, SC 29042; (803) 793-3351.

Abbreviations: ESL = English as a Second Language; TOEFL = Test of English as a Foreign Language; ALIGU = American Language Institute of Georgetown University; GPA = Grade Point Average; SAT = Scholastic Aptitude Test; GED = General Equivalency Diploma.

ANTHROPOLOGY

V6 STATE UNIVERSITY OF NEW YORK AT BINGHAMTON
MA Program in Development Anthropology.
Specialization: Includes courses in development anthropology, ecology and development, and economic anthropology.
Dates: Late Aug.–May.
Location: Binghamton, New York: on campus.
Instruction: *Methods:* discussion groups, lectures, case studies, individualized instruction, independent study/research. *By:* faculty.
Highlights: Sponsor has offered program previously. Master's degree upon completion of 30 hours of coursework. Issues I-20AB, IAP-66. Foreign nationals on tourist visas are not eligible to enroll. A foreign student counselor/adviser is available. Orientation, friendship family, and host student programs. 33% foreign enrollment in 1985.
Eligibility: *Academic:* bachelor's degree in anthropology or social science preferred.
Language: English proficiency on advanced level is required. TOEFL: 550.
Professional: none.
Cost: About $10,100 inclusive. *Scholarships:* full.
Housing: In dormitories.
Application: *Deadline:* Feb. 15. *Fee:* $35; not refundable. *Scholarship deadline:* Feb. 15.
Contact: Development Anthropology Program, Dept. of Anthropology, SUNY at Binghamton, Binghamton, NY 13901; (607) 777-2737.

DEMOGRAPHY

V7 EAST-WEST POPULATION INSTITUTE
Graduate Study Program.
Specialization: Demographic trends and estimation, fertility and the family in transition, economic development and human resources, urbanization, migration, and development.
Dates: Classes begin in August.
Location: Honolulu, Hawaii: on campus.
Instruction: *Methods:* discussion groups, lectures, case studies, field trips, individualized instruction, "hands-on" training, independent study/research, computer-assisted instruction. *By:* faculty, guest speakers/lecturers, research associates.
Highlights: Sponsor has offered short-term programs since 1969. Certificate. Practical training is a program component; participants are paid. Foreign nationals on tourist visas are not eligible to enroll. A foreign student counselor/adviser is available. Various support services are available. 15 total enrollment; 75% foreign enrollment in 1985.
Eligibility: *Academic:* bachelor's degree. *Language:* English proficiency on intermediate level is required. TOEFL: 550. *Professional:* none.
Cost: Varies. *Scholarships:* full only to citizens or permanent residents of Asian and Pacific countries.
Housing: In dormitories, apartments.
Application: *Deadline:* Dec 1. of prior year. *Fee:* none. *Scholarship deadline:* not given.
Contact: Award Services Officer, East-West Center, 1777 East-West Road, Honolulu, HI 96848; (808) 944-7404/7736. Cable: EASWESCEN. Telex: 743-0331.

V8 EAST-WEST POPULATION INSTITUTE
Summer Seminar Program.
Specialization: Demographic trends and estimation, fertility and the family in transition, economic development and human resources, urbanization, migration, and development.
Dates: Five weeks: classes begin in June.
Location: Honolulu, Hawaii: on campus.

Instruction: *Methods:* discussion groups, lectures, case studies, field trips, individualized instruction, "hands-on" training, independent study/research, computer-assisted instruction. *By:* faculty, guest speakers/lecturers, research associates.
Highlights: Sponsor has offered short-term programs since 1969. Certificate. Practical training is a program component; participants are paid. Foreign nationals on tourist visas are not eligible to enroll. A foreign student counselor/adviser is available. Various support services are available. 15 total enrollment; 75% foreign enrollment in 1985.
Eligibility: *Academic:* bachelor's degree. *Language:* English proficiency on intermediate level is required. TOEFL. *Professional:* prefer staff of organizations involved in population research or planning, or doctoral candidates doing dissertation research directly related to a workshop topic.
Cost: $1,225 inclusive. *Scholarships:* full only to citizens or permanent residents of Asian and Pacific countries.
Housing: In dormitories, apartments.
Application: *Deadline:* mid-Feb. *Fee:* none. *Scholarship deadline:* not given.
Contact: Summer Seminar Coordinator, East-West Population Institute, East-West Center, 1777 East-West Road, Honolulu, HI 96848; (808) 944-7404/7736. Cable: EASWESCEN. Telex: 743-0331.

V9 UNIVERSITY OF PENNSYLVANIA
Graduate Group in Demography.
Specialization: Master's degree program in demography.
Dates: Sept. 1–May 31.
Location: Philadelphia, Pennsylvania: on campus.
Instruction: *Methods:* discussion groups, lectures, independent study/research. *By:* faculty.
Highlights: Sponsor has offered program since 1963. Certificate upon completion of eight course units, exam, and research paper. Issues I-20AB, I-20MN, IAP-66. Foreign nationals on tourist visas are not eligible to enroll. A foreign student counselor/adviser is available. ESL and tutoring programs. 12 total enrollment; 40% foreign enrollment in 1985.
Eligibility: *Academic:* bachelor's degree. *Language:* English proficiency on advanced level is preferred. TOEFL. *Professional:* none.
Cost: $18,500 for tuition, meals, housing. *Scholarships:* full.
Housing: Not provided; sponsor assists in locating housing.
Application: *Deadline:* Feb. 1. *Fee:* $40; not refundable. *Scholarship deadline:* Feb. 1.
Contact: Chair, Graduate Group in Demography, University of Pennsylvania, 3718 Locust Walk, Philadelphia, PA 19104-6298; (215) 898-7768.

V10 UNIVERSITY OF MICHIGAN
Population and Development.
Specialization: For planners and administrators in developing countries to increase understanding of how demographic patterns relate to the development process. Includes economic development and planning, economic theory in planning and development, demography and population studies, historical experience of population policies, family planning, and theory application through computer exercises.
Dates: Late Aug.–late Dec.
Location: Ann Arbor, Michigan: on campus.
Instruction: *Methods:* lectures, discussion groups, case studies, field trips, individualized instruction, "hands-on" training, computer-assisted instruction, language labs. *By:* faculty.
Highlights: Sponsor has offered short-term programs since 1980. Certificate. Issues I-20AB, IAP-66. Foreign nationals on tourist visas are not eligible to enroll. A foreign student counselor/adviser is available. 10–15 total enrollment; 100% foreign enrollment in 1985.
Eligibility: *Academic:* bachelor's degree. *Language:* English proficiency on intermediate level is required. TOEFL. *Professional:* current or projected professional involvement in population and development planning.

Abbreviations: ESL = English as a Second Language; TOEFL = Test of English as a Foreign Language; ALIGU = American Language Institute of Georgetown University; GPA = Grade Point Average; SAT = Scholastic Aptitude Test; GED = General Equivalency Diploma.

189

Cost: $7,500 for tuition, program fees. *Scholarships:* full through sponsorship by various international organizations.
Housing: Arranged.
Application: *Deadline:* June 1. *Fee:* $20; not refundable. *Scholarship deadline:* June 1.
Contact: Director, Training Program in Population and Development, Dept. of Population Planning and International Health, School of Public Health, University of Michigan, Ann Arbor, MI 48109-2029; (313) 763-4320 or 763-4238. Cable: POPLANUM. Telex: 810-223-6056 UOFMAA.

ECONOMICS

V11 THE AMERICAN UNIVERSITY
Graduate Certificate in Applied Economics.
Specialization: Applied economics.
Dates: Classes begin in Sept., Jan., May, July.
Location: Washington, D.C.: on campus.
Instruction: *Methods:* discussion groups, lectures, case studies. *By:* faculty.
Highlights: Sponsor has offered program previously. Certificate. Issues I-20AB. Foreign nationals on tourist visas are not eligible to enroll. A foreign student counselor/adviser is available. Orientation and ESL programs.
Eligibility: *Academic:* bachelor's degree; undergraduate work in micro/macro economics, price and income theory, basic statistics. *Language:* English proficiency on advanced level is required. TOEFL: 600; or English Language Institute Placement Test. *Professional:* none.
Cost: $299 per semester hour for tuition. *Scholarships:* none.
Housing: Not provided; sponsor assists in locating housing.
Application: *Deadline:* none. *Fee:* none.
Contact: Programs Advisement Center, The American University, 4400 Massachusetts Ave. NW, Room 153 McKinley Bldg., Washington, DC 20016; (202) 885-2500.

V12 ECONOMICS INSTITUTE
Specialization: Economics and agricultural economics; intercultural program.
Dates: Year-round program.
Location: Boulder, Colorado: at institute.
Instruction: *Methods:* lectures, independent study, field trips, labs. *By:* faculty, guest speakers/lecturers.
Highlights: Sponsor has offered program since 1958. Credit. Certificate. Issues I-20. Extensive services for foreign nationals. 100% foreign enrollment in 1985. List of past participants is available.
Eligibility: *Academic:* bachelor's degree. *Language:* TOEFL or self-evaluation. *Professional:* none.
Cost: Varies with length of study. *Scholarships:* partial.
Housing: In dormitories, apartments, furnished rooms, with families.
Application: *Deadline:* not given. *Fee:* $50. *Scholarship deadline:* not given.
Contact: Admissions Office, Economics Institute, 1030 13th Street, Boulder, CO 80302; (303) 492-7337. Telex: 450385 ECONINST BLDR.

V13 UNIVERSITY OF VIRGINIA, ECONOMICS DEPARTMENT
Graduate Programs.
Specialization: Master's programs in economics.
Dates: Sept.–May.
Location: Charlottesville, Virginia: on campus.
Instruction: *Methods:* discussion groups, lectures, independent study/research. *By:* faculty.
Highlights: Sponsor has offered program since 1925. Master's degree. Issues IAP-66.

Foreign nationals on tourist visas are not eligible to enroll. A foreign student counselor/adviser is available. 40 total enrollment; 25% foreign enrollment in 1985.
Eligibility: *Academic:* bachelor's degree. *Language:* English proficiency on advanced level is required. TOEFL: 600. *Professional:* none.
Cost: $4,000 for tuition, books, and materials. *Scholarships:* partial.
Housing: Not provided; sponsor assists in locating housing.
Application: *Deadline:* May 1. *Fee:* $20; not refundable. *Scholarship deadline:* Feb. 1.
Contact: William R. Johnson, Dept. of Economics, University of Virginia, Rouss Hall, Charlottesville, VA 22901; (804) 924-3251.

V14 WILLIAMS COLLEGE, CENTER FOR DEVELOPMENT ECONOMICS
M.A. Program in Development Economics.
Specialization: Economic analysis and quantitative techniques relevant to economic policy-making in developing countries, designed for economists at public economic development agencies.
Dates: Nine months: classes begin in Sept. Refresher study required for most students: about June 1 to Aug. 20.
Location: Williamstown, Massachusetts: on campus; and Boulder, Colorado: at Economics Institute.
Instruction: *Methods:* discussion groups, lectures, case studies, field trips, individualized instruction, independent study/research, computer-assisted instruction. *By:* faculty.
Highlights: Sponsor has offered program since 1960. Master's degree. Issues IAP-66. Foreign nationals on tourist visas are not eligible to enroll. A foreign student counselor/adviser is available. Various support services are available. 25 total enrollment; 100% foreign enrollment in 1985. List of past participants is available.
Eligibility: *Academic:* bachelor's degree in economics; second class honor's degree or equivalent. *Language:* English proficiency on advanced level is required. TOEFL: 550. *Professional:* three years of experience in a public agency as an economist working on development problems.
Cost: $20,000 inclusive. Economics Institute: $6,000. *Scholarships:* none.
Housing: In furnished rooms at CDE House.
Application: *Deadline:* Dec. 1. *Fee:* none.
Contact: Christine Naughton, CDE Admissions Officer, Fernald House, Williams College, Williamstown, MA 01267; (413) 597-2110. Cable: ECONOMICS. Telex: 01469735.

V15 YALE UNIVERSITY
International and Development Economics.
Specialization: Economics.
Dates: Nine months: classes begin in Sept.
Location: New Haven, Connecticut: on campus.
Instruction: *Methods:* discussion groups, lectures, individualized instruction. *By:* faculty.
Highlights: Sponsor has offered program previously. Master's degree upon completion of eight courses. Foreign nationals on tourist visas are not eligible to enroll. A foreign student counselor/adviser is available. 15–20 total enrollment; 100% foreign enrollment in 1985.
Eligibility: *Academic:* bachelor's degree. *Language:* English proficiency on advanced level is required. TOEFL: 560. *Professional:* none.
Cost: $11,120 for tuition. *Scholarships:* none.
Housing: In dormitories if single; in apartments if married.
Application: *Deadline:* Jan. 2. *Fee:* $40; not refundable.
Contact: Prof. R.E. Evenson, Dept. of Economics, Yale University, 27 Hillhouse Ave., New Haven, CT 06520; (203) 436-4403.

Abbreviations: ESL = English as a Second Language; TOEFL = Test of English as a Foreign Language; ALIGU = American Language Institute of Georgetown University; GPA = Grade Point Average; SAT = Scholastic Aptitude Test; GED = General Equivalency Diploma.

GERONTOLOGY

V16 UNIVERSITY OF PENNSYLVANIA
Master of Arts in Social Gerontology.
Specialization: Multidisciplinary program combining liberal arts and sciences while focusing on a broad range of conceptual issues in the field of aging.
Dates: Sept.–May.
Location: Philadelphia, Pennsylvania: on campus.
Instruction: *Methods:* discussion groups, lectures, case studies, independent study/research. *By:* faculty.
Highlights: Sponsor has offered program since 1978. Master's degree upon completion of eight courses and fieldwork. Practical training is a program component; participants are not paid. Issues I-20AB, IAP-66. Foreign nationals on tourist visas are not eligible to enroll. A foreign student counselor/adviser is available.
Eligibility: *Academic:* bachelor's degree. *Language:* English proficiency on advanced level is required. TOEFL. *Professional:* none.
Cost: $20,000 inclusive. *Scholarships:* none.
Housing: Not provided; sponsor assists in locating housing.
Application: *Deadline:* July 15. *Fee:* $35; not refundable.
Contact: Janet Theophano, Administrative Coordinator, College of General Studies, University of Pennsylvania, 210 Logal Hall, Philadelphia, PA 19104; (215) 898-5390. Cable: PNSYL Phila PA. Telex: 710-670-0328.

HUMAN AND SOCIAL SERVICES

V17 BRANDEIS UNIVERSITY
Master of Management of Human Services.
Specialization: Includes a management laboratory project providing students with experience in the public, private, and nonprofit sectors.
Dates: June–May.
Location: Waltham, Massachusetts: on campus.
Instruction: *Methods:* lectures, discussion groups, case studies, "hands-on" training, independent study/research. *By:* faculty.
Highlights: Sponsor has offered program since 1977. Master's degree. Issues I-20AB, IAP-66. Foreign nationals on tourist visas are not eligible to enroll. A foreign student counselor/adviser is available. 35 total enrollment; 10% foreign enrollment in 1985.
Eligibility: *Academic:* bachelor's degree. *Language:* English proficiency on advanced level is required. TOEFL. *Professional:* two years of experience.
Cost: $10,000 for tuition. *Scholarships:* none.
Housing: In apartments.
Application: *Deadline:* Feb. 15. *Fee:* $25; not refundable.
Contact: Hazel Miele, Admissions, Heller Graduate School, Brandeis University, Waltham, MA 02254; (617) 647-2944.

V18 CLEVELAND STATE UNIVERSITY, COLLEGE OF EDUCATION
Short-Term Courses.
Specialization: Special topical programs on such issues as family counseling, substance abuse, human relations.
Dates: Two weeks: primarily during the summer.
Location: Cleveland, Ohio: on campus.
Instruction: *Methods:* discussion groups, lectures, case studies, field trips, independent study/research, computer-assisted instruction. *By:* faculty.
Highlights: Sponsor has offered program previously. A foreign student counselor/adviser is available. Unlimited total enrollment; about 1% foreign enrollment in 1985.

Eligibility: *Academic:* bachelor's degree. *Language:* English proficiency on intermediate level is required. TOEFL. *Professional:* none.
Cost: Varies. *Scholarships:* none.
Housing: Not provided; sponsor assists in locating housing.
Application: *Deadline:* rolling. *Fee:* $25; refundable.
Contact: Dr. Lewis E. Patterson, Associate Dean, College of Education, Cleveland State University, East 24 and Euclid, Cleveland, OH 44115; (216) 687-3737.

V19 DENVER INTERNATIONAL PROGRAM
Specialization: Human service organization work and study program at the School of Social Work of Denver University.
Dates: Apr.–Aug.
Location: Denver, Colorado: on campus of Denver University, at professional work site.
Instruction: *Methods:* discussion groups, lectures, field trips. *By:* faculty.
Highlights: Sponsor has offered program since 1979. Certificate. Practical training is a program component; participants are paid. Issues IAP-66. Foreign nationals on tourist visas are not eligible to enroll. A foreign student counselor/adviser is not available. Various support services are available. 15 total enrollment; 100% foreign enrollment in 1985.
Eligibility: *Academic:* master's degree or equivalent. *Language:* English proficiency on advanced level is required. TOEFL. *Professional:* three years of work experience and professional certification in social work, youth work, physical therapy, psychology, sociology, or community development. Participants must be between 23 and 45 years old.
Cost: $25,000 inclusive. *Scholarships:* full.
Housing: With families.
Application: *Deadline:* Sept. of previous year. *Fee:* none. *Scholarship deadline:* none.
Contact: Council of International Program, 1030 Euclid Ave., Suite 410, Cleveland, OH 44115; (216) 861-5478. Cable: CIPRO. Telex: 241423.

V20 GUILFORD COLLEGE
Social Services.
Specialization: Social services.
Dates: Aug.–late July.
Location: Greensboro, North Carolina: on campus.
Instruction: *Methods:* lectures, discussion groups. *By:* faculty.
Highlights: Sponsor has offered program since 1983. Certificate upon completion of 4–6 courses. Issues I-20AB, I-20MN. Foreign nationals on tourist visas are not eligible to enroll. A foreign student counselor/adviser is available.
Cost: $112 per credit hour for tuition. *Scholarships:* none.
Housing: Not provided; student makes own arrangements.
Application: *Deadline:* open. *Fee:* $20; not refundable.
Contact: Dean of Admissions and Financial Aid, Guilford College, 5800 W. Friendly Ave., Greensboro, NC 27410; (919) 292-5511.

V21 LESLEY COLLEGE GRADUATE SCHOOL
Human Services.
Specialization: Individually designed, independent study degree program in human services directed by college faculty and professionals in the field. Requires four three-hour meetings on campus.
Dates: To be arranged.
Location: Cambridge, Massachusetts: on campus.
Instruction: *Methods:* lectures, discussion groups, case studies, field trips, individualized instruction, "hands-on" training, independent study/research. *By:* faculty.
Highlights: Sponsor has offered program since 1971. Master's degree. Practical training may be a program component. Issues I-20AB. A foreign student counselor/adviser is available. 5% foreign enrollment in 1985.

Abbreviations: ESL = English as a Second Language; TOEFL = Test of English as a Foreign Language; ALIGU = American Language Institute of Georgetown University; GPA = Grade Point Average; SAT = Scholastic Aptitude Test; GED = General Equivalency Diploma.

Eligibility: *Academic:* bachelor's degree. *Language:* English proficiency is required. TOEFL. *Professional:* none.
Cost: $7,200 for tuition. *Scholarships:* none.
Housing: Not provided.
Application: *Deadline:* open. *Fee:* $35; not refundable.
Contact: Margot Chamberlain, Program Advisor, Graduate School, Lesley College, 29 Everett Street, Cambridge, MA 02238; (617) 868-9600, Ext. 426.

V22 PURDUE UNIVERSITY, DEPARTMENT OF CHILD DEVELOPMENT & FAMILY STUDIES
Master's Degree in Child Development & Family Studies.
Specialization: Child development, early childhood education, family studies.
Dates: One year: classes begin in Aug., Jan., June.
Location: West Lafayette, Indiana: on campus.
Instruction: *Methods:* discussion groups, lectures, "hands-on" training, independent study/research. *By:* faculty.
Highlights: Sponsor has offered program previously. Certificate upon completion of 36 semester credit hours and practicum. Practical training is a program component; participants are not paid. Issues I-20AB.
Eligibility: *Academic:* bachelor's degree; GRE. *Language:* English proficiency on advanced level is required. TOEFL. *Professional:* none.
Cost: $6,050 for tuition, health insurance. *Scholarships:* partial.
Housing: In apartments, furnished rooms.
Application: *Deadline:* Feb. 15. *Fee:* none. *Scholarship deadline:* Feb. 15.
Contact: Dept. of Child Development and Family Studies, Purdue University, CDFS Bldg., West Lafayette, IN 47906; (317) 494-2932.

V23 SAINT JOSEPH COLLEGE, GRADUATE DIVISION
Graduate Programs in Child Welfare.
Specialization: Master's and certificate programs in child welfare. Intensive short summer courses.
Dates: Classes begin in Sept., Jan., June.
Location: West Hartford, Connecticut: on campus.
Instruction: *Methods:* discussion groups, lectures, individualized instruction, "hands-on" training, computer-assisted instruction, language laboratories, science laboratories. *By:* faculty, guest speakers/lecturers.
Highlights: Sponsor has offered program since 1959. Certificate. Practical training may be a program component; participants are not paid. Issues I-20AB. Foreign nationals on tourist visas are eligible to enroll. A foreign student counselor/adviser is not available. 30 total enrollment; 2% foreign enrollment in 1985.
Eligibility: *Academic:* bachelor's degree. *Language:* English proficiency on intermediate level is required. TOEFL. *Professional:* none.
Cost: $165 per credit hour for tuition. *Scholarships:* none.
Housing: In dormitories.
Application: *Deadline:* one week prior. *Fee:* $15; not refundable.
Contact: Claire Markham, Graduate Dean, Saint Joseph College, West Hartford, CT 06117; (203) 232-4571.

V24 SPRINGFIELD COLLEGE
Human Services Administration.
Specialization: Master's degree program comprising 32 semester hours of study.
Dates: One year: classes begin in Sept.
Location: Springfield, Massachusetts: on campus, at professional work site.
Instruction: *Methods:* discussion groups, lectures, individualized instruction, "hands-on" training, independent study/research. *By:* faculty.

Highlights: Sponsor has offered program since 1953. Master's degree upon completion of coursework and comprehensive exam. Practical training is a program component; participants are not paid. Issues I-20AB, IAP-66. Foreign nationals on tourist visas are not eligible to enroll. A foreign student counselor/adviser is available. International center. Unlimited total enrollment; 40% foreign enrollment in 1985.
Eligibility: *Academic:* bachelor's degree. *Language:* English proficiency on intermediate level is required. TOEFL: 550. *Professional:* none.
Cost: About $9,700 for tuition, books and materials, meals, housing, registration. *Scholarships:* partial.
Housing: In dormitories, apartments.
Application: *Deadline:* May 1. *Fee:* $25; not refundable. *Scholarship deadline:* May 1.
Contact: Dr. Gordon Diem, Springfield College, Box 1750, Springfield, MA 01109; (413) 788-3194.

V25 SPRINGFIELD COLLEGE
Summer Master's Degree in Human Services Administration.
Specialization: Independent study program consists of 3–5 two-week summer sessions on campus, credit for transfer work, and ten credits of independent study.
Dates: Two weeks: August.
Location: Springfield, Massachusetts: on campus. Independent study at home or other appropriate site.
Instruction: *Methods:* discussion groups, lectures, individualized instruction, independent study/research. *By:* faculty.
Highlights: Sponsor has offered program since 1972. Certificate upon completion of 32 semester hours of credit and comprehensive exam. Issues I-20AB, IAP-66. Foreign nationals on tourist visas are not eligible to enroll. A foreign student counselor/adviser is available. International Center. Unlimited total enrollment; no foreign enrollment in 1985.
Eligibility: *Academic:* bachelor's degree. *Language:* English proficiency on intermediate level is required. TOEFL: 550. *Professional:* employment in human services agency preferred.
Cost: $4,400–$5,300 for tuition, registration. *Scholarships:* none.
Housing: In dormitories.
Application: *Deadline:* open. *Fee:* $25; not refundable.
Contact: Dr. Gordon Diem, Director, HSAD Summer Master's Program, Springfield College, Box 1750, Springfield, MA 01109; (413) 788-3194.

V26 TEMPLE UNIVERSITY, SCHOOL OF SOCIAL ADMINISTRATION
Administration of the Social Services.
Specialization: Social work and social welfare administration.
Dates: Oct.–May.
Location: Philadelphia, Pennsylvania: on campus.
Instruction: *Methods:* discussion groups, lectures, case studies. *By:* faculty, guest speakers/lecturers.
Highlights: Sponsor has offered program since 1982. Certificate. A foreign student counselor/adviser is available. 30 total enrollment; no foreign enrollment in 1985.
Eligibility: *Academic:* master's degree. *Language:* not given. *Professional:* none.
Cost: $900 for tuition, books, and materials. *Scholarships:* none.
Housing: Not provided; sponsor assists in locating housing.
Application: *Deadline:* Oct. 1. *Fee:* none.
Contact: Prof. Felice Perlmutter, Ph.D., School of Social Administration, Temple University, Philadelphia, PA 19122; (215) 787-1206.

V27 UNIVERSITY OF PENNSYLVANIA
Post Master's Certificate in Social Work.
Specialization: Examination of a particular social work issue or problem to increase skill and understanding of an area of professional practice.

Abbreviations: ESL = English as a Second Language; TOEFL = Test of English as a Foreign Language; ALIGU = American Language Institute of Georgetown University; GPA = Grade Point Average; SAT = Scholastic Aptitude Test; GED = General Equivalency Diploma.

195

Dates: Sept.–June.
Location: Philadelphia, Pennsylvania: on campus, at professional work site.
Instruction: *Methods:* discussion groups, lectures, case studies, field trips, individualized instruction, "hands-on" training, independent study/research, computer-assisted instruction. *By:* faculty.
Highlights: Sponsor has offered program previously. Certificate upon completion of eight credit units, practicum, and research project. Practical training is a program component; participants are not paid. Issues I-20AB, IAP-66. Foreign nationals on tourist visas are not eligible to enroll. A foreign student counselor/adviser is available. 10 total enrollment.
Eligibility: *Academic:* master's degree. *Language:* English proficiency on advanced level is required. TOEFL: 525. *Professional:* five years of work experience.
Cost: $20,000 inclusive. *Scholarships:* none.
Housing: In dormitories.
Application: *Deadline:* Apr. 1. *Fee:* $30; not refundable.
Contact: Orneice Dorsey-Leslie, Admissions Director, School of Social Work, University of Pennsylvania, 3701 Locust Walk, Philadelphia, PA 19104; (215) 898-5521. Cable: PNSYL Phila Pa. Telex: 710-670-0328.

SOCIAL RESEARCH

V28 UNIVERSITY OF MICHIGAN
Summer Institute in Survey Research Techniques.
Specialization: Survey research.
Dates: June 30–July 25, July 28–Aug. 22.
Location: Ann Arbor, Michigan: on campus.
Instruction: *Methods:* lectures, "hands-on" training. *By:* faculty.
Highlights: Sponsor has offered program since 1947. Credit. Helps obtain visa. No services for foreign nationals. 29% foreign enrollment in 1985. List of past participants is available.
Eligibility: *Academic:* bachelor's degree. *Language:* TOEFL; Univ. of Michigan Language Test. *Professional:* none.
Cost: Varies. *Scholarships:* none.
Housing: Not provided.
Application: *Deadline:* May 1. *Fee:* none.
Contact: Professor Duane F. Alwin, Survey Research Center, P.O. Box 1248, Ann Arbor, MI 48106; (313) 764-6595.

V29 UNIVERSITY OF MICHIGAN and INTERUNIVERSITY CONSORTIUM FOR POLITICAL AND SOCIAL RESEARCH
Summer Program in Quantitative Methods of Social Research.
Specialization: Quantitative methods of social research: research design, statistics, data analysis, and social methodology.
Dates: June 30–Aug. 22.
Location: Ann Arbor, Michigan: on campus.
Instruction: *Methods:* lectures, discussion groups, "hands-on" training, computer-assisted instruction. *By:* faculty.
Highlights: Sponsor has offered program since 1963. Certificate. Participants may audit courses without credit. Issues IAP-66. Foreign nationals on tourist visas are eligible to enroll. A foreign student counselor is available. 400 total enrollment; 25% foreign enrollment in 1985.
Eligibility: *Academic:* bachelor's degree. *Language:* English proficiency on advanced level is required. *Professional:* none.
Cost: Not given. *Scholarships:* none.
Housing: Not provided; sponsor assists in locating housing.
Application: *Deadline:* June 1. *Fee:* not given.
Contact: Henry Heitowit, Director, ICPSR Summer Program, University of Michigan, P.O. Box 1248, Ann Arbor, MI 48106; (313) 764-8392.

All program information is subject to change without notice
and must be confirmed directly with the sponsor.

VISUAL AND PERFORMING ARTS

W1 GUILFORD COLLEGE
Specialization: Programs available in art, classics, drama, speech, and music. Designed for those persons with bachelor's degrees who desire expertise in other areas.
Dates: Aug.–late July.
Location: Greensboro, North Carolina: on campus.
Instruction: *Methods:* lectures, discussion groups. *By:* faculty.
Highlights: Sponsor has offered short-term programs since 1983. Certificate. Issues I-20AB, I-20MN. Foreign nationals on tourist visas are not eligible to enroll. A foreign student counselor/adviser is available. International Relations Club. 8% total foreign enrollment in 1985.
Eligibility: *Academic:* bachelor's degree. *Language:* English proficiency on advanced level is required. TOEFL: 500. *Professional:* none.
Cost: $112 per credit hour for tuition. *Scholarships:* none.
Housing: Not provided; student makes own arrangements.
Application: *Deadline:* open. *Fee:* $20; not refundable.
Contact: Dean of Admissions and Financial Aid, Guilford College, 5800 West Friendly Ave., Greensboro, NC 27410; (919) 292-5511.

W2 LESLEY COLLEGE GRADUATE SCHOOL
Arts and Culture.
Specialization: Individually designed, independent study degree programs, supervised by faculty and professionals in the field. Requires four three-hour meetings on campus.
Dates: To be arranged.
Location: Cambridge, Massachusetts: on campus.
Instruction: *Methods:* lectures, discussion groups, case studies, field trips, individualized instruction, "hands-on" training, independent study/research. *By:* faculty.
Highlights: Sponsor has offered program previously. Master's degree. Practical training may be a program component. Issues I-20AB. A foreign student counselor/adviser is available. 5% foreign enrollment in 1985.
Eligibility: *Academic:* bachelor's degree. *Language:* English proficiency is required. TOEFL. *Professional:* none.
Cost: $7,200 for tuition. *Scholarships:* none.
Housing: Not provided.
Application: *Deadline:* open. *Fee:* $35; not refundable.
Contact: Margot Chamberlain, Program Advisor, Lesley College Graduate School, 29 Everett Street, Cambridge, MA 02238; (617) 868-9600, Ext. 426.

W3 MARYWOOD COLLEGE
Painting, Ceramics, Weaving.
Specialization: For schoolteachers: watercolor painting, off-loom weaving, design weaving with microcomputers, ceramics—Raku.
Dates: Five weeks: classes begin in late June.
Location: Scranton, Pennsylvania: on campus.

Abbreviations: ESL = English as a Second Language; TOEFL = Test of English as a Foreign Language; ALIGU = American Language Institute of Georgetown University; GPA = Grade Point Average; SAT = Scholastic Aptitude Test; GED = General Equivalency Diploma.

Instruction: *Methods:* discussion groups, lectures, individualized instruction, "hands-on" training. *By:* faculty, guest speakers/lecturers.
Highlights: Sponsor has offered short-term programs since 1982. Certificate. Foreign nationals on tourist visas are eligible to enroll. A foreign student counselor/adviser is available. Orientation programs. 4% foreign enrollment in 1985.
Eligibility: *Academic:* bachelor's degree. *Language:* English proficiency on intermediate level is required. TOEFL: 550. *Professional:* none.
Cost: $145 per credit for tuition. *Scholarships:* none.
Housing: In apartments, or sponsor assists in locating housing.
Application: *Deadline:* none. *Fee:* none.
Contact: Sister M. Eamon O'Neill, Marywood College, 2300 Adams Ave., Scranton, PA 18509; (717) 348-6230.

ART

W4 SYRACUSE UNIVERSITY
Advertising Design/Illustration.
Specialization: Independent study degree program in advertising design or illustration; requires two weeks of residency for three consecutive summers and several long weekends during a two-year time period.
Dates: See Specialization above.
Location: Syracuse, New York: on campus, at major art centers.
Instruction: *Methods:* lectures, individualized instruction, "hands-on" training, independent study/research. *By:* faculty, guest speakers/lecturers.
Highlights: Sponsor has offered program since 1973. Certificate upon completion of research project. Foreign nationals on tourist visas are eligible to enroll. A foreign student counselor/adviser is not available. 15 total enrollment; 5% foreign enrollment in 1985.
Eligibility: *Academic:* associate or bachelor's degree. *Language:* English proficiency is required. *Professional:* three years of experience in advertising design or illustration.
Cost: $7,500 for tuition, books. *Scholarships:* none.
Housing: In apartments.
Application: *Deadline:* late spring for Illustration, early spring for Ad Design. *Fee:* $30; not refundable.
Contact: Mary Lou Bagdovitz, Independent Study Degree Program, Syracuse University, 610 E. Fayette Street, 302 Reid Hall, Syracuse, NY 13202; (315) 423-3269.

DRAMA AND THEATER ARTS

W5 BOSTON UNIVERSITY, THEATER INSTITUTE
Teachers of Theatre Program.
Specialization: Performing arts skills and teaching techniques for teachers; acting, dance, voice.
Dates: Six weeks: classes begin in late June.
Location: Boston, Massachusetts: on campus.
Instruction: *Methods:* discussion groups, lectures, field trips, "hands-on" training, independent study/research. *By:* faculty, guest speakers/lecturers.
Highlights: Sponsor has offered program since 1980. Certificate. Practical training is a program component; participants are not paid. Foreign nationals on tourist visas are eligible to enroll. A foreign student counselor/adviser is available. 100 total enrollment; 5% foreign enrollment in 1985.
Eligibility: *Academic:* bachelor's degree. *Language:* English proficiency on intermediate level is required. TOEFL: 550. *Professional:* two years of experience; secondary school teachers of drama preferred.

Cost: $1,800 for tuition, meals, housing. *Scholarships:* full.
Housing: Not provided; sponsor assists in locating housing.
Application: *Deadline:* May 31. *Fee:* $20; not refundable. *Scholarship deadline:* May 31.
Contact: Joyce Schmidt, Director, Boston University Theatre Institute, 1019 Commonwealth Ave., Boston, MA 02215; (617) 353-4363.

MUSIC

W6 MANHATTAN SCHOOL OF MUSIC and MANHATTAN DALCROZE INSTITUTE
Manhattan Dalcroze Institute Teacher Training Program.
Specialization: Daily work with children's classes.
Dates: Three weeks: classes begin in July.
Location: New York, New York: on campus.
Instruction: *Methods:* discussion groups, lectures, "hands-on" training. *By:* faculty.
Highlights: Sponsor has offered program since 1983. Certificate. Practical training is a program component; participants are not paid. Foreign nationals on tourist visas are eligible to enroll. A foreign student counselor/adviser is available. 50 total enrollment; 10% foreign enrollment in 1985.
Eligibility: *Academic:* bachelor's degree. *Language:* English proficiency on intermediate level is preferred. TOEFL: 550. *Professional:* experience as a classroom music teacher.
Cost: $1,624 for tuition, housing. *Scholarships:* none.
Housing: In dormitories.
Application: *Deadline:* one month prior. *Fee:* $25; refundable.
Contact: Neal Hatch, Manhattan School of Music, 120 Claremont Ave., New York, NY 10027; (212) 749-2802.

W7 MARYWOOD COLLEGE
Music Seminars.
Specialization: Theoretical and practical workshops in microcomputer literacy for musicians, Suzuki techniques, staging a musical, piano literature.
Dates: June 16–July 11.
Location: Scranton, Pennsylvania: on campus.
Instruction: *Methods:* lectures, practical training. *By:* faculty, guest speakers/lecturers.
Highlights: Sponsor has offered program previously. Credit. Issues I-20. Limited services for foreign nationals. List of past participants is available.
Eligibility: *Academic:* bachelor's degree. *Language:* TOEFL: 500. *Professional:* none.
Cost: $175–$325 for tuition, registration. $90–$150 for auditors. *Scholarships:* none.
Housing: Not provided; sponsor assists in locating housing.
Application: *Deadline:* June 1. *Fee:* none.
Contact: Sister M. Eamon O'Neill, I.H.M., Ed.D., Dean, Marywood College, Scranton, PA 18509; (717) 348-6230.

W8 UNIVERSITY OF CALIFORNIA, LOS ANGELES EXTENSION
Professional Designation in Film Scoring.
Specialization: Composing and arranging music for films and television.
Dates: One year: classes begin in June, Sept., Jan., and April.
Location: Los Angeles, California: on campus.
Instruction: *Methods:* discussion groups, lectures. *By:* faculty, guest speakers/lecturers.
Highlights: Sponsor has offered program previously. Certificate. Issues I-20AB. Foreign nationals on tourist visas are eligible to enroll. A foreign student counselor/adviser is available. ESL program. Unlimited total enrollment; about 10% foreign enrollment in 1985.
Eligibility: *Academic:* advanced music students or professional musicians. *Language:* English

Abbreviations: ESL = English as a Second Language; TOEFL = Test of English as a Foreign Language; ALIGU = American Language Institute of Georgetown University; GPA = Grade Point Average; SAT = Scholastic Aptitude Test; GED = General Equivalency Diploma.

199

proficiency on intermediate level is required. Placement exam. *Professional:* professional musicians preferred.

Cost: About $3,300 per quarter for tuition. *Scholarships:* none.

Housing: Not provided; student makes own arrangements.

Application: *Deadline:* three months to one year prior. *Fee:* $275; not refundable.

Contact: Foreign Student Advisor, UCLA Extension Advisory Service, 10995 Le Conte Avenue, Los Angeles, CA 90024; (213) 825-9351 or 206-6201. Cable: 9103427597. Telex: 9103427597.

APPENDIX

PROFESSIONAL ASSOCIATIONS

Specialized Study Options U.S.A. describes hundreds of short-term education and training programs available to foreign nationals. It does not exhaust the opportunities available for short-term training in the United States, however. Many professional associations conduct one- or two-day workshops and seminars as part of their annual national or regional conferences. Others offer continuing education programs of varying lengths for their members throughout the year.

Because the opportunities for very short-term training are so many and varied, it is best to contact these organizations directly for full information on their courses, conferences, and other study opportunities. The list below is a selection of 120 major professional associations, representing a variety of educational and professional fields. If you do not find an association in your chosen field, consult the annual Encyclopedia of Associations, published by Gale Research Company, Book Tower, Detroit, Michigan 48226, for complete information about virtually all U.S. professional associations.

Academy of International Business
World Trade Education Center
Cleveland State University
Cleveland, OH 44115

Agricultural Cooperative Development
   International
1012 Fourteenth Street, NW
Washington, DC 20005

AIESEC—United States
(International Association of Students in
   Economics and Business Management)
14 West 23rd Street
New York, NY 10010

AMA/International
(American Management Associations)
135 West 50th Street
New York, NY 10020

American Academy of Microbiology
1913 Eye Street, NW
Washington, DC 20006

American Academy of Physical Education
Texas Woman's University
P.O. Box 24142
Denton, TX 76204

American Accounting Association
5717 Bessie Drive
Sarasota, FL 33581

American Anthropological Association
1703 New Hampshire Avenue, NW
Washington, DC 20009

American Assembly of Collegiate Schools
   of Business
605 Old Ballas Road, Suite 520
Saint Louis, MO 63141

American Association for Adult and
   Continuing Education
1201 Sixteenth Street, NW
Washington, DC 20036

ASSOCIATIONS

American Association for the Advancement
of Science
1333 H Street, NW
Washington, DC 20005

American Association of Colleges for
Teacher Education
One Dupont Circle, NW, Suite 610
Washington, DC 20036

American Association of Engineering
Societies
345 East 47th Street
New York, NY 10017

American Association of Housing
Educators
Department of C.T.I.D.
Kansas State University
Justin Hall
Manhattan, KS 66506

American Association of Medical Assistants
20 North Wacker Drive, Suite 1575
Chicago, IL 60606

American Association of Nurse
Anesthetists
216 Higgins Road
Park Ridge, IL 60068

American Astronomical Society
1816 Jefferson Place, NW
Washington, DC 20036

American Bankers Association
1120 Connecticut Ave, NW
Washington, DC 20036

American Bar Association
Section of Legal Education
750 North Lake Shore Drive
Chicago, IL 60611

American Ceramic Society
65 Ceramic Drive
Columbus, OH 43214

American Chemical Society
Committee on Professional Training
1155 Sixteenth Street, NW
Washington, DC 20036

American Council on Pharmaceutical
Education
311 West Superior Street
Chicago, IL 60610

American Culinary Federation
P.O. Box 3466
St. Augustine, FL 32084

American Dental Association
211 East Chicago Avenue
Chicago, IL 60611

American Dietetic Association
430 Michigan Avenue
Chicago, IL 60611

American Electronics Association
2670 Hanover Street
Palo Alto, CA 94303

American Fisheries Society
5410 Grosvenor Lane
Bethesda, MD 20814

American Hotel and Motel Association
888 Seventh Avenue
New York, NY 10019

American Institute of Aeronautics and
Astronautics
1633 Broadway
New York, NY 10019

American Institute of Architects
1735 New York Avenue, NW
Washington, DC 20006

American Institute of Biological Sciences
1401 Wilson Boulevard
Arlington, VA 22209

American Institute of Chemical Engineers
345 East 47th Street
New York, NY 10017

American Institute of Cooperation
1800 Massachusetts Avenue, NW
Washington, DC 20036

American Institute of Mining,
Metallurgical and Petroleum Engineers
345 East 47th Street
New York, NY 10017

American Institute of Petroleum Geologists
Box 979
Tulsa, OK 74101

American Institute of Physics
335 East 45th Street
New York, NY·10017

American Library Association
50 East Huron Street
Chicago, IL 60611

American Management Associations
135 West 50th Street
New York, NY 10020

American Mathematical Society
P.O. Box 6248
Providence, RI 02940

American Medical Association
535 North Dearborn Street
Chicago, IL 60610

American Meteorological Society
45 Beacon Street
Boston, MA 02108

American Nuclear Society
555 North Kensington Avenue
LaGrange Park, IL 60525

American Occupational Therapy
   Association
1383 Piccard Drive, Suite 300
Rockville, MD 20850

American Optometric Association
Council on Optometric Education
243 North Lindbergh Boulevard
Saint Louis, MO 63141

American Osteopathic Association
212 East Ohio Street
Chicago, IL 60611

American Petroleum Institute
1220 L Street, NW
Washington, DC 20005

American Physical Therapy Association
1111 North Fairfax Street
Alexandria, VA 22314

American Political Science Association
1527 New Hampshire Avenue, NW
Washington, DC 20036

American Psychological Association
1200 Seventeenth Street, NW
Washington, DC 20036

American Public Health Association
1015 Fifteenth Street, NW, Suite 300
Washington, DC 20005

American Society for Engineering
   Education
11 Dupont Circle, NW, Suite 200
Washington, DC 20036

American Society for Information Science
1010 Sixteenth Street, NW
Washington, DC 20036

American Society for Microbiology
1913 I Street, NW
Washington, DC 20006

American Society for Personnel
   Administration
606 North Washington Street
Alexandria, VA 22314

American Society for Public
   Administration
1120 G Street, NW, Suite 520
Washington, DC 20005

American Society for Quality Control
230 West Wells Street, Suite 7000
Milwaukee, WI 53203

American Society for Training and
   Development
600 Maryland Avenue, SW, Suite 305
Washington, DC 20025

American Society of Actuaries
1835 K Street, NW, Suite 515
Washington, DC 20006

American Society of Agronomy
677 South Segoe Road
Madison, WI 53711

American Society of Allied Health
   Professions
1101 Connecticut Avenue, NW, Suite 700
Washington, DC 20036

American Society of Civil Engineers
345 East 47th Street
New York, Ny 10017

American Society of Landscape Architects
1733 Connecticut Avenue, NW
Washington, DC 20009

American Society of Mechanical Engineers
345 East 47th Street
New York, NY 10017

American Statistical Association
806 Fifteenth Street, NW, Suite 640
Washington, DC 20005

American Studies Association
University of Pennsylvania
307 College Hall
Philadelphia, PA 19104

American Veterinary Medical Association
930 North Meacham Road
Schaumburg, IL 60196

Archaeological Institute of America
P.O. Box 1901, Kenmore Station
Boston, MA 02215

Association for Continuing Higher
  Education
College of Graduate and Continuing
  Studies
University of Evansville
1800 Lincoln Avenue
Evansville, IN 47714

Association for International Practical
  Training
American City Building, Suite 217
Columbia, MD 21044

Association of American Geographers
1710 Sixteenth Street, NW
Washington, DC 20009

Association of Collegiate Schools of
  Architecture
1735 New York Avenue, NW
Washington, DC 20006

Association of Collegiate Schools of
  Planning
Department of City and Regional Planning
University of California
Berkeley, CA 94720

Association of Independent Conservatories
  of Music
11021 East Boulevard
Cleveland, OH 44106

Association of Schools of Journalism and
  Mass Communication
College of Journalism
University of South Carolina
1621 College Street
Columbia, SC 29208-0251

Association of U.S. University Directors of
  International
Agricultural Programs
University of Illinois
1301 West Gregory Drive
Urbana, IL 61801

Association of University Programs in
  Health Administration
1911 North Fort Meyer Drive, Suite 503
Arlington, VA 22209

Association of University Summer Sessions
Indiana University
Maxwell Hall 254
Bloomington, IN 47405

Audio Engineering Society
60 East 42nd Street, Room 2520
New York, NY 10065

College Art Association of America
149 Madison Avenue
New York, NY 10016

Council on Education for Public Health
1015 Fifteenth Street, NW, Suite 403
Washington, DC 20005

Council on Social Work Education
1744 R Street, NW
Washington, DC 20009

Crop Science Society of America
677 South Segoe Road
Madison, WI 53711

Electronic Industries Association
2001 Eye Street, NW
Washington, DC 20006

Food Processors Institute
1401 New York Avenue, NW, Suite 400
Washington, DC 20005

Geological Society of America
P.O. Box 9140
3300 Penrose Place
Boulder, CO 80301

Human Resource Planning Society
P.O. Box 2553, Grand Central Station
New York, NY 10163

Institute of Certified Financial Planners
P.O. Box 3668
Charlottesville, VA 22903

Institute of Electrical and Electronics
  Engineers
345 East 47th Street
New York, NY 10017

Institute of Financial Education
111 East Wacker Drive
Chicago, IL 60601

Institute of Real Estate Management
430 North Michigan Avenue
Chicago, IL 60611

Instrument Society of America
P.O. Box 12277
67 Alexander Drive
Research Triangle Park, NC 27709

Insurance Institute of America
Providence Road
Malvern, PA 19355

International Association for Financial
  Planning
5775 Peachtree-Dunwoody Road, Suite
  120-C
Atlanta, GA 30342

International Association of Independent
  Producers
P.O. Box 2801
Washington, DC 20013

International Communication Association
8140 Burnet Road
P.O. Box 9589
Austin, TX 78666

International Council on Education for
  Teaching
One Dupont Circle, NW, Suite 616
Washington, DC 20036

International Personnel Management
  Association
1617 Duke Street
Alexandria, VA 22314

International Society of Certified
  Electronics Technicians
2708 West Berry, Suite 8
Fort Worth, TX 76109

International Society of Tropical Foresters
c/o Society of American Foresters
5400 Grosvenor Lane
Bethesda, MD 20814

Linguistic Society of America
1325 Eighteenth Street, NW, Suite 211
Washington, DC 20036-6501

National Academy of Television Arts and
  Sciences
110 West 57th Street
New York, NY 10019

National Association for Practical Nurse
  Education and Service
10801 Pear Tree Lane
Saint Louis, MO 63074

National Association of Credit
  Management
475 Park Avenue South
New York, NY 10016

National Association of Purchasing
  Management
P.O. Box 418
496 Kinderkamack Road
Oradell, NJ 07649

National Association of Schools of Art and
  Design
11250 Roger Bacon Drive, Number 5
Reston, VA 22090

National Association of Schools of Dance
11250 Roger Bacon Drive, Number 5
Reston, VA 22090

National Association of Schools of Music
11250 Roger Bacon Drive, Number 5
Reston, VA 22090

National Association of Schools of Theatre
11250 Roger Bacon Drive, Number 5
Reston, VA 22090

National Association of Trade and
  Technical Schools
2251 Wisconsin Avenue
Washington, DC 20007

National Center for Financial Education
25 Van Ness Avenue, Suite 390
San Francisco, CA 94102

National Commission for Cooperative
  Education
360 Huntington Avenue
Boston, MA 02115

National League for Nursing
Ten Columbus Circle
New York, NY 10019

North American Association of Summer
  Sessions
11728 Summerhaven Drive
Creve Coeur, MO 63146

Public Relations Society of America
845 Third Avenue
New York, NY 10022

Society of American Foresters
5400 Grosvenor Lane
Bethesda, MD 20814

Teachers of English to Speakers of Other
  Languages
Georgetown University
201 DC Transit Building
Washington, DC 20057

University Aviation Association
Box 2321
Auburn, AL 36830

University Film and Video Association
Department of Cinema and Photography
Southern Illinois University
Carbondale, IL 62901

INDEX I

SPONSORING INSTITUTIONS

Adelphi University, D16, D64, D65
Airco Computer Learning Center, F12
Alabama, University of
  Birmingham, Q17–Q19, Q26, Q32, Q33
  Center for Health Services Continuing
    Education, Q26
  Graduate School of Library Service, N5
  School of Nursing, Q32, Q33
  School of Public Health, Q17–Q19
  University Station, N5
American Cultural Exchange, M13
American Graduate School of International
  Management, D45
American University, D11, D66, D84,
  D85, F1, F9, G36, K7, K8, M14, P2,
  U1, U2, U35, U42, U56, V11
Arizona, University of
  Agricultural Engineering Department,
    A25
  School of Renewable Natural Resources,
    A18, A24
Arkansas, University of
  Little Rock, G35
Arthur D. Little Management Education
  Institute, A9, D40, D46, D83, M6
Associated Technical Institute, F10
Atlantic, College of the, O9, S9, S13

Baltimore, University of, D14
Battelle, D67
Bexley Hall, R1
Boston University, E1, Q5
  Metropolitan College, B3, L5
  School of Public Health, Q15
  Theater Institute, W5
Brandeis University, V17
Brenau College, D1, Q36

California State University
  Chico, I1
  Long Beach, G1
California, University of
  Berkeley Extension, G42
  Davis Extension, A7
  Los Angeles Extension, E9, H8, L8,
    Q8A, W8
  Santa Cruz, F5
Calvin College, G2, R5
Carnegie Mellon University, H10
Center for the Advanced Studies of the
  Americas (CASA), C2
Central Connecticut State University, J1
Central Michigan University, U3
  Atlantic Region, D68
Central Missouri State University, J3
Central Washington University, M12
Cincinnati, University of, S12
Clarissa School of Fashion Design, I3
Clemson University, K1, M1, O1, P1, T1,
  U53, V1
Cleveland State University
  College of Education, G3, V18
Colgate Rochester Divinity School, R1
Colorado School of Mines, H1, H2, S1
  Special Programs and Continuing
    Education, H13
Colorado State University
  Department of Range Science, A37
  International School for Water
    Resources, A22, A23
  International School of Forestry and
    Natural Resources, A1
Columbia Theological Seminary, R2
Columbia University, D47
Computer Learning Center of Los
  Angeles, F11, F13, F14

Laredo State University, D49
La Salle University, R7
Lesley College, G30, M3
  Graduate School, C5, G7, G8, G19,
  Q27, T4, U8, V2, V21, W2
Linguistic Society of America, K2
Loma Linda University, Q16
Long Island University
  Brooklyn Campus, U28, U29, V3

Manhattan Dalcroze Institute, W6
Manhattan School of Music, W6
Marquette University
  Institute for Catholic Media, E5
Maryland Eastern Shore, University of,
  A11
Maryland Institute, G18
Maryland, University of, I10
  Baltimore, O6
Maryville College—St. Louis, G38
Marywood College, G34, W3, W7
Massachusetts Institute of Technology,
  D3, D4, D73, D86, F4, H4, H9,
  H11, H12, J4, O7, S4
Medicine and Dentistry of New Jersey,
  University of
  New Jersey Dental School, Q9
  School of Health Related Professions,
  I11, Q7, Q30
Michigan State University
  Special Institute for Studies of
  Nonformal Education, G32
Michigan, University of, V10, V28, V29
  Institute of Public Policy Studies, U19
  Law School, L2
Middlebury College, K3
Minnesota, University of, A13, A35, C7,
  C8
  School of Public Health, Q6
Mississippi State University, A12
Monterey Institute of International
  Studies, G26, G39, K4, K9, K10
Murray State University, D26
  Mid-America Remote Sensing Center,
  M17

Nebraska, University of
  Omaha, D22, D31, D41
New Mexico Institute of Mining and
  Technology, S10
New Mexico, University of
  College of Education, G14
New York University
  Graduate School of Business
  Administration, D74

Graduate School of Public
  Administration, U9, U45
  Institute of Public Administration, U7
  School of Continuing Education, D39,
  D82, E11, E12
Nicholls State University, D50
North Carolina, University of, Chapel Hill
  School of Medicine, T6
  School of Public Health, Q20
North Dakota State University, S5
Northeastern University
  Center for Management Development,
  D27
Northern Illinois University, U11
  International and Special Programs, U10
Northwest Regional Educational
  Laboratory, G9

Ohio State University, A20, A21, G44,
  U12
  Department of Architecture, B1
  International Programs in Agriculture,
  A33
Ohio University, C1, E7
Oklahoma State University, A6, H5, J2

Pace University, D5, D51, D52, D63,
  D75, E13, Q25, U13
Pacific School of Religion, R8
Pennsylvania, University of, B2, B6, B9,
  L3, M8–M10, U32, U33, V9, V16,
  V27
Pittsburg State University
  Continuing Education, M4
Pittsburgh, University of, D32
  Institute of Training and Organizational
  Development, M11, U52
Plaza Three Academy, B10, D37
Pratt Institute, B4
Princeton Theological Seminary, K5, R9
Public Administration, Institute of, U22,
  U27, U44
Purdue University, D42
  Department of Child Development &
  Family Studies, V22

Radcliffe College, E14
Rochester, University of, D43, G11

St. John's University
  School of Theology, R10
Saint Joseph College
  Graduate Division, V23
Saint Martin's College, D76, H6
Saint Mary's College of California, D53
Sam Houston State University, N2

San Diego State University
  International Population Center, Q11
San Jose State University
  Department of Urban & Regional
    Planning, B5
School for International Training, G16,
  U30, U31
School of World Mission, R3
Simmons College, N1
Smith College, C6, D77
Sonoma State University, M7
South Dakota State University, M18, M19
South Florida, University of, A26
  College of Public Health, Q21
Southeast Missouri State University, D54
Southern California College, R4
Southern California, University of
  International Business Education and
    Research Program, D60
Southern Colorado, University of, G21, G25
Southern Illinois University
  Carbondale, E4, E8, S11
  Edwardsville, O3
  School of Journalism, E4, E8
Southwestern Legal Foundation
  Academy of American and International
    Law, L7
Spalding University, G20
Spartan Health Sciences University, Q1
Springfield College, V24, V25
Stanford Alumni Association, E15
Stanford University
  Food Research Institute, F7
State University of New York
  Binghamton, V6
  Buffalo, D6, G40
  Geneseo, College at, G10, O4, Q4, T5
Swarthmore College, S6
Syracuse University, D78, N3, V4, W4
  Maxwell School of Citizenship & Public
    Affairs, U14, U15

Temple University
  School of Social Administration, V26
Tennessee, University of
  Knoxville, O8
Texas A&M University, D28, D29
  Center for Executive Development, S7
  College of Veterinary Medecine, Q46
Texas Tech University
  Center for Applied International
    Development Studies, U48
Texas, University of
  Dallas, E6
Texas Woman's University, N4

Union College, H7
U.S. Department of Agriculture Graduate
  School, D15, G27, G41, U23, U36,
  U46
Utah State University
  Department of Agricultural Education
  Department of Range Science, A38, A39
  International Irrigation Center, A27–A32

Virginia Commonwealth University
  Department of Public Administration,
  U20
Virginia Polytechnic Institute & State
  University, I2, I9, I12
Virginia, University of
  Economics Department, V13
Voorhees College, D10, F6, G12, O5, P4,
  S3, V5

Wadams Hall Seminary-College, R11
Wake Forest University, D79, Q3
Washington and Lee University, D33
Washington State University, A19
  Hotel and Restaurant Administration,
  D90
Washington University, C10, K6
Washington, University of
  College of Engineering, H14
  Department of Chemistry, S8
  Graduate School of Public Affairs, U43
Wesley Theological Seminary, R12
Wesleyan University, M5
West Virginia University, U21
Westark Community College, F15
Western Carolina University and the
  Tennessee Valley Authority, M16
Western Michigan University, C9, D61
Western Montana College, G13
Wheelock College Graduate School, G22
Williams College, D34
  Center for Development Economics,
  V14
Wisconsin, University of
  Department of Urban and Regional
    Planning, B7
  Law School, Law Extension, L4
  Library & Information Science, N6
  Madison, A14, A41, B7, G43, L4, Q8
  Milwaukee, N6
World Affairs, Institute of, A4, D19
World Trade Education Center, D62

Xavier University, D80

Yale University, V15

INDEX II

STATES

Alabama, N5, Q17–Q19, Q26, Q32, Q33
Arizona, A18, A24, A25, B10, D37, D45
Arkansas, F15, G35

California, A7, B5, D35, D53, D60, D87,
    E9, E15, F5, F7, F11, F13, F14, G1,
    G26, G31, G37, G39, G42, H8, I1, I4,
    K4, K9, K10, L8, M7, Q8A, Q11,
    Q16, R3, R4, R6, R8, W8
Colorado, A1, A3, A10, A22, A23, A37,
    A40, D25, D70, G21, G25, H1, H2,
    H13, M15, S1, V12, V19
Connecticut, A4, D19, F8, G17, G28, J1,
    M5, Q12, Q28, Q34, Q41, U16–U18,
    U34, U37–U41, U49–U51, U55, V15,
    V23

District of Columbia, A5, C2, D11, D66,
    D68, D84, D85, D88, E10, F1, F9,
    G27, G29, G36, G41, K7, K8, M14,
    P2, R12, U1–U3, U22, U23, U27,
    U35, U36, U42, U46, U49, U56, V11

Florida, A26, B8, D48, Q21, U25

Georgia, D1, Q36, R2, U54

Hawaii, D21, D55, D56, D89, V7, V8

Idaho, A36
Illinois, A34, C11, C12, D9, D13, D20,
    D57–D59, D72, D81, E4, E8, F2,
    O3, Q13, Q14, Q35, S11, U10, U11,
    U58
Indiana, C4, D42, U26, V22

Kansas, M4
Kentucky, D26, G20, M17, Q2

Louisiana, D50

Maine, O9, S9, S13
Maryland, A11, D14, D15, G18, I10, O6,
    Q10, Q24, Q40
Massachusetts, A9, B3, C5, C6, D3, D4,
    D27, D34, D40, D46, D73, D77,
    D83, D86, E1, E14, F4, F10, F12,
    G7, G8, G15, G16, G19, G22, G30,
    H4, H9, H11, H12, J4, L1, L5, M3,
    M6, N1, O7, Q5, Q15, Q23, Q27,
    Q37–Q39, S4, T2, T4, U5, U6, U8,
    U47, U57, V2, V14, V17, V21, V24,
    V25, W2, W5
Michigan, A17, C9, D8, D61, G2, G32,
    L2, Q1, R5, U19, V10, V28, V29
Minnesota, A13, A35, C7, C8, Q6, R10
Mississippi, A12
Missouri, C10, D54, G38, J3, K6
Montana, G13

Nebraska, D22, D31, D41
New Hampshire, D24
New Jersey, G23, G24, G33, I11, K5, Q7,
    Q9, Q30, R9
New Mexico, G14, S10
New York, A2, B4, D5, D6, D16, D23,
    D36, D39, D43, D44, D47, D51,
    D52, D63–D65, D74, D75, D78,
    D82, E3, E11–E13, F16, G10, G11,
    G40, H7, I5–I8, N3, O4, Q4, Q22,
    Q25, Q43, Q44, R1, R11, R13, T5,
    U7, U9, U13, U14, U15, U24, U28,
    U29, U45, V3, V4, V6, W4, W6
North Carolina, D12, D71, D79, E2, F3,
    G5, L6, M2, M16, O2, P3, Q3, Q20,
    Q45, S2, T3, T6, V20, W1
North Dakota, S5

Ohio, A20, A21, A33, B1, C1, D62, D67, D80, E7, G3, G44, S12, U12, V18
Oklahoma, A6, H5, J2
Oregon, A15, A16, G9

Pennsylvania, B2, B6, B9, C3, D2, D17, D32, D38, D69, G34, H10, I3, L3, M8–M11, R7, S6, U32, U33, U52, V9, V16, V26, V27, W3, W7
Puerto Rico, Q29

South Carolina, D10, F6, G12, K1, M1, O1, O5, P1, P4, S3, T1, U53, V1, V5
South Dakota, M18, M19

Tennessee, M16, O8
Texas, D7, D28–D30, D49, E6, L7, N2, N4, Q46, S7, U48

Utah, A8, A27–A32, A38, A39, Q42

Vermont, G16, K3, U30, U31
Virginia, D33, I2, I9, I12, Q31, U20, U44, V13

Washington, A19, D17, D76, D90, H6, H14, M12, M13, S8, U4, U43
West Virginia, U21
Wisconsin, A14, A41, B7, D18, E5, G43, L4, N6, Q8

INDEX III

FIELDS OF STUDY

Music, W1, W6–W8
  Computer literacy for musicians, W7
  Education, G31
  Film scoring, W8
  Kodaly method, G31
  Piano literature, W7
  Suzuki technique, W7
  Therapy, T4

Natural resources management, A1, M12
  Energy resources, M6–M11
  Regional resources, M16
  Water management, A22–A32
Nonprofit and nongovernmental
  organizations, U28, U44, U45
  Fundraising, U39
Nutrition, A11, I1, I10–I12, Q19, U24
Nursing, Q31–Q35
  Administration, Q35
  Clinical, Q32, Q35
  Education, Q35
  Primary health care, in, Q31
  Public health, Q34

Oceanography, S13

Painting, W3
Paralegal, L8
Parks and recreation, U53, U54
Performing arts, W1, W5–W7
Personnel management (See Human
  resources management)
Pesticides, A33
Petroleum
  Engineering, S1
  Management, M6
  Refining, S1
Philosophy, M2
Physical sciences, S1–S13
Physical therapy, Q36
Physics, P3, S2
  Biophysics, O6
  Geophysics, S1
Plant pathology, A33–A352
Political science, M2, V4, V5
Professional development, M13–M15
Project management, D83, U17, U47–U52
Psychology, M2, T1–T6
  Expressive therapies, T4
  Family therapy, T2
Public administration, U1–U57
  Auditing, U37
  Comparative, U7
  Consulting skills, U22
  Cultural resources, U23

Development studies, U7, U9, U11,
  U17, U24–U33, U50, U51
Financial management, U4, U11, U12,
  U17, U20, U35–U39, U47
Health services (See Health services;
  Public health)
Human resources, U4, U11, U12, U17,
  U20, U40, U41
International, U7, U9
Investment management, U47
Law enforcement, U43
Local government, U4, U10, U17
Management, U1–U21
National, U10
Nongovernmental organizations, U28,
  U44, U45
Project management, U17, U47–U52
Public information, U42
Public policy, U5, U11, U12, U20, U46
Quantitative social science methods
  applied to, U19
Regional planning, U24
Systems analysis, U55
Taxation, U56
Public health, Q37–Q41
  Developing countries, in, Q15–Q21
  Epidemiology, Q10, Q15
  Nursing, Q34
  Nutrition, Q19
  Occupational health, Q37
  Systems management, Q22–Q26
  Urban health planning, Q41
Public relations, D84
Publishing, E10–E15
Purchasing, D85

Range management, A37–A39
Records management, N1, N6
Recreation resources, U53, U54
Regional planning, U24
Regional resources management, M16
Religion and theology, M2, R1–R13
  Christianity, R5–R12
  Development, role of nongovernmental
    organizations in, U28
  Ecumenical and multidenominational
    studies, R1, R2
  Television production, in, E5
Remote sensing, M17–M19
Robotics, F4
Rural development, A40, A41
Russian language, K3, K4
Russian studies, C11, C12

Seed improvement, A12
Social research, V28, V29

COMPLETE THIS ORDER FORM AND MAIL TO:
Publication Service
Institute of International Education
809 United Nations Plaza
New York, New York 10017
USA

All orders must be prepaid. Check/money orders should be made payable to **Institute of International Education.** IIE pays domestic postage. **Overseas please add $7.00.**

For more information about IIE books, please call (212) 984-5412.

Quantity	Title	Price	Total
	English Language and Orientation Programs in the United States	$ 8.95	
	Financial Resources for International Study	FREE	
	Study in U.S. Colleges and Universities	FREE	
	Specialized Study Options USA Vol 1: Technical Education	$19.95	
	Specialized Study Options USA Vol 2: Professional Development	$19.95	
		TOTAL COST	$

Name: _____

Address: _____

City/State/Country: _____

Zip code: _____ Telephone Number: _____

COMPLETE THIS ORDER FORM AND MAIL TO:
Publication Service
Institute of International Education
809 United Nations Plaza
New York, New York 10017
USA

All orders must be prepaid. Check/money orders should be made payable to **Institute of International Education.** IIE pays domestic postage. **Overseas please add $7.00.**

For more information about IIE books, please call (212) 984-5412.

Quantity	Title	Price	Total
	English Language and Orientation Programs in the United States	$ 8.95	
	Financial Resources for International Study	FREE	
	Study in U.S. Colleges and Universities	FREE	
	Specialized Study Options USA Vol 1: Technical Education	$19.95	
	Specialized Study Options USA Vol 2: Professional Development	$19.95	
		TOTAL COST	$

Name: _____

Address: _____

City/State/Country: _____

Zip code: _____ Telephone Number: _____